THE PRESIDENCY AND SOCIAL MEDIA

The media have long played an important role in the modern political process and the 2016 presidential campaign was no different. From Trump's tweets and cable-show-call-ins to Sanders's social media machine to Clinton's "Trump Yourself" app and podcast, journalism, social and digital media, and entertainment media were front and center in 2016. Clearly, political media played a dominant and disruptive role in our democratic process. This book helps to explain the role of these media and communication outlets in the 2016 presidential election.

This thorough study of how political communication evolved in 2016 examines the disruptive role communication technology played in the 2016 presidential primary campaign and general election and how voters sought and received political information. *The Presidency and Social Media* includes top scholars from leading research institutions using various research methodologies to generate new understandings—both theoretical and practical—for students, researchers, journalists, and practitioners.

Dan Schill is Associate Professor in the School of Communication Studies and Affiliate Professor in Political Science at James Madison University, where he teaches courses in advocacy, political communication, research methods, and media and politics. His research focuses on communication, politics, media, and technology.

John Allen Hendricks is Chair of the Department of Mass Communication and Professor at Stephen F. Austin State University, where he teaches courses in communication theory, research methods, First Amendment law, and media and politics. Dr. Hendricks has authored/edited more than ten books on the topics of media/politics, social media/new media technologies, and the broadcasting industry.

"*The Presidency and Social Media* is the essential and authoritative guide on the use and impact of social media in the 2016 presidential campaign. This impressive and comprehensive volume exposes the good, the bad, and the ugly influence of social media in 2016 but also provides clues to future campaigns. The volume, without question, is the go to source for understanding the evolving role of media in political campaigns."

—Robert E. Denton, Jr., W. Thomas Rice Chair, Pamplin College of Business and Head Department of Communication, Virginia Tech

"Social media played an unprecedented—and complicated—role in the 2016 presidential election. Schill and Hendricks have assembled work by impressive scholars that examines this phenomenon from multiple perspectives. The volume is relevant beyond the electoral context, as the tactics employed in the campaign have carried over to governing in unanticipated ways. This rich and comprehensive work is destined to be a landmark in studies of social media, especially as scholars, practitioners, and the public seek to understand the consequences of social-media driven elections and 'government by tweet.'"

—Diana Owen, Associate Professor of Political Science, Georgetown University

THE PRESIDENCY AND SOCIAL MEDIA

Discourse, Disruption, and Digital Democracy in the 2016 Presidential Election

Edited by Dan Schill and John Allen Hendricks

Routledge
Taylor & Francis Group
NEW YORK AND LONDON

First published 2018
by Routledge
711 Third Avenue, New York, NY 10017

and by Routledge
2 Park Square, Milton Park, Abingdon, Oxon, OX14 4RN

Routledge is an imprint of the Taylor & Francis Group, an informa business

Library of Congress Cataloging-in-Publication Data
Names: Schill, Daniel J., editor. | Hendricks, John Allen, editor.
Title: The presidency and social media : discourse, disruption, and digital democracy in the 2016 presidential election / edited by Dan Schill and John Allen Hendricks.
Description: New York, NY : Routledge, [2018] | Includes bibliographical references and index.
Identifiers: LCCN 2017023941 (print) | LCCN 2017047058 (ebook) | ISBN 9781315112824 (Master) | ISBN 9781351623193 (WebPDF) | ISBN 9781351623186 (ePub) | ISBN 9781351623179 (Mobipocket/Kindle) | ISBN 9781138081536 (hbk : alk. paper) | ISBN 9781138081543 (pbk : alk. paper) | ISBN 9781315112824 (ebk)
Subjects: LCSH: Presidents—United States—Election—2017. | Social media—Political aspects—United States. | Internet in political campaigns—United States. | Communication in politics—Technological innovations—United States. | Political campaigns—Technological innovations—United States.
Classification: LCC JK526 2016 (ebook) | LCC JK526 2016 .P737 2018 (print) | DDC 324.7/3—dc23
LC record available at https://lccn.loc.gov/2017023941

ISBN: 978-1-138-08153-6 (hbk)
ISBN: 978-1-138-08154-3 (pbk)
ISBN: 978-1-315-11282-4 (ebk)

Typeset in Bembo
by Apex CoVantage, LLC

CONTENTS

FIGURES

TABLES

FOREWORD

Until the 1970s, the media's role in American presidential elections was not heavily studied. Political scientists had not yet grasped the fact that political parties and voters were no longer the only important actors in the campaign, and journalism schools were only beginning to expand into the field of mass communication research.

We now know a great deal about the media and presidential elections, particularly when it comes to the traditional news media—television and newspapers. Of course every presidential campaign offers something new and thus something new to study. Donald Trump's 2016 candidacy presented the press with the novelty of covering a candidate who was himself a novelty. Preliminary research on the traditional media's coverage of the Trump candidacy suggests that we need to rethink some of our long-held assumptions about how they report a presidential campaign. The 2020 campaign is likely to require a similar adjustment. The traditional media are conducting internal reviews of what they did in 2016 with an eye toward changing their coverage next time.

Nevertheless, whatever we can learn from studies of traditional media is secondary to what we need to know about the role of social media in presidential politics. Election scholarship has always been a lagging enterprise. Changes in how campaigns are conducted are slow to capture the attention of a critical mass of research scholars. Even as late as 2012, Matthew Hindman's marvelous 2005 article on Howard Dean's campaign—"the first digital campaign" in Matt's words—was among a tiny set of studies that sought to inform us on social media's election role.

We're finally starting to catch up with social media's political impact, and this book contributes mightily to what's been missing. There's a lot to be learned in its pages. Want to know about social media use during the campaign? It's presented in abundance. Want to know about media effects? There are remarkable findings in several of the chapters. Want to know about candidate messaging? If you followed the 2016 campaign closely, you might think you already know everything worth knowing. This book will convince you otherwise. Want to know about media content? It's here, including that of political humor.

The level of scholarship is equally remarkable, given how soon after the election this book is being published. But I'm not surprised by the quality of the work, given the exceptional scholars who have written the book's chapters.

If Howard Dean's campaign was the first truly digital campaign, the 2016 campaign was the first full-blown digital campaign, just as the Trump presidency is the first full-blown digital presidency. Although Barack Obama was the first Twitter president, Trump is the first one on steroids. But Trump's tweets are just the surface of the transformation and are far less important than what's taking place largely out of public sight. Social media usage at the citizen level are having a large effect on what we know, don't know, and only think we know. An understanding of this subterranean world is critical if we are to understand the implications for our democracy. This book is a step toward that understanding.

There's so much remarkable scholarship in this book that it's almost unfair to ask what's underrepresented. There is at least one thing that I would have liked to have heard more about—"fake news." The digital-data site BuzzSumo found that, by the end of the 2016 campaign, the number of Facebook shares, reactions, and comments stemming from fake news stories exceeded the number originating in response to actual news stories. Fake news is hardly a new phenomenon. The idea behind it goes back at least to the mythological Trojan Horse that the Greeks parked at the gates of Troy. What's different today is the speed, penetration, and scalability of such messaging, and the ability of actors halfway around the world to influence its flow. It's a threatening development in urgent need of scholarly attention.

If the Brave New World that is social media is teeming with both threat and opportunity for our democracy, it's also teeming with research possibilities. This book represents a significant advance in what we know of that world, one that today's readers will discover in its pages and one that future readers will discover to an even greater extent from the future research that this book guides and inspires.

Those of us in the fields of media and political research owe a king-size debt to the authors of this edited volume. They have helped open our eyes to the present and future of presidential politics.

Thomas E. Patterson
Harvard University
Cambridge, Massachusetts USA
April, 2017

PREFACE

The media have long played an important role in the modern political process and the 2016 presidential campaign was no different. From Trump's tweets and cable-show-call-ins to Sanders's social media machine to Clinton's "Trump Yourself" app and podcast, journalism, social and digital media, and entertainment media were front and center in 2016. The purpose of this book is to better understand the role of these media and communication outlets in the historic 2016 presidential election. In particular, in five sections, it provides a detailed examination of the disruptive role communication technology played in the 2016 presidential primary campaign and general election.

This book studies the notable trend of the increasing centrality of digital and social media in our public affairs. A Pew Research study found that 91% of U.S. adults acquired political information in a given week, but that information sources were scattered across 11 different types of media (Gottfried, Barthel, Shearer, & Mitchell, 2016). When Americans were asked which information source they found most helpful, the number one response was cable news. However, only 24% cited that source. The remainder were spread across social media (14%), local television (14%), news websites and apps (13%), radio (11%), network nightly news (10%), late-night comedy (3%), and local newspapers (3%), among others. As MIT's William Powers (2016) observed, "the old influence hierarchy has been shattered, replaced by a new mosaic of influence in which social media play a growing role" (para. 7).

In total, according to the same Pew Research study, 44% of all U.S. adults reported having learned about the 2016 presidential election in the past week from social media. And among those social outlets, the candidates' social media profiles, namely Facebook and Twitter profiles, were the most popular sources of political content, significantly outpacing candidate websites or emails. And what information was on these profiles? Positive and issue-based content was extensive, but negative information ruled the day as the candidates exchanged biting insults, attack videos, and video-based assaults on each other's character. Characterizing the tone of the 2016 campaign, David Plouffe, Barack Obama's 2008 campaign manager, compared it to a popular post-apocalyptic action movie, writing: "this campaign was not the Lincoln-Douglas debates, it was 'Mad Max: Fury Road'" (2016, para. 13).

Candidates also realized that the fastest way to gather mainstream media coverage was to put out a statement or comment on social media and avoid paying for ad placement. In fact, a March 2016 *New York Times* analysis found that Donald Trump spent less on paid advertising than any other major primary candidate ($10 million) at that point in the campaign, but earned nearly $2 billion in free media coverage, more than doubling the next-best candidate in earning free media and totaling significantly more than his Republican rivals combined (Confessore & Yourish, 2016). Much of this Trump coverage was a response to controversial tweets and Facebook video posts, in addition to cable news call-ins by the candidate. For example, Trump's December 7 proposal to ban all Muslims from the U.S. was retweeted more than 646,000 times and generated 50 million interactions on Facebook, according to reporting by *USA Today* (Singer, 2016). Put another way, Matt Taibbi (2016) in *Rolling Stone* observed,

> [Trump] is the first to realize the weakness in the system, which is that the watchdogs in the political media can't resist a car wreck. The more he insults the press, the more they cover him. . . . It doesn't know how to turn the cameras off, even when it's filming its own demise.
>
> *(paras. 143–144)*

Of course, not all of the coverage was positive, but, in 2016, the candidates demonstrated that social media was a direct pipeline to voters and mainstream media coverage.

Trump's media strategy was relatively lacking in precedent and journalists scrambled to cover him with traditional journalistic standards and practices, including objectivity norms, poll-driven news, and ratings-based journalism. In effect, because Trump could seize the news cycle with a controversial tweet or inflammatory comment at a rally, he tested news desks' editorial control. *FiveThirtyEight*'s Nate Silver (2016) put it well:

> Trump has hacked the system and exposed the weaknesses in American political institutions. He's uncovered profound flaws in the Republican Party. He's demonstrated that third-rail issues like racism and nationalism can still be a potent political force. He's exploited the media's goodwill and taken advantage of the lack of trust the American public has in journalism.
>
> *(para. 44)*

News organizations had column inches and airtime to fill and Trump coverage ensured a steady stream of clicks and eyeballs.

It is not hyperbole to say that reality TV star Donald Trump would not have been the Republican nominee without the media—in all its forms: journalistic, digital, social, and entertainment, among others. Never before has there been a major party nominee created outside the traditional parties' apparatuses. Based on a review of preprimary news coverage, Harvard's Thomas Patterson (2016) concluded: "Trump is arguably the first bona-fide media-created presidential nominee. Although he subsequently tapped a political nerve, journalists fueled his launch" (p. 5).

The book proceeds in five parts, beginning with an overview section examining social media use in 2016. In the opening chapter, we tell the story of the 2016 presidential election with emphasis on the disruptive role social media played, social media discourses, and the implications digital campaigning pose for our democracy. In Chapter 2, Michael Beam, Paul Haridakis, Myiah Hutchens, and Jay Hmielowski study how Americans used various news sources during the 2016 election and revealed that social networking sites (SNSs) were used less frequently for news compared to online search engines and news aggregators and much less frequently compared to local media and interpersonal discussion. Building on this broad analysis, Sharon Jarvis and Jay Jennings narrow the focus to the opinions and media habits of Trump supporters in Chapter 3. They find that, compared to those supporting other Republican candidates, Trump supporters consumed similar amounts of news from the same sources, but that they voiced less trust in the media and government and lower levels of political participation and community engagement than their conservative peers. Section one concludes in Chapter 4 with a case study of Twitter use in the 2016 Ohio primary election by Jeffrey Kuznekoff, Leland Spencer, and Robert Burt. They find that it wasn't the *amount* of social media buzz that correlated to a campaign's success, but that the candidate with the highest positive sentiment on social media ended up receiving the nomination (even though they didn't have the most mentions).

The second section features three media effects chapters. In Chapter 5, Raluca Cozma turns her attention to the Iowa caucus and finds that voters in this Midwestern state were highly concerned about issues such as terrorism and foreign policy, but that viewing local television—one of the top sources of political information—was correlated with a decline in interest in international issues. Chapter 6 focuses on how social networking impacts users' trust in government, feelings of political efficacy, and beliefs that they can understand and influence political affairs. In this chapter, Ben Warner, Molly Greenwood, Freddie Jennings, and Josh Bramlett use a nationwide survey to conclude that the production and consumption of political content on social media is linked to feeling more qualified and informed about politics and government. In 2016, more and more Americans relied on streaming television services, such as Netflix, and in Chapter 7, Sarah Krongard and Jacob Groshek identify a positive relationship between streaming video and both online and offline political talk.

The presidential candidates extensively used social media to create political images in 2016 and the four chapters in section three consider these discourses. In Chapter 8, David Painter and Katherine Rizzo employ computer-assisted content analysis to analyze the tone of candidate rhetoric on Twitter, in televised debates, and in campaign speeches. Similarly, in Chapter 9, Kate Kenski and Christine Filer investigate how frequently the Democratic and Republican nominees mentioned "change" and "experience" in their tweets and, perhaps counterintuitively, Democrats referenced change three times as often as the Republican candidates did. In a critical analysis of Trump's rhetoric, in Chapter 10, Zac Gershberg argues that the Republican nominee's "paranoid style" crossed traditional media boundaries and took control of the media agenda, especially on social media channels. Comedians had a field day in 2016 and some of the most frequently shared videos, especially on YouTube, were from late-night talk-show programs. It appeared that the shows were evolving their format to create short videos that would go viral the next day. Tapping into this trend, candidates appeared on these programs in an attempt to reach voters. Wrapping up this section in Chapter 11, Dannagal Young and Johanna Lukk review these appearances and show how the candidates use humor strategically and how policy was discussed at a higher rate in these interviews than on traditional news programs.

In the fourth section, three chapters focus on the branding tactics the candidates used in their digital campaigns. Sarah Oates and Wendy Moe use concepts from marketing and political communication in Chapter 12 to trace how elements of political brands for Trump and Clinton resonated through traditional and social media in the primary and general elections. Social media sites such as Instagram, Facebook, and Snapchat are inherently visual mediums. In Chapter 13, Terri Towner surveys users and shows that political photos and infographics on social networks were a stronger predictor of candidate evaluations than attention to textual campaign content. Notably, attention to digital video on social media, however, did show the same effect on candidate evaluations. In the final chapter in this section, Kim Hixson analyzes the tactics each campaign used on Twitter. Noting the negative tone of the tweet campaign, Hixon describes how Clinton was more likely than Trump to address issues, urge voters to go to the polls, recruit volunteers, ask for votes, and criticize her opponent. Alternatively, Trump was more likely to be personable in his tweets by thanking supporters, inviting them to campaign events, and celebrating the successes of the campaign.

The final section of the book shifts away from studying candidate-created social media messages to considering citizen-created content. In Chapter 15, for example, Andrew Ross and Damian Rivers scrutinize the increasingly popular use of Internet memes. In this chapter, a critical discourse analysis reveals how memes mix humor, delegitimization strategies, and intertextuality to generate an active and highly participatory digital culture. Social and digital media continues to be more popular among younger voters. Alison Novak explains how many younger voters engaged the digital campaign through the new social media platform Brigade in Chapter 16. As noted previously, jokes from late-night comedians were frequently shared on social networks in 2016. The book concludes in Chapter 17 with Steve Farnsworth, Bob Lichter, and Deanne Canieso's unpacking of how Trump dominated the late-night comedic discourse in every phase of the campaign.

The 2016 social media ecosystem was a rich tapestry of messages, cultures, and events, and this book only scratches the surface of this rich topic. And although it typically takes decades to fully understand an election's impact, this book begins to research the central and disruptive role social and digital media had in our mediated democracy. Undoubtedly, the 2016 campaign will be studied by scholars and future campaigns, and it serves as an illustration of the paradigm shift that is occurring in political communication.

References

Confessore, N., & Yourish, K. (2016, March 15). $2 billion worth of free media for Donald Trump. *New York Times*. Retrieved from https://nyti.ms/2jQTVYm

Gottfried, J., Barthel, M., Shearer, E., & Mitchell, A. (2016, February 4). The 2016 president campaign: A news event that's hard to miss. *Pew Research Center*. Retrieved from www.journalism.org/2016/02/04/the-2016-presidential-campaign-a-news-event-thats-hard-to-miss/

Patterson, T. E. (2016). Pre-primary news coverage of the 2016 presidential race: Trump's rise, Sanders' emergence, Clinton's struggle. *Shorenstein Center on Media, Politics and Public Policy*. Retrieved from https://shorensteincenter.org/wp-content/uploads/2016/06/Pre-Primary-News-Coverage-Trump-Sanders-Clinton-2016.pdf

Plouffe, D. (2016, November 11). David Plouffe: What I got wrong about the election. *New York Times*. Retrieved from https://nyti.ms/2kksbZ7

Powers, W. (2016, February 23). Who's influencing election 2016? *Medium*. Retrieved from https://medium.com/@socialmachines/who-s-influencing-election-2016-8bed68ddecc3

Silver, N. (2016, March 30). How Trump hacked the media. *FiveThirtyEight*. Retrieved from http://53eig.ht/1WXYCKd

Singer, P. (2016, January 7). Trump took over Twitter with proposed Muslim ban. *USA Today*. Retrieved from http://usat.ly/1OQMq7Z

Taibbi, M. (2016, February 24). How American made Donald Trump unstoppable. *Rolling Stone*. Retrieved from http://rol.st/1oAKCKU

ACKNOWLEDGMENTS

The editors express appreciation to each contributor of this book for their diligent work on each study and their eagerness to assist at each stage of the editing process. Without each contributor's desire to better understand the relationship between media and politics, this book would not have come to completion.

The editors wish to acknowledge all at Routledge in New York who assisted with the development of this book. First, we thank Natalja Mortensen, Senior Editor, Political Science, who, at the project's beginning, supported and guided our book proposal through the peer review and acceptance stages; and, toward the project's conclusion, María Landschoot, Editorial Assistant, Political Science who steered our book manuscript through the final stages of publication. Second, the editors also wish to thank Peter Lloyd at T&F and the production team at Apex. Lastly, the editors wish to express gratitude to the reviewers who offered wise advice that indeed enhanced the value of the finished product.

Dan Schill would like to recognize his colleagues at James Madison University for their continued collegiality, encouragement, and strong support for research and teaching. John Allen Hendricks wishes to acknowledge the continued support of Stephen F. Austin State University (SFA) in Nacogdoches, Texas. Notably, this book was the beneficiary of a grant from the SFA Research Enhancement Program. Finally, Dr. Hendricks is appreciative of his graduate assistant, Aliaa Sadik Hussein Alyassri, for her diligence and meticulous eye for details.

Dan Schill is deeply thankful for Jessica, Ellie, and Bennett. John Allen Hendricks remains grateful to Stacy, Abby, and Haydyn.

Dan Schill
James Madison University
Harrisonburg, Virginia USA

John Allen Hendricks
Stephen F. Austin State University
Nacogdoches, Texas USA
April, 2017

ABOUT THE EDITORS

Dan Schill (Ph.D., University of Kansas) is an Associate Professor in the School of Communication Studies and Affiliate Professor in Political Science at James Madison University, where he teaches courses in advocacy, political communication, media and politics, and research methods. His research focuses on communication, politics, media, and technology. He has published four books on political communication topics, including *Political Communication in Real Time* (with Rita Kirk and Amy Jasperson, Routledge, 2017), *Communication and Midterm Elections* (with John Allen Hendricks; Palgrave Macmillan, 2015), *Presidential Campaigning and Social Media* (with John Allen Hendricks; Oxford University Press, 2014), and *Stagecraft and Statecraft: Advance and Media Events in Political Communication* (Lexington Books, 2009). Other work has appeared in *American Behavioral Scientist*, *Mass Communication & Society*, *Review of Communication*, and *PS: Political Science & Politics*. He has also received top paper awards from the Political Communication divisions of the International Communication Association, National Communication Association, and the Central States Communication Association. In addition to his academic research, Dr. Schill frequently conducts research for media outlets with frequent-collaborator Dr. Rita Kirk. In the 2008, 2012, and 2016 presidential campaigns, he organized and moderated on-air dial focus groups for CNN and provided real-time analysis of debates, convention speeches, and campaign ads. He also served as an American Political Science Association Congressional Fellow during the 111th Congress, where he worked on technology and communication issues in the U.S. Senate.

John Allen Hendricks (Ph.D., University of Southern Mississippi) is Chair of the Department of Mass Communication and Professor of Mass Communication at Stephen F. Austin State University in Nacogdoches, Texas. He has authored/edited ten books on the topics of media/politics, social media/new media technologies, and the broadcasting industry. Some of his books include: *Communication and Midterm Elections: Media, Message, and Mobilization* (with Dan Schill, Palgrave Macmillan, 2016); *Presidential Campaigning and Social Media: An Analysis of the 2012 Campaign* (with Dan Schill, Oxford University Press, 2015); *Social Media and Strategic Communications* (with Hana Noor Al-Deen, Palgrave MacMillan, 2013); *Social Media: Usage and Impact* (with Hana Noor Al-Deen; Lexington Books, 2012); *Techno Politics in Presidential Campaigning: New Voices, New Technologies, and New Voters* (with Lynda Lee Kaid; Routledge, 2011); and *Communicator-in-Chief: How Barack Obama Used New Media Technology to Win the White House* (with Robert E. Denton, Jr.; Lexington Books, 2009), which was the recipient of the National Communication Association's Applied Research Division's 2011 Distinguished Scholarly Book Award. Dr. Hendricks is Founding Editor of the "Studies in New Media" for Lexington Books/Rowman & Littlefield in Lanham, Maryland. He serves on the Editorial Advisory Board of *Journal of Broadcasting & Electronic Media* and *Social Media + Society*. He was President of the Broadcast Education Association (BEA) from 2015–2016 and served on its Board of Directors for eight years.

ABOUT THE CONTRIBUTORS

Michael A. Beam (Ph.D., The Ohio State University) is an Assistant Professor in the School of Communication Studies at Kent State University. His research interests include political communication and new communication technologies.

Josh C. Bramlett (M.S., Arkansas State University) is a doctoral student in the Department of Communication at the University of Missouri. His research focuses on political campaign communication, political comedy, and the political uses of social media.

Robert N. Burt (Bachelor of Integrative Studies, Miami University) is a recent graduate of the Department of Interdisciplinary and Communication Studies at Miami University.

Deanne Canieso is a doctoral student in Communication at George Mason University and has more than ten years of experience in project management, legislative affairs, and strategic communications, with experience in support of nonprofit associations, media campaigns, and health policy programs. Her professional involvement has encompassed developing legislative toolkits, press releases, video profiles, talking points, and policy briefs highlighting key public health issues. Her research interests are at the intersection of policy and health communication with primary interest in research that addresses mental health distress among disproportionately affected populations.

Raluca Cozma (Ph.D., Louisiana State University) is an Associate Professor of Journalism in the A.Q. Miller School of Journalism and Mass Communications at Kansas State University. Cozma's research examines the state and evolution of foreign correspondence and political communication and the role of social media in these fields. Her research has been published in venues such as the *Newspaper Research Journal*, *Journalism Studies*, *Journal of Broadcasting & Electronic Media*, and the *International Journal of Press/Politics*.

Stephen J. Farnsworth (Ph.D., Georgetown) is Professor of Political Science and International Affairs at the University of Mary Washington, where he directs the University's Center for Leadership and Media Studies. Farnsworth is the author or co-author of five books and dozens of scholarly articles on U.S. elections, the mass media, the presidency, public opinion, and Virginia politics. His most recent book is *The Global President: International Media and the U.S. Government* (co-authored with S. Robert Lichter and Roland Schatz). Farnsworth is a 2017 recipient of the Outstanding Faculty Award from the State Council of Higher Education for Virginia and has received three campus-wide teaching awards at Mary Washington.

Christine R. Filer is a doctoral candidate in the Department of Communication at the University of Arizona. Her research interests include political campaigns, media and politics, public opinion, and social media.

Zac Gershberg (Ph.D., Louisiana State University) is an Assistant Professor of Multiplatform Journalism and Media Studies in the Department of Communication, Media, and Persuasion at Idaho State University. He specializes in teaching and researching media history, journalism ethics, and political communication. Before entering academia, he worked as a reporter in Hawaii and he now contributes a column on media issues for the *Idaho State Journal* in Pocatello, Idaho.

Molly M. Greenwood (M.A., Marquette University) is a doctoral candidate in the Department of Communication at the University of Missouri. Her primary aim is to improve understanding of how mediated political communication messages impact individuals' political learning, efficacy, and engagement. In particular, she studies political comedy on social media, political campaign debates, and gender in political communication.

Jacob Groshek (Ph.D., Indiana University) researches the democratic utility of communication technologies and the ways in which the structure, content, and uses of online and mobile media may influence sociopolitical change. Additional research pursuits include applied econometric analyses, data mining, and visualizing social media content. He has over 45 peer-reviewed publications and some of his more notable work is featured in *Journal of Communication*, *New Media & Society*, *Social Scientific Computer Review*, and in volumes published by Oxford and Routledge, among others. Dr. Groshek also sits on the editorial boards of *Communication Yearbook* and the *Journal of Information Technology and Politics*, as well as regularly reviews for more than two dozen journals. He recently completed his term as Head of the Communication Technology Division of the Association for Education in Journalism and Mass Communication (AEJMC) and he has received top paper awards at the faculty and student levels in international competitions.

Paul M. Haridakis (Ph.D., Kent State University) is a Professor in the School of Communication Studies at Kent State University. His research interests include media use and effects, social media and other new communication technologies, political communication, freedom of speech, and media history.

Thomas Kim Hixson (Ph.D., Southern Illinois University) is Department Head of the Journalism and Communication Department at Utah State University. His research interests include social media use in politics, presidential campaigns, and media uses and gratifications. He has held elective office as a state legislator and city council president.

Jay D. Hmielowski (Ph.D., The Ohio State University) is an Assistant Professor in the Edward R. Murrow College of Communication at Washington State University. His research interests include political and environmental communication.

Myiah J. Hutchens (Ph.D., The Ohio State University) is an Assistant Professor in the Edward R. Murrow College of Communication at Washington State University. Her research interests include political communication and political discussion.

Sharon E. Jarvis (Ph.D., University of Texas at Austin) is an Associate Professor of Communication Studies and Associate Director of the Annette Strauss Institute for Civic Life at the University of Texas at Austin, where she teaches and conducts research on political communication, language use, and persuasion. She is the author of *The Talk of the Party: Political Labels, Symbolic Capital & American Life* (Rowman & Littlefield) and a co-author of *Political Keywords: Using Language that Uses Us* (Oxford University Press).

Freddie J. Jennings (M.A., University of Arkansas) is a doctoral student at the University of Missouri in the Department of Communication. His research centers on information processing and political identities. He studies the impact of the wide array of political communication that makes up the evolving informational landscape of American democracy, including political comedy, partisan media, presidential debates, and social media.

Jay T. Jennings (Ph.D., Temple University) is a Postdoctoral Research Fellow at the Annette Strauss Institute for Civic Life at the University of Texas at Austin.

His research focuses on political and civic engagement in the U.S. and more specifically on the relationship between social institutions and the capacity of citizens to effectively participate in politics. His work draws on the fields of political psychology, public opinion, and political communication.

Kate Kenski (Ph.D., University of Pennsylvania, 2006) is an Associate Professor in the Department of Communication at the University of Arizona. She is co-author of the award-winning book *The Obama Victory: How Media, Money, and Message Shaped the 2008 Election* (2010, Oxford University Press). Her current research focuses on campaign use of new media, incivility in online forums, and multimedia teaching strategies to mitigate cognitive biases.

Sarah Krongard is a doctoral student in Emerging Media Studies at Boston University's College of Communication. She received her Bachelor's degree in Cinema and Media Studies from Wellesley College and her Master's degree in Technology, Innovation, and Education from the Harvard Graduate School of Education. Through her research, Sarah examines the capacity for popular culture to facilitate healthy social and emotional development. She is specifically interested in television's role in socialization, particularly as the medium continues to evolve.

Jeffrey H. Kuznekoff (Ph.D., Ohio University, 2012) is an Assistant Professor in the Department of Interdisciplinary and Communication Studies at Miami University. His research interests include: computer-mediated communication, interpersonal communication, and instructional communication. His most recent work examines the influence of student text messaging, during classroom lecture, on student learning and investigating issues of gender voice in multiplayer video gaming. His research appears in *Communication Education*, *New Media & Society*, and *PloS ONE*.

S. Robert Lichter (Ph.D., Harvard) is Professor of Communication at George Mason University, where he also directs the Center for Media and Public Affairs. He has previously served on the teaching or research faculties of Yale, Columbia, Princeton, Georgetown, and George Washington universities. Lichter has authored or co-authored numerous books, monographs, and scholarly and popular articles on the news and entertainment media. His most recent book is *Politics is a Joke: How TV Comedians are Remaking Political Life* (co-authored with Jody Baumgartner and Jonathon Morris).

Johanna M. Lukk (M.A., University of Delaware) works as a Project Coordinator at The Archer Group, an advertising firm located in Wilmington, DE.

Wendy W. Moe (Ph.D., University of Pennsylvania) is a Professor of Marketing and Director of the Master's degree in Marketing Analytics at the Robert H.

Smith School of Business, University of Maryland. She is a recognized expert in online marketing and social media and is the author of *Social Media Intelligence* (Cambridge University Press). Professor Moe's research has appeared in numerous leading journals. In addition to her academic work, Professor Moe has consulted for numerous corporations and government agencies, helping them develop and implement state-of-the-art statistical models in the context of web analytics, social media intelligence, and forecasting.

Alison N. Novak (Ph.D., Drexel University) is an Assistant Professor of Public Relations and Advertising at Rowan University. Her work examines media discourses and effects on Millennial political and civic engagement. She is the author of *Media, Millennials, and Politics: The Coming of Age of the Next Political Generation* and the editor of *Defining Identity and the Changing Scope of Culture in the Digital Age*. Her work has been published in *First Monday*, *Review of Communication*, and *The Journal of Information, Technology, and Politics.* She is a contributor to the *Huffington Post* and has been featured in *Wired Magazine*, *Redbook Magazine*, and *CBS News.*

Sarah Oates (Ph.D., Emory University) is Professor and Senior Scholar at the Philip Merrill College of Journalism at the University of Maryland, College Park. She studies political communication in places as diverse as Russia, the U.S., and the U.K. A former journalist, she has published extensively on media and democratization, including her most recent book, *Revolution Stalled: The Political Limits of the Internet in the Post-Soviet Sphere* (Oxford University Press).

David Lynn Painter (Ph.D., University of Florida) is an Assistant Professor in the Communication Department at Rollins College. Dr. Painter's 20-year professional background and his academic research interests focus on political campaign communication, with particular expertise in social media engagement and television advertising. Since 2009, he has authored 14 publications in scholarly volumes and more than 25 papers competitively selected for presentation at national and international conferences.

Thomas E. Patterson (Ph.D., University of Minnesota) is Bradlee Professor of Government and the Press at Harvard University's Kennedy School of Government. He is author of the book *Informing the News: The Need for Knowledge-Based Journalism*, published in October 2013. His earlier book, *The Vanishing Voter*, looks at the causes and consequences of electoral participation, and his book on the media's political role, *Out of Order*, received the American Political Science Association's Graber Award as the best book of the decade in political communication. His first book, *The Unseeing Eye*, was named by the American Association for Public Opinion Research as one of the 50 most influential books on public opinion in the past half century. He is also the author of *Mass*

Media Election: How Americans Choose Their President (1980), and two general American government texts: The American Democracy and We the People. His articles have appeared in *Political Communication, Journal of Communication*, and other academic journals, as well as in the popular press. His research has been funded by the Ford, Markle, Smith-Richardson, Pew, Knight, Carnegie, and National Science foundations.

Damian J. Rivers (Ph.D., University of Leicester, U.K.) is an Associate Professor of Communication at Future University Hakodate (Hakodate, Japan). His research interests are varied and include critical applied linguistics, discourses of authority in educational contexts, rhetoric and knowledge representation, the native-speaker criterion, and the management of multiple identities. In addition to numerous international journal publications, he has co-edited four book volumes, including *Native-Speakerism in Japan: Intergroup Dynamics in Foreign Language Education* (2013, Multilingual Matters), *Social Identities and Multiple Selves in Foreign Language Education* (2013, Bloomsbury), *Isms in Language Education: Oppression, Intersectionality, and Emancipation* (2017, Mouton De Gruyter), and *The Sociolinguistics of Hip-Hop as Critical Conscience: Dissatisfaction and Dissent* (2017, Palgrave Macmillan). He also served as solo editor for the project *Resistance to the Known: Counter-Conduct in Language Education* (2015, Palgrave Macmillan) and is currently a co-author of the volume *Beyond Native-Speakerism: Current Explorations and Future Visions* (2018, Routledge).

Katherine Rizzo (A.B., Rollins College) is a communication studies scholar and public relations professional whose academic and professional background includes multiple conference presentations and industry awards. Rizzo's research and professional interests focus on political communication and analyses of big data related to the promotion of social and political issues.

Andrew S. Ross (Ph.D., University of Canberra) is a Lecturer at Southern Cross University (Gold Coast, Australia) and has more than ten years of experience as a language teacher in Australia, Thailand, and Japan. Currently, he is interested in the discourses that occur within and across digital social media platforms, but other interests include emotional identities in language education, the sociolinguistics of resistance, and approaches to teaching and learning in higher education settings. His work has appeared in such venues as the *Journal of Language, Identity and Education*, the *Australian Review of Applied Linguistics*, and *Discourse, Context and Media*. He is currently co-editor of the volume *The Sociolinguistics of Hip-Hop as Critical Conscience: Dissatisfaction and Dissent* (2017, Palgrave Macmillan).

Leland G. Spencer (Ph.D., University of Georgia) is an Assistant Professor in the Department of Interdisciplinary and Communication Studies and an Affiliate Faculty Member in the Department of Media, Journalism, and Film and the Women's, Gender, and Sexuality Studies Program at Miami University. An award-winning scholar, Leland co-edited (with Jamie Capuzza) *Transgender Communication Studies: Histories, Trends, and Traditions* (Lexington, 2015) and has published research in several academic journals, including the *Western Journal of Communication*, the *Southern Communication Journal*, *Communication Studies*, *QED: A Journal in GLBTQ Worldmaking*, and *Queer Studies in Media and Popular Culture*, among others.

Terri L. Towner (Ph.D., Purdue University) is an Associate Professor of Political Science at Oakland University in Michigan. Her research focuses on American politics, public opinion, new media coverage of elections and political institutions, and the politics of race, class, and gender. Towner is currently working on a book project titled *The Internet and the 2016 Presidential Campaign*. Her research has been published as book chapters and journal articles, most recently in: *Social Sciences*; *The Journal of Women, Politics & Policy*; *Presidential Campaigning and Social Media: An Analysis of the 2012 Election*; *The Journal of Political Marketing*; *Social Science Computer Review*; *New Media & Society*; *Techno-Politics in Presidential Campaigning: New Voices, New Technologies, and New Voters*; and *The Howard Journal of Communications*.

Benjamin R. Warner (Ph.D., University of Kansas) is Assistant Professor in the Department of Communication at the University of Missouri. His research examines the effects of political communication on attitudes such as partisan polarization and political efficacy. In particular, he studies political messages in social media, political satire, televised presidential debates, and campaign advertising.

Dannagal G. Young (Ph.D., University of Pennsylvania) is an Associate Professor at the University of Delaware, where she studies the content and effects of political communication, with a focus on political entertainment. Her research on the psychology and influence of political satire has been published in academic journals including *Media Psychology*, *Political Communication*, and the *International Journal of Press/Politics*. Young's writing has appeared in the *Columbia Journalism Review*, *The Atlantic*, and the *New York Times*. Young is a Research Fellow with the University of Delaware's Center for Political Communication, a Distinguished Fellow of the University of Pennsylvania's Annenberg Public Policy Center, and was awarded the University of Delaware's Excellence in Teaching Award in 2014.

PART 1

Media Use

Political Engagement and Digital Democracy

1

DISCOURSE, DISRUPTION, AND DIGITAL DEMOCRACY

Political Communication in the 2016 Presidential Campaign

Dan Schill and John Allen Hendricks

Digital and social media were influential in past presidential elections, but in 2016, the digital campaign was the story as online communication played a significant and integral role during the primary and general elections for both Trump and Clinton. "It is not an exaggeration to say that political campaigns today *are* social media campaigns" (Hendricks & Schill, 2017). Social and digital media disrupted long-standing campaign norms and practices—including how the candidates ran their campaigns, how the media covered the news, and how citizens received and shared information—in what *New York Times* media columnist Jim Ruttenberg (2016) characterized as a "media hurricane" (para. 12). Old distinctions were made quaint and erased. As Stanford's Nate Persily (2017) concluded:

> the 2016 campaign broke down all the established distinctions that observers had used to describe campaigns: between insiders and outsiders, earned media and advertising, media and nonmedia, legacy media and new media, news and entertainment, and even foreign and domestic sources of campaign communication.
>
> *(pp. 63–64)*

Or, as Michael Slaby (2016), the Chief Integration and Innovation Officer for President Obama's 2012 and 2016 campaigns, summarized: "The 2016 cycle has been categorized by unprecedented unpredictability, not as much from the perspective of technology disruption, but a whole-scale shift in the norms of campaign communications" (para. 19). In 2016, history, logic, and even facts themselves appeared not to matter (Ignatius, 2016; Rampell, 2016). Alex Conant, a senior strategist for Republican primary challenger Marco Rubio, described the 2016 media/politics ecosystem this way: "There was no news cycle—everything was one big fire hose. News was constantly breaking and at the end of the day hardly anything mattered. Things would happen; 24 hours later, everyone was talking about something else" (para. 14). And although television news and other legacy media sources remained influential, digital media drove the national conversation and social media were Donald Trump's primary communication channel. Brad Parscale, Trump's digital director, made this exact point: "Facebook and Twitter were the reason we won this thing. Twitter for Mr. Trump. And Facebook for fundraising" (quoted in Lapowsky, 2016, para. 3). The purpose of this chapter is to describe and discuss how these digital and social media outlets disrupted political discourse and participation in the 2016 presidential election and to illustrate how communication technologies are impacting our continuously evolving digital democracy.

Donald Trump and Hillary Clinton

After long and hard-fought primaries for both political parties, the 2016 general-election candidates were chosen by a very polarized electorate. New York real estate billionaire Donald J. Trump clinched the Republican Party's nomination on July 22, 2016, and former Secretary of State Hillary Rodham Clinton clinched the Democratic Party nomination on July 26, 2016. Trump had 16 opponents in the Republican primary compared to Clinton's five opponents in the Democratic primary (Andrews, Lai, Parlapiano, & Yourish, 2016). Trump cast himself throughout the campaign as a "change agent" who would "drain the swamp" in Washington. In seemingly constant, pungent, and pointed tweets and in large campaign rallies, his "America First," outsider message resonated with many voters outside of the nation's capital who had grown weary of hollow political promises from establishment politicians. Trump was the first president ever elected who had never served in the military or in elected office prior to his victory, and his lack of political experience was a significant part of his appeal to voters. Trump's change message was accepted to the point that voters were willing to overlook an audio recording of Trump bragging that he had sexually abused women in the past. The outsider, populist message resonated with voters to the point that not even a significant fundraising advantage could propel Clinton into the Oval Office. To no avail, Clinton outspent Trump fairly significantly. In total, she spent \$1.4 billion whereas he spent \$932.3 million (Gold & Narayanswamy, 2016). Clinton won the popular vote 48.5% (65,853,516) to Trump's 46.4% (62,984,825) whereas Trump won the needed electoral college votes, 306 to 232, to become the nation's 45th commander-in-chief (Krieg, 2016).

Both candidates held high unfavorable ratings among the American public throughout the election and both appeared to be deeply flawed at times. In fact, Clinton and Trump were the most unpopular candidates ever ("2016 campaign," 2016; Collins, 2016). Clinton, the Washington-entrenched, status-quo politician, was consistently plagued with scandals surrounding her perceived lack of honesty and transparency ranging from giving paid speeches to Wall Street firms to using a personal server for emails during her tenure as U.S. secretary of state. She was further dogged by an alleged unethical relationship with her family's foundation during her tenure as secretary of state. Yet, the issue that appeared to most damage her reputation in the campaign was Clinton's response to the attack on two U.S. government CIA facilities in Benghazi, Libya resulting in the death of four American diplomats and security personnel, including a U.S. ambassador. The *Chicago Tribune*, in an editorial about the attacks, stated: "On the question of how Clinton and the Obama administration reacted, we see more than enough evidence to reaffirm our opinion that the secretary of state failed a crucial chance to show decisive, principled leadership" ("Editorial: Benghazi," 2016, para. 4). After extensive public hearings, a U.S. House Select Committee published an 800-page report on the incident that found that Secretary Clinton "promoted a false narrative for public consumption" both during and after the attacks ("Editorial: Benghazi," 2016, para. 5).

Following on the heels of the Benghazi scandal, it was revealed that, while secretary, Clinton refused to use the Department of State official email account and instead chose to set up a personal and private server in her New York home to conduct official government business. Many of the emails sent via this unsecured server were marked as "classified," containing national security secrets that allowed Clinton's critics to question her judgment and honesty even more vociferously. Eventually the Clinton team provided the State Department with 55,000 pages of emails and 30,490 individual email messages to review and archive (Graff, 2016). Clinton deleted more than 30,000 emails that she claimed contained "records of communications about private matters, like yoga routines, her daughter's wedding and her mother's funeral" (Chozick & Schmidt, 2015, para. 1). The mishandling of classified materials prompted the FBI to start an investigation into whether Clinton had violated federal laws. The FBI eventually ruled that Clinton should not be charged, but the investigation hung over the election and it resulted in an "October Surprise" when the FBI director suddenly sent a letter to several committees on Capitol Hill informing them that the FBI was reopening its investigating into Clinton's handling of the emails based upon new evidence. This provided fertile fodder for Trump to consistently remind voters that Clinton had a penchant for not being honest and trustworthy. For example, an oft-repeated chant at Trump rallies was "lock her up!" In fact, when Clinton called for Trump to release his taxes for the sake of transparency, he replied she needed to release the 30,000 emails she deleted. That kind of attack resonated with many voters in 2016. In the end, after all of the investigations by FBI Director James Comey and his agency and the attacks Clinton endured on the campaign trail, it was determined that Clinton had not broken any laws related to the email scandal nor the Benghazi attacks.

Many anti-Clinton attacks came from and were amplified by emails and documents that were hacked from a cyberattack on the Democratic National Committee and an email phishing hack on Clinton campaign manager John Podesta, and subsequently released on the anti-secrecy website WikiLeaks (see Cohen, 2017 for a timeline). The hacked documents were promoted by Trump surrogates and Trump himself, who said "I love WikiLeaks" at an October 10 rally. In January 2017, the Office of the Director of National Intelligence released a report which concluded that Russian President Vladimir Putin ordered these hacks as part of an "influence campaign" to help Trump and hurt Clinton, as well as to undermine public faith in the U.S. election system. The report detailed "a Russian messaging strategy that blends covert intelligence operations—such as cyber activity—with overt efforts by Russian government agencies, state-funded media, third-party intermediaries, and paid social media users or 'trolls'" ("Assessing Russian Activities," 2017, p. ii). Extensive connections between Trump campaign officials and Russia were revealed during the campaign, leading to multiple post-election investigations. In a March 20, 2017 hearing, FBI Director Comey publicly confirmed that the FBI was probing "the nature of any links between individuals associated with the Trump campaign and the Russian government, and whether there was any coordination between the campaign and Russia's efforts" (cited in Cohen, 2017, para. 68).

Trump, the impetuous and egotistical New York real estate tycoon and reality TV star, also had his share of scandals and missteps during the campaign: insulting the parents of a dead war hero, an arm-flapping impersonation of a disabled reporter, and mocking John McCain's five-year internment in a Vietnam POW camp (Thrush, 2016). Like Clinton, Trump also gained a reputation for not always telling the truth and being transparent. Breaking a long tradition that started with President Richard Nixon, he refused to publicly release his taxes claiming that he could not because he was being audited by the IRS (Disis, 2017). This provided his opponents with the ability to question what he said his net worth was, thereby questioning his business acumen, which was a cornerstone of his campaign strategy, as well as allowing opponents to question whether he had engaged in any unethical business dealings. In the presidential debate, Clinton stated:

> First, maybe he's not as rich as he says he is. Maybe he's not as charitable as he claims to be. Third, we don't know all of his business dealings, but we have been told through investigative reporting that he owes about $650 million to Wall Street and foreign banks. Or maybe he doesn't want the American people, all of you watching tonight, to know that he's paid nothing in federal taxes.
>
> *(Wilke, 2016, para. 7)*

Regarding Clinton's allegation that he had paid nothing in federal taxes, he quickly retorted: "That makes me smart" (Wilke, 2016, para. 9).

Using Twitter, Trump was quick to troll his opponents with mean-spirited insults. In the primaries, he threatened to expose alleged secrets about Texas Senator Ted Cruz's wife and suggested his supporters check out an alleged sex tape of a former Miss Universe pageant winner who criticized him. There were numerous tweets that caught people's attention and were outright inaccurate, but it was the *Access Hollywood* tape that perhaps provided the biggest scandals for the Trump campaign. On the 2005 tape, Trump used lewd language in which he bragged about kissing and groping women and trying to have sex with them. He asserted, "when you're a star, they let you do it" (Fahrenthold, 2016, para. 1). The future president added that when you are famous you can do anything to women such as "Grab them by the p—y, you can do anything" (Fahrenthold, 2016, para. 19). Although Trump apologized "if anyone was offended" about what he had said on the audiotape, he simultaneously defended it as innocuous "locker-room banter." He went on the counter-attack and turned the scandal into a spectacle about Bill Clinton's infidelities by having a press conference prior to the second presidential debate with three women whom had accused the former U.S. president of sexual assault in the past (Fahrenthold, 2016, para. 21). After the press conference, he had the women sit in the Trump family seats to confront the Clintons during the debate.

Prolific, attention-grabbing tweets were front and center to the Trump approach to political communication. In 2016, Trump could jolt the news cycle with Twitter missives fired off consecutively in the early morning, throughout the day, and into the evening. Corey Lewandowski, Trump's former campaign manager, called Twitter "a very, very powerful weapon" and argued that "Trump's Twitter account is the greatest bully pulpit that has ever existed" (quoted in Rucker & Paquette, 2017, paras. 14–15). Unlike Clinton, Trump was perceived by his supporters as being authentic on social media, especially on Twitter, even though (and perhaps because) his tweets were often insulting and inaccurate. This approach was not new for Trump. As Rucker and Paquette note: "prolific, indiscriminate and often deceptive tweeting has been a central part of Trump's public identity for years" (2017, para. 7). Trump was fond of referring to himself as "the Ernest Hemingway of Twitter" (quoted in Rucker & Paquette, 2017, para. 20) and experts agreed, such as Amanda Hess, who called Trump a "modern social media master" (2016, para. 3). In addition to gaining followers, his social media strategy proved to be successful in garnering free media coverage (Wells et al., 2016). MediaQuant, an analytics firm, estimated that Trump received more than \$3.4 billion in free media coverage with about \$372 million alone just from traditional media outlets covering his outlandish, attention-grabbing tweets (Samuelsohn, 2016). Comparatively, Hillary Clinton received only \$1.4 billion in free media with only \$93 million of free media being generated from her tweets. It appeared that Trump understood that "the beast that is social media constantly has to be fed with information" (Barrett, 2016, para. 12).

Social Media: Campaign Digital Teams

In 2016, politicians had to meet the voters on their turf—social media ("Election 2016," 2016). Facebook had 231 million monthly active users in North America and Canada alone, with 1.86 billion monthly active users around the world ("Number of monthly active Facebook users in the United States and Canada," 2017). Twitter had 67 million monthly active users with 310 million users worldwide ("Number of monthly active Twitter users in the United States," 2017). YouTube boasted 1.3 billion users with 5 billion videos being watched every day with more than 30 million visitors each day (YouTube Statistics, 2017). And Instagram had 77.5 million users in America and that number is expected to grow to 116 million users by 2020. Worldwide, there were 500 million Instagram users ("Number of Instagram users in the United States," 2017). Overall, *Statistica.com* reported that "an estimated 31 percent of the world's population was using social networking, with North America having the highest penetration rate—59 percent of the country's population" ("Number of Instagram users in the United States," 2017, para. 2). Clearly, to be competitive, politicians now must integrate social media into campaign strategies.

Further, the Pew Research Center found that 69%, or over two-thirds of all American adults, used social media (Smith, 2017). Among 18- to 29-year-olds, social media usage rose to 86%. With news applications, push notices, and seemingly non-stop social media notifications, for most of the electorate, the campaign was always with them as smartphones dominated as a means to access news and information. Specifically, in 2017, the Pew Research Center found that nearly 80% of Americans owned a smartphone compared to only 35% just five years prior (Smith, 2017). The same Pew study found that 92% of 18- to 29-year-olds had a smartphone whereas an impressive 74% of 50- to 64-year-olds had smartphones. The study indicated there had been an increase in smartphone adoption in all age, income, and geographic demographics. The study also found that, overall, 88% of Americans used the Internet, over half (51%) owned a tablet, and 77% had broadband Internet service at home. Thus, because the electorate was on the Internet and smartphones were accessing social media, so too were the presidential candidates. Indeed, the candidates' campaigns engaged in impressive digital strategies to target specific demographics among the American electorate. Patterson (2016) stated:

> Politicians use social platforms to gauge voter interest and identify what truly matters to him or her. If an individual is regularly advocating for women's rights and posting about it on Facebook or Twitter, for example, social data can pick up on this and help politicians better target these individuals with the right messaging. With the right data-driven strategy, candidates identify the right audiences on social media for both donating and voting.
>
> *(para. 5)*

Both Clinton and Trump had digital teams who were very adept at using social media platforms to develop the right data-driven messages, more so than in any previous elections. In fact, Johnson (2016) said, "the 2016 presidential election has been the most digital race in American history—making it full of lessons for marketers" (para. 2). The Clinton campaign based in Brooklyn included: Jenna Lowenstein, digital director for the Clinton campaign; Katie Dowd, senior digital advisor; Teddy Goff, chief digital strategist; Elan Kriegel, director of analytics; and Andrew Bleeker, digital marketing advisor (Hendricks & Schill, 2017). There were more than 100 people working on the Clinton digital team employing all types of social media platforms such as Facebook, Twitter, Instagram, Tumblr, Snapchat, and YouTube (Allen, 2017). If there was a social media platform, Clinton's team generated content for it. And Clinton created her own platforms with video- and social-centric websites and mobile applications. The Clinton website's highly visual and modular design allowed for fast customization and served as a hub to house content from multiple digital and social media platforms, including seamless integration with Twitter and Facebook. Additionally, the Clinton mobile app was inspired by popular games such as Farmville, Hay Day, and Tiny Tower, and when users would complete one of four challenges—such as checking in for an organizing event, sharing a video with friends, or sharing results from online policy quizzes—they would be rewarded with points on a common leaderboard and could even win bonuses such as signed campaign merchandise (Sifry, 2016).

Of the 100 Clinton digital team members, dozens were assigned to typing posts on social media each day. The Clinton team was clever in its use of social-networking platforms and created games such as "Trump Yourself" that enabled users to take Trump quotes, such as, "If you need Viagra, you're probably with the wrong girl," and apply it to their profiles on Facebook and Twitter (Chen, 2016). Clinton and Trump both used social media to raise money. There were options to donate money on Twitter, Facebook, and YouTube and then supporters could post on their newsfeeds that they did so to try and build momentum for their favorite candidate. Patterson (2016) noted:

> [Users who donate] become surrogates for a campaign that candidates can use to their advantage, especially when factoring in big data that already exists within social platforms. This data is unique in that it can help politicians target potential voters and donors.
>
> *(para. 11)*

In addition to email, a key digital fundraising tool was the humble text message. Supporters who provided their cell phone number when visiting the campaign website or at a rally received daily text messages promoting upcoming events, driving the campaign's message of the day, or asking for contributions. According to Corasaniti (2015), "What gives texting its political power is its ability to cut through a lot of other advertising noise: targeted posts on Facebook and Twitter, web video commercials and the pitter-patter of emails pleading for campaign contributions" (para. 16).

Trump's digital campaign primarily consisted of the marketing agency Giles-Parscale, the targeting and analytics firm Cambridge Analytica, and the staffers from the Republican National Committee. The Trump digital team was led by political novice Brad Parscale, a San Antonio marketing entrepreneur who had built web pages for the Trump family's business and charities (Green & Issenberg, 2016). Two top aides, Steve Bannon and Jared Kushner, had extensive digital and social media experience as Chairman of Breitbart News Network and Publisher of the *New York Observer*, respectively. On the data side, even though Trump called data "overrated," his campaign hired Matt Braynard and Witold Chrabaszcz, both data strategists, to work with political data firm L2 to use data and analytics from both the Trump social media platforms and the RNC database, which provided Trump access to information on more than 200 million people ("The role of technology," 2016, para. 5; Vogel & Samuelsohn, 2016). Trump generated the bulk of the campaign's fundraising online and used extensive message-testing to A/B test social media content; Trump's campaign said they used Facebook to run "40,000 to 50,000 variants of its ads, testing how they performed in different formats, with subtitles and without, and static versus video, among other small differences" (Lapowsky, 2016, para. 9). And perhaps more integral to the Trump campaign's digital team than the data analytics team was his social media team. Justin McConney, Trump's 29-year-old director of new media, met with the Republican candidate each morning and discussed what should be posted or tweeted and then the candidate wrote the message. When Trump was on the campaign trail and not in the office, Dan Scavino, the campaign's director of social media, played the role of McConney (Schreckinger, 2015; Sherman, 2016). Trump would personally write his tweets using his Samsung smartphone and occasionally had an aide type for him (Schreckinger, 2015).

Social Media: Trump vs. Clinton

In the general election, both Trump and Clinton utilized the primary social media platforms. However, Trump had more followers and more engagement than Clinton on most social media platforms. On Facebook, Socialbakers.com—a social media analytics company—reported that Trump had 15.9 million followers compared to Clinton's 9.9 million followers. Trump was averaging an addition of 296,000 fans per week compared to Clinton's 232,000 fans per week (see Figure 1.1). In terms of engagement, Trump averaged 7.0 million interactions per week compared to Clinton's 2.9 million weekly interactions. When comparing the distribution of interactions between the two candidates—which includes reactions, comments, and shares—again Trump averaged more than Clinton. Specifically, Trump had 184 million interactions compared to Clinton's 78.7 million interactions. Interestingly, Trump's interactions with followers were higher with videos and status updates (see Figure 1.2).

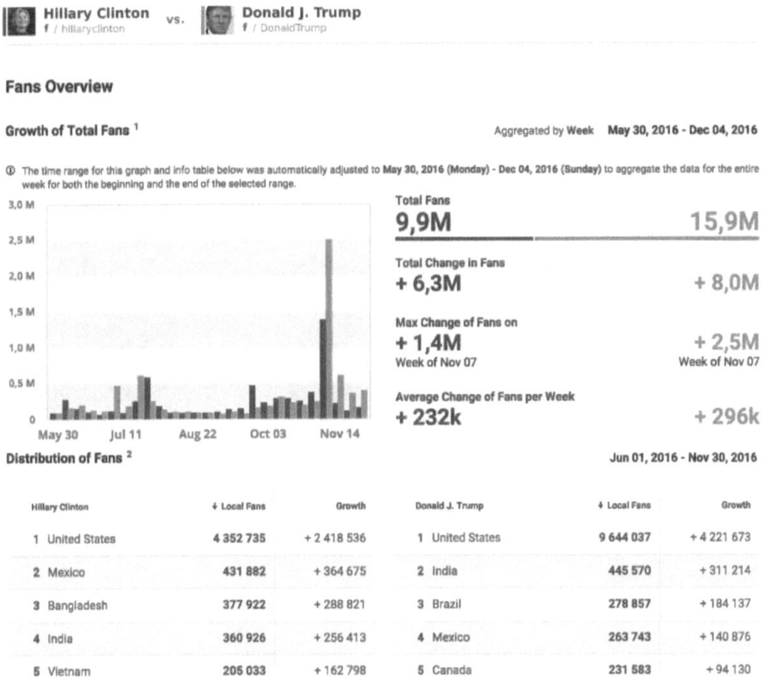

FIGURE 1.1A Facebook: Hillary Clinton vs. Donald J. Trump—Fans Overview

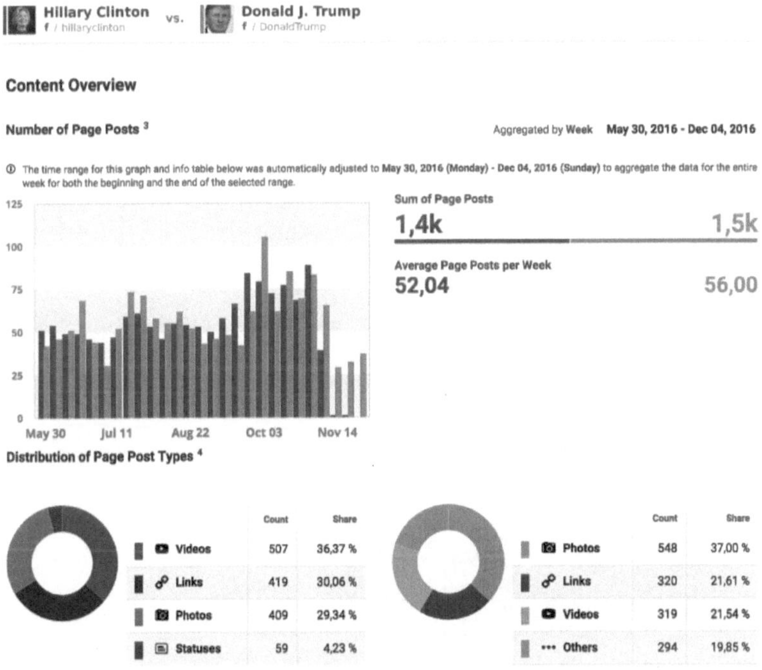

FIGURE 1.1B Facebook: Hillary Clinton vs. Donald J. Trump—Content Overview

Source: Facebook Overview (2016). *Socialbakers.com*. Reprinted with permission.

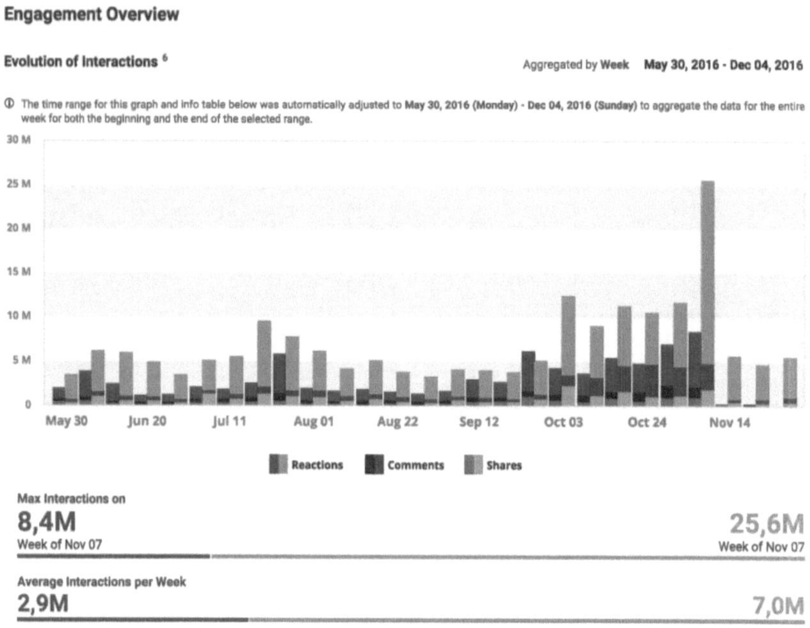

FIGURE 1.2A Facebook: Hillary Clinton vs. Donald J. Trump—Engagement Overview

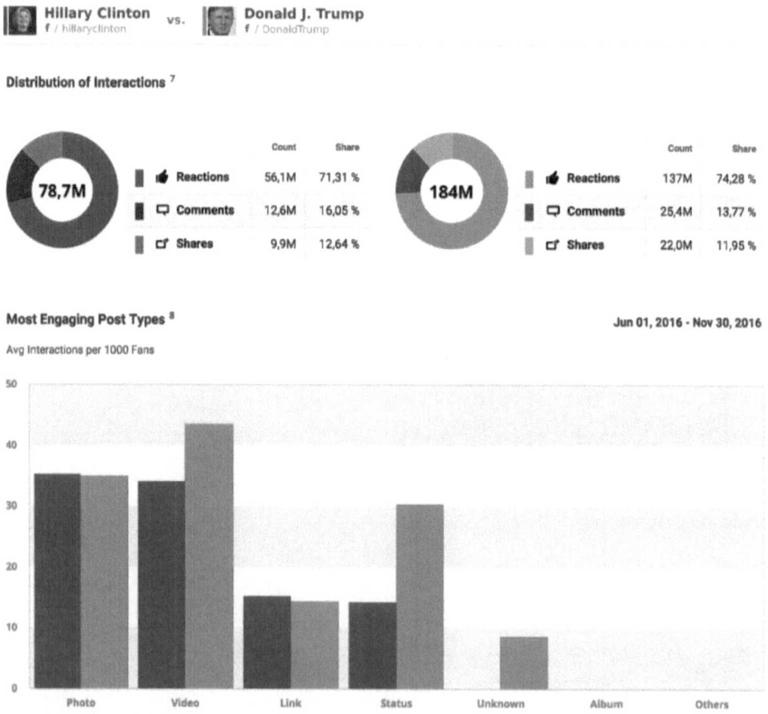

FIGURE 1.2B Facebook: Hillary Clinton vs. Donald J. Trump—Distribution of Interactions

Source: Facebook Overview (2016). *Socialbakers.com*. Reprinted with permission.

Donald Trump was notorious for using his Twitter account @realDonaldTrump to hurl insults at his opponents and take on the mainstream media when they disagreed with him. This bombastic approach not only influenced the news cycles, but also gained him many new followers just to see what he was going to say in the next tweet. Although not all of these accounts were likely to be actual users, Trump had 16.7 million Twitter followers compared to Clinton's 11.5 million. Trump averaged 302,000 new followers per week compared to Clinton's 187,000 (see Figure 1.3). In total, during the general-election period (from May 30, 2016 to December 4, 2016) Clinton's Twitter profile posted about 1,900 messages (averaging 71 per week) compared to Trump's 2,700 messages (101 per week). The most engaging tweet for each candidate was Clinton's "To

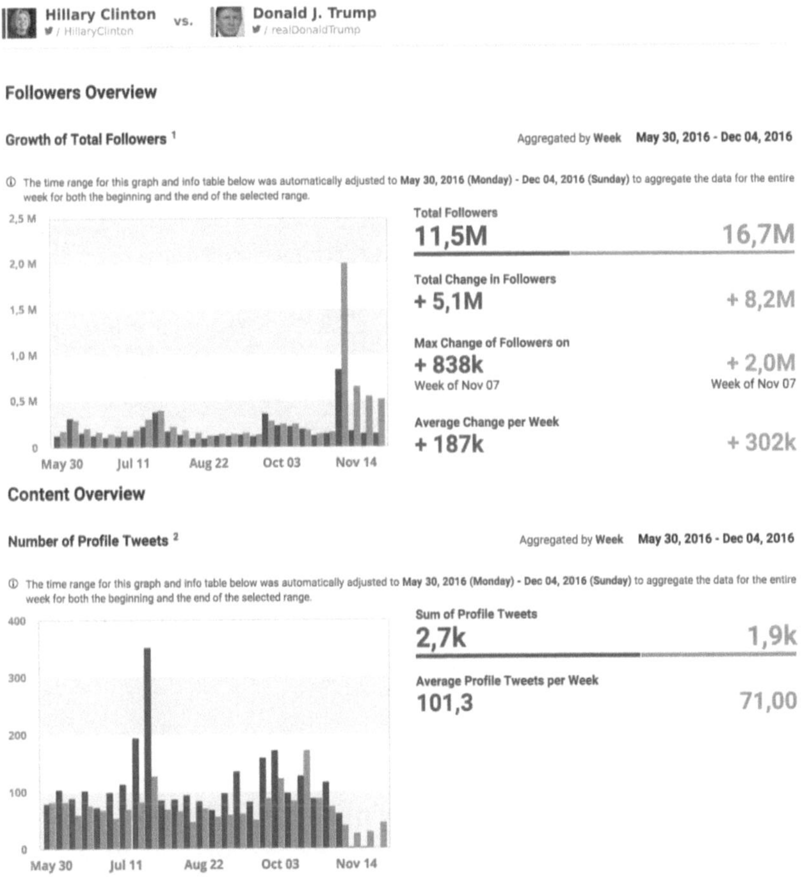

FIGURE 1.3 Twitter: Hillary Clinton vs. Donald J. Trump—Followers Overview

Source: Twitter Overview (2016). *Socialbakers.com*. Reprinted with permission.

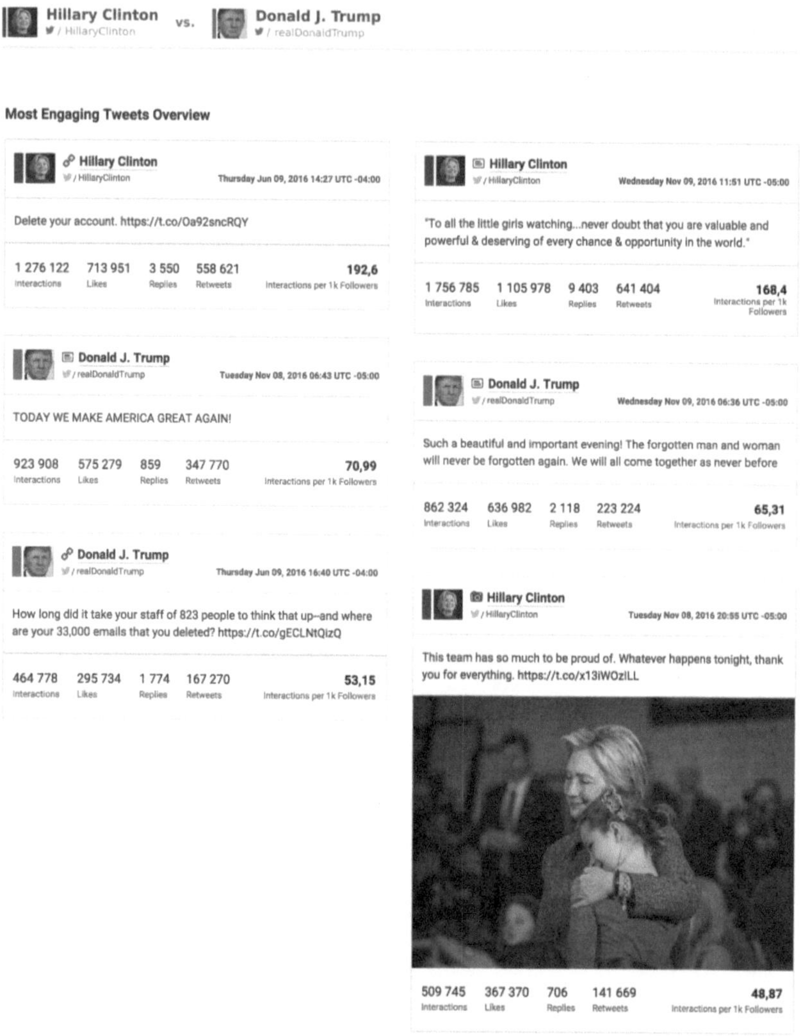

FIGURE 1.4 Twitter: Hillary Clinton vs. Donald J. Trump—Most Engaging Tweets Overview

Source: Twitter Overview (2016). *Socialbakers.com*. Reprinted with permission.

all the little girls watching . . . never doubt that you are valuable and powerful & deserving of every chance & opportunity in the world" tweet that garnered 1.7 million interactions the day after the election compared to Trump's most engaging tweet, which was on election day and stated, "TODAY WE MAKE AMERICA GREAT AGAIN!" (tweeted by the candidate in all caps) that garnered 923,908 interactions (see Figure 1.4). Overall, Trump's Twitter account had 79.5

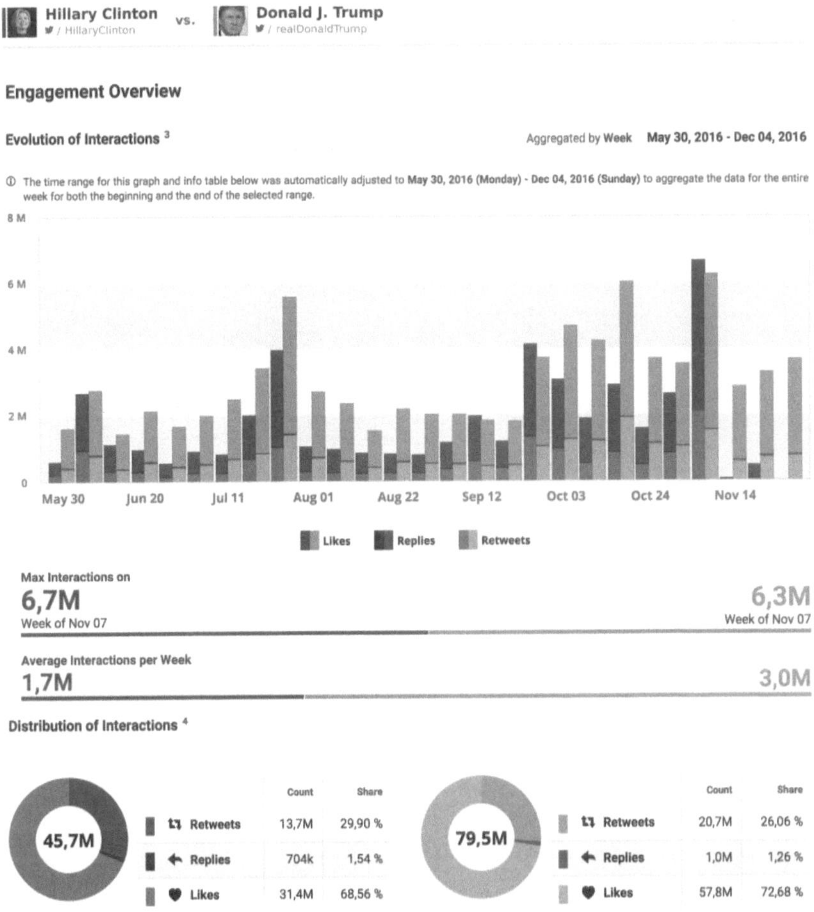

FIGURE 1.5 Twitter: Hillary Clinton vs. Donald J. Trump—Engagement Overview

Source: Twitter Overview (2016). *Socialbakers.com*. Reprinted with permission.

million interactions whereas Clinton's account had 45.7 million interactions (see Figure 1.5). Clinton's more traditional and less provocative tweets failed to gain the type of traction that Trump's tweeting gained during the campaign.

Both Trump and Clinton had YouTube channels during the 2016 campaign. Based on the social media metrics, this is the only social media outlet that Clinton prevailed in against her Republican opponent. Clinton had about 135,000 subscribers to her YouTube channel "Hillary Clinton" compared to Trump's 104,000 subscribers to his YouTube channel "Donald J. Trump for President." During the general-election period, Trump posted 139 videos compared to Clinton's 87 videos and Trump averaged 5.15 videos per week compared to Clinton's average

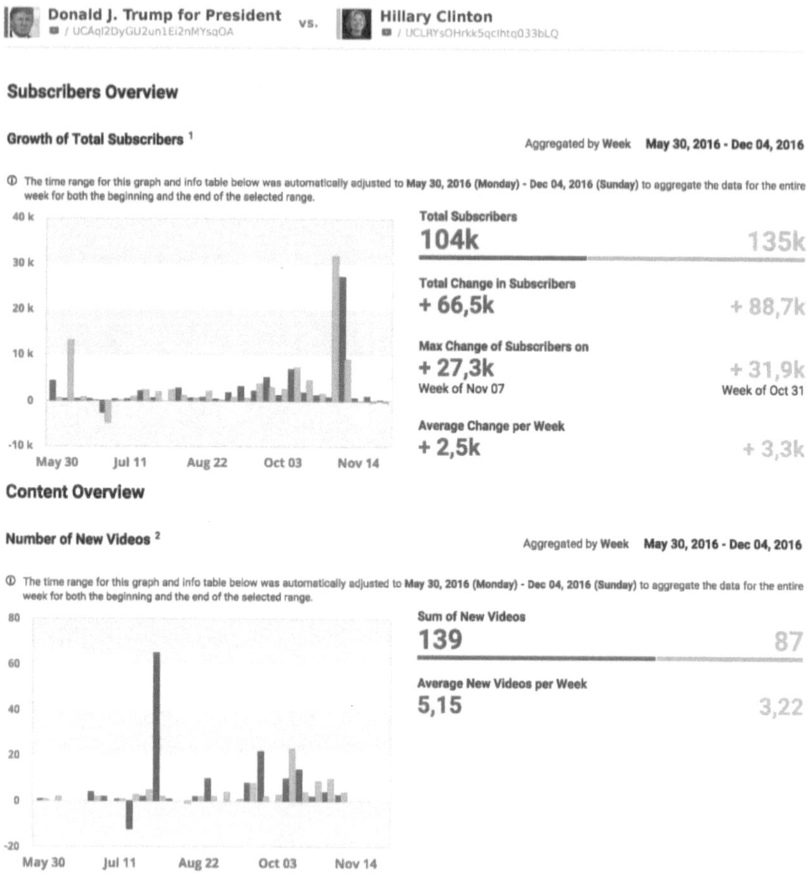

FIGURE 1.6 YouTube: Donald J. Trump for President vs. Hillary Clinton—Subscribers Overview

Source: YouTube Overview (2016). *Socialbakers.com*. Reprinted with permission.

of 3.22 videos per week (see Figure 1.6). In terms of YouTube engagement, Clinton experienced 870,000 interactions compared to Trump's 402,000 interactions. The Clinton channel averaged 26.2 million views compared to Trump's 19.9 million views (see Figures 1.7 and 1.8).

As noted, Instagram has a large number of active users and that number is expected to continue to rapidly increase in the coming years. Accordingly, both candidates had Instagram accounts. Interestingly, although 58% of Instagram users are female and 42% are male (Seligson, 2016), gender did not appear to help Clinton with followers on the social-networking platform. Trump had 4.3 million followers compared to Clinton's 3.8 million. In total, Trump's profile had 533 posts compared to Clinton's 321 posts with Trump having 457

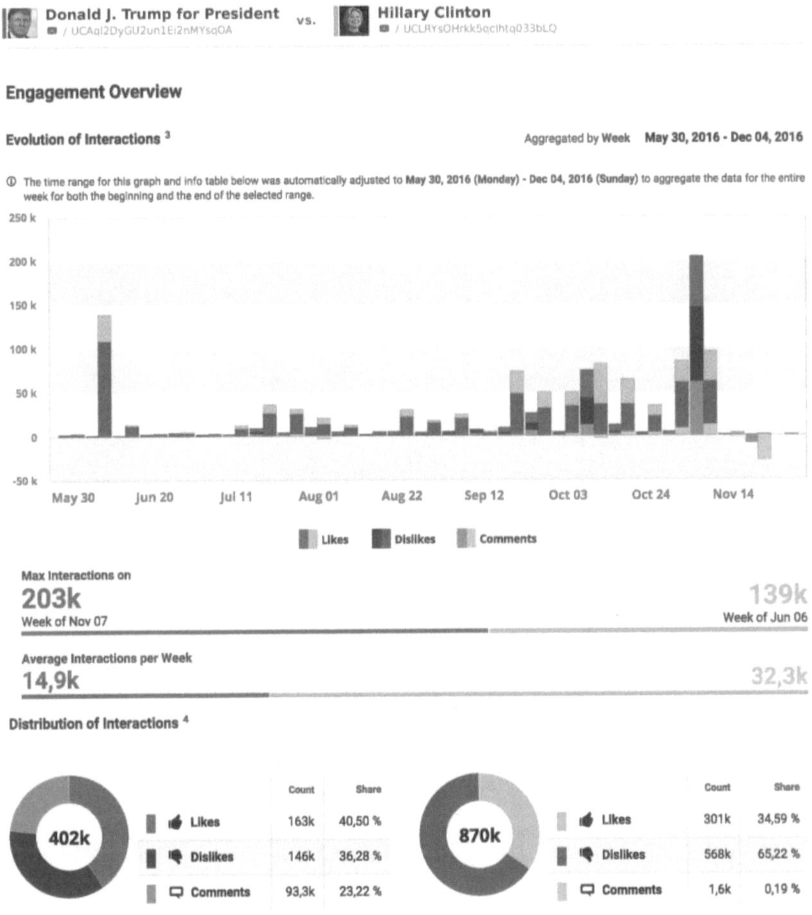

FIGURE 1.7 YouTube: Donald J. Trump for President vs. Hillary Clinton—Engagement Overview

Source: YouTube Overview (2016). *Socialbakers.com*. Reprinted with permission.

photos compared to Clinton's 252 photos (see Figure 1.9). In turn, Trump's Instagram account experienced 50.1 million interactions whereas Clinton only experienced 29.8 million. To illustrate the disparity between the two accounts, during the week of November 7, 2016, Trump's Instagram account had 6.9 million interactions compared to Clinton's 4.4 million interactions (see Figure 1.10).

Beyond the numbers, Jennifer Stromer-Galley (2016) computationally analyzed Clinton and Trump's Facebook and Twitter content and found stark differences in the ways the candidates used social media in terms of the issues and amount

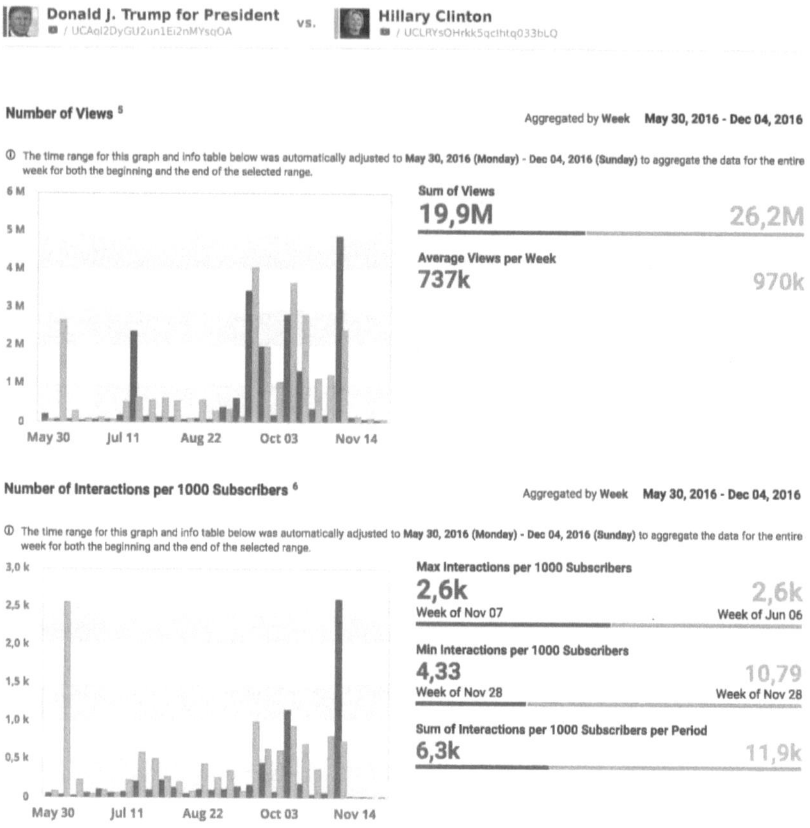

FIGURE 1.8 YouTube: Donald J. Trump for President vs. Hillary Clinton—Number of Views

Source: YouTube Overview (2016). *Socialbakers.com.* Reprinted with permission.

of evidence in the posts. Namely, Clinton posted three times as many messages as Trump about issues, such as education, the economy, and women's issues. And Trump's posts were characterized as broad generalizations or generic claims with little evidence in contrast to Clinton's posts, which routinely provided facts and backing for her positions (Stromer-Galley, 2016).

The campaigns used both positive and negative messaging. On the positive front, the candidates typically used social media to: (1) create an appealing image of the candidate, often with behind-the-scenes or throwback images and videos; (2) show images from rallies and media events to indicate popularity and connect the candidate to voters and issues; (3) messaging images, videos, and tweets designed to be forwarded by supporters; and (4) fundraising appeals. The dominant positive social media tactic in 2016 was constructing a positive

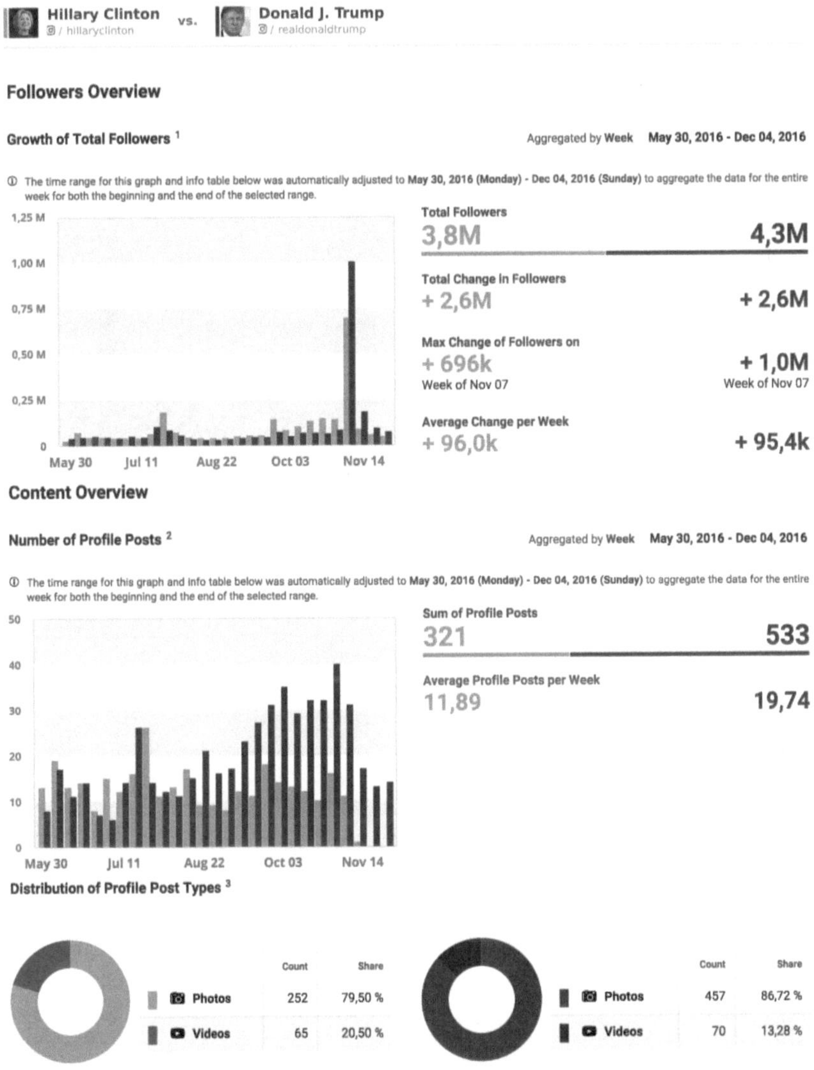

FIGURE 1.9 Instagram: Hillary Clinton vs. Donald J. Trump—Followers Overview

Source: Instagram Overview (2016). *Socialbakers.com*. Reprinted with permission.

political image through visual images. These images usually depicted the candidate on the campaign trail, meeting with voters, or throwback images from the candidate's past. For example, in a May 5, 2016 tweet and Facebook post, Trump wrote "Happy Cinco De Mayo! The best taco bowls are made in Trump Tower Grill. I love Hispanics!" along with a picture of the Republican nominee

FIGURE 1.10 Instagram: Hillary Clinton vs. Donald J. Trump—Engagement Overview

Source: Instagram Overview (2016). *Socialbakers.com*. Reprinted with permission.

giving a thumbs-up at his desk as he supposedly got ready to eat a taco bowl (see Figure 1.11). This tweet was widely shared and discussed on both traditional and social media, including a counter-post from Clinton. Figure 1.12 further illustrates this strategy—a Snapchat post of the Marco Rubio campaign bus being refueled along with the text "Feed the beast." Old photos were also common. The Clinton campaign, for instance, frequently used photos of their candidate as a young adult, First Lady, and secretary of state to show Clinton's long-term commitment to public service (see Figure 1.13 for an example). Second, and relatedly, candidates regularly posted pictures from rallies and campaign events to demonstrate popularity and breadth of support (see Figure 1.14). When voters followed either candidate on social media, they got the strong impression

FIGURE 1.11 Donald Trump Twitter Post, "Happy #CincoDeMayo!," May 5, 2016

that both candidates were well liked because of picture after picture of adoring crowds in state after state.

All of these posts were "social-media-genic" and designed to be shared, clicked, and commented upon. The campaigns tapped into popular social media trends, such as text-over-image memes and hashtags. Campaigns often called on supporters to share and like social media content. For example, on March 20, 2016, Bernie Sanders asked his supporters to "Join our social media push today" and "show the world what a REAL grassroots campaign looks like" (see Figure 1.15, see also, Figure 1.13). Campaigns even created dedicated apps to

FIGURE 1.12 Marco Rubio Snapchat Post, "Feed the Beast," March 18, 2016

facilitate social sharing. For instance, to rally supporters and encourage supporters to share a positive final message about the campaign, the Clinton campaign created a "Love Trumps Hate" app where supporters could create a customized short video by choosing the photo, style, and message to share with their friends on Facebook, Twitter, and other social platforms (Ng, 2016). Finally, fundraising

FIGURE 1.13 Hillary Clinton Instagram Post, "Like This If You Think Kids and Families Deserve a Champion in the White House," November 3, 2016

was also common on digital and social channels, as in this September 4, 2016 Facebook video from Trump calling on supporters to donate to "claim your spot on the Trump Board of Directors" to get a certificate and "special campaign updates" (see Figure 1.16).

Despite the positive messaging, it was the negative approaches that got the most attention in 2016. Negative campaigning was front and center—as candidates posted goading tweets, attack videos, and opponent-vilifying memes. In the primaries and continuing into the general election, for instance, Trump's social media feeds were full of insults hurled at his opponents that ranged from calling

FIGURE 1.14 Hillary Clinton Instagram Post, "'Let's Make History!'—Hillary," November 7, 2016

Senator Marco Rubio "Little Marco" because of his small stature to nicknaming Senator Ted Cruz "Lyin' Ted" and Secretary Hillary Clinton "Crooked Hillary." Trump ridiculed Governor Jeb Bush for having "low energy" and demeaned Senator Rand Paul's looks by saying that he had never attacked the senator on his looks, but that there was plenty of subject matter there to do so (Hampson, 2016). And the candidates frequently traded barbs over social media, as their supporters liked and commented along. In perhaps the most notable example, in June of 2016, after President Obama endorsed Clinton, Trump tweeted: "Obama

FIGURE 1.15 Bernie Sanders Instagram Post, "Join Our Social Media Push Today!," March 20, 2016

just endorsed Crooked Hillary. He wants four more years of Obama—but nobody else does!" Five minutes later, the Clinton campaign—borrowing from the popular online expression that is the online equivalent "kill yourself"—tersely tweeted back: "Delete your account." Twitter exploded as this post became a globally trending topic on Twitter and users responded with often-humorous text-, GIF-, and emoji-filled posts. Ultimately, the "delete your account" response

FIGURE 1.16 Donald Trump Facebook Post, "Donate Now for Special Trump Invitations and Updates!," September 4, 2016

was retweeted over 550,000 times, gained over 700,000 likes, and kicked off the popular hashtag "#DeleteYourAccount."

Throughout the campaign, voters amplified candidate-created messages through sharing and forwarding. Supporters attended rallies with the hopes of getting a picture of themselves with the candidate (i.e., a "selfie") that they could share with their friends and family online. This was such a large trend that the *New York Times* called 2016 the "Selfie Election" and said that the candidates often spent an hour or two exhausting a line of eager selfie seekers (Peters & Parker, 2015). Celebrities, well-known journalists, and others with large online followings had particularly large influence, as Kapko (2016) noted:

> The 2016 presidential election isn't the first event for which social media has been used as a political tool, but today it carries tremendous weight and influence over the electorate. Hillary Clinton and Donald Trump both use social to their advantages, but it's often the surrogates, supporters and influencers who shape perceptions, according to whatever views serve their preferred candidate's interests.
>
> *(para. 2)*

Social Media: An Expanding Outlet for Political Information

Social media outlets are providing users the ability to gather news as well as allowing the candidates to actually control entire news cycles. Undeniably, users are gathering news from social media. The Pew Research Center found that 63% of Twitter and Facebook users gather news from the social-networking platforms (Barthel, Shearer, Gottfried, & Mitchell, 2015). Marissa Lang (2016), of the *San Francisco Chronicle*, stated: "More people than ever get their news mainly from social networks like Facebook, Twitter and Snapchat. Candidates have discovered the quickest way to make news is to put out a statement or comment in a social media post" (para. 6). And many of these users are active—roughly one-third of social media users report they often or sometimes comment, discuss, or post about government and politics (notably, this also means that nearly seven in ten do not actively participate) (Duggan & Smith, 2016).

Voters are relying more and more on social media to provide news and this has caught the attention of politicians. Sarma (2016) argued that social media became a legitimate media tool for politicians as opposed to simply using it as a supplement to what is being placed on social media:

> Twitter and other forms of social media are reshaping how politicians communicate with voters, cutting out the journalistic middleman, and popularizing political criticism. Not only has the wall separating voters from politicians been overrun, but American news media consumption

> habits have changed. User-generated political content on social media sites can have the far-reaching impact formerly reserved for journalists and newscasters. Increasingly, Americans are relying upon viral media content on social networks as a primary source of information. User-driven and spreading virally, social media presents a whole new ballgame for politics, the potential of which has of yet not been significantly explored.
>
> *(para. 5)*

Social media began to erode the power of the media elites by allowing candidates to bypass traditional campaigning techniques such as seeking the support of media and political elites. Read (2016) said:

> Trump's ascendancy is far from the first material consequence of Facebook's conquering invasion of our social, cultural, and political lives, but it's still a bracing reminder of the extent to which the social network is able to upend existing structure and transform society—and often not for the better.
>
> *(para. 3)*

This paradigm shift for social media's role in the political process was in part due to Donald Trump's strategy of using social media—particularly Twitter—at all times of the day to communicate campaign ideas and throw insults at opponents, which, in turn, drove the day's news cycle. This social media campaign strategy was a vast departure from the sanitized way in which social media was used in the 2012 presidential campaign (Lang, 2016). Social flow, a social media data analytics company, found that Donald Trump's social media messages were getting the attention of users and the electorate. Social Flow found "Trump had become the most talked-about person on the planet" (Lang, 2016, para. 25). Del Vecho (2016) noted that social media condenses news and information into short videos, and even GIFs, with very little information for the social media user to walk away with any substantive knowledge about a subject—especially about politics. "Political GIFs are the new sound bites this campaign season," the *New York Times* reported (Bilton, 2016, para. 1). Similarly, Del Vecho stated:

> While these videos are a good way to help understand current happenings, they are far from representative of the events from which they extract sound bites. Instead, these videos paraphrase speeches, reducing them to a catchphrase with only a few sentences of context, which makes them yes, easily digestible and appealing, but hardly a reliable source for a comprehensive understanding of present issues. Consequently, social media users who rely solely on these types of videos for their news believe their decisions to be informed before they have even been given all the information.
>
> *(para. 3)*

Importantly, Anderson (2016) reminds us that "the majority of social media users are not swayed by what they see in their networks" (para. 10). Generally speaking, social media users do not change their minds based on what they are exposed to on social media. A Pew Research Center study found that 82% of social media users say they have never changed their views on a candidate and 79% indicated they have never changed their political views (Anderson, 2016).

Digital and Social Media Implications

Observers have noted that social media is the next big technological intervention in American politics. The medium of radio in the 1930s and 1940s brought Franklin D. Roosevelt into the homes of families around the nation whereas in the 1950s and 1960s the medium of television placed politicians such as John F. Kennedy and Richard Nixon in the homes of Americans. In the 2000s and 2010s, the Internet and social media have now placed politicians such as Donald Trump and Bernie Sanders in the hands of Americans with smartphones. In the early days, the Internet was seen by many as a boon to democracy and several benefits of digital media were evident in 2016. The Internet has enabled outsiders on the right such as Donald Trump and Ted Cruz and Bernie Sanders on the left to have a national platform that likely would not have existed several election cycles earlier. Social media allow politicians to bypass mainstream media and political elites and reach the voters directly for support through votes and financial donations. The Internet enabled Bernie Sanders to raise hundreds of millions of dollars to compete against Hillary Clinton. However, this transition from traditional media such as television and radio to social media is not considered to be a positive transition by everyone.

Yes, communication technologies expanded the availability and reach of information, introduced new voices into the public sphere and empowered citizens, and allowed political outsiders to more easily fundraise and engage, but they also allowed for the spreading of fake news, rewarded harsh and extreme political rhetoric, and lessened democratic institutions (Balz, 2017). Persily (2017) summarized the threat that digital democracy poses: "The premium placed on virality of messages, the threat to accountability posed by unrestrained anonymity, and the undercutting of sovereignty presented by an open Internet pose novel challenges for democracy in the United States" (p. 72). Echoing this point, Carr (2015) stated:

> Social media favors the bitty over the meaty, the cutting over the considered. It also prizes emotionalism over reason. The more visceral the message, the more quickly it circulates and the longer it holds the darting public eye. In something of a return to the pre-radio days, the fiery populist now

> seems more desirable, more worthy of attention, than the cool wonk. It's the crusty Bernie and the caustic Donald that get hearted and hash-tagged, friended and followed.
>
> *(para. 11)*

Americans notice the effect social media are having on political talk, as polling has found that a majority of Americans say political discussions occurring on social media are less respectful and civil, and angrier compared to other venues where people engage in political dialogue (Duggan & Smith, 2016).

Social media also reinforce people's beliefs. In essence, social media is an echo chamber where people feel more comfortable surrounding themselves in "filter bubbles" of friends who perpetuate similar beliefs. Although the empirical data on this topic is mixed, Lee (2016) found:

> Liberal Facebook users see more liberal articles on their newsfeeds. Conservatives see more conservative articles. The Facebook researchers argued that this wasn't really Facebook's fault—it simply reflects the kinds of friends social media users have and the kinds of articles they share. But regardless of whose fault it is, the result is the same.
>
> *(para. 25)*

Not only was social media in general, and Facebook specifically, a place where users found information that reinforced their already-held beliefs, but it also served as a platform for fake or inaccurate political news and information. Federal investigators found that operatives for Russia used "bots" to blitz social media with millions of Twitter and Facebook posts carrying links to pro-Trump stories—some fictional—on conservative sites such as Breitbart News and Infowars, in addition to Kremlin-backed Sputnik News and RT News (Stone & Gorgon, 2017). Fake news was widespread on social media. In fact, in a case study of social media users in the battleground state of Michigan, researchers at the Oxford Internet Institute found that 23% of the content shared on Twitter in the final days of the election were links to fake news, about the same amount shared to professional news stories over the same period (Blood, 2017; Howard, Bolsover, Kollanyi, Bradshaw, & Neudert, 2017). Regarding social media's tendency to serve up a cacophony of reinforcing beliefs for users that sometimes was inaccurate, *The Economist* reported:

> if any technology helped Mr. Trump win, it was social media rather than data science. He and Steve Bannon, his controversial campaign boss and now his chief strategist, understood how the Facebook and Twitter-driven media landscape worked. Whether a piece of news spreads online does not depend on whether it is true and coherent, but whether it is

> surprising, shocking and confirms prejudices. It can bounce endlessly in virtual echo-chambers—even if it is patently false.
>
> *(para. 7)*

And, after the election, social media users acknowledged that fake news and inaccurate information created confusion among the electorate. The Pew Research Center found that 64% of American adults believe "fabricated news stories cause a great deal of confusion about the basic facts of current issues and events" (Mitchell, Barthel, Holcomb, & Weisel, 2016, para. 2). Further, the Pew study found that 57% of Republicans and 64% of Democrats believe that fake news causes confusion. Also, 39% of Americans believe they can recognize fake news as it scrolls through their newsfeeds and nearly a third of American adults have seen fake political news on the Internet. Interestingly, 23% of the respondents say they have shared fake news (Mitchell et al., 2016). Read (2016) asserted:

> Of course, lies and exaggerations have always been central to real political campaigns; Facebook has simply made them easier to spread, and discovered that it suffers no particular market punishment for doing so—humans seem to have a strong bias toward news that confirms their beliefs, and environments where those beliefs are unlikely to be challenged.
>
> *(para. 9)*

Conclusion

Finally, although social and digital media clearly played a major role in the 2016 U.S. presidential campaign, it is worth remembering that the precipitating cultural and historical factors of Trump's victory long predated Twitter, Breitbart News, and "filter bubbles." As Daniel Kreiss (2016) argued:

> The Internet did not bring about a "post-fact" or "post truth" era, nor did it bring about conspiracy theories, white nationalism, conservative identity and its farcical villains, and the distrust of institutionalized ways of producing knowledge, from journalism to science . . . While social media might increase the speed of half-truths, rumors, and outright lies, it did not create the cynical public that does not understand, or care to, how knowledge producing institutions work.
>
> *(para. 5)*

Trump's Electoral College victory can be seen as a culminating event of American's distrust of government and media institutions, anxiety towards economic and cultural change in the country, and partisan sorting and polarization. Equally valid is a reading of the election as a failure of the Clinton campaign. Any campaign where a nominee strongly wins the popular vote (Clinton outpaced

Trump by almost 2.9 million voters), yet loses the Electoral College by significant margins plainly made strategic and tactical mistakes (see Ball, 2016). In the end, a single issue didn't determine the election outcome; instead, a multidimensional constellation of factors was at work, of which social media was a bright star. Whether this election set a new standard or if it will be a historical one-off remains an open question, and one that will only be answered with time.

References

2016 campaign: Strong interest, widespread dissatisfaction. (2016, July 7). *Pew Research Center.* Retrieved from www.people-press.org/2016/07/07/2016-campaign-strong-interest-widespread-dissatisfaction/

Allen, N. (2017, January 9). How Hillary Clinton's digital strategy helped lead to her election defeat. *The [London] Telegraph.* Retrieved from www.telegraph.co.uk/news/2017/01/09/hillary-clintons-digital-strategy-helped-lead-election-defeat/

Anderson, M. (2016, November 7). Social media causes some users to rethink their views on an issue. *Pew Research Center.* Retrieved from www.pewresearch.org/fact-tank/2016/11/07/social-media-causes-some-users-to-rethink-their-views-on-an-issue/

Andrews, W., Rebecca Lai, K. K., Parlapiano, A., & Yourish, K. (2016, July 26). Who is running for president? *The New York Times.* Retrieved from www.nytimes.com/interactive/2016/us/elections/2016-presidential-candidates.html

Assessing Russian activities and intentions in recent US Elections. (2017, January 6). *Office of the Director of National Intelligence.* Intelligence Community Assessment 2017–01D. Retrieved from www.dni.gov/files/documents/ICA_2017_01.pdf

Ball, M. (2016, November 15). Why Hillary Clinton lost. *Atlantic.* Retrieved from www.theatlantic.com/politics/archive/2016/11/why-hillary-clinton-lost/507704/

Balz, D. (2017, April 22). A scholar asks, 'Can democracy survive the Internet?' *Washington Post.* Retrieved from http://wapo.st/2p3eh1c

Barrett, J. (2016, September 21). 3 ways social media is warping politics more than ever. *Digital Trends.* Retrieved from www.digitaltrends.com/social-media/how-social-media-is-warping-politics-more-than-ever/

Barthel, M., Shearer, E., Gottfried, J., & Mitchell, A. (2015, July 14). The evolving role of news on Twitter and Facebook. *Pew Research Center.* Retrieved from www.journalism.org/2015/07/14/the-evolving-role-of-news-on-twitter-and-facebook/

Bilton, N. (2016, January 6). Political GIFs are the new sound bites this campaign season. *New York Times.* Retrieved from http://nyti.ms/1mGMvVf

Blood, D. (2017, March 27). Fake news is shared as widely as the real thing. *Financial Times.* Retrieved from www.ft.com/content/99ea2fae-107c-11e7-b030-768954394623

Carr, N. (2015, September 2). How social media is ruining politics. *Politico.* Retrieved from www.politico.com/magazine/story/2015/09/2016-election-social-media-ruining-politics-213104

Chen, Y. (2016, September 26). #ImWithHer: Inside the Clinton campaign's social strategy. *Digiday.com.* Retrieved from http://digiday.com/marketing/imwithher-look-inside-clinton-campaigns-social-strategy/

Chozick, A., & Schmidt, M. S. (2015, March 10). Hillary Clinton tries to quell controversy over private email. *The New York Times.* Retrieved from www.nytimes.com/2015/03/11/us/hillary-clinton-email.html

Cohen, M. (2017, March 22). Timeline: What we know about the Trump campaign, his administration and Russia. *CNN.com*. Retrieved from http://cnn.it/2lUZR0i

Collins, E. (2016, August 31). Poll: Clinton, Trump most unfavorable candidates ever. *USA Today*. Retrieved from http://usat.ly/2cesCEv

Corasaniti, N. (2015, August 18). Texting comes of age as a political messenger. *New York Times*. Retrieved from http://nyti.ms/1E07YAx

Del Vecho, G. (2016, August 3). The role of social media in the 2016 election. *The Duke Chronicle*. Retrieved from www.dukechronicle.com/article/2016/08/social-media-election-role

Disis, J. (2017, January 26). Will it end with Trump? *CNN.com*. Retrieved from http://money.cnn.com/2017/01/23/news/economy/donald-trump-tax-returns/

Duggan, M., & Smith, A. (2016, October 25). The political environment on social media. *Pew Research Center*. Retrieved from http://pewrsr.ch/2eCBi5c

Editorial: Benghazi: What the report reveals about Hillary Clinton. (2016, June 28). *The Chicago Tribune*. Retrieved from www.chicagotribune.com/news/opinion/editorials/ct-benghazi-hillary-clinton-obama-rhodes-edit-0629-jm-20160628-story.html

Election 2016: Campaigns as a direct source of news. (2016, July 18). *Pew Research Center*. Retrieved from www.journalism.org/2016/07/18/election-2016-campaigns-as-a-direct-source-of-news/

Fahrenthold, D. A. (2016, October 8). Trump recorded having extremely lewd conversation about women in 2005. *Washington Post*. Retrieved from www.washingtonpost.com/politics/trump-recorded-having-extremely-lewd-conversation-about-women-in-2005/2016/10/07/3b9ce776-8cb4–11e6-bf8a-3d26847eeed4_story.html?utm_term=.fcd78d19d3f9

Gold, M., & Narayanswamy, A. (2016, December 8). Trump donors continued to give millions after his election victory. *The Washington Post*. Retrieved from www.washingtonpost.com/news/post-politics/wp/2016/12/08/trump-donors-continued-to-give-millions-after-his-election-victory

Graff, G. M. (2016, September 30). What the FBI files reveal about Hillary Clinton's email server new documents tell the full, strange story of a technophobic VIP, a sloppy State Department, and the jerry-rigged computer that held it all together. *Politico Magazine*. Retrieved from www.politico.com/magazine/story/2016/09/hillary-clinton-emails-2016-server-state-department-fbi-214307

Green, J., & Issenberg, S. (2016, October 27). Inside the Trump bunker, with days to go. *Bloomberg Businessweek*. Retrieved from www.bloomberg.com/news/articles/2016-10-27/inside-the-trump-bunker-with-12-days-to-go

Hampson, R. (2016, September 25). In the primary debates, Trump showed what he'll bring to battle with Clinton. *USA Today*. Retrieved from www.usatoday.com/story/news/politics/elections/2016/09/25/donald-trump-primary-debate-lessons-hillary-clinton/90900576/

Hendricks, J. A., & Schill, D. (2017). The social media election of 2016. In R. E. Denton, Jr. (Ed.), *The 2016 U.S. presidential campaign: Political communication and practice*. New York, NY: Palgrave Macmillan.

Hess, A. (2016, February 18). How Trump wins Twitter: Everyone knows he's the best on social media: Here's why. *Slate*. Retrieved from www.slate.com/articles/technology/future_tense/2016/02/donald_trump_is_the_best_at_twitter_here_s_why.html

Howard, P. N., Bolsover, G., Kollanyi, B., Bradshaw, S., & Neudert, L. (2017). Junk news and bots during the U.S. Election: What were Michigan voters sharing over Twitter? Data Memo 2017.1. Oxford, UK: Project on Computational Propaganda. Retrieved from http://comprop.oii.ox.ac.uk/2017/03/26/junk-news-and-bots-during-the-u-s-election-what-were-michigan-voters-sharing-over-twitter/

Ignatius, D. (2016, August 4). Why facts don't matter to Trump's supporters. *Washington Post*. Retrieved from http://wapo.st/2axzs4x

Johnson, L. (2016, October 6). Hillary Clinton's digital staff gives 6 marketing lessons they've learned from this bizarre election. *Adweek*. Retrieved from www.adweek.com/digital/hillary-clintons-digital-staff-gives-6-marketing-lessons-theyve-learned-bizarre-election-173919/

Kapko, M. (2016, September 29). How social media is shaping the 2016 presidential election. *CIO.com*. Retrieved from www.cio.com/article/3125120/social-networking/how-social-media-is-shaping-the-2016-presidential-election.html

Kreiss, D. (2016). Social media did not give us Donald Trump and it is not weakening democracy. *U.S. Election Analysis 2016*. Retrieved from www.electionanalysis2016.us/us-election-analysis-2016/section-6-internet/social-media-did-not-give-us-donald-trump-and-it-is-not-weakening-democracy/

Krieg, G. (2016, December 22). It's official: Clinton swamps Trump in popular vote. *CNN.com*. Retrieved from http://cnn.it/2hsLMFp

Lang, M. (2016, April 5). 2016 presidential election circus: Is social media the cause? *San Francisco Chronicle*. Retrieved from www.govtech.com/social/2016-Presidential-Election-Circus-Is-Social-Media-the-Cause.html

Lapowsky, I. (2016, November 15). Here's how Facebook actually won Trump the presidency. *Wired*. Retrieved from www.wired.com/2016/11/facebook-won-trump-election-not-just-fake-news/

Lee, T. B. (2016, March 14). How the Internet is disrupting politics. *Vox.com*. Retrieved from www.vox.com/2016/3/14/11211204/sanders-trump-disrupting-politic

Mitchell, A., Barthel, M., Holcomb, J., & Weisel, R. (2016, December 15). Many Americans believe fake news is sowing confusion. *Pew Research Center*. Retrieved from www.journalism.org/2016/12/15/many-americans-believe-fake-news-is-sowing-confusion/

Ng, V. (2016). Love Trumps hate. *Personal Website*. Retrieved from http://victor.ng/love-trumps-hate

Number of Instagram users in the United States from 2015 to 2020 (in millions). (2017). *Statistica.com*. Retrieved from www.statista.com/statistics/293771/number-of-us-instagram-users/

Number of monthly active Facebook users in the United States and Canada as of 4th quarter 2016 (in millions). (2017). *Statistica.com*. Retrieved from www.statista.com/statistics/247614/number-of-monthly-active-facebook-users-worldwide/

Number of monthly active Twitter users in the United States from 1st quarter 2010 to 4th quarter 2016 (in millions). (2017). *Statistica.com*. Retrieved from www.statista.com/statistics/274564/monthly-active-twitter-users-in-the-united-states/

Patterson, D. (2016, May 31). Election tech: Why social media is more powerful than advertising. *Tech Republic*. Retrieved from www.techrepublic.com/article/election-tech-why-social-media-is-more-powerful-than-advertising/

Persily, N. (2017). Can democracy survive the Internet? *Journal of Democracy*, *28*(2), 63–76.

Peters, J. W., & Parker, A. (2015, July 4). Facing a selfie election, presidential hopefuls grin and bear it. *New York Times*. Retrieved from http://nyti.ms/1GX3xCi

Rampell, C. (2016). When the facts don't matter, how can democracy survive? *Washington Post*. Retrieved from http://wapo.st/2ebbezB

Read, M. (2016, November 9). Donald Trump won because of Facebook. *New York Magazine*. Retrieved from http://nymag.com/selectall/2016/11/donald-trump-won-because-of-facebook.html

The role of technology in the presidential election. (2016, November 20). *The Economist*. Retrieved from www.economist.com/news/united-states/21710614-fake-news-big-data-post-mortem-under-way-role-technology

Rucker, P., & Paquette, D. (2017, January 7). How a week of Trump tweets stoked anxiety, moved markets and altered plans. *Washington Post*. Retrieved from www.washingtonpost.com/graphics/politics/week-of-trump-tweets/

Ruttenberg, J. (2016, April 24). In this Snapchat campaign, election news is big and then it's gone. *New York Times*. Retrieved from http://nyti.ms/1qKDtsi

Samuelsohn, D. (2016, June 15). Trump's Twitter army: New data show the GOP nominee's followers are exactly what the Dems hoped they weren't: Reliable voters. *Politico*. Retrieved from http://politi.co/24QmtOC

Sarma, M. D. (2016). Tweeting 2016: How social media is shaping the presidential election. *Inquiries Journal, 8*(09). Retrieved from www.inquiriesjournal.com/articles/1454/tweeting-2016-how-social-media-is-shaping-the-presidential-election

Schreckinger, B. (2015, October 1). Meet the man who makes Donald Trump go viral. *Politico*. Retrieved from www.politico.com/story/2015/09/trumps-social-media-guy-214309

Seligson, H. (2016, June 7). Why are more women than men on Instagram? *The Atlantic*. Retrieved from www.theatlantic.com/technology/archive/2016/06/why-are-more-women-than-men-on-instagram/485993/

Sherman, E. (2016, March 25). Two Trump insiders behind the campaign's social network explosion. *Fortune*. Retrieved from http://fortune.com/2016/03/25/trump-scavino-mcconney-social-media/

Sifry, M. L. (2016, July 26). Clinton 2016 tech aims to make mobile participation fun (and have fun with Trump. *Civicist*. Retrieved from http://civichall.org/civicist/clinton-2016-tech-aims-make-mobile-participation-fun-fun-trump

Slaby, M. (2016, October 12). The new normal: Digital defines presidential campaigns. *The Hill*. Retrieved from http://thehill.com/blogs/pundits-blog/presidential-campaign/300535-the-new-normal-digital-defines-and-revolutionizes

Smith, A. (2017, January 12). Record shares of Americans now own smartphones, have home broadband. *Pew Research Center*. Retrieved from www.pewresearch.org/fact-tank/2017/01/12/evolution-of-technology/

Stone, P., & Gorgon, G. (2017, March 20). FBI's Russian-influence probe includes a look at Breitbart, InfoWars news sites. *McClatchy DC Bureau*. Retrieved from www.mcclatchydc.com/news/politics-government/white-house/article139695453.html

Stromer-Galley, J. (2016). In the age of social media, voters still need journalists. *U. S. Election Analysis 2016*. Retrieved from www.electionanalysis2016.us/us-election-analysis-2016/section-6-internet/in-the-age-of-social-media-voters-still-need-journalists/

Thrush, G. (2016, December 9). 10 crucial decisions that reshaped America. *Politico Magazine*. Retrieved from http://politi.co/2gH6WPK

Vogel, K. P., & Samuelsohn, D. (2016, January 5). Trump quietly builds a data juggernaut: Defying skeptics, he puts tools in place to get out the vote. *Politico*. Retrieved from www.politico.com/story/2016/01/trump-builds-data-juggernaut-217391

Wells, C., Shah, D. V., Pevehouse, J. C., Yang, J., Pelled, A., Boehm, F., . . . & Schmidt, J. L. (2016). How Trump drove coverage to the nomination: Hybrid media campaigning. *Political Communication, Well, 33*(4), 669–676.

Wilke, C. (2016, September 26). Clinton destroys Trump on his missing tax returns. *CNN.com*. Retrieved from www.huffingtonpost.com/entry/donald-trump-tax-returns_us_57e9a316e4b0c2407cd8d472

YouTube Statistics. (2017). *Fortunelords.com*. Retrieved from https://fortunelords.com/youtube-statistics/

2

SOCIAL MEDIA, NEWS PLATFORMS, AND PARTISAN EXPOSURE

Voters' Media Preferences During the 2016 Presidential Campaign Season

Michael A. Beam, Paul M. Haridakis, Myiah J. Hutchens, and Jay D. Hmielowski

We have been studying the use of social media during U.S. presidential campaign seasons since the 2008 campaign, after Facebook and YouTube had become widely available. By the 2012 campaign season, Twitter emerged as an additional news and social-networking media platform. Twitter's role in the 2016 election was even more pronounced as presidential hopefuls, particularly Donald Trump, tweeted on an ongoing basis. The ultimate Democratic and Republican nominees, Hillary Clinton and Donald Trump, respectively, even selected Twitter to make their first official announcement of their vice presidential running mates.

Facebook communication also increased, as sharing of political fare was common. At the same time, however, there is evidence that use of Facebook and other social media were not without consternation. A recent Pew Research Center survey (Duggan & Smith, 2016) suggested that many users were frustrated with the tone and content of political fare on social media. By the end of the campaign, more than a third of social media users reported that they were worn out by the amount of political social media interaction. This is consistent with prior surveys during the 2012 election suggesting that a significant percentage of Facebook users defriended someone because of their political posts (see Haridakis, Lin, & Hanson, 2017).

Thus, despite the growing prevalence of these popular social-networking sites (SNSs) by campaigns, the effectiveness of social media is driven largely by the users, who have a number of media from which to choose to satisfy their informational needs during political campaigns. For example, some research has suggested that most news still comes from local media sources (e.g., Matsa, 2015; Mitchell, Gottfried, Barthel, & Shearer, 2016). Research conducted during the prior two presidential campaigns in 2008 and 2012 suggested that television was used more often than social media as a source of political information (e.g., Haridakis & Hanson, 2011; Haridakis, Hanson, Lin, & McCullough, 2015). Furthermore, 2012 data show that people are likely to get news online by browsing to a website that aggregates news or a search engine (Mitchell, Rosenstiel, & Christian, 2012).

Of course, heavier use of other media does not necessarily diminish the influence of social media use. Two points are important to note. First, although social media had not supplanted older media such as television for most voters in 2008 and 2012, they did emerge as valuable complementary sources of political information for some, particularly younger, voters (Haridakis et al., 2015). Politically engaged users also may use social media at the same time as other media (e.g., as second screens) (Schill & Kirk, 2015). Second, although many voters may not receive political information from social media directly, they often receive it indirectly through their selection of other media sources. Political candidates and their surrogates influence the agenda of mainstream network and cable news media (Kreiss, 2016; Schill & Kirk, 2015) who republish their social media communications—exposing their audiences to these communications.

Thus, as technological platforms and sources of news evolve, people have greater choice in where they choose to receive their news. With increased choice, media sources are likely to fragment and target audience members' individual and group differences (Stroud, 2011). Accordingly, it remains important when assessing the uses and effects of social media during political campaign seasons to also examine the extent to which SNSs are selected as sources of news information vis-à-vis the selection of other partisan and nonpartisan media sources that people choose to satisfy their needs and expectations based on their individual and group differences.

Although we cannot account for every individual attribute of potential voters that may influence media choice, in this chapter we survey Americans to examine their selection of news sources chosen most often for news information during the 2016 presidential campaign based on specific salient group differences. During the campaign, voters were often identified or described by the media in accordance with group characteristics (e.g., Millennials, African Americans, Hispanics), or with a combination of group characteristics (e.g., working class, White males). Here we focus on several demographic groups that received significant media attention that dealt with the way presidential candidates were reaching out to these blocs of voters and speculation as to which candidate group members would ultimately support. These include the following demographic variables: age, gender, race/ethnicity, income level, and religious affiliation.

The campaign was rife with examples of media coverage and discussion of various demographic group-related issues. Some well-publicized examples include those arguably related to race/ethnicity (e.g., the building of a wall across the southern border of the U.S., immigration and the handling of undocumented immigrants, well-publicized incidents of police shootings of African Americans, and inner-city violence), age group (e.g., affordable college education, handling of student loan debt, affordable healthcare), income group (e.g., anger among working- and middle-class Americans over the disparity of wealth in the country, the ongoing loss of jobs, tax cuts, affordable child care, renegotiation of trade agreements such as NAFTA), gender (e.g., Trump's attitude and behavior toward women, coverage of Clinton as the first female presidential candidate, women's rights and eliminating historical barriers such as the "glass ceiling"), and religious affiliation (e.g., the debate revolving around same-sex marriage and religious freedom, and abortion).

In addition to demographic group differences, partisanship also is an important group difference endemic during political elections (see Haridakis et al., 2017). As more people rely on social media for news, partisan news sources may proliferate more rapidly than nonpartisan sources due to a tendency to connect with others who share one's political predispositions (Pariser, 2011; Sunstein, 2007). Accordingly, in addition to segmenting our analysis according to demographic groups, we consider voter partisanship. We examine the role of partisanship in selecting partisan and nonpartisan news sources. Lastly, we examine the relationship between social media use and partisan and nonpartisan news sources.

Demographic Group Differentiation in Political Media Use

Much of the research on group differences in the uses and effects of social media for political news has focused on partisan and political ideological differences (see Bakshy, Messing, & Adamic, 2015; Flaxman, Goel, & Rao, 2016). Nonetheless, a body of research does exist that has addressed other group differentiated media use and effects in political and other contexts. In the case of social media use, for example, Lenhart (2009) noted that Latinos and African Americans were more likely to have a SNS profile than were Whites. Hendricks and Schill (2015) noted that minorities used Twitter more than did Whites during the 2012 campaign. Yun (2015) also asserted that younger voters, women, and ethnic minorities were more likely than older people, males, and Whites to use social media to express their political views. Yun (2015) observed that supporters of third-party candidates were more likely to use social media to express their political views than were Democrats and Republicans.

Thus, it appears that social media platforms can provide voice to groups that historically have been more politically marginalized and/or isolated from the political process. Bekafigo and McBride (2013) suggested that this was the case with Twitter, in particular. Finding that non-White minorities were engaged in election conversations during recent gubernatorial elections, they asserted that Twitter may be providing a political outlet for minorities.

At the same time, there has been a great deal of discussion of a digital divide among some of these demographic groups that cannot be ignored. On balance, early adopters of social-networking sites for political use during the 2008 presidential election appeared to parallel a stereotypical profile of early adopters of communication technology, generally. According to Ancu's (2015) review, these early adopters tended to be wealthy and White. This differed from the typical SNS users at the time who on balance had lower incomes and were younger. In addition, African Americans and Hispanics tended to use SNSs more than did their White counterparts.

Although the reasons for demographic disparity in SNS use are not always straightforward, such disparity has been found consistently. In a 2012 presidential campaign study, Barbera and Rivero (2015) found that women made up a minority of Twitter users. Wicks and his colleagues (2014) found that politically engaged adolescents tended to come from higher income households and were likely to use social media for political activities. Younger people also have been found to blog more (Sweetser & Kaid, 2008), and those 18–29 appear more likely to use social network sites such as Facebook for political expression and other purposes (see Bennett, Wells, & Freelon, 2011). Over 40% of young adults (18–24) learned about the 2012 Republican presidential nomination from Facebook (Baumgartner, Morris, & Morris, 2015). They also were more likely to follow candidates on Facebook and Twitter than were their older counterparts.

Partisan Group Differentiation in Media Use and Exposure

In addition to demographic group differences, party affiliation is an additional group-related variable that influences media selection during political campaign seasons. Increased access to biased partisan media and greater levels of political polarization have coincided with the rise of digital and social media, leading some scholars to call for research focused on partisan media selection (e.g., Hmielowski, Beam, & Hutchens, 2016; Pariser, 2011; Sunstein, 2007). In fact, strong partisan SNS users have reported paying more attention to political posts, indicating that partisanship is an important factor motivating social media news use (Mitchell, Gottfried, Kiley, & Matsa, 2014).

Research on partisan selective exposure has provided evidence that Democrat and Republican partisans often turn to different sources when given news choices that have an ideological slant. Selective exposure research is rooted in cognitive dissonance theory (Festinger, 1957, 1964), which posits that people will favor pro-attitudinal information over counter-attitudinal information to avoid the psychological discomfort associated with conflicting attitudes. According to this theory, dissonant information will be likely to increase uncertainty and psychological discomfort, whereas attitude-consistent information will lead to reinforced confidence in preexisting attitudes and beliefs.

Political communication scholars have renewed their interest in selective exposure research after the diffusion of Internet technologies that gave people greater access to news information, such as SNSs, search engines, and news aggregators (Stroud, 2014). The Internet allows for unprecedented flow of information, which weakens traditional gatekeepers' control over the news (Dylko, Beam, Landreville,

& Geidner, 2012). In fact, the algorithms that underlie these online tools can serve as gatekeepers themselves (Hargittai, 2000). Some scholars have worried that, consistent with the theory of cognitive dissonance, people who rely on personalized and filtered news might not be exposed to information that is inconsistent with their beliefs (Pariser, 2011; Sunstein, 2007). Additionally, as people increasingly turn to SNSs to curate their news, there is a danger of developing an echo chamber in which attitude-consistent ideas drown out opposing views.

Evidence shows there has been an increase in partisan news exposure over time, which has political consequences (Coe et. al, 2008). Ideologically consistent sources of online news are more likely to be rated as interesting (Iyengar & Hahn, 2009) and selected to read (Garrett & Stroud, 2014). Furthermore, algorithmic systems such as social media (Bakshy et al., 2015; Flaxman et al., 2016) and search engines (Flaxman et al., 2016) can facilitate partisan selective exposure. Research on news aggregators is mixed, as Flaxman and his colleagues (2016) found that online news aggregator users are less ideologically segregated compared to other news platforms, but Beam (2014) found that people spend more time reading pro-attitudinal news when aggregators use personalized algorithms.

However, research also has indicated that when given the choice, online newsreaders are less likely to avoid counter-attitudinal information than select pro-attitudinal information (Garrett, 2009; Garrett, Carnahan, & Lynch, 2013). Instead, algorithmic online news systems have been linked to increased overall news exposure, including more diverse political perspectives and topics (Beam & Kosicki, 2014; Flaxman et al., 2016; Messing & Westwood, 2014). Bakshy and his colleagues (2015) showed that despite algorithmic sorting and network self-selection, Facebook users are still exposed to counter-attitudinal news. In fact, news containing counter-attitudinal perspectives were more likely to be read when endorsed by peers through social network sites (Messing & Westwood, 2014). That is, algorithmic online news platforms can facilitate both increased pro- and counter-attitudinal news (Flaxman et al., 2016).

Moving beyond partisan news, research has consistently suggested that mainstream nonpartisan news sources garner the greatest attention (Mitchell et al., 2016). Indeed, Benkler (2006) argued that the rise of the Internet allows for a more reflective news environment that facilitates online communities to engage in political discourse. He also showed that mainstream news collectors still dominate the flow of political news information online. Research has also shown that despite a rise in user control to news gatekeeping, elite mainstream news organizations still produce the majority of news shared online (Dylko et al., 2012). So, access to personally relevant news made possible by algorithmic and social recommendations on SNSs could be related to increased overall news consumption. But what classifies as "news" consumption has become increasingly compromised in recent years by the proliferation of "fake news" (Allcott & Gentzkow, 2017). That is particularly true in digital and social media platforms, where dissemination of information is easier in an environment devoid of traditional media gatekeepers. Researchers are currently debating the influence of candidate misinformation proffered by fake news on election outcomes (see Allcott & Gentzkow, 2017; Weeks & Garrett, 2014).

Research Questions

In light of the above research, we examine demographic and partisan differences in the use of news platforms and partisan news sources. First, we examine differences in online news use among our subgroups of interest, including online news platforms and offline sources of news such as local media and word of mouth. Next, we investigate exposure to partisan and nonpartisan news based on political group affiliation. Lastly, we ask if use of SNSs and other algorithmic online news platforms is related to differences in partisan and nonpartisan news use. Formally:

RQ1: How does selection of SNSs (Facebook and Twitter) for news during the presidential campaign compare to selection of other sources (online search, online news aggregators, local media, word of mouth)?

RQ2: Do patterns in news use differ across demographic and partisan subgroups (age, gender, race/ethnicity, income, religion, and party affiliation)?

RQ3: Is there a difference in the frequency of the selection of partisan and nonpartisan news sources for partisans and nonpartisans?

RQ4: Do people who use SNSs and other online platforms for news differ in their patterns of exposure to partisan or nonpartisan news?

Method

Data were collected via an Internet survey with a sample provided by the polling firm YouGov from October 24 to October 30, 2016. YouGov utilizes a sample-matching procedure, wherein they initially over-sample and then create a final sample that matches national population characteristics. A sampling frame to generate the final sample is created using benchmarks from large, high-quality probability samples. YouGov's sample-matching procedure has been empirically compared to random sampling procedures and found to exhibit little to no selection bias (Ansolabehere & Rivers, 2013; Ansolabehere & Schaffner, 2014; Rivers & Bailey, 2009). Indeed, scholars empirically demonstrated that sample-matching procedures generate samples better than other Internet panels, and are equivalent to the random methods used to create well-respected surveys such as the American National Election Survey.

The data used here consist of 500 sample-matched participants using frames that matched respondents on gender, age, race, education, party identification, ideology, political interest, voter registration, and voter turnout. Weights are provided by YouGov based on propensity scores created via age, gender, race/ethnicity, years of education, and ideology.

Measures

Media Measures

Individuals were asked to report how often they get news from a variety of sources on a 6-point scale ranging from never (0) to several times per day (5). The various sources were: news from a local news organization (M = 2.96, SD = 1.40); news from a national news organization often characterized as liberal or favoring the Democratic party (i.e., *New York Times, MSNBC*) (M = 2.08, SD = 1.62); news from a national news organization often characterized as not favoring a particular political party (i.e., *CBS, NBC, ABC*) (M = 2.52, SD = 1.46); news from a national news organizations often characterized as conservative, or favoring the Republican Party (i.e., *FOX News, Wall Street Journal*) (M = 2.12, SD = 1.63); word of mouth from friends, family, co-workers, and neighbors (M = 2.28, SD = 1.38); news linked from a website that aggregates news stories from a variety of sources, such as Google News or Yahoo! News (M = 1.79, SD = 1.63), and using a search engine for news such as Google or Bing (M = 1.73, SD = 1.54). Facebook and Twitter news use were created by averaging responses to two questions using the same six-point scale. Facebook news use was assessed by asking participants how often they read news on Facebook without following the links and how often they clicked on news links shared from Facebook (M = 1.60, SD = 1.55, $p < .001$). Twitter news use was assessed by asking participants how often they read news on Twitter without following the links and how often they clicked on news links shared from Twitter (M = .76, SD = 1.24, $p < .001$). On both SNSs, reading news on the site and clicking news links from posts were highly correlated ($r_{Facebook} = .73$, $r_{Twitter} = .83$).

Personal Characteristics

The demographic predictors used in this study were age (M = 46.07, SD = 17.52), gender (51.5% female), race (66.9% White, 11.7% African American, 14.4% Hispanic, 2.1% Asian, 5% other), income (4-point scale ranging from < $30K per year [1] to more than $150K per year [4], median and mode = 2, $30K to less than $75K per year),[1] and religious affiliation (Born Again/ Evangelical Christian = 21.2%, Other Christian = 32.5%, Non-religious = 34.8%, Other religions = 11.5%). Additionally, we examined political party identification on a 5-point scale ranging from Republican (-2) to Democrat (2). Participants who affiliated with a major party were coded as partisans (coded -2 (26.5%), 2 (39.1%)). If participants did not affiliate with a major party, they were asked if they agreed more often with one of the major parties (coded -1 (8.4%), 1 (6.4%)). If respondents noted no affiliation or lean, they were coded "0" (19.6%).

Analysis

One-way analysis of variance (ANOVA) tests are used to examine differences between groups using different news platforms and partisan patterns of news exposure. Bonferroni post-hoc comparisons are employed to compare specific subgroups when differences across groups are detected. Lastly, paired-sample *t*-tests are used to compare differences in patterns of news exposure within particular categories of users. Analyses were computed in SPSS with sample weighting enabled and listwise deletion when data was missing.

Results

When we assessed both the news media-use patterns of the sample as a whole and when we segmented participants into the various demographic groups, we found far more similarities than differences in the relative reliance on social-networking sites and in news and partisan media diets during the 2016 election season. Table 2.1 summarizes overall and group differences for the six specific sources of news information during the 2016 election season: Facebook, Twitter,

TABLE 2.1 News Use by Demographic Groups, Religion, and Partisan Affiliation

	Facebook	*Twitter*	*Aggregator*	*Search*	*Local Media*	*Word of Mouth*
Total	1.60 ^{w} (1.55)	.76 ^{v} (1.24)	1.79 ^{x} (1.63)	1.73 ^{x} (1.54)	2.96 ^{z} (1.40)	2.28 ^{y} (1.38)
Age Group						
18–29	1.85 ^{ab,xy} (1.38)	1.26 ^{a,w} (1.46)	1.73 ^{a,x} (1.49)	1.71 ^{a,x} (1.31)	2.45 ^{a,z} (1.22)	2.08 ^{a,y} (1.27)
30–49	1.88 ^{a,x} (1.56)	1.00 ^{a,w} (1.35)	1.99 ^{a,x} (1.59)	1.99 ^{a,x} (1.67)	2.85 ^{ab,z} (1.39)	2.27 ^{a,y} (1.41)
50–64	1.37 ^{bc,w} (1.63)	.42 ^{b,v} (.97)	1.82 ^{a,x} (1.80)	1.82 ^{a,x} (1.65)	3.29 ^{c,z} (1.41)	2.43 ^{a,y} (1.44)
65+	1.22 ^{c,x} (1.64)	.17 ^{b,w} (.51)	1.44 ^{a,x} (1.55)	1.11 ^{b,x} (1.20)	3.30 $^{bc},^{z}$ (1.41)	2.28 ^{a,y} (1.33)
Gender						
Male	1.55 ^{a,w} (1.63)	.87 ^{a,v} (1.34)	1.95 ^{a,x} (1.74)	1.90 ^{a,x} (1.60)	2.99 ^{a,z} (1.38)	2.38 ^{a,y} (1.40)
Female	1.65 ^{a,x} (1.48)	.65 ^{a,w} (1.14)	1.65 ^{b,x} (1.51)	1.58 ^{b,x} (1.47)	2.95 ^{a,z} (1.42)	2.17 ^{a,y} (1.35)
Race						
White	1.48 ^{a,w} (1.54)	.59 ^{b,v} (1.09)	1.71 ^{a,x} (1.59)	1.51 ^{b,w} (1.41)	2.89 ^{a,z} (1.42)	2.25 ^{a,x} (1.31)

	Facebook	*Twitter*	*Aggregator*	*Search*	*Local Media*	*Word of Mouth*
African American	1.55 ^{a,x} (1.68)	1.08 ^{a,w} (1.56)	1.86 ^{a,xy} (1.78)	2.06 ^{ab,y} (1.84)	3.35 ^{a,z} (1.25)	2.46 ^{a,y} (1.73)
Hispanic	2.01 ^{a,y} (1.42)	1.15 ^{a,x} (1.52)	1.84 ^{a,y} (1.58)	1.81 ^{ab,y} (1.40)	2.82 ^{a,z} (1.85)	2.03 ^{a,y} (1.26)
Asian	1.74 ^{a,yz} (1.36)	1.09 ^{ab,y} (1.08)	1.83 ^{a,yz} (1.29)	2.79 ^{a,z} (1.88)	2.90 ^{a,z} (1.30)	1.66 ^{a,yz} (1.56)
Income						
<$30k	1.66 ^{a,x} (1.50)	.77 ^{a,w} (1.20)	1.71 ^{a,x} (1.65)	1.56 ^{a,x} (1.63)	2.81 ^{a,z} (1.44)	2.18 ^{a,y} (1.41)
$30k-<$75k	1.42 ^{a,w} (1.51)	.73 ^{a,v} (1.28)	1.71 ^{a,x} (1.54)	1.72 ^{a,x} (1.41)	2.92 ^{a,z} (1.34)	2.18 ^{a,y} (1.33)
$75k-<$150k	1.79 ^{a,x} (1.64)	.70 ^{a,w} (1.23)	1.98 ^{a,x} (1.70)	1.92 ^{a,x} (1.55)	3.16 ^{a,z} (1.36)	2.50 ^{a,y} (1.32)
$150k+	1.97 ^{a,x} (1.82)	1.15 ^{a,w} (1.29)	2.43 ^{a,xy} (1.83)	2.36 ^{a,xy} (1.62)	3.57 ^{a,z} (1.49)	2.94 ^{a,y} (1.49)
Religion						
Christian	1.55 ^{a,x} (1.60)	.69 ^{a,w} (1.19)	1.80 ^{a,x} (1.63)	1.90 ^{a,x} (1.55)	3.01 ^{a,z} (1.34)	2.33 ^{a,y} (1.38)
Evangelical	1.71 ^{a,x} (1.64)	.76 ^{a,w} (1.27)	1.56 ^{a,x} (1.58)	1.61 ^{a,x} (1.56)	3.15 ^{a,z} (1.41)	2.42 ^{a,y} (1.42)
No Religion	1.49 ^{a,w} (1.48)	.77 ^{a,v} (1.30)	1.79 ^{a,x} (1.67)	1.66 ^{a,x} (1.51)	2.81 ^{a,z} (1.42)	2.12 ^{a,y} (1.35)
Party						
Republican	1.54 ^{a,x} (1.56)	.49 ^{a,w} (1.04)	1.63 ^{a,x} (1.54)	1.55 ^{a,x} (1.52)	3.00 ^{b,z} (1.34)	2.21 ^{a,y} (1.36)
Lean Republican	1.35 ^{a,x} (1.50)	.55 ^{ab,w} (1.01)	2.12 ^{a,y} (1.72)	1.37 ^{a,x} (1.30)	2.82 ^{ab,z} (1.50)	2.54 ^{a,yz} (1.25)
No Party	1.68 ^{a,y} (1.67)	.99 ^{b,x} (1.28)	1.87 ^{a,yz} (1.74)	1.79 ^{a,yz} (1.63)	2.47 ^{a,z} (1.45)	2.15 ^{a,z} (1.39)
Lean Democrat	1.43 ^{a,x} (1.55)	.49 ^{ab,w} (.87)	1.76 ^{a,xy} (1.64)	1.87 ^{a,xy} (1.42)	2.81 ^{ab,z} (1.45)	2.01 ^{a,y} (1.23)
Democrat	1.69 ^{a,x} (1.50)	.91 ^{b,w} (1.40)	1.80 ^{a,x} (1.61)	1.88 ^{a,x} (1.56)	3.23 ^{b,z} (1.32)	2.37 ^{a,y} (1.43)

Note: Means with standard deviations in parentheses. $^{A\text{-}C}$ superscripts denote differences in Bonferroni post-hoc comparisons across the subcolumn, $^{W\text{-}Z}$ superscripts denote differences in paired-sample *t*-tests across rows. Differing superscripts denote statistically significant differences between comparison groups. Sig. subcolumn one-way ANOVA analyses listed below.

Age: Facebook: $F(3,496) = 6.99, p < .001$, Twitter: $F(3,496) = 19.92, p < .001$, Search: $F(3,496) = 6.76, p < .001$, Local: $F(3,496) = 9.88, p < .001$
Gender: Aggregators: $F(1,598) = 4.29, p < .05$. Search: $F(1,498) = 5.48, p < .05$
Race: Twitter: $F(3,470) = 6.09), p < .001$, Search: $F(3,470) = 4.81, p < .01$.
Income: Local: $F(3.495) = 2.97, p < .05$, Word of Mouth: $F(3,495) = 3.47, p < .05$
Party: Twitter: $F(4,495) = 3.86, p < .01$, Local: $F(4,495 = 5.24), p < .001$

online news aggregators, Internet searches, local media, and word-of-mouth, interpersonal communication.

First, RQ1 asked if there are differences in frequency of use of SNSs for news compared to other news sources. The top line of Table 2.1 shows that local media was the most frequently used source for news across our sample. Word of mouth (interpersonal communication) was the second-most-used source of news information for our full sample. Next, search engines and news aggregators were used at a similar frequency, leaving the two SNS news sources to fall as the least used sources of news. Comparing Facebook and Twitter, we find that Facebook was used significantly more frequently than Twitter across our sample for news. In all, then, when assessing the news use across the entire sample, there were statistically significant differences in news use patterns with all other types of news sources being used more frequently than SNSs (see Table 2.1).

Next, RQ2 asked if there were differences in news use patterns among our subgroups of interest. We examined differences *within* subgroup categories (across the rows in Table 2.1) and *between* subgroup categories (across the columns in Table 2.1). First, we consistently found that local media was the top-rated source for news within all subgroup categories. Older people and partisans were more likely to view news on local media compared to those who were younger and didn't associate with either political party. Next, word-of-mouth was consistently rated the second-most frequently used source of news among all of our subgroups except for Asians, for whom Internet searching was the second-most used news source. However, due to a low sample size, we didn't find significant differences across media sources in Asians Americas, except that they were using Twitter significantly less than other sources of news. Frequency of using word of mouth for news was consistent between all of our subgroups. Taken together, we found local media and word of mouth to be entrenched and frequently used sources of news for all our participants.

More patterns of subgroup differences emerged when looking at online platforms for news. First, there were few differences in patterns for those who used search engines and news aggregators for news. Results in Table 2.1 show that men were using online news aggregators and Internet search engines more frequently than women. People over 65 and Whites used search engines for news less than those under 65 and Asians Americans.

Facebook was the second-least-used news source for most subgroups—with a few notable exceptions. Those within the 18- to 29-year-old age group, Hispanics, and Evangelical Christians used Facebook for news more often than news aggregators and Internet search engines. For those over the age of 65 and those with annual incomes under $30,000, Facebook was used more for news than were Internet search engines, but less often than news aggregators. Women used Facebook for news more often than search engines and used Facebook and news aggregators at a similar frequency. In each subgroup described above, the differences were observed in mean values, but comparisons showed that in all of these cases the differences between frequency of news exposure through Facebook, news aggregators, and Internet searches were not statistically significant. Partisan groups also showed few significant differences between using Facebook, news aggregators, and Internet searches for news. Within other demographic subgroup categories, Facebook was used significantly less frequently than news aggregators and Internet search for news. We found few differences between subgroups except that younger people were using Facebook for news more than those who are older.

Lastly, Twitter was consistently the least-used source of news for members of each demographic and partisan subgroup with no exceptions. Looking between subgroup categories, we found that older, White, and Republican participants reported significantly less use of Twitter than those who were younger, African American, Hispanic, Democratic, or nonpartisan (see Table 2.1). Taken together, we conclude that there were some significant differences in subgroup patterns of using online platforms for news. Whereas this was true, social media were among the least-used sources for news for everyone during the 2016 election, even compared to other online news platforms.

The next analyses, summarized in Table 2.2, focused on the pattern of nonpartisan and partisan news exposure. RQ3 asked if those who affiliate with different parties differ in nonpartisan and partisan news exposure. First, consistent

TABLE 2.2 Partisan News Exposure and Party Affiliation

	Nonpartisan	*Liberal*	*Conservative*
Total	2.52^{z}	2.08^{y}	2.12^{y}
	(1.46)	(1.62)	(1.63)
Party			
Republican	2.27^{a,y}	1.33^{a,x}	2.97^{b,z}
	(1.99)	(1.33)	(1.66)
Lean Republican	1.99^{a,y}	1.05^{a,x}	3.27^{b,z}
	(1.41)	(1.31)	(1.49)
No Party	2.00^{a,z}	1.90^{b,z}	1.93^{a,z}
	(1.47)	(1.47)	(1.55)
Lean Democrat	3.19^{b,z}	2.77^{c,z}	1.66^{a,y}
	(1.16)	(1.47)	(1.27)
Democrat	2.96^{b,z}	2.80^{c,z}	1.47^{a,y}
	(1.41)	(1.60)	(1.34)

Note: Means with standard deviations in parentheses. $^{A\text{-}C}$ superscripts denote differences in Bonferroni post-hoc comparisons across the subcolumn, $^{X\text{-}Z}$ superscripts denote differences in paired-sample *t*-tests across rows. Differing superscripts denote statistically significant differences between comparison groups. Significant subcolumn one-way ANOVA analyses listed below.

Nonpartisan: $F(4{,}495) = 12.66$, $p < .001$, Liberal: $F(4{,}495) = 27.49$, $p < .001$, Conservative: $F(4{,}495) = 27.94$, $p < .001$

with past research, partisans were more likely to view pro-attitudinal partisan news compared with counter-attitudinal news. Democrats were more likely than Republicans to view liberal news, whereas Republicans were more likely than Democrats to view conservative news. Participants who did not affiliate with either party fell between Democrats and Republicans in their use of partisan news. Interestingly, Democrats were more likely to view nonpartisan news compared with Republicans and people unaffiliated with a political party. Democrats viewed nonpartisan news and liberal news at a similar rate, whereas Republicans viewed more conservative news than nonpartisan news. Lastly, those who did not identify or lean toward either party reported no significant differences in their selection of nonpartisan, conservative, or liberal news.

Moving to our last research question (RQ4), Table 2.3 illustrates a general trend that heavy users of online platforms for news were more likely to be exposed to *all* types of news compared to non-users. This was true across Facebook, Twitter, news aggregators, and Internet search engines for nonpartisan and liberal news. This pattern of increased news exposure also persisted for conservative news for users of Facebook, news aggregators, and search engines. However, Twitter users did not show any differences in their exposure to conservative news compared to non-users. When examining differences across the rows in Table 2.3, there was a general trend where online news platform non-users viewed nonpartisan news at a higher rate than partisan news. In contrast, heavy users of Facebook, news aggregators, and search engines for news showed similar rates of exposure to nonpartisan, liberal, and conservative news. Again, heavy Twitter users were an outlier as they viewed nonpartisan and liberal news at a higher rate than conservative news. We conclude that there were significant differences in the patterns of partisan and nonpartisan news for users of online platforms for news, where users showed increased news exposure in all categories. The one caveat is the consistent finding that Twitter news use was not related to increased conservative news use.

Discussion

This study continues a line of research that investigates the importance of social media in U.S. political campaigns. On balance, these results suggest that during the 2016 presidential election season, reliance on social-networking sites (Facebook and Twitter) was rather anemic. This is consistent with findings during the prior two presidential election seasons (Haridakis & Hanson, 2011; Haridakis et al., 2015). We found that other outlets, including local media, word of mouth, Internet search, and online news aggregators, were more commonly used for news information. The consistency of these findings over the three presidential campaigns that occurred since the emergence of social media suggests that although SNSs may have been used less than other sources of news, they do

TABLE 2.3 Partisan News Exposure Patterns and Users of Algorithmic Online News Platforms

	Nonpartisan	*Liberal*	*Conservative*
Facebook			
Not User	$2.34^{a,z}$ (1.50)	$1.78^{a,y}$ (1.69)	$1.98^{a,y}$ (1.72)
Average User	$2.53^{ab,z}$ (1.43)	$2.12^{a,y}$ (1.49)	$2.09^{ab,y}$ (1.57)
Heavy User	$2.96^{b,z}$ (1.38)	$2.76^{b,z}$ (1.64)	$2.61^{b,z}$ (1.52)
Twitter			
Not User	$2.44^{a,z}$ (1.48)	$1.85^{a,y}$ (1.64)	$2.03^{a,y}$ (1.68)
Average User	$2.42^{a,z}$ (1.34)	$2.34^{b,z}$ (1.40)	$2.40^{a,z}$ (1.55)
Heavy User	$3.08^{b,z}$ (1.45)	$2.89^{b,z}$ (1.51)	$2.23^{a,y}$ (1.44)
News Aggregator			
Not User	$2.19^{a,z}$ (1.59)	$1.63^{a,y}$ (1.75)	$1.80^{a,y}$ (1.85)
Average User	$2.55^{ab,z}$ (1.37)	$2.06^{b,y}$ (1.47)	$2.05^{a,y}$ (1.43)
Heavy User	$2.96^{b,z}$ (1.43)	$2.83^{c,z}$ (1.60)	$2.83^{b,z}$ (1.64)
Internet Search			
Not User	$2.09^{a,z}$ (1.54)	$1.55^{a,y}$ (1.63)	$1.83^{a,yz}$ (1.79)
Average User	$2.55^{b,z}$ (1.34)	$2.11^{b,y}$ (1.52)	$2.09^{a,y}$ (1.52)
Heavy User	$3.20^{c,z}$ (1.54)	$2.96^{c,z}$ (1.63)	$2.79^{b,z}$ (1.58)

Note: Means with standard deviations in parentheses. Heavy users comprised of people reporting over 1 SD of mean use. $^{A\text{-}C}$ superscripts denote differences in Bonferroni post-hoc comparisons across the subcolumn, $^{Y\text{-}Z}$ superscripts denote differences in paired-sample *t*-tests across rows. Differing superscripts denote statistically significant differences between comparison groups. Significant subcolumn one-way ANOVA analyses listed below.

Facebook: Nonpartisann: $F(2,497) = 10.34, p < .001$, Liberal: $F(2,497) = 4.94$ $p < .01$, Conservative: $F(2,497) = 4.18, p < .05$
Twitter: Nonpartisan: $F(2,497) = 14.08, p < .001$, Liberal: $F(2,497) = 5.93, p < .01$
News Aggregator: Nonpartisan: $F(2,497) = 16.16, p < .001$, Liberal: $F(2,497) = 7.82, p < .001$, Conservative: $F(2.497) = 12.04, p < .001$
Search: Nonpartisann: $F(2,497) = 19.53, p < .001$, Liberal: $F(2,497) = 22.40, p < .001$, Conservative: $F(2,497) = 8.67, p < .001$

appear to be firmly entrenched as complementary sources for news during campaign seasons. Furthermore, our results showed that Facebook was used for news far more frequently than Twitter, despite increased candidate use of Twitter as a political platform.

In the case of SNS use, these findings challenge at least some older digital divide assumptions that traditionally under-privileged groups may be disadvantaged in the digital age due to limited access to newer media technologies in comparison to more privileged groups. African Americans and Hispanic Americans used Twitter for news more than Whites. Furthermore, we found no gender or income gap in SNS use for news. Of course, definitive conclusions about the extent of any technology divide must be tempered by the fact that the survey conducted for this study was administered online. Therefore, participants, by definition were connected. Thus, their access does not necessarily reflect the extent of access of their demographic counterparts. Nonetheless, among the participants of this study, frequency of use across platforms was not disparate.

Moving to partisan selective exposure, these data suggested that partisans were more likely to turn to pro-attitudinal partisan news than counter-attitudinal news, which is consistent with past work on partisan selective exposure (e.g., Garrett, 2009; Stroud, 2011). However, we also found that heavier users of Facebook for news were also heavier consumers of news overall—including nonpartisan news, conservative news, and liberal news. This suggests that although algorithmically and socially driven systems may facilitate increased partisan news exposure, people may be using Facebook as a gateway to engaging in more news overall. In fact, it is possible that Facebook helps those who are less inclined to read news and politics to engage through easy access to personally relevant news. We found a similar pattern for news aggregators and search engines (see also Beam & Kosicki, 2014). Furthermore, if nonpartisan sources of news continue to be a steady component of news content in users' online news routines, as found here among heavier Facebook users, then worries about algorithmic echo chambers and filter bubbles may be overstated.

Our results revealed some cause for concern, however, when focusing on differential patterns of nonpartisan news use. Republicans were significantly less likely to select nonpartisan news than conservative news, whereas Democrats viewed nonpartisan news and liberal news at a similar frequency. Democrats were also more likely to view nonpartisan news compared to Republicans. These findings suggest the possibility that partisan news may be trumping less biased news for conservative partisans. There has been a growing public notion, especially from conservative partisans, that the mainstream media has a liberal bias. For example, throughout the 2016 campaign Donald Trump called mainstream media "crooked" and "dishonest" (Ingram, 2016; Trump, 2016). Past research has not found consistent evidence for ideological bias in mainstream news (Lichter, 2014). Instead, this body of research has been mixed depending on context, methods, and theories (Lichter, 2014). Our results indicate that the continuing growth in audience fragmentation does result in differential patterns of both partisan and nonpartisan media use.

Future Research

Taken together, these results indicate more research is needed to look at the *flow* of news. Among the online sources measured, but for the above few exceptions, news aggregators and general Internet searching were used more often than Facebook and Twitter. For example, our results show that the average person views Twitter between *Never* and *Less than a few times a month*. This is important to note, because although we have given greater attention to the use and potential effects of social media during recent campaigns, we should not ignore reliance on and effects of other (and sometimes older) forms of online platforms that continue to be relied on by many users. The results suggest that candidates who want to reach these voters are best served if they make sure their message reaches the local media, which was the most used source of news during the campaign. For example, 2016 election victor Donald Trump frequently posted campaign messages directly to Twitter throughout the campaign. Our results indicate that most Internet users, especially Republican partisans, were not using the platform. However, Trump's tweets were often covered and amplified by other mainstream news organizations. Therefore, to the extent this messaging was successful, people were most likely to learn about the posts through an alternate source—such as traditional media or word of mouth that were used more often (see Conway, Kenski, & Wang, 2015 for a discussion of politicians' use of Twitter and intra-media agenda setting).

In addition, the importance of interpersonal communication should be stressed here in relation to SNSs and other online platforms, as well. Past research has found that use of online social media for political news and information is positively related to interpersonal political discussion with others, particularly for partisans (Haridakis et al., 2017). Our data showed that word-of-mouth interaction was one of the most-used avenues for news during the campaign for most groups. Although it was used more often than SNSs, it is likely that discussion was a major aspect on Facebook, too. Future research should give greater attention to the specific role of online discussion in SNSs. Facebook, in particular, is a specific medium of connection with family and friends, so it is likely that it provided an additional tool for dialogue and dissemination of news and political information among and between family and friends. If this is true, then word-of-mouth interaction, when coupled with SNS interaction, likely made interpersonal and group discussion even more pronounced than when we assess word-of-mouth communication and SNSs separately. Thus, although we have long recognized the importance of interpersonal communication in political campaigns (Lazarsfeld, Berelson, & Gaudet, 1944), it may be occurring more than ever before.

If future research confirms our speculation here, it has significant implications for putting in perspective other findings that have suggested that people's media diets have become more concentrated. That is, if selective exposure to media content can create echo chambers, we need to integrate interpersonal communication in the discussion. News aggregators and search engines use algorithms to select news recommendations for users (Pariser, 2011). Mainstream media often take a partisan slant (Entman, 2010), and people like to talk to like-minded others (Mutz, 2006). Thus, all of these sources of information have a potential propensity to create echo chambers. However, past research has indicated there are many conditions where people seek counter-attitudinal information (e.g., Hart et al., 2009). Our communication theories should work to integrate uses of interpersonal and mediated channels of information to disentangle patterns of biased and non-biased political information effects.

Conclusion

In conclusion, we have illustrated that patterns of SNS news use are relatively consistent across demographic subgroups. Although social media is one of the least-used sources of news, those who use social media for news indicate greater exposure to all types of news. SNSs might, then, be helpful in facilitating political news attention and interest. Over the last three U.S. general elections, social media has become entrenched as a tool for candidates to disseminate their messages directly to the public. We believe this reorganization of the flow of news warrants further attention. However, we are hesitant to join the growing chorus that singles out SNSs as a primary driver of filter bubbles and echo chambers. Although we demonstrate evidence that partisan news use is prevalent, evidence here shows that SNSs are rarely used as frequently as other news outlets. In a media environment with increased choice, SNSs should be assessed alongside other sources of news, rather than in isolation.

Note

1 < $30K per year = 36.1%, $30K—<$75K = 39.8%, $75K—<$150K = 19.2%, $150K+ = 4.9%

References

Allcott, H., & Gentzkow, M. (2017, January). Social media and fake news in the 2016 Election. [White paper]. Retrieved from https://web.stanford.edu/~gentzkow/research/fakenews.pdf

Ancu, M. (2015). Here comes everybody, or not: An analysis of the social media consumer of campaign content. In J. Hendricks & D. Schill (Eds.), *Presidential campaigning and social media* (pp. 218–231). New York, NY: Oxford University Press.

Ansolabehere, S., & Rivers, D. (2013). Cooperative survey research. *Annual Review of Political Science, 16*, 307–329. doi:10.1146/annurev-polisci-022811-160625

Ansolabehere, S., & Schaffner, B. F. (2014). Does survey mode still matter? Findings from a 2010 multi-mode comparison. *Political Analysis, 22*(3), 285–303. doi:10.1093/pan/mpt025

Bakshy, E., Messing, S., & Adamic, L. A. (2015). Exposure to ideologically diverse news and opinion on Facebook. *Science, 348*, 1130–1132. doi:10.1126/science.aaa1160

Barbera, P., & Rivero, G. (2015). Understanding the political representativeness of Twitter users. *Social Science Computer Review, 33*, 712–729. doi:10.1177/0894439314558836

Baumgartner, J. C., Morris, D. S., & Morris, J. S. (2015). Of networks and knowledge: Young adults and the early 2012 republican presidential primaries and caucuses. In J. Hendricks & D. Schill (Eds.), *Presidential campaigning and social media* (pp. 44–57). New York, NY: Oxford University Press.

Beam, M. A. (2014). Automating the news: How personalized news recommender system design choices impact news reception. *Communication Research, 41*(8), 1019–1041. doi:10.1177/0093650213497979

Beam, M. A., & Kosicki, G. M. (2014). Personalized news portals: Filtering systems and increased news exposure. *Journalism & Mass Communication Quarterly, 91*(1), 59–77. doi:10.1177/1077699013514411

Bekafigo, M. A., & McBride, A. (2013). Who tweets about politics? Political participation of Twitter users during the 2011 gubernatorial elections. *Social Science Computer Review, 31*, 625–643. doi:10.1177/0894439313490405

Benkler, Y. (2006). *The wealth of networks: How social production transforms markets and freedom.* New Haven, CT: Yale University Press.

Bennett, W. L., Wells, C., & Freelon, D. (2011). Communicating civic engagement: Contrasting models of citizenship in the youth web sphere. *Journal of Communication, 61*, 835–856. doi:10.1111/j.1460–2466.2011.01588.x

Coe, K., Tewksbury, D., Bond, B. J., Drogos, K. L., Porter, R. W., Yahn, A., & Zhang, Y. (2008). Hostile news: Partisan use and perceptions of cable news programming. *Journal of Communication, 58*, 201–219. doi:10.1111/j.1460–2466.2008.00381.x

Conway, B. A., Kenski, K., & Wang, D. (2015). The rise of Twitter in the political campaign: Searching for intramedia agenda-setting effects in the presidential primary. *Journal of Computer-Mediated Communication, 20*(4), 363–380. doi:10.1111/jcc4.12124

Duggan, M., & Smith, A. (2016, October 25). The political environment on social media. *Pew Research Center.* Retrieved from www.pewinternet.org/2016/10/25/the-political-environment-on-social-media/

Dylko, I., Beam, M. A., Landreville, K. D., & Geidner, N. W. (2012). Filtering 2008 presidential election news on YouTube by elites and non-elites: An examination in the democratizing potential of the Internet. *New Media & Society, 14*(5), 832–849. doi:10.1177/1461444811428899

Entman, R. M. (2010). Media framing biases and political power: Explaining slant in news of campaign 2008. *Journalism, 11*(4), 389–408. doi:10.1177/1464884910367587

Festinger, L. (1957). *A theory of cognitive dissonance.* Stanford, CA: Stanford University Press.

Festinger, L. (1964). *Conflict, decision, and dissonance.* Stanford, CA: Stanford University Press.

Flaxman, S., Goel, S. & Rao, J. M. (2016). Filter bubbles, echo chambers, and online news consumption. *Public Opinion Quarterly, 80*(S1), 298–320. doi:10.1093/poq/nfw006

Garrett, R. K. (2009). Echo chambers online? Politically motivated selective exposure among Internet news users. *Journal of Computer Mediated Communication, 14*(2), 265–285.

Garrett, R. K., Carnahan, D., & Lynch, E. K. (2013). A turn toward avoidance? Selective exposure to online political information, 2004–2008. *Political Behavior, 35*(1), 113–134. doi:10.1007/s11109-011-9185-6

Garrett, R. K., & Stroud, N. J. (2014). Partisan oaths to exposure diversity: Differences in pro-and counterattitudinal news consumption. *Journal of Communication, 64*(4), 680–701. doi:10.1111/jcom.12105

Hargittai, E. (2000). Open portals or closed gates? Channeling content on the World Wide Web. *Poetics, 27*, 233–253.

Haridakis, P., & Hanson, G. (2011). Campaign 2008: Comparing YouTube, social networking and other media use among younger voters and older voters. In J. A. Hendricks & L. L. Kaid (Eds.), *Techno-politics and presidential campaigning: New technologies, new voices, and new voters* (pp. 61–82). New York, NY: Routledge.

Haridakis, P. M., Hanson, G. L., Lin, M.-C., & McCullough, J. (2015). Fitting social media into the media landscape during a 2012 republican primary. In J. Hendricks & D. Schill (Eds.), *Presidential campaigning and social media* (pp. 106–121). New York, NY: Oxford University Press.

Haridakis, P. M., Lin, M. C., & Hanson, G. L. (2017). The influence of political intergroup differences and social media use on political discussion and polarization. In G. Richardson (Ed.), *Social media and politics: A new way to participate in the political process (Vol 1: Candidates, campaigns and political power)* (pp. 219–242). Santa Barbara, CA: Praeger.

Hart, W., Albarracín, D., Eagly, A. H., Lindberg, M., Lee, K. H., & Brechan, I. (2009). Feeling validated vs. being correct: A meta-analysis of exposure to information. *Psychological Bulletin, 135*, 555–588. doi:10.1037/a0015701

Hendricks, J. A., & Schill, D. (2015). The presidential campaign of 2012: New media technologies used to interact and engage with the electorate. In J. Hendricks & D. Schill (Eds.), *Presidential campaigning and social media* (pp. 1–14). New York, NY: Oxford University Press.

Hmielowski, J. D., Beam, M. A., & Hutchens, M. J. (2016). Structural changes in media and attitude polarization: Examining the contributions of TV news before and after the Telecommunications Act of 1996. *International Journal of Public Opinion Research, 18*(2), 123–143. doi:10.1080/15205436.2014.902968

Ingram, M. (2016, November 22). Trump has the media between a rock and a very hard place. *Fortune*. Retrieved from http://fortune.com/2016/11/22/trump-media-rock/

Iyengar, S., & Hahn., K. S. (2009). Red media, blue media: Evidence of ideological selectivity in media use. *Journal of Communication, 59*, 19–39.

Kreiss, D. (2016). Seizing the moment: The presidential campaigns' use of Twitter during the 2012 electoral cycle. *New Media & Society, 18*, 1473–1490. doi:10.1177/1461444814562445

Lazarsfeld, P. F., Berelson, B., & Gaudet, H. (1944). *The people's choice: How the voter makes up his mind in a presidential campaign*. New York, NY: Columbia University Press.

Lenhart, A. (2009). Adults and social network websites. *Pew Research Center*. Retrieved from www.pewinternet.org/2009/01/14/main-findings-13/

Lichter, S. R. (2014). Theories of media bias. In K. Kenski & K. H. Jamieson (Eds.), *Oxford handbook of political communication*. New York, NY: Oxford University Press. doi:10.1093/oxfordhb/9780199793471.013.44

Matsa, E. M. (2015). Early morning, noon, and late evening slots drive growth in local TV news. *Pew Research Center*. Retrieved from www.pewresearch.org/fact-tank/2015/07/15/early-morning-noon-and-late-evening-slots-drive-growth-in-local-tv-news/

Messing, S., & Westwood, S. J. (2014). Selective exposure in the age of social media: Endorsements trump partisan source affiliation when selecting news online. *Communication Research, 41*(8), 1042–1063. doi:10.1177/0093650212466406

Mitchell, A., Gottfried, J., Barthel, M., & Shearer, E. (2016). The modern news consumer. *Pew Research Center.* Retrieved from www.journalism.org/2016/07/07/the-modern-news-consumer/

Mitchell, A., Gottfried, J., Kiley, J., & Matsa, K. E. (2014). Political polarization & media habits. *Pew Research Center,* Retrieved from www.journalism.org/2014/10/21/political-polarization-media-habits/

Mitchell, A., Rosenstiel, T., & Christian, L. (2012). What Facebook and Twitter mean for news. *Pew Research Center's Project for Excellence in Journalism.* Retrieved from www.stateofthemedia.org/2012/mobile-devices-and-news-consumption-some-good-signs-for-journalism/what-facebook-and-twitter-mean-for-news/

Mutz, D. C. (2006). *Hearing the other side: Deliberative versus participatory democracy.* New York, NY: Cambridge University Press.

Pariser, E. (2011). *The filter bubble: What the Internet is hiding from you.* New York, NY: Penguin.

Rivers, D., & Bailey, D. (2009). Inference from matched samples in the 2008 U. S. national elections. In *Proceedings of the joint statistical meetings* (pp. 627–639). Alexandria, VA: American Statistical Association.

Schill, D., & Kirk, R. (2015). Issue debates in 140 characters: Online talk surrounding the 2012 debates. In J. Hendricks & D. Schill (Eds.), *Presidential campaigning and social media* (pp. 198–217). New York, NY: Oxford University Press.

Stroud, N. J. (2011). *Niche news: The politics of news choice.* New York, NY: Oxford University Press.

Stroud, N. J. (2014). Selective exposure theories. In K. Kenski & K. H. Jamieson (Eds.), *Oxford handbook of political communication.* New York, NY: Oxford University Press. doi:10.1093/oxfordhb/9780199793471.013.009

Sunstein, C. (2007). *Republic.com 2.0.* Princeton, NJ: Princeton University Press.

Sweetser, K. D., & Kaid, L. L. (2008). Stealth soapboxes: Political information efficacy, cynicism and uses of celebrity weblogs among readers. *New Media & Society, 10,* 67–91. doi:10.1177/1461444807085322

Trump, D. J. [realDonaldTrump]. (2016, October 16). The election is absolutely being rigged by the dishonest and distorted media pushing Crooked Hillary—but also at many polling places—SAD [Tweet]. Retrieved from https://twitter.com/realDonaldTrump/status/787699930718695425

Weeks, B. E., & Garrett, R. K. (2014). Electoral consequences of political rumors: Motivated reasoning, candidate rumors, and vote choice during the 2008 U. S. Presidential Election. *International Journal of Public Opinion Research, 26*(4), 401–422. doi:10.1093/ijpor/edu005

Wicks, R. H., Wicks, J. L., Morimoto, S. A., Maxwell, A., & Schulte, S. R. (2014). Correlates of political and civic engagement among youth during the 2012 presidential campaign. *American Behavioral Scientist, 58,* 622–644. doi:10.1177/0002764213515226

Yun, H. J. (2015). The spirals of newly transcending political voices: Social media purify the atmosphere of political dialogues in cyberspace. In J. Hendricks & D. Schill (Eds.), *Presidential campaigning and social media* (pp. 154–170). New York, NY: Oxford University Press.

3

TRUMP SUPPORTERS VS. REPUBLICAN VOTERS

How Frustration With the Media Separated the GOP in 2016

Sharon E. Jarvis and Jay T. Jennings

On November 8, 2016, Donald J. Trump was elected the 45th president of the U.S. This outcome came as a surprise to the prevailing campaign news narrative. Outlets ranging from the *New York Times* to the *Washington Post* to the *Wall Street Journal* had informed readers that Democratic nominee Hillary Clinton's chances for victory were nearly inevitable (Hook, 2016; Katz, 2016; Rampell, 2016). Headlines posted to the FiveThirtyEight website, founded by predictive model expert Nate Silver, informed: "Trump has a Better Chance of Cameoing in another 'Home Alone' Movie with Macaulay Culkin—or Playing in the NBA Finals—than Winning the Republican Nomination" (Fossett, 2016). In the months before the election, members of the chattering class labeled a Trump victory "a fantasy," suggesting that "it would take video evidence of a smiling Hillary drowning a litter of puppies while terrorists surrounded her with chants of 'Death to America'" for him to prevail (Arrietta-Kenna, 2016, para. 4). Media elites offered to eat crickets on CNN as well as printouts of their *Washington Post* columns should Trump be victorious (Arrietta-Kenna, 2016; Wang, 2016). On the morning of Election Day, even Trump admitted that he didn't think he was going to win (Arrietta-Kenna, 2016, para. 5).

In the days following the election, journalists and pundits worked to read meaning into the unexpected results. One conversation on November 9, 2016 on MSNBC's *Hardball with Chris Matthews* began with host Matthews asking Republican operative John Brabender, "Why is there a silent majority for Donald Trump that didn't get picked up by pollsters?" Brabender offered three arguments: (1) there were a lot of blue-collar Democrats in states such as "Wisconsin, Michigan, and Pennsylvania . . . who were going to vote for Donald Trump. But believe me, they're not answering the phone and telling people publicly they're voting for Donald Trump"; (2) "Donald Trump was made toxic to a

lot of college-educated moderate women who are not going to publicly go out and say, I'm voting for Donald Trump. But . . . he didn't lose by the margins everybody thought"; and (3) "non-college-educated women overwhelmingly voted for Donald Trump in these states." In response to these observations, Matthews asked,

> Why weren't they going to talk to pollsters? What is it about the pollsters? Do they see the pollsters as the media, as the establishment, as Ivy Leaguers? What is it about them that makes them think that they can put a lawn sign up, but they're not going to tell somebody who they're voting for on the phone?
>
> *(Matthews, 2016)*

This chapter examines such sentiments by focusing on the relationship(s) between Trump supporters, their regard for the media, and their perceptions of political participation and engagement. Inspired by the theme of this edited volume, by Trump's unexpected victories (in both the primaries and the general election), and by scholarship pointing to a lack of trust and an abundance of frustration in parts of the Republican base (Cramer, 2016; Grossman & Hopkins, 2016; Hochschild, 2016; Mann & Ornstein, 2012; Vance, 2016), we advance three questions: Where did Trump supporters get their news in campaign 2016? How did they feel about the media? And, how did they regard political participation and engagement? We answer these questions by analyzing findings from a national survey conducted in the spring of 2016 and by comparing the responses of early Trump supporters to other Republican voters. This approach allows us to shed light on the seeds of the Trump movement that led to his nomination and surprising victory.

Republicans, News Use, and Trust

The Republican Party has had an adversarial relationship with "the media" for decades (Cappella & Jamieson, 1997; Jarvis, 2005). Hemmer (2016a; 2016b) explains how conservatives have regarded elections to be rigged against them dating at least back to the early 1950s, because—in their minds—liberal gatekeepers held all the keys to the mainstream media. She details how a first generation of right-leaning journalists, book publishers, and media activists banded together at that time to critique the press and to produce more ideologically preferable content. A second generation emerged in the late 1960s with the Richard Nixon presidency and their public charges of bias. One of the more notable indictments at that time was voiced by Vice President Spiro Agnew when he alluded to how news outlets did not reflect the views of the public by stating, "In the United States today, we have more than our share of nattering nabobs of negativism. They have formed their own 4-H club—the hopeless, hysterical hypochondriacs of history" (Ladd, 2012; Remnick, 2006).

Years later, these charges were still in vogue. In 1992 for instance, George Herbert Walker Bush encouraged Republican voters to "annoy the media: Re-elect Bush," placing this phrase on bumper stickers and campaign hats (Ayers, 1992; Lichter & Noyes, 1996). In 1996, Robert Dole admonished crowds, saying, "Voters are not angry enough at the media" and "Don't read that stuff! Don't watch television! Don't let them make up your mind for you!" He elaborated, "When do the American people rise up and say, 'Forget the media in America! We're going to make up our minds! You're not going to make up our minds!'" (Seelye, 1996). In 2012, Mitt Romney addressed the topic with a softer touch during his comedic speech at the Al Smith Dinner, asserting, "Now I never suggest that the press is biased. I recognize they have their job to do and I have my job to do. My job is to lay out a positive vision for the future of the country. And their job is to make sure no one else finds out about it" (Romney, 2012).

Polls from the Pew Research Center show that conservative voters have embraced this anti-media perspective. Data reveal how individuals who identify as right-leaning are "tightly clustered around a single news source" (with 47% reporting Fox News as the main source of information), show higher levels of distrust of news sources, are unlikely to encounter political content they agree with on Facebook, and are likely to have friends who share their opinions (with 66% suggesting that most of their close friends agree with them about the role of government). In contrast, those who identify as left-leaning rely on a greater range of news outlets (often including NPR and the *New York Times*), express more trust than distrust of the news, and report interacting with political content they find disagreeable on Facebook such that they must "block or 'defriend'" others in their networks (Mitchell, Gottfried, Kiley, & Matsa, 2014). Survey findings further reveal that only 13% of conservative Republicans and 18% of moderate/liberal Republicans trust information "from national news organizations a lot" versus 31% of liberal Democrats and 24% of conservative/moderate Democrats (Mitchell, Gottfried, Barthel, & Shearer, 2016). Additionally, conservative Republicans are more likely to believe "the news media tend to favor one side" (87%) than are conservative to moderate Democrats (57%) (Mitchell et al., 2016). Throughout his campaign and during the early months of his presidency, Trump attacked the integrity of the media extensively; data collected one month prior to the 2016 presidential election suggest that just 14% of Republican voters voiced trust in the fourth estate at that time (Swift, 2016).

The Republican Party, too, has long harbored an uneasy relationship to government. Aldrich (1995) maintains that the central cleavage between the two major parties in the U.S. has been the role and size of government, with Democrats preferring more and Republicans favoring less. Hemmer (2016a) details how conservative elites publicly praised the virtues of smaller government in the 1950s, a sentiment that would intensify over the next 50 years (Jarvis, 2005).

Lakoff's (1996) stance that conservatives have a distinct relationship to government describes motivations that underlie this perspective. Employing a parenting metaphor, he contends that conservatives obey a Strict Father model in which ideal citizens are responsible, self-disciplined, and self-reliant. Guided by this mindset, conservatives view social programs as amoral because they reward those who were not disciplined enough to "sink or swim by themselves" (p. 273). Lakoff maintains that these individuals "know what is good for them better than their government" and strongly resent "any governmental meddling or interfering" (p. 273). Survey data underscore these claims. Polls continue to show that Republicans and conservatives prefer a smaller government presence than do Democrats and liberals (Doherty, Kiley, Tyson, & Jameson, 2015).

Republicans: A Party in Transition

Classic works point to unique aspects of Republican Party culture. Consider research published prior to 2010. At that time, the GOP was regarded as having a corporate style, where power flowed downward from the Republican National Committee, members identified as insiders (even when out of power), individualism was prized, identification was stronger to the party (than to an interest group or other organizational bloc), order was embraced, and conflict was hidden (Freeman, 1986). Baumer and Gold (1995) add that Republicans were positively viewed as tough on enemies (both foreign and domestic), favoring entrepreneurial activity and low taxes, and upholding traditional values. These authors also note how the GOP was viewed negatively for helping the wealthy (at the expense of the poor), for holding an overly aggressive perspective on international relations, and for imposing their values on others.

In comparing the cultural priorities of the Republican and Democratic Parties, Freeman (1986) viewed the commitment to smaller government, individualism, and values as serving an important "social function" facilitating "trust" for the GOP. She observed,

> People normally trust those who are like them to think like them and do what they would do. People understand others who are like themselves. Organizations or communities whose members trust each other function more smoothly and take direction more willingly than those where trust is more limited. Republicans trust their party, and their leaders, to do what they think is right more than Democrats do because they are socially homogenous.
>
> *(p. 351)*

This trust began to erode, however, with time. Anger that had been brewing over economic policies and spending during the final years of George W. Bush's presidency, as well as during the start of Barack Obama's first term, led to the rise of the Tea Party faction of the party in the 2010 election cycle (Skocpol & Williamson, 2016). The tone and approach of the core of the GOP also changed. Mann and Ornstein (2012) describe how at this time the party became "an insurgent outlier," an organization that was "ideologically extreme, contemptuous of the inherited social and economic policy regime, scornful of compromise, unpersuaded by conventional understandings of facts, evidence and science, and dismissive of the legitimacy of its political opposition" (p. xiv). They detail how the governing style of many Republicans on Capitol Hill abandoned an older notion of "respecting adversaries" and embraced a "take-it-or-leave-it" type of bargaining that was supported by "shrill voices" on "talk radio, blogs, and Twitter" (p. 26). Conservative television news, in particular, started allocating coverage to "extreme and outrageous" actions (p. 62), rewarded "sensationalism" over "sensible centrism" (p. 62), and began to eschew "facts" (p. 67). Consumers of this content, in turn, became "significantly less optimistic" about the future of the country (p. 61).

Given these dynamics, scholars have invited renewed attention to the nature, composition, and motivations of leaders and followers on the right (Grossman & Hopkins, 2015; 2016). Pertaining to the eventual Trump candidacy, three books shed light on what conservative citizen anger sounded like heading into the 2016 campaign. Cramer's (2016) *The Politics of Resentment: Rural Consciousness in Wisconsin and the Rise of Scott Walker* described how people in the Badger State made sense of politics and their role in it. After five years of listening to people in rural areas, Cramer discovered deep resentment toward cities, urbanities, universities, government, and the media. Her interviewees felt a deep lack of respect from those entities; the people she talked to believed that they were hardworking and being overlooked, that policy makers were allocating resources to less deserving people in cities, and that an urban mindset, propagated by the press, looked down on them as uneducated and racist. Such feelings, Cramer detailed, led them to support candidates who critiqued and policies that rolled back government.

Vance's (2016) *Hillbilly Elegy: A Memoir of a Family and Culture in Crisis* offered another take on people's anger and mistrust toward elites and government. Written by a Yale Law School graduate, who was born in Kentucky and grew up in Ohio, it told of his family's poverty and of his community's learned helplessness and harmful cultural tendencies. In recounting interactions with family members and friends, he revealed a lack of agency in Appalachia and the Rust Belt as well as a propensity to blame others (and the government) for difficult conditions. Further, Hochschild's (2016) *Strangers in Their Own Land: Anger and Mourning on the American Right* addressed the great paradox of "opposition to federal help from people and places that need it" (p. 5). To do so, she spent five years interviewing Tea Party members in Louisiana and paid close attention to how they felt about politics. Similar to depictions in the Cramer and Vance books, the people she studied were (1) frustrated that others (often racial minorities and immigrants) were "cutting in line" to receive special treatment from government and (2) tired of being mocked and disrespected by the liberal media. Connecting back to Mann's and Ornstein's (2012) analysis, the people represented in these three works were rarely hopeful about the country's future.

Although none of these books were written about Trump's campaign directly, they all shed light on how many potential Republican voters have moved from Freeman's (1986) model organized by a hierarchical coalition prizing order and loyalty to Mann's and Ornstein's (2012) paradigm united by frustration and anger. Additionally, even though Republicans had been campaigning against the media and government since the 1950s, Trump's rhetoric took such charges to a more incendiary level (Folkenflik, 2016; Parker & Chozick, 2015). From June 2015 through November 2016, he routinely took issue with political leaders, the government, his Republican opponents, the media in general, specific news outlets in particular, and high-profile journalists. So pervasive were his charges that the *New York Times* catalogued the "People, places, and things Donald Trump has insulted," a list that topped 300 targets by the time Trump was inaugurated in January of 2017 (Lee & Quealy, 2017).

Guided by understandings of the traditional Republican base, changes to the party, and the unexpected candidacy—and victory—of Trump, this chapter turns to address: Where did Trump supporters get their news in campaign 2016? How did they feel about the media? And, how did they regard political participation and engagement?

Data

The Texas Media & Society Survey was created by the Annette Strauss Institute for Civic Life at the University of Texas at Austin. Fielded by the GfK Group, it employed a probability-based sampling strategy to recruit participants; 3,743 were sampled for participation and 2,015 completed the survey. Data collection took place between May 24, 2016 and June 14, 2016 and respondents included 1,009 Americans and an additional over-sample of 1,006 Texans. (Note: The results presented below include the full sample including our over-sample of Texans. Each of the results presented were tested to see if controlling for the Texas over-sample influenced the results. Because those tests showed no substantial differences, we did not include such controls in our models.) The survey included items about journalism and the media, politics and civic engagement, and discussion networks and communities, and it was available in both English and Spanish.

The date of the survey allows us insight into Trump's early supporters. It was fielded at a time when many in the nation had already voted in their state primaries and yet the nomination had not yet been formally or informally won. In late May and early June, Trump was leading in the delegate count, but two legitimate contenders in Ted Cruz and John Kasich were still in the race. One hundred and ninety-five of our participants told us they voted for Trump in their state primaries and 355 others told us they voted for other Republican candidates. Unlike the general election, in which true support for a candidate is muddled by partisan allegiances, primary elections allow for a clearer understanding of candidate preferences. At the time of the survey, Trump supporters voted for him because of his political stances and the campaign he had run up until that point—not because he was a Republican. The following paragraphs compare the media habits, trust in the media and government, and perceptions of political participation and engagement of those who supported Trump in the primaries versus those who voted for other Republican candidates. We excluded all respondents who had not voted in a primary at the time of the survey.

Results

A first concern addressed attention to the news. The data show very small differences between Trump supporters and other Republican voters on this measure (see Figure 3.1). That is, 36% of Trump supporters said they followed "national news" very closely compared to 37% of those who voted for other Republican candidates. Additionally, 36% of Trump supporters watched "political news" closely compared to 38% of other Republican voters. For "international news," there was no difference, with 17% of both groups following very closely.

A second matter concerned where people got their news. Because demographic differences are expected to influence news seeking, it is important to control for key differences in the sample. Trump supporters were significantly less likely to have a college degree than those who supported other Republican candidates (33% versus 51%). Trump supporters were also slightly older, slightly more likely to be White, and slightly less conservative than supporters of other candidates.

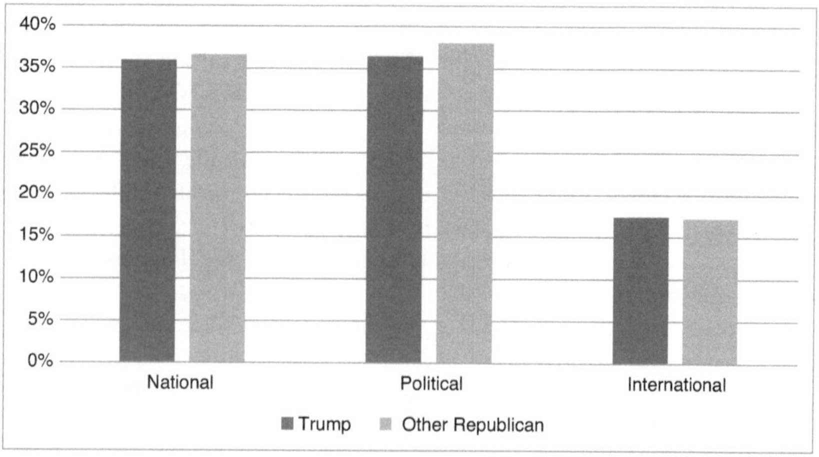

FIGURE 3.1 Percent Following News Very Closely by Type of News

In the following analyses, age, education, race, and ideology were all controlled for in logit models predicting the probability of voting for Trump versus other Republican primary candidates. In the first model, the probability of voting for Trump was estimated based on whether or not the respondent used various media sources for news. Figure 3.2 features probabilities of voting for Trump for respondents who sought news via Facebook, MSNBC, Fox News, Drudge Report, *New York Times*, and local newspapers. As it illustrates, news choice did not predict any statistically significant differences between Trump supporters and other Republican voters. The only source where there appeared to be a difference is that individuals seeking news on the Drudge Report were about 10% less likely to vote for Trump. However, as is the case with the other news sources, this result was not significant even at the 90% confidence level. Figures 3.1 and 3.2, then, provide evidence that Trump supporters were not significantly different from other Republicans in attention to the news or in outlet choice.

A third matter was trust in the media. The data show that on this measure, Trump supporters departed from other Republican voters. Respondents were asked if it was "impossible for journalists to objectively report the news" and those who agreed with that statement were much more likely to support Trump. Figure 3.3 presents the predicted probabilities for how strongly individuals agreed or disagreed with this statement on journalistic objectivity. Again, the model controlled for age, education, race, and ideology. The figure displays the point

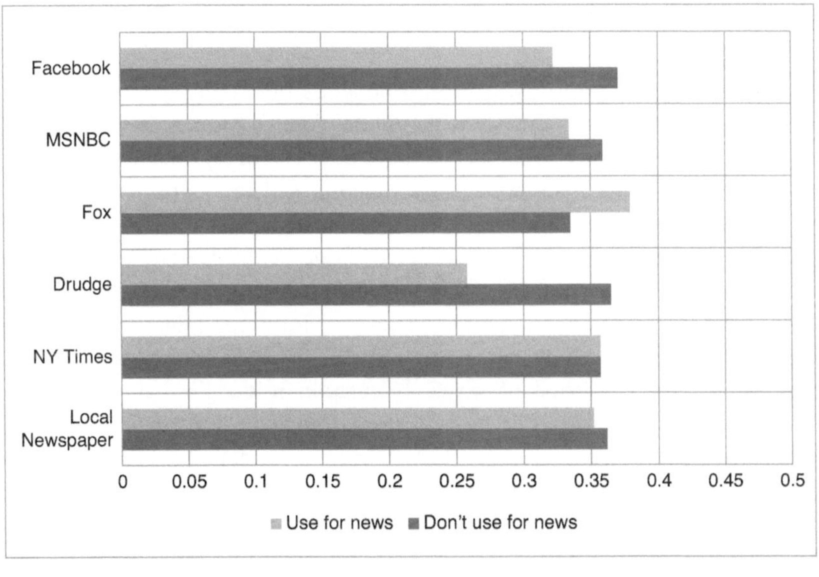

FIGURE 3.2 Probability of Voting for Trump vs. Other Republicans by News Media Choice

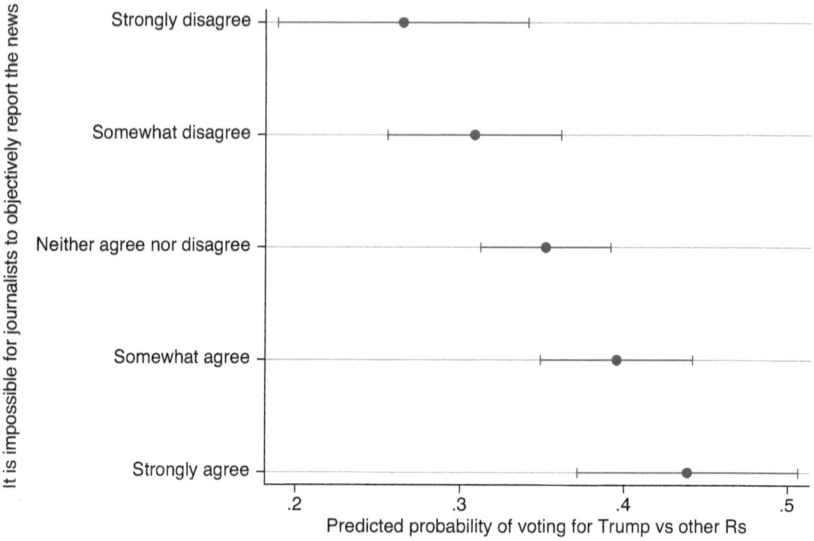

FIGURE 3.3 Voting for Trump and Journalist Objectivity

estimate and the 95% confidence bands. Here, those who strongly disagreed with the statement, and therefore believed in a journalist's ability to remain objective, were only estimated to vote for Trump 28% of the time. Those who strongly agreed with the statement on the other hand were estimated to vote for Trump 42% of the time. The difference between these two groups was statistically significant.

Another way we measured trust in journalistic objectivity was to ask people what types of disclosures journalists should be required to include when reporting on certain topics. The Texas Media & Society Survey included eight different questions about requirements for disclosures. These options ranged from the notion of reporters disclosing their partisan affiliations to if they had been a victim of a crime. Some people preferred none of the options for disclosure, indicating they trusted the journalist to remain objective. Others preferred all eight types of disclosures, indicating a severe distrust in journalists to report objectively. The mean preference was just over two disclosures and the least popular was the disclosure of sexual orientation if the journalist reports on same-sex marriage (24%). The most preferred disclosure was partisan affiliation if the journalist reports on politics (37%). Figure 3.4 graphs the total number of disclosure preferred by respondents and their predicted probability of voting for Trump. There it appears that those selecting all eight disclosures were predicted to vote for Trump 49% of the time, whereas those selecting zero disclosures were only predicted to vote for Trump 32% of the time. The difference between these two extremes was statistically significant. Those who selected two disclosures,

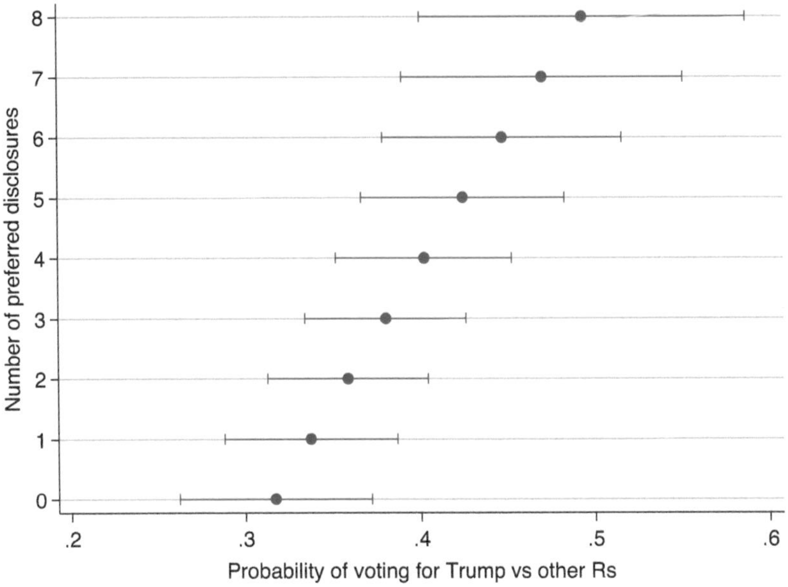

FIGURE 3.4 Voting for Trump and Journalist Disclosures

which was the mean response, were predicted to vote for Trump 35% of the time. Those who preferred more disclosures and therefore had less trust in journalistic objectivity were much more likely to vote for Trump than those who preferred few or no disclosures.

A fourth topic regarded trust in government. Figure 3.5 shows the predicted probability of voting for Trump across levels of trust in the federal government. Again, these results included controls for age, education, race, and ideology and compared voting for Trump versus other Republican primary candidates. Respondents who believed you can never trust the federal government to do what is right were estimated to vote for Trump 45% of the time, whereas those who believed you can trust the federal government all of the time were estimated to vote for Trump only 18% of the time. This variation between the extreme responses was significantly different, but so was the difference between those who said you can trust the government "most of the time" (24%) and "hardly ever" (38%). These results provide strong evidence that Trump supporters were much more distrustful of the federal government than those who voted for other Republican candidates.

Frustration with the media and the government also appeared in responses to an open-ended prompt asking participants to "offer all of their thoughts and feelings about voting." After reading the responses closely, Trump supporters voiced more frustration and a greater need for change than did those

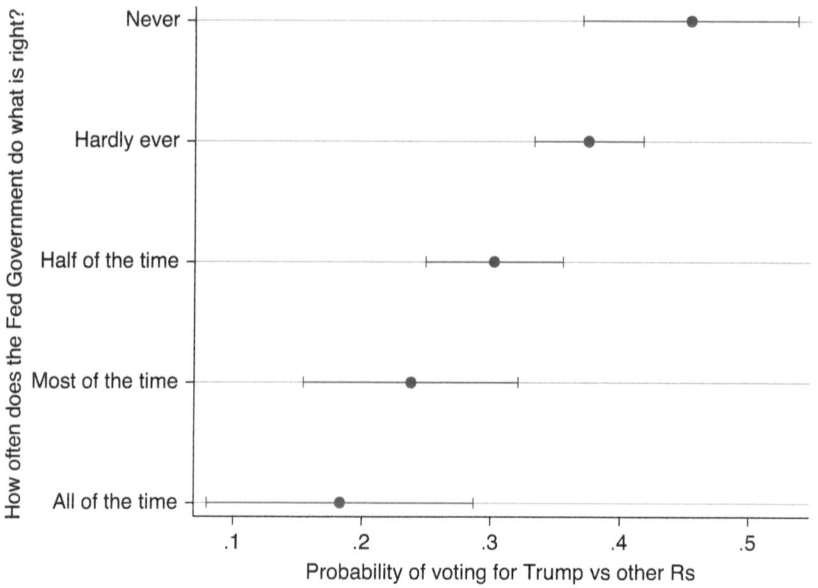

FIGURE 3.5 Trust in Federal Government and Voting for Trump

who voted for other Republicans. To begin, several Trump supporters pointed to problems with the status quo, stating "it is all rigged," "we need a change. Establishment runs the show," and "I love voting but lately hearing some of the Republican talk makes me feel my vote don't count." Other Trump supporters put an even sharper point on this sentiment, offering: "Our Founding Fathers are rolling over in their graves because of the way our government" is run and "truly I believe that this country IS great but our government sucks . . . Sorry YOU ASKED." One of the longer responses connected a set of concerns from the 2016 campaign together, lamenting,

> I think if you are not a legal citizen you should not be able to vote, I also believe that if you have been on any government program for longer than a year you should not be able to vote. I think it should be up to the men and women who go out every day and fight hard to earn a living who have the right to say which way our country is going. I also think if you are a reporter or a celebrity you need to keep your opinion to yourself. Too many people look at a celebrity like they are a god or something and follow blindly on how their idol thinks.

In these open-ended responses, then, the early Trump supporters imparted both a connection to the idea of the U.S. and a deep dissatisfaction with how it is being reported on and run.

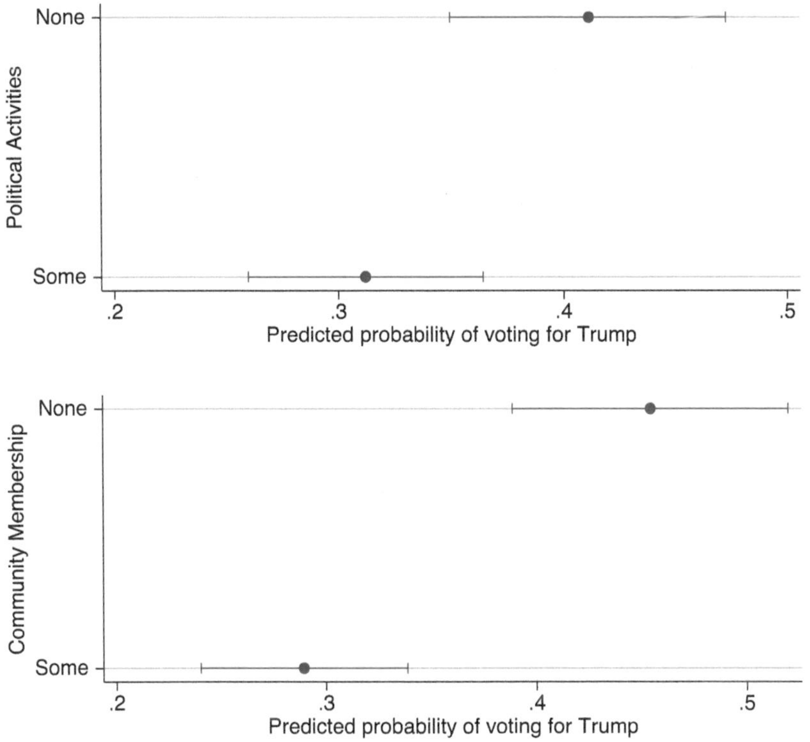

FIGURE 3.6 Political Activities/Community Group Membership and Voting for Trump

A final matter addressed regard for political participation and engagement. In addition to be distrusting of both the media and government, Trump supporters were also less likely than other Republican voters to participate in politics and to be involved in their communities. The Texas Media & Society Survey asked about various political activities that respondents had participated in as well as community groups they had been a member of over the past year. Figure 3.6 presents the results from both batteries of questions and estimates the likelihood of voting for Trump based on whether a person had participated in any political activities or been a member of any groups. In both cases, those in the "none" category were much more likely to support Trump than vote for other Republican primary candidates. The probability of voting for Trump of those who had some type of political participation was 31% versus 41% for those who had no political activities in the past year. Those with some type of community group membership had an estimated 29% chance of voting for Trump whereas those with no memberships had a 45% probability of voting for Trump. These results provide evidence that Trump supporters were significantly less involved in both politics and their communities.

Discussion

The findings showed both similarities and differences between Trump supporters and traditional Republican voters. To begin, both groups followed the news at similar rates and sought content from the same outlets. All 550 respondents, then, were likely to have encountered voluminous coverage of Trump, much of it positive (Confessore & Yourish, 2016). Stories, particularly in 2015, portrayed him as exceeding expectations, leading the horse race, and connecting with audiences (Patterson, 2016a). Content analyses found that individuals at Trump rallies were more commonly quoted in the news extolling him than were advocates for other candidates (Patterson, 2016a; 2016b). Further, Trump's own words were more regularly recirculated than those of his opponents (Patterson, 2016a; 2016b). So unprecedented and ever-present was his reportage that political scholar Patterson observed, "Trump is arguably the first bona-fide media-created presidential nominee. Although he subsequently tapped a political nerve, journalists fueled his launch" (Patterson, 2016a, p. 5; see also Patterson, 2016b; 2016c; 2016d).

And yet, Trump struck this nerve with specific kinds of people. The data suggest that his supporters were significantly less likely than other Republicans to trust journalists (either their objectivity or backgrounds), to trust in the federal government, or to be involved in politics or their communities. In a sense, Trump did particularly well with *political isolates*—individuals who were less prone to have faith in governing and media institutions or to interact with others in political or community groups. These data shed insight to the questions advanced by Matthews at the start of this chapter. The Trump supporters in our analysis *would indeed be less likely* to be exposed to other individuals who might be offended by Trump's bombastic behavior *and would also be less likely* to be in situations where they would have to communicate their support of him to others. In many ways, these Trump supporters more closely resemble the angry and frustrated individuals studied by Mann and Ornstein (2012) than the loyal Republican base united by a shared sense of trust in their party discussed by Freeman (1986).

As detailed earlier, a hallmark of Trump's candidacy was attacking foils—be it President Obama, the government, his political opponents, the media, news outlets, or individual journalists. Many in the press recirculated these charges, guided by an "insider" sense that audiences would find him unpalatable, a bully, and not fit for the presidency (Folkenflik, 2016; Pope, 2016). The data suggest that Republican voters who had been active in politics and community groups did just that. In contrast, those who were less connected to groups or participation embraced him. Perhaps, for this latter group, months of coverage underscoring how a famous businessman and political outsider was exceeding expectations and attacking American institutions and actors served as a winning and welcome message.

A key theme of the first section of this edited volume addresses media use, political participation, and engagement. The data, here, show that Trump supporters and other Republican voters received the same story about campaign 2016 from the press. The separation between these groups is not that the former was more *tuned out* than the latter; rather they were truly *turned off* by government and the journalists who write about it.

References

Aldrich, J. (1995). *Why parties? The origin and transformation of political parties in America.* Chicago, IL: University of Chicago Press.

Arrietta-Kenna, R. (2016, December 28). The worst political predictions of 2016. *Politico.* Retrieved from www.politico.com/magazine/story/2016/12/the-worst-political-predictions-of-2016-214555

Ayers, B. D. (1992, October 28). The 1992 campaign: Campaign trail; Bush eases hammering of the press. *New York Times.* Retrieved from www.nytimes.com/1992/10/28/us/the-1992-campaign-campaign-trail-bush-eases-hammering-of-the-press.html

Baumer, D. C., & Gold, H. J. (1995). Party images and the American electorate. *American Politics Research, 23*(1), 33–61.

Cappella, J. N., & Jamieson, K. H. (1997). *Spiral of cynicism: The press and the public good.* New York, NY: Oxford University Press.

Confessore, N., & Yourish, K. (2016, March 17). Measuring Trump's big advantage in free media. *New York Times*, p. A3.

Cramer, K. (2016). *The politics of resentment: Rural consciousness in Wisconsin and the rise of Scott Walker.* Chicago, IL: University of Chicago Press.

Doherty, C., Kiley, J., Tyson, A., & Jameson, B. (2015, November). Beyond distrust: How Americans view their government. *Pew Research Center.* Retrieved from www.people-press.org/2015/11/23/beyond-distrust-how-americans-view-their-government/

Folkenflik, D. (2016, June 1). Why Trump called a press conference to bash the press. *NPR.* Retrieved from www.npr.org/2016/06/01/480247326/trump-calls-a-press-conference-to-bash-the-press

Fossett, K. (2016, November 6). 16 worst predictions of 2016. *Politico.* Retrieved from www.politico.com/story/2016/11/2016-election-worst-predictions-230806

Freeman, Jo. (1986). The political culture of the democratic and republican parties. *Political Science Quarterly, 101*(3), 327–356.

Grossman, M., & Hopkins, D. A. (2015). Ideological republicans and group interest Democrats: The asymmetry of American party politics. *Perspectives on Politics, 13*(1), 119–139.

Grossman, M., & Hopkins, D. A. (2016). *Asymmetric politics: Ideological republicans and group interest democrats.* New York, NY: Oxford University Press.

Hemmer, N. (2016a). *Messengers of the right: Conservative media and the transformation of American politics.* Philadelphia, PA: University of Pennsylvania Press.

Hemmer, N. (2016b, August 30). How conservative media learned to play politics. *Politico.* Retrieved from www.politico.com/magazine/story/2016/08/conservative-media-history-steve-bannon-clarence-manion-214199

Hochschild, A. (2016). *Strangers in their own land: Anger and mourning on the American right.* New York, NY: The New Press.

Hook, J. (2016, November 6). Hillary Clinton leads Donald Trump by 4 points in latest poll. *Wall Street Journal*. Retrieved from www.wsj.com/articles/hillary-clinton-leads-donald-trump-by-4-points-in-latest-poll-1478440818

Jarvis, S. E. (2005). *The talk of the party: Political labels, symbolic capital & American life*. Lanham, MD: Rowman & Littlefield.

Katz, J. (2016, November 8). The upshot: Who will be president? *New York Times*. Retrieved from www.nytimes.com/interactive/2016/upshot/presidential-polls-forecast.html

Ladd, J. M. (2012). *Why Americans hate the media and how it matters*. Princeton, NJ: Princeton University Press.

Lakoff, G. (1996). *Moral politics: What conservatives know that liberals don't*. Chicago, IL: University of Chicago Press.

Lee, J. C., & Quealy, K. (2017, January 20). The 305 people, places and things Donald Trump has insulted on Twitter: A complete list. *New York Times*. Retrieved from www.nytimes.com/interactive/2016/01/28/upshot/donald-trump-twitter-insults.html

Lichter, S. R., & Noyes, R. E. (1996). *Good intentions make bad news: Why Americans hate campaign journalism* (2nd ed.). Lanham, MD: Rowman & Littlefield Press.

Mann, T. E., & Ornstein, N. J. (2012). *It's even worse than it looks: How the American constitutional system collided with the new politics of extremism*. New York, NY: Basic Books.

Matthews, C. (2016, November 9). HARDBALL with Chris Matthews. *MSNBC*. Retrieved from www.msnbc.com/transcripts/hardball/2016-11-09

Mitchell, A., Gottfried, J., Barthel, M., & Shearer, E. (2016, July 7). The modern news consumer. *Pew Research Center for Journalism & Media*. Retrieved from www.journalism.org/2016/07/07/party-id-and-news/

Mitchell, A., Gottfried, J., Kiley, J., & Matsa, K. E. (2014, October 21). Political polarization & media habits. *Pew Research Center for Journalism & Media*. Retrieved from www.journalism.org/2014/10/21/political-polarization-media-habits/

Parker, A., & Chozick, A. (2015, October 7). Donald Trump's act seems to be wearing out its welcome. *New York Times*. Retrieved from www.nytimes.com/2015/10/08/us/politics/donald-trumps-bombast-seems-to-be-wearing-out-its-welcome.html

Patterson, T. (2016a, June). *Pre-primary news coverage of the 2016 presidential race: Trump's rise, Sanders' emergence, Clinton's struggle*. Harvard Kennedy School Shorenstein Center on Media, Politics and Public Policy (in Conjunction with Media Tenor). Cambridge, MA: Harvard University.

Patterson, T. (2016b, July). *News coverage of the 2016 presidential primaries: Horse race reporting has consequences*. Harvard Kennedy School Shorenstein Center on Media, Politics and Public Policy (in Conjunction with Media Tenor). Cambridge, MA: Harvard University.

Patterson, T. (2016c, September). *News coverage of the 2016 national conventions: Negative news, lacking context*. Harvard Kennedy School Shorenstein Center on Media, Politics and Public Policy (in Conjunction with Media Tenor). Cambridge, MA: Harvard University.

Patterson, T. (2016d, December). *News coverage of the 2016 general election: How the press failed voters*. Harvard Kennedy School Shorenstein Center on Media, Politics and Public Policy (in Conjunction with Media Tenor). Cambridge, MA: Harvard University.

Pope, K. (2016, November 9). Here's to the return of the journalist as the malcontent. *Columbia Journalism Review*. Retrieved from www.cjr.org/criticism/journalist_election_trump_failure.php

Rampell, C. (2016, October 28). If the GOP collapses, democracy loses. *Washington Post*, p. A17.

Remnick, D. (2006, July 10). Nattering nabobs. *New Yorker*. Retrieved from www.newyorker.com/magazine/2006/07/10/nattering-nabobs

Romney, M. (2012, October 18). Remarks to the Al Smith Dinner. New York, NY. Retrieved from www.realclearpolitics.com/articles/2012/10/18/mitt_romneys_speech_at_the_al_smith_dinner_115842.html

Seelye, K. (1996, October 26). Dole is imploring voters to 'rise up' against the press. *New York Times*. Retrieved from www.nytimes.com/1996/10/26/us/dole-is-imploring-voters-to-rise-up-against-the-press.html

Skocpol, T., & Williamson, V. (2016). *The tea party and the remaking of republican conservatism*. New York, NY: Oxford.

Swift, A. (2016, September 14). Americans' trust in mass media sinks to new low. *Gallup.com*. Retrieved from www.gallup.com/poll/195542/americans-trust-mass-media-sinks-new-low.aspx

Vance, J. D. (2016). *Hillbilly elegy: A memoir of a family and culture in crisis*. New York, NY: Harper.

Wang, S. (2016, November 18). Why I had to eat a bug on *CNN*. *New York Times*. Retrieved from www.nytimes.com/2016/11/19/opinion/why-i-had-to-eat-a-bug-on-cnn.html

4

ONLINE COMMUNICATION REGARDING OHIO'S 2016 PRESIDENTIAL PRIMARY

Jeffrey H. Kuznekoff, Leland G. Spencer, and Robert N. Burt

Writing in 2008, Trent and Friedenberg observed that "as recently as 2002, only 55 percent of all candidates for the United States Senate utilized a website" (p. 399). Only a few years later, of course, the thought that anyone might run for elected office on the national, state, or even most local levels without at least a website registers as untenable. Indeed, candidates in the present era not only use websites to communicate their messages, but also use a variety of social media platforms (e.g., Facebook, Instagram, Twitter).

At least since the presidential election of 2008, communication scholars have carefully observed the rapidly increasing importance of social media in electoral politics. Gronbeck averred that "the evolution of oral to literate to electronic political cultures has brought with it both shifting modes of doing politics and changing relationships between Leaders and the Led" (2009, p. 240). Going even further, Hendricks (2014) suggested that social media may become *the* factor that determines electoral outcomes. As such, scholars have analyzed politicians' use of social media for its role in fundraising, voter mobilization, and information dissemination, among other functions (Glassman, Strauss, & Shogan, 2011; Parmelee & Bichard, 2012). Some studies have gone beyond the functional and candidate-based approaches to consider everyday citizens' and voters' participatory use of social media to generate their own content and arguments about issues and candidates on sites such as YouTube and Twitter (Hanson, Haridakis, Cunningham, Sharma, & Ponder, 2010; Murthy, 2015).

In our view, these studies that focus on voter-generated content and its ways of moving—in both the sense of "going viral" but also persuading by moving the passions—best capture the potential and importance of social media for electoral politics. Voters have become more politically involved in recent elections through various social media sites; in particular, Twitter invites closer scholarly scrutiny for its uniquely viral possibilities, the interconnectivity and uncertainty invited by the ubiquity of hashtagging in the platform, and the site's structural insistence on brevity (Murthy, 2015).

Although less than a decade old, Twitter has made a considerable impact on electoral politics, as some studies already attest (Gronbeck, 2009; Hendricks, 2014). Beyond a focus on candidates' use and deployment of Twitter, we examine social media content about each candidate. More specifically, we use NUVI, a social media analysis platform, to collect and analyze social media content—not just *of* and *from* candidates, but *about* candidates and the election itself. Taking the 2016 presidential primary in the state of Ohio as a case study, we focus on the geography, valence, timing, and concentration of social media content and, through this approach, deepen what political communication scholars can know about elections, not just from an instrumental perspective, but also a constitutive one.

Our argument unfolds in a series of five related movements. First, we elucidate previous research about the use and influence of social media in electoral politics. Next, we examine the uses and gratifications approach as it applies to election politics on social media, and we consider Twitter's particular importance, including dominant modes for making sense of Twitter in communication scholarship. We then explain NUVI and its usefulness for this chapter's methodological approach. Following that, our case study of the Ohio 2016 primary election illustrates how the public conversation surrounding the primary developed online. We conclude with reflections about the future of social media in political communication and the potential for social media analysis as an analytical tool for communication scholars and practitioners.

Social Media and Electoral Politics

Many studies of social media in electoral politics take what we understand as a modified "uses and gratifications" style approach, focusing on how candidates use various forms of social media to promote their brands, raise money, and organize voters (Glassman et al., 2011; Gronbeck, 2009; Parmelee & Bichard, 2012). Hendricks (2014), for example, compared Obama's and Romney's number of Facebook likes and Twitter followers throughout the final months of the 2012 campaign, charting key dates when the campaigns gained followers. Glassman et al. (2011) found that 205 representatives and senators had Twitter accounts and shared approximately 116 tweets per day.

The key distinguishing feature of social media, interactivity, means that candidates' web presence does more than simply digitize campaign leaflets. Candidates, we suggest, take a secondary role to the citizens and voters who generate content. Bor (2014) argued that social networks certainly allow candidates to share their identities and politics with their audiences, but by their very nature, social media platforms represent a loss of control for candidates as well (see also, van Dijck, 2013). According to the Pew Internet and American Life Project, 66% of U.S.

adults who use social media (39% of all U.S. adults) have engaged in political-oriented activities on social-networking sites, and 20% have used social media to follow elected officials and candidates (Rainie, Smith, Schlozman, Brady, & Verba, 2012). Such political activities include: promoting material on political/social issues, encouraging others to vote, and posting links to political stories, to list a few. This leaves candidates with limited control of what their constituents and voting population share among their friends, unless the social media users are posting on the candidate's own page. After all, as Barnett (2015) observed, social media allow the formation of publics *and* counterpublics.

Bor (2014) found that campaigns frequently managed voters' interactions with their social media pages, including deleting negative comments, even though the campaigns appreciated the ability to receive real-time feedback from their constituents throughout the campaign. Sometimes, of course, managing users' social media behavior proves impossible, as Senator George Allen found out when he derided one of his opponent's supporters with a racial epithet in 2006. Someone filmed the encounter, posted it on YouTube with viral results, and ended Allen's chances for election—not to mention his future political aspirations (Gronbeck, 2009). In 2012, Mitt Romney ran into the same issue when news clips from his campaign turned into a humorous parody titled, "Will the real Mitt Romney please stand up" (Penney, 2016). One clip included statements such as, "I'm not concerned about the very poor," which painted an unfavorable portrait of the candidate.

Twitter in particular has been a highly used source for the world of politics. From 2009–2011, the hashtag #TCOT (top conservatives on Twitter), as well as many other hashtags relating to the Tea Party movement, grew in popularity among users and helped gain support for the movement itself. The hashtag phenomenon within Twitter can help create a topic for people to talk about, and a way for users to see what others in the social media sphere have to say. Just as #TCOT trended for most of the year, #BigBird gained popularity in just a matter of minutes when Mitt Romney made a comment during the debate about Big Bird. In just five minutes after the comment, #BigBird became the top trending hashtag on Twitter, getting 17,000 tweets per minute (Wallsten, 2015). The near instantaneous ability for a topic or hashtag to go viral, which may help campaign messages spread, could be why politicians view Twitter as a good way to connect with their constituents, with many members of Congress having accounts on the site, especially if their constituents are more urban, young, and minorities (Murthy, 2015).

Uses and Gratifications

Although originally focused on mass media effects, the uses and gratifications approach has been helpful in explaining how people intentionally seek particular media and the reasons behind this behavior (Katz, 1959). As Rubin noted,

"Uses and gratifications emphasizes individual choice. People choose among available communication or functional alternatives. They make their choices based on their wants, interests, and expectations" (2009, p. 149). In other words, people make intentional choices about the media they seek and the media people do use can function to gratify a particular need. Although situated in traditional mass media (i.e., television), this approach has been extended to examine individuals' use of social media. For example, Quinn (2016) used uses and gratifications to examine users' privacy concerns and privacy behaviors when on social media.

Furthermore, we know that both campaigns and the public use social media to talk about political issues. As noted earlier, nearly 40% of all U.S. adults have engaged in political activities via social media (Rainie et al., 2012), and this number is only going to grow over time. This increasingly important communication channel has received much scholarly attention. When discussing social media use during the 2008 presidential campaign, Hanson et al. (2010) noted "social media provided an opportunity for ordinary citizens to create their own political content, distribute it online, and comment on the content created by others" (p. 585). One of the key aspects of social media is the interactive element, the ability to create and comment on content made by others. Social media is an important communication channel for millions of people and, through social media, people will seek information and interaction with others to gratify their needs. We see this behavior occurring daily and, particularly in the 2016 presidential election, the use of social media has become a staple communication channel for candidates and voters. In the case of the present chapter, we are primarily interested in how the public engages in conversation regarding the political process through social media. We know, from the uses and gratifications approach, that individuals will likely use social media to engage in discussion of politics online; however, focusing on the nature of that online conversation may shed further light on how the public engages in conversation regarding the political process. Thus, we understand uses and gratifications as a theoretical lens through which we can understand why people would use social media to discuss politics; moving beyond a uses and gratifications approach, our chapter focuses not on why people are using social media, but *how* they are using social media, particularly Twitter, to converse with others regarding American politics.

Although much of the research on Twitter and politics has focused on the U.S., scholars from around the world have examined Twitter's influence in a number of contexts, including electoral politics in Germany, Kenya, and Kuwait (Bing, 2015; Miller & Ko, 2015; Tumasjan, Sprenger, Sandner, & Welpe, 2010). On the whole, these studies found that Twitter has created an alternative political world, causing participants who live under many different forms of government to get involved with campaigns and elections. Many researchers have also found the impact Twitter has on political communication in the realm of mainstream media. These studies suggested that news stations such as Fox News, CNN, and

MSNBC use Twitter as a tool for their coverage of political events and discussions (Chung, Tsay-Vogel, & Kim, 2015; Wallsten, 2015), particularly when news stations routinely air citizen tweets.

Whereas we have so far reviewed research focused on candidates' use of Twitter, some scholars focus on the populist function and form of social media. Such research best approximates our approach to understanding the role of social media in political communication because it recognizes the uniqueness of social media as a *form* (Murthy, 2015; van Dijck, 2013). During the 2012 primary, Ron Paul was one of the top positively mentioned candidates on Twitter during many debates, but he was hardly a front-runner in many polls. This may be due to the fact that he used Twitter the most frequently out of any other candidate during the primaries, creating a "buzz" around himself which raised his sentiment levels in the Twitter sphere (Murthy, 2015). Candidates' goals on Twitter include generating energy around their campaign brand and likely to gratify the need of spreading the candidates' message. The more mentions a candidate gets, the more buzz surrounds their entire campaign, but inspiring buzz depends mostly on the Twitter population, the everyday citizen, interacting with the political world through the social media world. For example, a candidate may post a tweet; however, the ability for that message to reach a truly wider audience rests with other Twitter users. Thus, examining the online conversation regarding candidates may help the scholarly community understand the vital role that social media now plays in the political process.

Ohio Presidential Primary

With a population of nearly 12 million, the seventh highest state population in the country, and 16 total seats in the U.S. House of Representatives, Ohio is continually identified as a battleground state in national elections and a swing state in the general presidential election every four years. As Coffey, Green, Cohen, and Brooks (2011) noted, Ohio is "a prize worth fighting for in national elections. Another reason is that Ohio is a good *bellwether* state, predicting the winning candidates and parties more often than other large states" (p. 3). Although this status as a battleground state or as a prize worth winning has changed over the country's history, we certainly do see Ohio continue to take a prominent role in national elections. As noted by Coffey et al., "by the twenty-first century, Ohio had become a key swing state in national campaigns, a fulcrum on which control of the federal government rested for both major political parties" (2011, p. 3). This status as a swing state points towards the importance of examining presidential primary results in the state, as results in Ohio may have the potential to influence future primaries.

Outside of the primary season, Ohio also plays a prominent role in the general election. Warren (2016) interviewed John Green, Director of the Ray C. Bliss Institute of Applied Politics, and asked why Ohio was an important state for presidential politics. In general, Ohio has "been a good microcosm of the country as a whole. No state is a perfect mirror but Ohio comes very close . . . When the U.S. is divided politically, that division tends to run right through Ohio" (Warren, 2016, para. 10). In the case of the present chapter, examining social media content regarding the 2016 presidential primary in Ohio should allow us to better understand the role of social media in facilitating public discussion of the political process. Furthermore, this analysis may be of use when understanding primaries in other states and, perhaps, the general election.

Research Questions

As previously stated, most research that has been conducted on social media and political communication focuses on candidates, when social media, especially Twitter, as a form relies on citizen-generated content as well as citizen-inspired dissemination of elites' content. Thus far, research has primarily examined how candidates use social media to engage the public; however, this perspective limits our view of social media and political communication. This chapter extends past research by shifting the focus from candidate tweets to the broader conversation occurring around a political event on social media. In addition, this chapter focuses on the battleground state of Ohio, an important state to win in both the Republican and Democratic primaries. Using the social media analysis platform NUVI, we collected and examined social media content regarding the 2016 Ohio presidential primary, and the results of that primary, against the backdrop of these research questions:

RQ1: How did people in Ohio use social media to discuss the 2016 Ohio presidential primary?
RQ2: What top words, phrases, and hashtags emerged about the candidates?
RQ3a: Does the valence of social media content vary by political party?
RQ3b: Does the valence of social media content vary by candidate?

Method

We used the social media analysis platform NUVI to collect social media content regarding the 2016 Ohio presidential primary. As a social media analytic platform, NUVI allows users to monitor, in near real time, online and social media content about a particular topic, brand, organization, or person. NUVI conducts real-time analyses, allowing users to make sense of (potentially) millions of tweets, posts, or other online content quickly. This collection and analysis is accomplished through the creation of "monitors," essentially search parameters. Each monitor is made up of various search terms and criteria that NUVI uses to select content for inclusion in later analysis. When the monitor finds a piece of social media content that fits the search parameters, which NUVI calls a mention, that content is captured in the monitor and included in visualizations or analyses within NUVI. The benefit of this analytic platform is the ability to *collect* tens of thousands of mentions in near real time and generate *analyses* of that content.

This method of data collection and analysis differs from past approaches, which relied on using standalone applications that typically performed one or two specific functions. For example, Parmelee and Bichard (2012) noted that various companies created thousands of different applications for use with Twitter. However, those applications typically served only one or two minor functions, such as aggregating Twitter content. NUVI and other social media analysis platforms move beyond this approach by integrating multiple functions into a single platform. For example, NUVI analyzes mentions captured by monitors and identifies trending topics, hashtags, concepts, and keywords. In addition, NUVI identifies individuals who might influence the online conversation and performs a sentiment analysis, which uses natural language processing to determine the overall tone of each mention (i.e., negative, positive, or neutral). NUVI also measures the reach and spread of collected content. Reach is simply the total number of people who could have seen mentions collected, whereas spread refers to the total number of people who could have seen mentions collected due to that content being shared (i.e., retweeted, shared, favorited) (NUVI, n.d.).

Monitors

For the present chapter, we created separate NUVI monitors for each of the main presidential candidates from the Democratic and Republican parties running in the Ohio primary on March 15, 2016. Andrews, Lai, Parlapiano, and Yourish (2016) identified Hillary Clinton and Bernie Sanders as the main candidates for the Democratic nomination and the following candidates for the Republican nomination: Ted Cruz, John Kasich, Marco Rubio, and Donald Trump. The monitor for each candidate included keywords, phrases, hashtags (e.g., #imwithher, #feelthebern, "make America great again"), and the official social media accounts (Twitter, Facebook, and Instagram) for each respective candidate (see Appendix 4.1). We only included those accounts associated with each candidate's campaign and did not include accounts associated with each candidate's current position or office. For example, we did not include Cruz's Instagram account because @sentedcruz was directly tied to his position as senator and not his campaign for Republican nominee for president.

We also created a single monitor that focused on the general discussion of the Ohio primary, using hashtags and keywords that focused solely on the words "Ohio," "primary," and "2016." We set up each monitor to collect only social media content geotagged within the state of Ohio. This restriction allowed us to focus on how Ohioans, or at least those currently in Ohio, discussed the primary on social media. The collection period spanned from 12:00am Monday, March 14, 2016, to 12:00am Thursday, March 17, 2016, providing us with 72 hours of social media content. In total, we collected 57,041 mentions for the candidate monitors during this time period, which accounted for the day before the Ohio primary, the day of the primary, and the day after. Over 99% of those mentions were from Twitter; the remaining <1% were from Facebook and Instagram.

Results

Our first research question broadly examined how people in Ohio used social media to discuss the 2016 Ohio presidential primary. However, it is also important to consider this content alongside the results of the primary. Andrews, Bloch, Bowers, and Giratikanon (2016) reported that Clinton won the Democratic primary with 56.5% of the vote compared to Sanders's 42.7%. Kasich, the governor of Ohio, won the Republican primary with 46.8%, whereas Trump received 35.6%, Cruz had 13.1%, and Rubio had 2.9% (see Table 4.1 for a summary). The six candidate monitors collected a combined total of 57,041 mentions during the 72-hour time period. Trump (22,437) had the most mentions, followed by Sanders (10,688), Clinton (8,027), Kasich (7,823), Cruz (5,420), and Rubio (2,646). In terms of reach, the number of people who could have viewed mentions about the candidate, Trump potentially reached 91,371,182 people, followed by Clinton (38,854,978), Sanders (30,833,855), Cruz (17,521,914), Kasich (13,178,165), and Rubio (11,026,569). For spread, we found that Trump (13,817,153) had the greatest spread, followed by Kasich (7,771,996), Sanders (5,202,078), Clinton (4,661,027), Rubio (2,409,338), and Cruz (2,148,102).

Over the course of the data collection period, nearly half (48.96%) of all mentions occurred on Tuesday, March 15, whereas nearly 29.5% were on Monday, March 14, and the remaining 21.5% were on Wednesday, March 16. On the evening of the primary, between the hours of 8 and 10pm EST, Clinton, Kasich, Rubio, and Trump all had large spikes in the number of mentions they

TABLE 4.1 Summary of Twitter Content by Candidate and Party

	Mentions			*Sentiment*			*Results*★	
	Total	*Reach*	*Spread*	*Positive*	*Negative*	*Neutral*	*Votes*	*% of Vote*
Democrat								
Clinton	8,027	38,854,978	4,661,027	39%	12%	51%	679,266	57%
Sanders	10,688	30,833,855	5,202,078	31%	12%	58%	513,549	43%
Republican								
Cruz	5,420	17,521,914	2,148,102	36%	15%	50%	267,592	13%
Kasich	7,823	13,178,165	7,711,996	44%	14%	43%	956,762	47%
Rubio	2,646	11,026,569	2,409,338	28%	23%	50%	59,418	3%
Trump	22,437	91,371,182	13,817,153	35%	19%	48%	727,585	36%

★ Primary results retrieved from Andrews, Block, Bowers, & Giratikanon. (2016)

received; however, both Cruz and Sanders received only mild increases in mentions or no significant bump in mentions. In particular, Kasich, who won the Republican nomination, had until this point in time been eclipsed by Trump and was on par with Cruz. However, Kasich received a massive jump in mentions moving from 140 mentions during 7–8pm, to 1,007 from 8–9pm, and 1,354 from 9–10pm. This spike in mentions corresponds to the announcement of the projection that Kasich would win Ohio. Rubio experienced a similar spike in traffic; however, it is worth noting that until Tuesday evening, Rubio received the fewest mentions out of all the candidates. When Rubio announced that he was dropping out of the race, primarily due to his loss in his home state of Florida on the same night, his mentions spiked from 68 during 7–8pm to 1,049 the following hour. Despite losing Ohio to Kasich, Trump also experienced a spike in mentions, moving from 402 between 7–8pm to 1,061 during 8–9pm and 1,025 from 9–10pm. The spike in mentions of Trump likely relates to his loss in the Ohio primary and the bitter battle between him and other Republican candidates.

When examining sharing of social media content (i.e., retweets), we found that the top accounts that "reshared" content within each monitor appear to be from individuals and not from news organizations. However, we also examined influence, defined this way: "NUVI analyzes influence based on the profile's Klout score. NUVI also augments this score based on how people react to their content in this the selected topic" (NUVI, n.d., p. 19). With regard to influence, we found that official news organization Twitter accounts were among the top influencers for each monitor. For example, the account @DispatchAlerts appears as one of the top influencers on several of the monitors; and that account is operated by *The Columbus Dispatch*, a newspaper focusing on news in Columbus, Ohio's capital city. That being said, individuals also appeared as top influencers for each monitor. Candidates had as many as seven out of the top ten influencers appear to be individuals rather than news organizations.

When we examined the top accounts for reach and spread, we found that the official candidate accounts were each the top for their respective monitors and, at times, in the top 5 accounts for each other's monitors. For example, @hillaryclinton was the top account for reach and spread on Clinton's monitor and @JohnKasich was the number two account on that same monitor. A mix of news organizations, such as @fox8news (Cleveland), @FOX19 (Cincinnati), as well as individual accounts also appeared as the top accounts for reach and spread. Based on our examination of this content, it appears that official Twitter accounts of each respective campaign, news organizations, and individuals account for the most reach and spread, whereas the top influencers appear to be individuals.

The second research question focused on trending content, specifically the top words, phrases, and hashtags that emerged concerning the candidates. Table 4.2 contains the top five trending keywords and hashtags for each candidate. In

TABLE 4.2 Trending Keyword, Keyword Frequency, and Hashtags by Candidate

	Trending Keyword	*N*	*Topic Keyword Frequency*	*N*	*Trending Hashtags*	*N*
Democrat						
Clinton	Ohio	663	hillary clinton	4,609	#primaryday	483
	Vote	342	#imwithher	2,458	#sheswithus	395
	bernie sanders	341	#hillary2016	554	#ohioprimary	246
	Donald	319	#hillaryclinton	497	#supertuesday	221
	Somebody	311	hillary clinton for president	58	#hillyes	174
Sanders	Vote	1,098	#feelthebern	4,728	#ohioprimary	529
	Bernie	557	bernie sanders	3,808	#primaryday	518
	Ohio	409	#berniesanders	1,132	#ohio	305
	hillary clinton	327	#bernie2016	1,004	#gotvforbernie	289
	hillary	168	#bernie	541	#stillsanders	218
Republican						
Cruz	vote	315	ted cruz	2,443	#pjnet	542
	cruz	174	#cruzcrew	1,478	#nevertrump	276
	donald	150	#choosecruz	724	#tcot	253
	ohio	138	#tedcruz	488	#ohprimary	229
	america	80	#cruz2016	211	#flprimary	196
Kasich	john	3,322	john kasich	4,554	#ohioprimary	509
	ohio	1,391	#kasich	1,399	#ohio	441
	vote	335	#kasich4us	699	#trump	222
	donald	255	#johnkasich	392	#primaryday	218
	cnn projects john	232	#kasichforus	56	#trump2016	156
Rubio	florida	196	marco rubio	1,698	#primaryday	239
	campaign	150	#rubio	327	#kasich	105
	donald	119	#marcorubio	247	#trump	95
	presidential campaign	118	#rubio2016	60	#breaking	92
	president	100	#marcorubio2016	20	#cruz	89
Trump	donald	9,927	donald trump	12,680	#supertuesday	882
	vote	1,278	#trump2016	5,465	#ohioprimary	871
	ohio	1,204	#makeamericagreatagain	3,161	#votetrump	779
	america	1,026	#trumptrain	1,698	#ohio	764
	president	925	#donaldtrump	650	#trump	630

addition, the table also includes the top five keywords used in that candidate's respective monitor. For example, "#feelthebern" was used in 4,728 mentions about Bernie Sanders. For trending keywords, "donald" appears as a trending word for Clinton, Cruz, Kasich, and Rubio. Within the Republican candidates, no other individual candidate emerged as a top 5 trending keyword for the other candidates. However, for both Democratic candidates, the other person appeared as a trending keyword. For Clinton, "bernie sanders" was a trending keyword and both "hillary clinton" and "hillary" were trending keywords for Sanders. Thus, it would appear that mentions captured in respective candidates' monitors do indeed include references to their opponents, but in general this was isolated within the respective parties.

Lastly, we posed a two-part research question that examined valence of social media content by political party (RQ3a) and by candidate (RQ3b). The NUVI monitors provided both a percentage and the raw number of mentions that qualified as positive, negative, or neutral. Positive mentions include words that NUVI interprets as having a positive connotation, whereas negative mentions have language that NUVI interprets as being negative. For example, the word "unqualified" was used in some of the mentions in reference to a particular candidate and those mentions were labeled as being negative. Neutral mentions are content that cannot be placed in either the positive or negative category.

We conducted a chi-square to determine if there was a difference in sentiment between the two parties and that test was statistically significant (X^2 (2, N = 57,041] = 422.131, $p < .001$, Cramer's V = 0.086). Between the two Democratic candidates, 54% of mentions were neutral, 34% were positive, and 12% were negative. For the Republican candidates, 47% of mentions were neutral, 36% were positive, and 17% were negative. The Republican candidates had a higher percentage of positive mentions and a higher percentage of negative mentions than the Democratic candidates. Within the Democratic party we did find a statistically significant difference between Clinton and Sanders (X^2 (2, N = 18,715) = 123.36, $p < .001$, Cramer's V = 0.0812). Clinton had a greater frequency of positive mentions (39%) than Sanders did (31%), Sanders had more neutral mentions (58%) than Clinton did (51%), and 12% of mentions for both candidates were negative. We also found a statistically significant difference between the four candidates in the Republican party (X^2 (6, N = 38,326) = 363.68, $p < .001$, Cramer's V = 0.0689). Kasich had the largest percentage of positive mentions (44%), followed by Cruz (36%), Trump (35%), and Rubio (28%). In terms of negative mentions, Rubio had the greatest percentage of negative mentions (23%), followed by Trump (19%), Cruz (15%), and Kasich (14%) (see Table 4.3). Within both parties, the candidate who received the highest percentage of positive mentions also won that party's Ohio primary.

TABLE 4.3 Sentiment by Party and Candidate

	Positive		*Negative*		*Neutral*		*Total*
	N	%	N	%	N	%	
Democrat	6,319	34%	2,200	12%	10,196	54%	18,715
Republican	13,719	36%	6,667	17%	17,940	47%	38,326
Total	20,038		8,867		28,136		57,041
Clinton	3,056	39%	937	12%	4,034	51%	8,027
Sanders	3,263	31%	1,263	12%	6,162	58%	10,688
Total	6,319		2,200		10,196		18,715
Cruz	1,924	36%	789	15%	2,707	50%	5,420
Kasich	3,382	44%	1,088	14%	3,353	43%	7,823
Rubio	738	28%	586	23%	1,322	50%	2,646
Trump	7,675	35%	4,204	19%	10,558	48%	22,437
Total	13,719		6,667		17,940		38,326

Discussion

The goal of the present chapter was to examine social media content regarding the 2016 Ohio presidential primary. In particular, we focused on content generated from within the state of Ohio and examined how that content discussed the six major candidates in both political parties. We argue that social media, particularly during a major presidential primary, allows citizens to engage with others concerning candidates and this use of social media may gratify particular needs. Past research (Glassman et al., 2011; Hanson et al., 2010; Murthy, 2015; Parmelee & Bichard, 2012) has certainly explained the increasing role that social media and social-networking sites play in political campaigns in the U.S. However, the continuing evolution of social media, and the way the citizenry uses social media to discuss politics, warrants continued attention and scholarly study.

Perhaps the most significant finding from our research was that more social media content *does not* equate to winning the nomination, despite the adage that campaigns ought to generate buzz or the celebration of any publicity as time in the spotlight. In both the Democratic and Republican Ohio primaries, the candidates with the most mentions were not the winners of their respective races. Kasich had roughly 8,000 mentions compared to Trump's 22,000 mentions, yet Kasich (the governor of Ohio) won the primary by over 10% points or over 200,000 votes. Clinton had about 2,000 fewer mentions than Sanders, yet won the Democratic primary by roughly 14% points or over 150,000 votes. According to our results, the candidate with more positive sentiment, in each respective party, won the primary of that party. For Clinton, 39% of mentions were positive compared to 31% for Sanders. In the Republican race, Kasich had 44% positive mentions compared to Cruz 36%, Trump 35%, and Rubio 28%. Linked with this finding is our result concerning negative sentiment. Rubio had a higher percentage of negative mentions than even Trump, 23% to 19%, respectively. Kasich had the lowest percentage of negative mentions out of all the Republican candidates (14%). During the primary, when it became obvious that Rubio lost his home state of Florida and would place last in Ohio, he dropped out of the race. This translated into a large spike in mentions about Rubio; however, up to this point in time he had received relatively little social media traffic.

As noted above, more content or more tweets do not appear to signal an election win for the candidate. Indeed, the nature and valence of that conversation also come into play. For instance, in the general election Trump made heavy use of Twitter and much media attention focused on that usage (Diamond, 2016). Nearly daily, news programs reported on tweets Trump sent and also those of the Democratic candidate Hillary Clinton. However, negative online content may very well harm candidates' chances of winning their respective race. Data collected for our research indicates that Trump had a higher percentage of negative content than Kasich did, despite Trump receiving nearly three times as many mentions as Kasich. However, Trump lost the Ohio primary to Kasich by over 225,000 votes.

We also found that, within the respective political parties, at least one other candidate's name typically appeared as a trending keyword. For instance, both Sanders and Clinton appeared as trending words on each other's monitor, while Trump appeared as a trending word for the three other Republican candidates. This finding seems to indicate that social media content for each candidate can, and does, cross over to include other candidates. As noted earlier, when candidates extend their messages to social media, they lose some control over those messages (Bor, 2014; van Dijck, 2013). However, it also seems that candidates and citizens can use social media to accomplish traditional goals of political advertising or even to fulfill particular needs. For instance, Benoit's (2001) functional approach noted that campaigns use political advertising to acclaim, attack, or defend, and applying this approach to social media content could be a fruitful area for future research. We posit that campaigns rely on social media to perform those same functions; however, not just the candidates can acclaim, attack, or defend. Supporters and attackers can also engage in acclaiming, attacking, or defending. For example, supporters of Sanders used #feelthebern to demonstrate their support of Sanders. However, the same hashtag could be used to attack Clinton or even other candidates, or in the same tweet a citizen might acclaim one candidate while attacking her or his opponent. In the context of the uses and gratifications approach, social media may allow for both functions. First, candidates and the public can intentionally seek which social media sites they want to use for particular reasons. Second, posting, sharing, and commenting on content may gratify some need, at the very least a need for interaction or perhaps to feel as if one is part of the process by spreading the message of one's preferred candidate through retweeting.

Overall, the findings from this chapter provide a couple implications for future research. First, social media analysis platforms do represent a way of collecting a vast amount of online content fairly quickly. The use of these platforms should help communication scholars come to a stronger understanding of online communication in a variety of contexts. Second, scholars can use the content collected to examine existing approaches to communication research. For example, we previously noted Benoit's (2001) functional approach as something that likely does occur on social media; however, shifting the application of this approach from candidate messages to content generated by the public likely will help us understand how the general public communicates about the candidates, and this shift is made realistically possible by social media analysis platforms.

Limitations

Although the sentiment tool in NUVI offers great promise, as we explored in the results about valence, we also caution that the way sentiment is determined seems to focus on individual words, when phrases would offer a better sense of the sentiment intended. Although we could manually change how a mention was coded (i.e., from negative to positive), doing manual corrections of a large volume of tweets becomes impractical as the amount of content increases. For instance, Kaplan (2015) reported that by October 2015, the 2016 presidential election had generated more than 1 billion posts, likes, shares, and comments on Facebook. One person, spending 1 second viewing each piece of content, would take 31.7 years to look at all 1 billion pieces of content. Thus, in order to efficiently examine a large volume of content, scholars will need to rely on computers to aid in the analysis. We suspect NUVI's software, and the software of other social media analysis platforms, on this point will likely improve over time. However, the sentiment analysis is currently a blunt instrument. It helps to catch large spikes in negative or positive traffic, which it reports accurately.

Conclusion

This chapter sought to examine social media content about the 2016 Ohio presidential primary by collecting messages about each major candidate. Our primary finding was that the amount of social media buzz a campaign creates may not indicate that campaign's success, but the valence the buzz generated, at least in this case, served as a barometer for how a candidate performed. In both the Democratic and Republican primaries, the candidate with the highest positive sentiment ended up receiving the nomination, and neither of those candidates had the most mentions in their respective parties. Of course this chapter does not demonstrate a causal link between valence and election outcomes, but the point stands that astute analysts and observers must pay attention to not just how much social media content someone generates, but also what kind of buzz circulates, when, and how it changes throughout a dynamic campaign cycle.

Certainly more research should be done on the role of social media in the U.S. political process, and we invite scholars of political communication and social media to expand the focus beyond just how candidates use social media and instead include how the voting public uses social media. Our chapter represents an initial foray into this extension of past communication research, and we are hopeful that this new area of research will continue to grow.

References

Andrews, W., Bloch, M., Bowers, J., & Giratikanon, T. (2016, March 17). Ohio primary results. *The New York Times*. Retrieved from www.nytimes.com/elections/2016/results/primaries/ohio

Andrews, W., Lai, K.K.R., Parlapiano, A., & Yourish, K. (2016). Who is running for President? *The New York Times*. Retrieved from www.nytimes.com/interactive/2016/us/elections/2016-presidential-candidates.html

Barnett, J. T. (2015). Fleshy metamorphosis: Temporal pedagogies of transsexual counterpublics. In L. G. Spencer & J. C. Capuzza (Eds.), *Transgender communication studies: Histories, trends, and trajectories* (pp. 155–169). Lanham, MD: Lexington Books.

Benoit, W. L. (2001). The functional approach to presidential television spots: Acclaiming, attacking, defending 1952–2000. *Communication Studies*, *52*(2), 109–126. doi:10.1080/10510970109388546

Bing, N. (2015). Kenya decides: Kiswahili, social media and politics in Kenya's 2013 general elections. *Journal of African Media Studies*, 7(2), 165–183. doi:10.1386/jams.7.2.165_1

Bor, S. E. (2014). Candidates' use of social network sites to control their campaign message. In R. E. Denton (Ed.), *Studies of communication in the 2012 presidential campaign* (pp. 195–204). Lanham, MD: Lexington Books.

Chung, D. S., Tsay-Vogel, M., & Kim, Y. S. (2015). Who's following Twitter? Coverage of the microblogging phenomenon by U.S. cable news networks. *International Journal of Communication*, *9*, 3369–3393.

Coffey, D. J., Green, J. C., Cohen, D. B., & Brooks, S. C. (2011). *Buckeye battleground: Ohio, campaigns, and elections in the twenty-first century*. Akron, OH: University of Akron Press.

Diamond, J. (2016, September 30). Donald Trump quintuples down. *CNN*. Retrieved from www.cnn.com/2016/09/30/politics/trump-overnight-media-tweets/

Glassman, M. E., Strauss, J. R., & Shogan, C. J. (2011). *Social networking and constituent communications: Member use of Twitter during a two-month period in the 111th congress* (Congressional Research Service Report No. R43018). Retrieved from https://fas.org/sgp/crs/misc/R43018.pdf

Gronbeck, B. E. (2009). The Web, campaign 07–08, and engaged citizens. In R. E. Denton (Ed.), *The 2008 presidential campaign: A communication perspective* (pp. 228–243). Lanham, MD: Rowman & Littlefield.

Hanson, G., Haridakis, P. M., Cunningham, A. W., Sharma, R., & Ponder, J. D. (2010). The 2008 presidential campaign: Political cynicism in the age of Facebook, MySpace, and YouTube. *Mass Communication and Society, 13*, 584–607. doi:10.1080/15205436.2010.513470

Hendricks, J. A. (2014). The new-media campaign of 2012. In R. E. Denton (Ed.), *The 2012 presidential campaign: A communication perspective* (pp. 133–156). Lanham, MD: Rowman & Littlefield.

Kaplan, R. (2015, October 15). Election 2016 gets more than a billion interactions on Facebook. Retrieved from www.cbsnews.com/news/election-2016-gets-more-than-a-billion-interactions-on-facebook/

Katz, E. (1959). Mass communications research and the study of popular culture: An editorial note on a possible future for this journal. *Studies in Public Communication, 2*, 1–6. Retrieved from http://repository.upenn.edu/asc_papers/165

Miller, N. W., & Ko, R. S. (2015). Studying political microblogging: Parliamentary candidates on Twitter during the February 2012 election in Kuwait. *International Journal of Communication, 9*, 2933–2953.

Murthy, D. (2015). Twitter and elections: Are tweets, predictive, reactive, or a form of buzz? *Information, Communication & Society, 18*(7), 816–831. doi:10.1080/1369118X.2015.1006659

NUVI, Inc. (n.d.). *NUVI training manual: Version 2.0.* Lehi, UT.

Parmelee, J. H., & Bichard, S. L. (2012). *Politics and the Twitter revolution: How tweets influence the relationship between political leaders and the public.* Lanham, MD: Lexington Books.

Penney, J. (2016). Motivations for participating in 'viral politics': A qualitative case study of Twitter users and the 2012 US presidential election. *Convergence, 22*(1), 71–87. doi:10.1177/1354856514532074

Quinn, K. (2016). Why we share: A uses and gratifications approach to privacy regulation in social media use. *Journal of Broadcasting & Electronic Media, 60*, 61–86. doi:10.1080/08838151.2015.1127245

Rainie, L., Smith, A., Schlozman, K., Brady, H., & Verba, S. (2012, October 19). Social media and political engagement. *Pew Internet and American Life Project.* Retrieved from www.pewinternet.org/files/old-media//Files/Reports/2012/PIP_SocialMediaAndPoliticalEngagement_PDF.pdf

Rubin, A. M. (2009). Uses and gratifications: An evolving perspective of media effects. In. R. L. Nabi & M. B. Oliver (Eds.), *The sage handbook of media processes and effects* (pp. 147–159). Los Angeles, CA: Sage.

Trent, J. S., & Friedenberg, R. V. (2008). *Political campaign communication: Principles and practices* (6th ed.). Lanham, MD: Rowman & Littlefield.

Tumasjan, A., Sprenger, T. O., Sandner, P. G., & Welpe, I. M. (2010). Predicting elections with twitter: What 140 characters reveal about political sentiment. *The International AAAI Conference on Web and Social Media, 10*, 178–185.

van Dijck, J. (2013). *The culture of connectivity: A critical history of social media.* New York, NY: Oxford University Press.

Wallsten, K. (2015). Non-elite Twitter sources rarely cited in coverage. *Newspaper Research Journal, 36*(1), 24–41. doi:10.1177/0739532915580311

Warren, J. (2016, March 9). The battle in the buckeye state: Why Ohio is such a key presidential prize. *U.S. News and World Report.* Retrieved from www.usnews.com/opinion/articles/2016-03-09/why-ohio-is-so-key-in-2016

APPENDIX 4.1

Monitors

Hillary Clinton

Official sites: Facebook: hillaryclinton, Twitter: @hillaryclinton, Instagram: @hillaryclinton

Keywords and Hashtags: "Hillary Clinton," "Hillary Clinton for President," #hillaryclinton, #imwithher, #iamwithher, #hillary2016, #makeamericawhole, "make america whole again," "Hillary for America," #hillaryforamerica, #madampresident

Bernie Sanders

Official sites: Facebook: berniesanders, Twitter: @berniesanders, Instagram: @berniesanders

Keywords and Hashtags: "Bernie Sanders," "Bernie Sanders for President," #berniesanders, #bernie, #feelthebern, #bernie2016, #sanders2016, "Bernie for America"

Ted Cruz

Official sites: Facebook: tedcruz, Twitter: @tedcruz, Instagram: excluded, his Instagram account is designated as his senate position not his campaign

Keywords and Hashtags: "Ted Cruz," "Ted Cruz for President," #tedcruz, #tedcruz2016, #cruz2016, #ted2016, #cruzcrew, #trusted, #choosecruz

John Kasich

Official sites: Facebook: johnkasich, Twitter: @johnkasich, Instagram: @ johnkasich

Keywords and Hashtags: "John Kasich," "John Kasich for President," "Kasich for President," #johnkasich, #kasich, #kasich4us, #kasichforamerica, "Kasich for America," "John Kasich for America," #kasichforus, "Kasich for us"

Marco Rubio

Official sites: Facebook: marcorubio, Twitter: @marcorubio, Instagram: @marcorubiofla

Keywords and Hashtags: "Marco Rubio," "Marco Rubio for President," "Rubio for president," #marcorubio, #rubio, #rubio2016, #marcorubio2016, "Rubio for America," #rubioforamerica

Donald Trump

Official sites: Facebook: donaldjtrump, Twitter: @realdonaldtrump, Instagram: @realdonaldtrump

Keywords and Hashtags: "Donald Trump," "Donald J Trump," #trumptrain, "Donald Trump for President," "Trump for President," #donaldtrump, #donaldjtrump, #trump2016, #makeamericagreatagain, "make america great again," "Trump for America," #trumpforamerica, "Donald Trump for America"

Ohio Monitor

Keywords and Hashtags: "Ohio 2016," "Ohio 2016 primary," #oh2016, #ohio2016, #oh16

PART 2

Media Effects

Traditional Media and Social Media Distribution

5

FOREIGN POLICY AND PRESIDENTIAL ELECTIONS

A Look at the Iowa Caucuses

Raluca Cozma

Are foreign news and foreign policy foreign concepts to Americans? Researchers tend to agree that, in the absence of an immediate threat to their health and safety, U.S. audiences are generally ignorant about, and uninterested in, news about foreign affairs (Aldrich, Gelpi, Feaver, Reifler, & Sharp, 2006; Delli Carpini & Keeter, 1996). As cited by Hamilton and Lawrence (2010), *New York Times* columnist James Reston once famously remarked, "The people of the United States will do anything for Latin America except read about it" (p. 630). When they do consume international news, it's often by accident, as a by-product of seeking entertainment on soft news media (Baum, 2002). Is that still the case, in an age when information technologies have led to the highest levels of political, economic, and social globalization in history? Using the 2016 Iowa caucuses as a case study, this chapter reviews the history of foreign policy as an issue that candidates, the media, and the electorate pay attention to during presidential elections. To tease out the perceived importance of foreign affairs in the 2016 primaries and patterns in voters' consumption of domestic and international news, the chapter analyzes survey data from the Iowa Caucus Poll, which was conducted among registered voters by Iowa State's Center for Survey Statistics and Methodology from January 5 to January 22, 2016. The telephone survey captured respondents' media-use patterns and interest in foreign news and foreign policy leading up to the Iowa caucuses, which took place February 1, 2016. The January poll correctly captured the top favorite candidates from each party, with Democrat Hillary Clinton and Republican Ted Cruz leading their respective parties and ultimately winning the Iowa caucuses a week later.

This study falls at the intersection of international and political communication and dissects the effects on issue opinions and attitudes of news media use in general and of consumption of an endangered but so vital form of journalism in particular: foreign correspondence. As the world is more interconnected than ever, reduction in resources dedicated to foreign news is a troubling trend. Media executives blame this dangerous decline on decreased readership or ratings and justify closing of foreign bureaus on U.S. audiences' disinterest in foreign news and foreign policy, although the need to inform the public about dangers within and without the country's borders is as high as ever. That is problematic because public opinion on vital issues related to foreign policy is central to representation, democratic accountability, and policymaking. Indeed, in a review of more than 50 years of research on public opinion and foreign policy, Aldrich and colleagues (2006) found that, especially in the case of military interventions, the foreign policies of American presidents have been largely influenced by their perceptions of public opinion on those issues.

Given the state's first-in-the-nation status, Iowa represents an ideal testing ground for the issues deemed important during presidential elections. No previous study has explored Iowans' consumption of foreign news and how that relates to issue opinions and attitudes during presidential campaigns. Considering that several international events and issues (such as the Syrian crisis, the Ukrainian-Russian conflict, the threat of ISIS, the Iran deal, international trade policy, and several terrorist attacks around the world) during the 2016 primaries had the potential to have far-reaching effects, the Iowa Caucus Poll surveyed Iowa voters about their news-consumption habits and their interest in foreign news and foreign policy as they related to political decision-making. In addition to traditional news media use and issue concerns, other variables under scrutiny included social media use, party identification, candidate preference, and intention to vote.

News Sources of Political Information

According to normative standards of democratic citizenship, voters should make informed election choices. Modern politics is primarily mediated politics (Bennett & Entman, 2000; Esser & Strömbäck, 2014) and, although voters in Iowa have increased opportunities to meet candidates in person and engage in so-called retail politics (Redlawsk, Tolbert, & Donovan, 2011), citizens generally rely on mass media as the most important source for their political information diet. Nowadays, more than ever, they have access to myriad sources of political information. In addition to traditional news sources, citizens also have the Internet and social media to turn to for information about issues, candidates, and their campaigns.

Whereas mainstream mass media serve as the "Fourth Estate" that keeps politicians and corporations accountable, social media have emerged as the "Fifth Estate" (Metzgar & Maruggi, 2009), allowing citizens from all walks of life to generate their own content. Politicians took advantage of the new and low-cost platforms that afforded them to bypass traditional media filters and, starting with the 2004 election, have increased their presence on social-networking sites such as YouTube, Twitter, and Facebook (Hendricks & Denton, 2010). Research during the 2012 election (Kaye & Johnson, 2016) found that the number of people who relied on traditional news media for political fare began to decline to the benefit of digital media, mainly due to perceptions of bias and to increased ease of accessing alternative sources of information. Haridakis, Hanson, Lin, and McCullough (2015) found that during the Ohio Republican primary in 2012, the majority of citizens received their information about the election from television, with the Internet edging television out only among respondents under 35 years of age. Similar age differences emerged in the 2008 presidential campaign, when younger voters turned to the Internet more than their older counterparts (Sweetser & Kaid, 2008). The trend continued into 2016, when the Pew Research Center found that digital platforms continued to rise as a source of political information, although television was still cited as the top source of election news (Anderson, 2016).

With these findings in mind, the first research question sets out to examine the following:

> **RQ1**: *What were the main sources of information for likely voters leading up to the 2016 Iowa caucuses?*

Foreign News and Foreign Policy

Research has found that only during critical junctures, such as wars, do American audiences care about foreign policy and, most of the time, they have limited knowledge of international affairs (Aldrich et al., 2006; Holsti, 2004). Traditional news organizations themselves dedicate dwindling resources to foreign news coverage, with the number of U.S. foreign correspondents declining more than 20% between 2003 and 2011 (Kumar, 2011). This trend is often blamed by news executives on lack of public interest in foreign policy and on low newsstand sales or low ratings when their news outlets focus on foreign news (Hamilton & Lawrence, 2010). However, a recent comparative study of audiences and coverage of foreign affairs in 11 countries found that the U.S. public is not particularly disinterested in international news (Aalberg et al., 2013). On the contrary, the U.S. ranked as one of the countries with the highest level of interest in international affairs, whereas the supply of foreign news was one of the lowest. This same study revealed a positive correlation between the supply of international news and the public's knowledge of international events, organizations, and political leaders. The U.S. audiences were found to know very little about international events, a result that the authors attribute to the lack of supply rather than to a lack of interest.

The U.S. public has not always been dismissive of foreign affairs, though. Mead's historical research (2013) found that long before World War I and World War II, elections were decided by foreign policy questions, which were also driving economic growth. Gallup polls, which have asked Americans since the 1930s to name the most pressing problem facing the country today, found that war and international tensions were at the forefront of people's concerns through the end of the Vietnam War (Newport, 2003). At the end of the Cold War, however, Kissinger (2002) warned that, based on congressional sentiments and media coverage, which had transformed foreign policy into a "subdivision of public entertainment" (p. 27), Americans' concern for foreign affairs had reached an all-time low. Indeed, in 2016, the Pew Research Center found that six in ten Americans believed the U.S. should look inward and deal with its own problems, and about half were wary of economic globalization (Wike, 2016), a shift in priorities successfully exploited by the campaign of candidate Donald Trump and his "America first" foreign policy.

Chang, Shoemaker, and Brendlinger (1987) identified four variables that predict whether U.S. news organizations will cover events abroad: the normative deviance of the event, its relevance to the U.S., its potential for social change, and its geographical proximity. During the 2016 election, several global events and issues met these criteria. As such, the Syrian crisis, the rise of ISIS, the Iran nuclear deal, the rumors of Russia's involvement in campaign leaks, as well as the terror attacks in Paris (November 13) and San Bernardino (December 13) close to the 2016 primary season, ensured that international news topics were prominent in news media as well as in candidates' campaigns. How important were they to the American public, though? And were Americans really disinterested in foreign news in 2016? Using Iowa caucus-goers as the subject of analysis, the following research questions are formulated:

RQ2: *What was the level of interest in foreign news among likely voters before the 2016 Iowa caucuses?*

RQ3: *What is the relationship between media use, interest in foreign news, and concern for foreign policy among likely voters?*

Method

To answer the research questions proposed above, this study relies on data from the Iowa Caucus Poll, which was conducted by phone among registered voters by Iowa State's Center for Survey Statistics and Methodology during January 5–22, 2016. The survey closed a week before the Iowa caucuses, which makes it a good test of political information sources and perceived issue priorities on the precipice of the primary season.

The survey reached a total of 722 Iowa registered voters and included 356 Democrats, 283 Republicans, and 83 Independents. Slightly more women (51.4%) than men (48.6%) participated in the phone interviews, which averaged 10 minutes. By age, 383 respondents (53%) were over the age of 65, 191 respondents (26.5%%) were between 51 and 65 years old, 116 (16.6%) were ages 30 to 50, and only 28 (3.9%) were under 30. Among the respondents, 275 (38.1%) said they would definitely attend the Iowa caucuses, 138 (19.1%) said probably, 98 (13.6%) said they were unsure, 86 (11.9%) said they probably wouldn't vote, and 125 (17.3%) said they would definitely not participate in the Iowa caucuses.

Operationalization of Variables

Media use was measured by assessing consumption of political information from traditional sources such as cable news, national network news, local TV news, newspapers, radio, late-night comedy shows, and campaign advertising. The survey asked respondents how often they get political news from each of these sources (1 = never, 2 = sometimes, 3 = often, 4 = very often). Another question gauged *interest in foreign news* ("How interested are you in getting news about international affairs?"; 1 = not at all interested, 2 = somewhat interested, 3 = quite interested, 4 = very interested). A separate set of questions measured various uses of *social media*, but for the purposes of this study, only a consumption variable was included in the analysis, which measured how often respondents follow candidates and political parties on social media (1 = never, 2 = sometimes, 3 = often, 4 = very often). For *issue* concerns, a classic Gallup question (Newport, 2003) asked respondents to pick one problem facing the country that they thought was the most important. Answer options included the economy, dissatisfaction with government and congress, race relations and racism, immigration, unemployment, morality and religious issues, federal budget deficit, poverty and hunger, crime and violence, education, healthcare, gap between rich and poor, the judicial system, terrorism, environment, and foreign policy. To gauge *interest in foreign policy* more accurately, a separate follow-up question asked how important foreign policy was to respondents personally (1 = not at all important, 2 = somewhat important, 3 = quite important, 4 = very important). Control variables included *age*, *gender* (1 = male, 0 = female), *political party identification* (1 = Democrat, 2 = Independent/other, 3 = Republican), and *intention to vote in the primaries* (1 = will definitely attend the caucus in one's precinct, 2 = will probably attend, 3 = unsure, 4 = will probably not attend, 5 = will definitely not attend).

Results

The first research question dealt with the main sources of political information for Iowans leading up to the Iowa caucuses. For the political news source variables, the options "very often" and "often" were combined to get a better sense of what type of media respondents relied on as their top source of political news. Out of 722 respondents, 64.5% said national network TV news was their main source of political information. Local television (52.1%) was the next top source, followed by cable television (45.3%), newspapers (43.4%), the Internet (34.8%), and radio (30.6%). About a quarter of those surveyed said they get information from campaign advertising (27%), and only 10% said they get political information from late-night shows often or very often. Looking at differences by age, the Internet was the main source of information for younger voters. Nearly 82% of respondents under 30 years old got their political information online, compared to only 33% of caucus-goers over 50 years of age. Interestingly, the survey found more voters under 30 (31.8%) also read the newspaper for political news as compared to voters in the middle 30-to-50 age group (21.8%). Voters over 50 (49%) emerged as the most avid readers of print media for political information. In terms of following candidates and political parties on social media, cross-tabs with Bonferroni post-hoc analysis found that significantly more Millennials (40%) used social media for this purpose compared to only 32% of respondents in the 30–50 age group or 11% of respondents over the age of 50 ($X^2 = 57.36$, $df = 6$, $p < .001$).

As for gender differences, more women turn to national networks (women = 65.5%, men = 58.3%) and local TV news (women = 53.7%, men = 44.5%) for their political information, whereas men (39%) are more likely to get their news from radio compared to women (29.4%). The analysis found no significant gender differences between users of Internet, newspapers, or campaign ads. More women (21.5%) followed candidates on social media than men (14.1%).

Descriptive analysis also examined differences in political news consumption by political affiliation. Chi-square analysis found that Democrats were significantly more likely to get their news from national network television (72.4% compared to only 54.8% of Republicans, $X^2 = 21.92$, $df = 1$, $p < .001$) and newspapers (51.8% of Democrats compared to 35.4% of Republicans, $X^2 = 18.79$, $df = 2$, $p < .001$), whereas Republicans were significantly more likely to rely on cable news (53.6% compared to 41.5% of Democrats, $X^2 = 11.57$, $df = 2$, $p < .01$). Cross-tab analysis found no other significant differences. Among Democrats, twice as many of Bernie Sanders's supporters relied on the Internet (58.9%) compared to Hillary Clinton supporters (31.6%, $X^2 = 25.45$, $df=3$, $p < .001$). On the Republican side, cable news (47.9%) was the top source of information for supporters of Ted Cruz, who went on to win the Iowa caucuses. Donald Trump supporters relied heavily on cable news as well (57.1%), and even more so on national network news (58.9%). Only 17.2% of respondents said they followed candidates or a political party on social media, such as Facebook or Twitter, with a significant difference between Democrats (37%) and Republicans (19.7%, $X^2 = 33.84$, $df = 2$, p $< .001$).

The second research question asked about the level of public interest in foreign news. Of the 722 respondents, 22.4% said they were very interested in getting news about international affairs and 31.2% said they were "quite interested" in foreign news. Using the foreign news interest scale, where 1 meant not at all interested and 4 meant very interested, independent-samples *t*-tests and analyses of variance tests were conducted to test differences by age group, gender, and party affiliation. No statistically significant differences were found among age or gender groups, where the average interest level was 2.7 out of 4. The only significant difference was found among partisans, where Bonferroni post-hoc analysis found that Democrats (M = 2.78, SD = .89) were more interested in foreign news than Independents/others (M = 2.5, SD = .87; f = 4.21, p = .02) and marginally more interested than Republicans (M = 2.63, SD = .88; f = 4.21, p = .09). Analysis of variance (f = 5.82, $d.f.$ = 4, p < .001) with Bonferroni post-hoc tests also found that respondents who said they would definitely attend the Iowa caucuses had a significantly higher interest in foreign news (M = 2.87, SD = .92) than respondents who said they were unsure if they would vote (M = 2.43, SD = .77, p < .001), probably would not vote (M = 2.54, SD = .83, p = .01), and definitely would not vote (M = 2.61, SD = .91, p = .05).

Finally, the last research question set out to examine the relationship between media use, interest in foreign news, and concern for foreign policy. Among the problems facing the country at the time the survey was conducted, terrorism emerged as the top concern for 21.2% of respondents, followed by the economy (18.6%), dissatisfaction with government and Congress (10.1%), and the gap between rich and poor (8.9%). Foreign policy was deemed the most important issue facing the nation by only 4.8% of respondents. However, a follow-up question gauged how important foreign policy was to respondents personally as an issue on its own (rather than part of an issue ranking with only one top choice). Four out of every 10 respondents (40.3%) said foreign policy was very important and 28.1% answered it was quite important.

To answer the third research question, a three-stage hierarchical regression analysis was conducted where perceived importance of foreign policy was the dependent variable and control variables of age, gender, party affiliation, and intention to vote were entered in a first stage, media and social media use variables were included as independent variables in the second stage, and interest in foreign news was added in the third stage. The first model in Table 5.1 shows that, when looking only at demographics, being older and a Republican were positively correlated with seeing foreign policy as important. This model, although statistically significant [F(4, 428) = 5.347, p < .001], explains only 4% of the variation in the dependent variable. Party affiliation loses its statistical significance once media-use variables enter the mix. As shown in the second model in Table 5.1, which explains 12% of the variation in the dependent variable [F(13,419) = 4.740, p < .001], respondents who rely on cable news are more concerned with foreign policy, whereas reliance on local television news predicts the opposite. No other types of sources of information have a significant predictive power in the second model. In the third model [F(14,418) = 11,070, p < .001], which explains the highest variance of all, at 27%, party identification returns as a significant explanatory variable, with being Republican having a significant and positive correlation with concern for foreign policy, and interest in foreign news emerges as a predictor as well. Once again, reliance on cable news

TABLE 5.1 Summary of Hierarchical Regression Analysis for Variables Predicting Perceived Importance of Foreign Policy ($N = 434$)

Variable	*Model 1*	*Model 2*	*Model 3*
Demographics	*B (SE)*	*B (SE)*	*B (SE)*
Age	.009 (.003)***	.006 (.003)*	.004 (.003)
Gender	–.081 (.08)	–.132 (.07)	–.113 (.07)
Party	.093 (.04)*	.079 (04)	.103 (.04)**
Intention to vote	.051 (.02)	.034 (.03)	.020 (.02)
Media Use			
Cable news		.443 (.08)***	.294 (.07)***
Network news		.161 (.09)	.134 (.08)
Local TV		–.233 (.09)**	–.139 (.08)
Newspapers		.085 (.08)	.018 (.07)
Radio		.151 (.08)	.092 (.08)
Internet		.102 (.08)	–.053 (.08)
Late-night shows		.014 (.13)	–.028 (.11)
Campaign ads		–.073 (.09)	–.090 (.08)
Candidate social media		–.008 (.04)	–.003 (.04)
Foreign News			
Foreign news			.389 (.04)***
R^2	.042	.128	.270
F	4.739***	4.740***	11.070***

Note: Gender: 1 = male, 0 = female; Party: 1 = Democrat, 2 = Independent, 3 = Republican.
***$p < .001$,
**$p < .01$,
*$p < .05$.

is positively correlated with concern for foreign policy, but local television loses its negative predictive power once we account for interest in foreign news. In other words, the three models indicate that the strongest indicators for increased perceptions of foreign policy as an important issue are consumption of cable news in general and consumption of foreign news in particular, with Republicans being more likely than Democrats to see foreign policy as an important issue.

Discussion

Following the end of the Cold War in the early 1990s, the U.S. and other countries around the world entered a new era of global economics that, in turn, created new global threats, heralded by the September 11 terrorist attacks at the beginning of the century (Wanta, Golan, & Lee, 2004). Given that the rhythm of globalization and the scope of terrorist threats has only increased since then, one would expect an uptick in the salience of international events in the media and in the public's interest in foreign policy. Trends in news coverage, however, point in the opposite direction, with U.S. media, especially television, dedicating ever-more limited attention to foreign affairs (Shanor, 2003; Aalberg et al., 2013). That is a worrisome fact, considering that in a study examining the determinants of political knowledge, Jerit, Barabas, and Bolsen (2006) found that the quality of the information environment is more responsible for political ignorance than individual-level factors such as education and socio-economic status.

This study offers reasons for optimism, however, showing that U.S. audiences are interested in international news, with 53.6% of Iowans saying they are quite or very interested in foreign news. The percentage is very similar to the one found by Aalberg et al. (2013) in their comparative study of 11 countries, which showed that 52% of the U.S. audience has interest in international news coverage. However, given that the majority of respondents (52%) in this study rely heavily on local television for political information, it is unlikely that they are getting substantive exposure to news about foreign affairs. Indeed, the regression analysis found that local television was the only type of news source that had a negative relationship with seeing foreign policy as important. Whereas it appears that local television satisfies Iowans' general needs for news, a practical recommendation based on the findings of the present study would be to include more political coverage and foreign correspondence on local television news broadcasts. Data from the Pew Research Center indicate that only 3% of local television airtime is dedicated to stories on politics and government (Jurkowitz et al., 2013), whereas CNN dedicates the largest amount of coverage to overseas reporting, or about a quarter of its news stories. On the bright side, cable news did emerge as one of the top three sources of political information (with 43% of respondents saying they turn to it often or very often), and correlated positively with concern for foreign policy. The findings in this study found similar media-use patterns to those in previous elections (Kaye & Johnson, 2016) and is consistent with Pew Research Center data on Americans' heavy reliance on television news, regardless of type, for political information in the 2016 election (Anderson, 2016).

In a departure from recent election years, however, when the economy usually emerges as the most important issue for voters, terrorism was cited as the most important problem facing the country by the respondents in this study (21%), and four in ten respondents said foreign policy was very important, reflecting not only national security concerns in the aftermath of the Paris and San Bernardino attacks, but also signaling to the media and the candidates that they need to address global issues that could have an impact on the country. Interestingly, the findings on the role of partisanship were mixed. Democrats indicated a higher interest in foreign news than both Independents and Republicans, whereas Republicans were more likely than Democrats to think that foreign policy was a very important issue. This could be explained by the focus of the candidates' campaigns, with Republicans, and especially Donald Trump, making immigration a central issue of their platforms. Indeed, immigration was deemed the most important issue by 30% of Republicans, compared to only 14.9% of Democrats and 15.7% of Independents. In fact, for Democrats, the top issue was the economy (17.2% of Democrats), followed by the gap between rich and poor (16.1% of Democrats, compared to only 0.4% of Republicans). Future studies could examine how exactly news media covered the threat of terrorism during this period, given that it was such a salient issue for the public, and whether voters' concern for terrorism might have been the result of agenda setting by both the media and the candidates. News executives should reconsider further reduction in resources dedicated to foreign correspondence, given the public's appetite for international news.

Overall, this study showed that, just as in previous elections, voters spent a lot of time in front of screens, and computer screens have not yet supplanted television viewing, except for younger voters. Television maintained its long-held position as the top source of political information, and, not surprisingly, the Internet was the main source of information for younger voters. About 82% of respondents under 30 years of age said they get their political information online. However, reliance on the Internet for political news did not show any correlation with perceived importance of foreign policy, whereas being younger predicted lower interest in foreign policy. It is worrisome that Millennials dismissed foreign policy, as most of them were born in a post-Cold War era marked by increased globalization. Given that recent research (Garrett, 2009) points to an increase in insular political news exposure online, despite the fact that the Internet affords users unprecedented access to diverse sources of information from around the world, it is important for future studies to further categorize Internet use by partisan or established/alternative considerations. Although this study did capture use of social media for following candidates, with 40% of Millennials reporting that they follow candidates on Facebook or Twitter, this particular variable did not explain variance in voters' concern for foreign policy. This could also be due to the nature of the sample, which was heavily skewed in favor of an older population. In short, this study's findings on the influence of media use on concerns for foreign policy are limited and mixed. Only local and cable television news viewing appeared to make a difference, and in opposite directions. For respondents interested in foreign news, however, the negative effect of local television disappeared whereas the positive effect of cable news remained, suggesting that this group gets its needs for world news satisfied by channels such as CNN, Fox News, and MSNBC, which indeed do dedicate more resources and airtime to foreign correspondence.

Future studies should also gauge actual knowledge of foreign affairs, as previous studies have shown that the quality of news supply is a stronger predictor of knowledge than interest in foreign news and foreign policy or even than education and socio-economic status. The expressed high interest in foreign news and foreign policy in this study could be the result of a social desirability bias, which marred the results of many public opinion polls in the 2016 election (Edsall, 2016).

When considering the implications of this study's findings, one should also take into account the unique features of Iowa in the U.S. presidential election process. As a swing state with first-in-the-nation status, it benefits from a relatively vibrant local media, as candidates flock to the Hawkeye state to meet with potential voters numerous times over the course of their campaigns. For instance, Republican prospects made 344 visits to Iowa and Democrat contenders paid 90 visits to the state before the Iowa caucuses (Democracy in Action, 2016a, 2016b). Iowans are thus likely to learn more about issue debates, candidates, and issue positions than citizens in less contested states. Even student media in Iowa have been found to cite more news sources and favor issue to horse-race coverage compared to mainstream news outlets in their coverage of presidential elections (Burch & Cozma, 2016). Hayes and Lawless (2015) argue that states with less disputed political races tend to suffer from diminished news environments, which in turn translates into depressed political engagement. When even in a state with healthy and substantive local news coverage reliance on local television predicts decreased interest in foreign policy, one must wonder what the situation might be in states with reduced local exposure to political news.

References

Aalberg, T., Papathanassopoulos, S., Soroka, S., Curran, J., Hayashi, K., Iyengar, S., Jones, P. K., Mazzoleni, G., Rojas, H., Rowe, D., & Tiffen, R. (2013). International TV news, foreign affairs interest and public knowledge: A comparative study of foreign news coverage and public opinion in 11 countries. *Journalism Studies, 14*(3), 387–406.

Aldrich, J. H., Gelpi, C., Feaver, P., Reifler, J., & Sharp, K. T. (2006). Foreign policy and the electoral connection. *Annual Review of Political Science, 9*, 477–502.

Anderson, M. (2016, November 21). TV still the top source for election results, but digital platforms rise. *Pew Research Center.* Retrieved from www.pewresearch.org/fact-tank/2016/11/21/tv-still-the-top-source-for-election-results-but-digital-platforms-rise/

Baum, M. A. (2002). Sex, lies, and war: How soft news brings foreign policy to the inattentive public. *American Political Science Review, 96*(1), 91–109.

Bennett, W. L., & Entman, R. M. (Eds.). (2000). *Mediated politics: Communication in the future of democracy.* Cambridge, UK: Cambridge University Press.

Burch, A., & Cozma, R. (2016). Student election stories use more diverse news sources. *Newspaper Research Journal, 37*(3), 235–248.

Chang, T., Shoemaker, P. J., & Brendlinger, N. (1987). Determinants of international news coverage in the U. S. media. *Communication Research, 15*(4), 396–414.

Delli Carpini, M. X., & Keeter, S. (1996). *What Americans don't know about politics and why it matters.* New Haven, CT: Yale University Press.

Democracy in Action. (2016a, January 28). *Iowa Visits by Democratic Prospects in 2015–2016.* Retrieved from www.p2016.org/chrniowa/iavisits15d.html

Democracy in Action. (2016b, February 4). *Iowa Visits by Republican Prospects 2016.* Retrieved from www.p2016.org/chrniowa/iavisits15r.html

Edsall, T. B. (2016, May 11). How many people support Trump but don't want to admit it? *New York Times.* Retrieved from www.nytimes.com/2016/05/11/opinion/campaign-stops/how-many-people-support-trump-but-dont-want-to-admit-it.html

Esser, F., & Strömbäck, J. (2014). *Mediatization of politics: Understanding the transformation of western democracies.* New York, NY: Palgrave Macmillan.

Garrett, R. K. (2009). Echo chambers online? Politically motivated selective exposure among Internet news users. *Journal of Computer-Mediated Communication, 14*(2), 265–285.

Hamilton, J. M., & Lawrence, R. G. (2010). Foreign correspondence. *Journalism Studies, 11*(5), 630–633.

Haridakis, P. M., Hanson, G., Lin, M. C., & McCullough, J. L. (2015). Fitting social media into the media landscape during a 2012 Republican Primary. In J. A. Hendricks & D. Schill (Eds.), *Presidential campaigning and social media: An analysis of the 2012 campaign* (pp. 106–121). New York, NY: Oxford University Press.

Hayes, D., & Lawless, J. L. (2015). As local news goes, so goes citizen engagement: Media, knowledge, and participation in US House elections. *The Journal of Politics*, 77(2), 447–462.

Hendricks, J. A., & Denton, R. E., Jr. (Eds.). (2010). *Communicator-in-chief: How Barack Obama used new media technology to win the White House.* Lanham, MD: Lexington Books.

Holsti, O. R. (2004). *Public opinion and American foreign policy.* Ann Arbor, MI: The University of Michigan Press.

Jerit, J., Barabas, J., & Bolsen, T. (2006). Citizens, knowledge, and the information environment. *American Journal of Political Science, 50*(2), 266–282.

Jurkowitz, M., Hitlin, P., Mitchell, A., Santhanam, L., Adams, S., Anderson, M., & Vogt, N. (2013). The changing TV news landscape. *The Pew Research Center's Project for Excellence in Journalism: The State of the News Media 2013.* Retrieved from www.stateofthemedia.org/2013/special-reports-landing-page/the-changing-tv-news-landscape/

Kaye, B. K., & Johnson, T. J. (2016). Across the great divide: How partisanship and perceptions of media bias influence changes in time spent with media. *Journal of Broadcasting & Electronic Media, 60*(4), 604–623.

Kissinger, H. (2002). *Does America need a foreign policy? Toward a diplomacy for the 21st century.* New York, NY: Simon and Schuster.

Kumar, P. (2011). Foreign correspondents: Who covers what. *American Journalism Review*, December/January 2011. Retrieved from http://ajrarchive.org/article.asp?id=4997

Mead, W. R. (2013). *Special providence: American foreign policy and how it changed the world.* New York, NY: Routledge.

Metzgar, E., & Maruggi, A. (2009). Social media and the 2008 US presidential election. *Journal of New Communications Research, 4*(1), 141–165.

Newport, F. (2003, May 12). Americans clear that economy is most important problem facing country. *Gallup.* Retrieved from www.gallup.com/poll/8368/americans-clear-economy-most-important-problem-facing-country.aspx

Redlawsk, D. P., Tolbert, C. J., & Donovan, T. (2011). *Why Iowa? How caucuses and sequential elections improve the presidential nominating process.* Chicago, IL: University of Chicago Press.

Shanor, D. R. (2003). *News from abroad.* New York, NY: Columbia University Press.

Sweetser, K. D., & Kaid, L. L. (2008). Stealth soapboxes: Political information efficacy, cynicism and uses of celebrity weblogs among readers. *New Media & Society, 10*(1), 67–91.

Wanta, W., Golan, G., & Lee, C. (2004). Agenda setting and international news: Media influence on public perceptions of foreign nations. *Journalism & Mass Communication Quarterly, 81*(2), 364–377.

Wike, R. (2016, June 14). Where Americans agree, disagree on foreign policy. *Pew Research Center.* Retrieved from www.pewresearch.org/fact-tank/2016/06/14/where-americans-and-europeans-agree-disagree-on-foreign-policy/

6

THE EFFECTS OF POLITICAL SOCIAL MEDIA USE ON EFFICACY AND CYNICISM IN THE 2016 PRESIDENTIAL ELECTION

Exploring the Possibility of a Reinforcing Spiral

Benjamin R. Warner, Molly M. Greenwood, Freddie J. Jennings, and Josh C. Bramlett

In Barack Obama's farewell address to the nation, he focused his comments on the health of democracy. He warned that democracy is threatened when trust in democratic institutions is low, when political cynicism is rampant, and when citizens worry that corruption makes engaging in the democratic process pointless. In articulating the sociological trends that threaten democracy, Obama identified several factors such as economic inequality, racism, and hyper-partisanship. Among the various threats listed, Obama included a warning about social media—urging citizens not to retreat into their social media bubbles surrounded solely by like-minded others who reaffirm their preexisting beliefs ("President Obama's," 2017).

It is entirely appropriate for Obama to be the first president to include social media in his farewell address; after all, Facebook was launched the year his speech at the Democratic National Convention brought Obama into national prominence and his presidency substantially overlapped with the widespread adoption of numerous social media platforms. Indeed, he has been called the social media president by scholars of political communication (Katz, Barris, & Jain, 2013). The 2016 presidential election to replace him illustrated precisely how inseparable social media have become from political communication. The Pew Research Center reported that nearly 80% of Internet users and 68% of all adults in the U.S. use Facebook, with the adoption rate of various other platforms hovering between 25%–30% (Greenwood, Perrin, & Duggan, 2016). Social media were also a common source of news and political information in 2016, with 62% of U.S. adults reporting that they at least occasionally received news from social media

(Gottfried & Shearer, 2016). Two-thirds of Facebook users and just over half of Twitter users reported encountering political information on these platforms (Gottfried & Shearer, 2016). Usage patterns among the younger generations imply that these numbers presage even wider adoption of social media for political communication. Echelon Insights reported that social media were the primary way adults aged 18–49 found news about the 2016 election ("Social Sharing," 2016). Furthermore, the same study found that when people encounter news shared by a friend via social media they report trusting it more—a finding that suggests social media may be especially influential on user attitudes.

Communication research on the antecedents and consequences of social media use is expanding to match the pace of social media adoption. Much of this research has focused on the effects of social media on political participation (Bode, Vraga, Borah, & Shah, 2014; Boulianne, 2015; Gil de Zúñiga, Jung, & Valenzuela, 2012; Kim, Chen, & Gil de Zúñiga, 2013; Saldaña, McGregror, & Gil de Zúñiga, 2015). However, as Shelly Boulianne (2015) observed in a recent meta-analysis of the effects of social media on political participation, there is a paucity of research using panel surveys to disentangle the causal direction of associations between social media uses and effects. This is concerning because, as Slater (2007) observed, many media effects are likely to be cyclical such that the causes of media use are also effects. For example, people who are more interested in politics should be more likely to engage the political information they encounter via social media and this new information should also serve to enhance their political interest. Hence the need for panel studies that allow scholars to disentangle the direction of causal influence for associations observed in cross-sectional research.

Furthermore, though there is considerable research investigating a possible relationship between social media use and political participation, there is much less research exploring the associations between social media use and trust in democracy. This is unfortunate because, as Miller (1974) argued in some of the earliest theorizing about democratic trust, our political system will not survive long if most citizens do not believe that it produces outputs in congruence with the needs and desires of the people. Given the rapid expansion of social media as a source for political communication, it is important to understand whether the information people receive via these platforms bolsters or undermines their sense that democracy is working on their behalf.

In this chapter, we seek to expand scholarly understanding of the antecedents and effects of social media by examining the cross-lagged relationships between political uses of social media and three facets of democratic efficacy: political information efficacy, external political efficacy, and political cynicism. We present results from a two-wave panel study conducted during the 2016 U.S. presidential election to assess the associations between the consumption and production of political content on social media and these three outcomes. We find that political information efficacy is associated with an increase in both the production and consumption of political information on social media. Furthermore, though we identified an association between external political efficacy and the production/consumption of social media in the first wave of the data collection, the association vanished under the more rigorous tests imposed by the panel design. There was no evidence of any relationship between political cynicism and social media production/consumption. In what follows we will consider existing research on political uses of social media to generate theoretical expectations about the relationship between cynicism, efficacy, and political information efficacy (PIE), as well as the production and consumption of political content on social media.

Political Uses of Social Media

At the conclusion of the first decade of social media as a communication platform, considerable political communication research has investigated the potential effects of this emerging media. Much of this research has focused on whether social media use influences political participation both online and off (Boulianne, 2015). Because social media are interactive, they provide opportunities for individuals to directly engage elected officials, political journalists, and other citizens about the important issues of the day. However, because social media also allow people to customize their information environment, the influence of user choice is magnified. It is possible for those who prefer entertainment media to opt out of the political conversation whereas those who are politically minded may construct information echo chambers in which they only encounter perspectives that reinforce their preexisting beliefs.

Despite (or perhaps facilitated by) these concerns, current research suggests that social media use results in a small increase in users' levels of political participation (Boulianne, 2015). Specifically, Bode and colleagues (2014) found that, in a survey of young people during the 2008 election, those who reported greater political uses of social media also reported greater offline political participation. In another cross-sectional survey, Gil de Zúñiga et al. (2012) found a link between political uses of social media and social capital, online participation, and offline participation—a result observed later in similar research that examined even incidental/accidental exposure to political information online (Kim et al., 2013). To expand this evidence beyond cross-sectional associations, Gil de Zúñiga, Molyneux, and Zheng (2014) analyzed data drawn from a two-wave panel survey and found that social media use was associated with greater political expression. They concluded that this political expression allowed users to develop a "political face" (p. 627) that would facilitate greater political engagement offline in the future.

This research suggests that social media may increase the amount of political participation, particularly amongst those who use social media for political expression. However, political participation is only one possible outcome of social media use. It may also be the case that the political information encountered could increase users' confidence in their own political knowledge and therefore make them more willing to express themselves online, that the information could increase their faith that democratic participation has positive outcomes, or, conversely, increase their suspicion that democratic institutions are fundamentally corrupt and therefore that participation is a waste of time. In short, social media could bolster or undermine support for democracy.

Social Media and Political Efficacy

In theorizing the vital attitudes that influence democratic support, Campbell, Gurin, and Miller (1954) identified political efficacy as fundamental to a healthy democracy. They defined efficacy as "the feeling that individual political action does have, or can have, an impact upon the political process, i.e., that it is worthwhile to perform one's civic duties" (p. 187). Scholars have since divided this construct into various sub-dimensions (Craig, Niemi, & Silver, 1990). In particular, scholars have distinguished between internal and external political efficacy. Internal efficacy is defined as individuals' self-perceptions that they possess the understanding and ability required to participate meaningfully in politics whereas external efficacy measures the belief that political institutions are responsive to the demands of the public (Craig et al., 1990). Kaid, McKinney, and Tedesco (2007) proposed augmenting the concept of internal political efficacy to focus on the critical role that communication plays in information acquisition. They call their modified internal efficacy construct political information efficacy (PIE). PIE is defined as the extent to which individuals believe they have the information necessary to meaningfully engage in political participation. Beyond PIE and external political efficacy, scholars of political communication have long worried that increased political cynicism would poison the well of democratic goodwill. Miller (1974) defined cynicism as "the degree of negative affect toward the government, . . . the belief that the government is not functioning and producing outputs in accord with individual expectations" (p. 952). This classic definition has been augmented, in practice, to emphasize a suspicion that elected officials are more interested in their personal benefit than the well-being of the public (e.g., Agger, Goldstein, & Pearl, 1961). In what follows, we focus on these three important attitudes to generate a set of theoretical expectations about the influence of each on political uses of social media and, conversely, on the effects of political uses of social media on each attitude.

Political Information Efficacy

When Craig and colleagues (1990) investigated the sub-dimensions of political efficacy in items pilot tested in the American National Election Studies (ANES), they found clear confirmation of a distinction between internal and external political efficacy. They defined internal efficacy as "beliefs about one's own competence to understand and participate effectively in politics" (p. 290). Kaid and colleagues (2007) argued that, especially when considering the effects of political communication, the most salient element of internal political efficacy is "the voter's confidence in his or her own political knowledge and its sufficiency to engage the political process (to vote)" (p. 1096). The relationship between social media use and PIE is important because a *perceived* lack of knowledge is a critical barrier to participation among the least engaged individuals (Kaid et al., 2007). If people only use social media for political expression when they have sufficient confidence in their political knowledge, social media are another venue in which participation gaps will emerge. However, if social media foster increases in PIE, use of social media can close participation gaps in other contexts.

Cross-section research demonstrates a clear connection between the political uses of social media and PIE (Warner, Turner McGowen, & Hawthorne, 2012). However, it is unclear whether political uses of social media cause increases in PIE, whether PIE causes increases in political uses of social media, or whether the relationship is mutually reinforcing. Clues about this potential relationship can be identified in the work of Weeks, Ardèvol-Abreu, and Gil de Zúñiga (2016), who found that a small percentage of individuals (12%) were much more likely to consume, produce, and share political content on social media. They named these individuals prosumers and found that prosumers were much more likely to consider themselves opinion leaders in their networks, more likely to participate in politics both online and offline, and were more likely to attempt to persuade others about a political issue. In other words, when it comes to posting, commenting, sharing, and otherwise distributing political content on social media, those with the greatest confidence in their political knowledge should be the greatest producers. Therefore, we predict, H1: Political information efficacy will be associated with greater production of political content on social media.

Though people high in PIE should be more likely to produce political content on social media, those who consume more political content on social media should also become more confident in their political information. Early Twitter research found that the political content was primarily informational (Small, 2011), suggesting that people who see political content should gain knowledge. Furthermore, social media platforms facilitate incidental contact with political information and therefore reduce the effort required to learn about politics (Xenos, Vromen, & Loader, 2014). Social media also expand the size of people's communication networks and therefore increase the sources of political information to which people are exposed (Gil de Zúñiga et al., 2012). People may therefore learn about politics passively merely because political information is available in their social media environments. Indeed, Bode (2016) found experimental evidence of passive learning via social media, though she did not replicate this finding in the observational component of her study. Regardless of the extent of actual information acquisition, mere exposure to information could enhance people's perceptions that they are politically knowledgeable. In fact, Painter, Fernandes, Mahone, and Nashmi (2015) found that online media (including Facebook but not limited to social media) did increase PIE. Hence, we predict, H2: The consumption of political content on social media will result in greater political information efficacy.

External Political Efficacy

External political efficacy is "one's belief about her or his government's responsiveness to regular citizens' voices" (Lee, 2006, p. 416). For instance, people high in external political efficacy will believe that their vote matters. In her analysis of political web use in Western Europe and the U.S., Norris (1999) found that individuals with high political efficacy were more likely to go online to discuss politics. Kim and Khang (2014) argued that political participation, such as online discussion, is rooted in political efficacy because individuals expend the time and energy to engage others only when they believe that their effort can influence the political system. Individuals who feel they have little say in the government are less likely to use the Internet to engage in political information seeking or discussion (Mou, Atkin, & Fu, 2011). Similarly, Kenski and Stroud (2006) found a small positive relationship between external efficacy and online engagement. Because people are more likely to use social media to express their political views if they think that democratic participation is efficacious, we predict H3: External political efficacy will be associated with greater production of political content on social media.

Regarding the question of whether social media use should enhance political efficacy, the research is somewhat more mixed. In an examination of college students' Internet use, Lee (2006) found that receiving online political messages from public figures or agencies did not increase external political efficacy, although he notes the quality of those public sites was below the expectation of the students. However, the public-sector websites of the mid-2000s differ from today's interactive social media sites. In fact, Lee (2006) proposed that the Internet could potentially facilitate increased efficacy by helping users interact with politically active social groups, via instant messaging and commentary. Moreover, Jung, Kim, and Gil de Zúñiga (2011) found that online political messaging produced a significant and positive influence on political efficacy and political participation. We therefore expect H4: The consumption of political content on social media will result in greater external political efficacy.

Political Cynicism

Much of the same logic applies to expectations about the influence of cynicism on the production of political content on social media. People who distrust politicians and do not believe elected officials are working on behalf of voters should be less inclined to expend the necessary effort to follow and discuss the election via social media. Similar patterns have been observed with other online activities. For example, Pinkleton and Austin (2001) found that people's active information searches, characterized by the perception of newspapers as important sources, were associated with lower levels of cynicism. Cynicism has also been examined in social media contexts. Hanson, Haridakis, Cunningham, Sharma, and Ponder (2010) found that during the 2008 campaign, social-networking use was a negative predictor of cynicism, in that the more people used social-networking sites, the lower the levels of cynicism they expressed. Indeed, political cynicism may encourage citizens to essentially opt out of political media use (Crotty & Jacobson, 1980; Pinkleton, Austin, & Fortman, 1998) and avoid online political discussion (Mou et al., 2011). Therefore, we suspect H5: More politically cynical individuals will produce less political content via social media.

The likely effects on cynicism of encountering political information via social media are potentially mixed. On one hand, scholars have found that political media use activates governmental distrust and political cynicism (Capella & Jamieson, 1996; Moy & Pfau, 2000). As such, individuals who actively engage in political media tend to become more cynical of politicians and political institutions (Pinkleton et al., 1998). Conversely, interacting with friends and family about politics (even online) can have different effects on an individual's level of cynicism (Lin, Haridakis, & Hanson, 2016). Political discussion among friends and family may reduce cynicism (Jasperson & Hyun Jung, 2007). Hence, we pose a research question, RQ1: Will consuming political content on social media influence political cynicism?

Method

Procedure

A quota-stratified survey was collected through the Qualtrics online panel aggregator, which utilizes over 20 actively maintained market research panels. The sample was proportioned to match the most recent U.S. census data on age, gender, and race/ethnicity. Participants were contacted for the first wave after the two major party conventions but before the first presidential debate (August 26–September 6). The second wave was collected after the third debate and prior to the election (November 1–November 7). In total, 2,014 participants completed the first wave of the survey and 998 completed the second wave for a retention rate of .495. Of the 998 participants who completed both waves, 796 (80%) reported using some social media. Ninety-four percent of these social media users reported using Facebook, 37% reported using Twitter, and 27% reported using Instagram.

Of the social media users who completed both waves of the survey, the average age was 48.61 (*SD* = 18.61; *min.* = 18, *max.* = 86). The majority were male (*n* = 399, 50.1%), most reported being White (*n* = 559, 72%) compared to African American (*n* = 93, 11.4%) or Latinx/Hispanic (*n* = 88, 10.4%). A slight majority of the sample reported not having earned a four-year college degree (*n* = 414, 52%). The plurality of respondents reported a combined household income of less than $30,000 per year (*n* = 189, 24.6%) though the next most frequent income category was greater than $100,000 (*n* = 126, 16.4%). The next five income categories (from $40,000/year to $79,999/year) each contained roughly 10% of the sample, with the remaining categories ($80,000–$89,999 and $90,000–$99,999) each accounting for about 5% of the sample. The plurality of respondents identified with the Democratic Party (*n* = 403, 49.1%) compared to Republicans (*n* = 274, 34.6%) and independents (*n* = 119, 16.3%). Similarly, a plurality intended to vote for Democratic nominee Hillary Clinton (W1: *n* = 366, 45.9%; W2: *n* = 356, 44.7%) compared to those intending to vote for Republican nominee Donald Trump (W1: *n* = 262, 33.9%; W2: *n* = 278, 34.9%) or uncommitted to either candidate (W1: *n* = 168, 21.1%; W2: *n* = 162, 20.4%).

Measures

Social Media Variables

Respondents were asked to think about the social media platforms that they checked most frequently. They were then asked to respond, on a 5-point scale ranging from 0 = never to 4 = all the time, how often in the past week they had: "read a post about Clinton or Trump that you saw on social media," "clicked a link or watched a video about Clinton or Trump that you saw on social media," and "read comments (or a discussion) about Clinton or Trump that you saw on someone's social media post." These three items combine to indicate each user's consumption of political content on social media (W1: M = 1.83, SD = 1.15, α = .911; W2: M = 1.98, SD = 1.14, α = .905). To assess the production of political content on social media, respondents were asked how often, in the past week, they: "posted something about Clinton or Trump," "shared a link, video, meme, etc. about Clinton or Trump," "commented or responded to someone else's post about Clinton or Trump," and "'liked,' 'favorited,' or otherwise reacted to someone else's post about Clinton or Trump." The average response to these four items indicates each user's production of political content on social media (W1: M = 1.11, SD = 1.13, α = .938; W2: M = 1.19, SD = 1.15, α = .932).

Political Information Efficacy

PIE was measured with items adapted from the ANES (Craig et al., 1990) survey by Kaid et al. (2007). Respondents were asked to respond to the following four items on a 5-point agreement scale: "I consider myself well qualified to participate in politics," "I feel that I have a pretty good understanding of the important political issues facing our country," "I think I am better informed about politics and government than most people," and "If a friend asked me about the presidential election, I feel I would have enough information to help my friend figure out who to vote for." These four items were asked in both waves and combine to create an overall assessment of PIE within each wave (W1: M = 3.7, SD = .85, α = .858; W2: M = 3.68, SD = .87, α = .867).

Cynicism

Cynicism was measured on a 5-point agreement scale with a truncated version of a measure used in recent political communication research (McKinney & Warner, 2013; Warner et al., 2012) and adapted from items in the ANES (Craig et al., 1990) survey. Participants were asked to respond to the following four items: "Politicians cannot be trusted," "Politicians are more interested in power than what people think," "Politicians make promises that are never kept," and "Politicians are too greedy." The average response to these four items, when combined, was (W1: M = 3.89, SD = .78, α = .878; W2: M = 3.91, SD = .78, α = .873).

External Efficacy

External efficacy was measured on a 5-point agreement scale with four items developed in the ANES (Craig et al., 1990) and used in similar studies (Kushin & Yamamoto, 2010; Pinkleton & Austin, 2001): "My vote makes a difference," "I have a real say in what the government does," "I can make a difference if I participate in the electoral process," and "Voting gives people an effective way to influence what the government does" (W1: M = 3.47, SD = .98, α = .910; W2: M = 3.5, SD = 1.0, α = .910).

Results

All hypotheses were tested in a cross-lagged structural equation model (SEM) using *Lavaan* developed by Rosseel (2012) for the *R* ecosystem. Little (2013) recommends that longitudinal SEM begin with a measurement model to confirm the latent structure of the variables across time (i.e., a confirmatory factor analysis, or CFA). The longitudinal CFA was fit using a robust maximum likelihood estimator with correlated error terms across time in line with Little's (2013) recommendations regarding latent path models. The measurement model fit the data well: χ^2 (601) = 1165.85, p < .001, RMSEA = .034 (.032-.037), CFI = .972, NNFI/TLI = .968, SRMR = .034. The measurement model was then re-specified as a two-wave panel model in which all variables in the first wave were used as control variables for themselves in the second wave. In addition to this, the first-wave variables were regressed on: age category, gender, race/ethnicity, income, education, religiosity, and political partisanship.

The latent panel model created three data-points for each hypothesis: 1) the association between the variables at Time 1 when controlling for the covariates listed above; 2) the association between the variables at Time 2 when controlling for values of the same variable at Time 1; and 3) the cross-lagged association between one variable at Time 1 with another variable at Time 2 when controlling for values at Time 1. The cross-lagged relationships indicate the ability of one variable to predict increases or decreases in the value of another variable over time and thus represents the strongest evidence of a causal relationship outside of an experiment. The Time 2 relationships demonstrate an association between variables that remains even after controlling for earlier values of each variable—a powerful control that suggests a true relationship even if causal mechanisms of the relationship were not observed in the amount of time captured in the panel. The Time 1 relationships indicate an association that remains after removing variance explained by the control variables, providing evidence of an association that is nevertheless potentially spurious. The results of the cross-lagged analysis are presented in Table 6.1. The latent correlations between the variables within Wave 1 and Wave 2 are presented in Table 6.2.

The first hypothesis predicted that PIE would be associated with more frequent production of political content on social media. People with higher values of PIE at Time 1 were likely to increase their production of social media between waves (see Table 6.1). Furthermore, the association between PIE and political production of social media was present within waves at both Time 1 and Time 2 (see Table 6.2). The evidence therefore supported H1. In addition, though not hypothesized, there was a significant association between PIE and the consumption of political content. This held not only within waves but also across waves such that people who were higher in PIE at Time 1 were more likely to report increased consumption of political content on social media at Time 2.

H2 predicted that the relationship between PIE and political uses of social media would be mutually reinforcing such that those who consumed more political content on social media would become more confident in their political information. However, H2 was not supported. Those who reported frequent consumption of political information on social media at Time 1 were not more likely to see an increase in PIE at Time 2.

The third hypothesis predicted that those higher in external efficacy would be more willing to exert the effort to engage in political communication via social media. As can be seen in Table 6.1, values of external efficacy in Wave 1 did not significantly influence the production of political content on social media in Wave 2. Furthermore, within Wave 2 but while controlling for values at Wave 1, there was no significant correlation between external efficacy and social media production. However, within Wave 1, when controlling for traditional political variables, there was a significant association between external

TABLE 6.1 Latent Regression Paths for Final SEM Model

Path	*PIE* B (S.E.)	*Cynicism* B (S.E.)	*Efficacy* B (S.E.)	*Social Media Consumption* B (S.E.)	*Production* B (S.E.)
Time 1 (August 26–September 6)					
Age	.02 (.02)	–.01 (.02)	.06 (.02)[a]	–.09 (.02)[c]	–.08(.02)[b]
Female	–.40 (.08)[c]	–.16 (.08)[a]	–.03 (.08)	–.21 (.08)[b]	–.22(.08)[b]
African American	–.47 (.13)	–.30 (.14)[a]	.22 (.12)[a]	–.27 (.13)[a]	–.10(.13)
Asian	–.51 (.17)[b]	–.35 (.18)[a]	.01 (.14)	–.55 (.17)[b]	–.28(.15)[a]
Hispanic/Latino	–.21 (.14)	–.13 (.13)	.04 (.13)	–.11 (.12)	.17(.12)
Other Race	.13 (.27)	.29 (.25)	–.71 (.34)[a]	–.37 (.29)	–.01(.20)
Income	.01 (.02)	–.03 (.02)[a]	.03 (.01)[a]	–.01 (.01)	–.004(.01)
Education	.23 (.04)[c]	–.06 (.04)	.04 (.04)	.08 (.04)[a]	.05(.04)
Born Again	.07 (.09)	–.02 (.09)	.28 (.09)[c]	.26 (.09)[b]	.30(.09)[c]
Partisanship	.01 (.02)	.12 (.02)[c]	–.08 (.02)[c]	–.05 (.02)[a]	–.03(.02)
Time 2 (November 1–7)					
PIE T1	1.59 (.16)[c]	.07 (.06)	.04 (.06)	.15 (.06)[b]	.14(.05)[b]
Cynicism T1	0.13 (.08)	1.01 (.09)[c]	–.13 (.05)[b]	–.04 (.05)	–.02(.05)
Efficacy T1	–0.10 (.08)	–.14 (.06)[a]	1.11 (.10)[c]	–.05 (.06)	–.04(.05)
Soc. Media Con T1	0.13 (.08)	.08 (.07)	–.001 (.08)	1.07 (.11)[c]	.21(.07)[b]
Soc. Media Prod T1	–0.08 (.08)	–.04 (.07)	.03 (.08)	.25 (.08)[c]	1.30(.12)[c]

Results were generated using a robust Maximum Likelihood estimator using Lavaan in R. Statistical significance was determined through chi-square difference nested model comparisons in which each path was individually constrained to zero;

a = $p < .05$;
b = $p < .01$;
c = $p < .001$. Final model fit: χ^2 (931) = 1637.19, $p < .001$, RMSEA = .031 (.028-.033), CFI = .968, NNFI/TLI = .963, SRMR = .032. Partisanship was measured on a 1–7 scale from strong Democrat to strong Republican.

efficacy and social media production. Because this is the least rigorous test of the hypothesis and more rigorous tests revealed no relationship, we conclude that the data does not support H3.

The fourth hypothesis predicted that consumption of political content on social media would be associated with greater external efficacy across time. However, those who consumed more political content via social media at Time 1 were not more likely to see an increase in external efficacy at Time 2. Furthermore, after controlling for external efficacy at Time 1, there was no association between the consumption of political content on social media and external efficacy. As with social media production, social media consumption was associated with external

TABLE 6.2 Correlation Matrix for Latent Variables

	1	*2*	*3*	*4*	*5*
1. Social Media Prod.	1	.734[c]	.441[c]	−.082	.281[c]
2. Social Media Cons.	.444[c]	1	.432[c]	−.012	.231[c]
3. Political Inf. Efficacy	.226[c]	.167[a]	1	−.014	.431[c]
4. Political Cynicism	.042	.051	.048	1	−.336[c]
5. External Pol. Efficacy	.081	.106	.341[c]	−.098	1

Note:

a = $p < .05$;
b = $p < .01$;
c = $p < .001$. Time 1 correlations, controlling for demographic variables, are presented above the diagonal. Time 2 correlations, controlling for values of the same variable at Time 1, are presented below the diagonal. Correlations are drawn from the completely standardized solution of the final structural model.

efficacy at Time 1 when controlling for other influential variables. Given this evidence, we conclude that H4 was not supported.

The fifth hypothesis predicted that cynical people would be less likely to express themselves politically via social media. However, there was no significant association between cynicism and social media production. This was the case for the cross-lagged relationships over time (Table 6.1) and the within-wave associations at both Time 1 and Time 2 (Table 6.2). Thus, H5 was not supported. We also posed a research question to investigate whether the consumption of political content on social media would make users more cynical or, conversely, would reduce their cynicism. However, as with social media production, there was no significant association between consumption of political content on social media and cynicism in either the cross-lagged (Table 6.1) or within-wave correlations (Table 6.2).

In addition to the above associations, two additional relationships emerged as statistically significant. First, there was a negative and mutually reinforcing association between cynicism and external efficacy across time. People who had more cynical attitudes became less efficacious as the election unfolded. Conversely, those with greater external efficacy became less cynical over the course of the election. This is interpreted as evidence of predictive validity of the variables—as they are theorized to have a negative association—but also suggests a reinforcing character of these attitudes that, though beyond the scope of this chapter, may warrant further consideration.

Finally, the relationship between the production and consumption of political content on social media was significant in the cross-lagged analysis. People who saw more political content in their social media environments were more likely to create social media content over the course of the election. Similarly, those who produced more political content via social media were more likely to see political content in their social media environments over the course of the election. Furthermore, the correlation between these variables was significant and substantial at both Time 1 and Time 2. This suggests that these behaviors (consuming/producing) are not only logically correlated but also mutually reinforcing.

Discussion

This study set out to test the possibility of a mutually reinforcing relationship between political uses of social media and political efficacy. The results provided compelling evidence for the hypothesis that those with the most confidence in their political information would be most likely to produce political content on social media. However, external political efficacy and political cynicism do not appear to influence the extent to which individuals engage in political communication via social media. Furthermore, under the stringent standards of our panel design, there was no evidence of any effects of social media use on political efficacy. In what follows, the implications and limitations of these findings will be discussed along with directions for future research.

The finding that PIE is associated with greater production of social media is consistent with the prosumer (i.e., Weeks et al., 2016) view of social media use—that the political content is primarily generated by a highly engaged subgroup of the overall population. People higher in PIE were the most frequent producers and consumers of political content on social media. PIE therefore appears to exacerbate gaps between political sophisticates and others, as those higher in PIE at Time 1 increased their production and consumption of political content on social media over the course of the election when compared to those who were lower in PIE. However, this effect was only observed with PIE, not with external efficacy or cynicism. This suggests that, even if people doubt that their advocacy will be effective, even if they suspect that politicians are unresponsive to the demands of the public, they will utilize social media to express their political views provided they are confident that they possess enough information to do so with competence. This finding is promising because, though external efficacy and cynicism are relatively stable attitudes that are difficult to alter over the course of an election, PIE is easier to influence with political communication (Kaid et al., 2007). Debates, in particular, seem to be effective ways to increase PIE (McKinney & Warner, 2013). It is therefore likely that, by encouraging people to view these major events, scholars of political communication can increase the number of people willing to participate in the political conversation online.

These results also support a limited effects theory of social media. Those who reported frequent consumption of political information on social media did not experience an increase in PIE, external efficacy, or cynicism. We found no validation of hopes that social media might, through either incidental exposure or deliberate engagement with political information, improve the normative attitudes of users. Conversely, some may fear that the hostility of the political conversation on social media could increase the cynicism of users. We also found no evidence of any negative effects of social media use on these vital political attitudes. It is important to note that our limited effects findings are, in many ways, a function of the rigor of the panel design of the study. The strong association between PIE and social media use, observed in a cross-sectional design, could be falsely interpreted as evidence that social media use increases PIE—when in fact our evidence suggests that the relationship exists only in the other direction. Similarly, we observed a cross-sectional relationship between social media use and external efficacy that, were it not for the panel design, could be interpreted as evidence that social media use increases external efficacy. However, by including a second observation, we were able to demonstrate that not only does social media use not influence changes in external efficacy, but that the association observed at Time 1 vanished when we controlled for previous values at Time 2. In other words, the overreliance on cross-sectional designs in social media research (Boulianne, 2015) may inflate the perception of social media effects in the field.

As with any study, there are important limitations to consider. First, longitudinal designs are limited by the often-arbitrary decision about the amount of time lapse between observations. Here, we selected the time between the conventions and the election to capture the period of time where the campaign is most intense and people are starting to pay greater attention to the election. However, election coverage was strong throughout 2016; it is possible that by the end of the conventions people had already formed fairly stable levels of efficacy and cynicism. An earlier observation may therefore have captured more change both in political activity on social media and the key outcome variables. The ability to generalize values from the sample to the U.S. voting public is also undermined by the use of a non-probability sample. Though online opt-in panels have been shown to effectively reproduce relationships observed in probability samples and in publicly available population data (Ansolabehere & Schaffner, 2014), the Qualtrics panels have not been specifically verified and online panels are still relatively new in political communication research. Nevertheless, the diversity of the sample should provide confidence that the observed relationships provide a robust test of the hypotheses—if the hypothesized relationships existed in the population there should be evidence of them in this diverse national sample.

This study also presents exciting avenues for future research. First, though PIE appears to be central to the production of political content on social media, the findings observed here suggest that PIE also influences the consumption of political content. This relationship was not hypothesized and, as with any post-hoc interpretation, all interpretations are speculative. However, if this relationship is robust to replication, it will suggest that confidence in political information is not only a prerequisite to political expression on social media, but also to the decision to read political content that others post. It may be that, because people who are low in PIE are less likely to read political content posted by others, they are unable to gain from exposure to this information. This could explain the absence of social media effects. Future research should also test other important normative variables with similar panel designs such as political knowledge and partisan polarization. Finally, this study observed the potential for a mutually reinforcing relationship between the production and consumption of political content on social media. The act of generating political content appears to make people more willing to read content posted by others and the act of reading content posted by others appears to increase people's willingness to post their own opinions. The theoretical implications of this relationship should be considered further in future studies.

Conclusion

Political efficacy is vital to a healthy democracy (Campbell et al., 1954) precisely because people will not long tolerate a political order that they do not believe effectively produces legitimate outcomes (Miller, 1974). In his farewell address, Obama identified numerous contemporary threats to the effective execution of self-governance. The preceding study focused on one—social media—and found limited evidence these emerging media would do much to exacerbate or resolve these concerns. However, democracy is premised on the belief that self-government requires widespread participation. Our findings demonstrate that, at least on social media, participation is concentrated primarily among those who are already confident in their political knowledge. This finding emphasizes the importance of exposing individuals to communication events that are capable of instilling this confidence. As this confidence increases, the conversation online should become more inclusive and better represent the full diversity of voices in the vast tapestry of the U.S. electorate.

References

Agger, R. E., Goldstein, M. N., & Pearl, S. A. (1961). Political cynicism: Measurement and meaning. *The Journal of Politics*, *23*, 477–506.

Ansolabehere, S., & Schaffner, B. F. (2014). Does survey mode still matter? *Political Analysis*, *22*, 285–303. doi:10.1093/pan/mpt025

Bode, L. (2016). Political news in the news feed: Learning politics from social media. *Mass Communication and Society*, *19*(1), 24–48. doi:10.1080/15205436.2015.1045149

Bode, L., Vraga, E. K., Borah, P., & Shah, D. V. (2014). A new space for political behavior: Political social networking and its democratic consequences. *Journal of Computer-Mediated Communication*, *19*(3), 414–429. doi:10.1111/jcc4.12048

Boulianne, S. (2015). Social media use and participation: A meta-analysis of current research. *Information, Communication & Society*, *18*(5), 524–538. doi:10.1080/1369118X.2015.1008542

Campbell, A., Gurin, G., & Miller, W. E. (1954). *The voter decides*. Evanston, IL: Row, Peterson.

Capella, J. N., & Jamieson, K. H. (1996). News frames, political cynicism, and media cynicism. *Annals of the American Academy of Political and Social Science*, *546*, 71–85.

Craig, S. C., Niemi, R. G., & Silver, G. E. (1990). Political efficacy and trust: A report on the NES pilot study items. *Political Behavior, 12*, 289–314.

Crotty, W. J., & Jacobson, G. C. (1980). *American parties in decline.* Boston, MA: Little, Brown and Company.

Gil de Zúñiga, H., Jung, N., & Valenzuela, A. (2012). Social media use for news and individuals' social capital, civic engagement, and political participation. *Journal of Computer-Mediated Communication, 17*, 319–336. doi:10.1111/j.1083-6101.2012.01574.x

Gil de Zúñiga, H., Molyneux, L., & Zheng, P. (2014). Social media, political expression, and political participation: Pane analysis of lagged and concurrent relationships. *Journal of Communication, 64*, 612–634. doi:10.1111/jcom.12103

Gottfried, J., & Shearer, E. (2016, May 26). News use across social media platforms 2016. *Pew Research Center.* Retrieved from www.journalism.org/2016/05/26/news-use-across-social-media-platforms-2016/

Greenwood, S., Perrin, A., & Duggan, M. (2016, November 11). Social media update 2016. *Pew Research Center.* Retrieved from www.pewinternet.org/2016/11/11/social-media-update-2016/

Hanson, G., Haridakis, P. M., Cunningham, A. W., Sharma, R., & Ponder, J. D. (2010). The 2008 presidential campaign: Political cynicism in the age of Facebook, MySpace, and YouTube. *Mass Communication & Society, 13*(5), 584–607. doi:10.1080/15205436.2010.513470

How social sharing is reshaping the 2016 Race: Key takeaways from our research for BuzzFeed. (2016, April 22). *Echelon Insights.* Retrieved from https://medium.com/echelon-indicators/how-social-sharing-is-reshaping-the-2016-race-key-takeaways-from-our-research-for-buzzfeed-df008cbdc313#.tz1e8p227

Jasperson, A. E., & Hyun Jung, Y. (2007). Political advertising effects and America's racially diverse newest voting generation. *American Behavioral Scientist, 50*, 1112–1123.

Jung, N., Kim, Y., & Gil de Zúñiga, H. (2011). The mediating role of knowledge and efficacy in the effects of communication on political participation. *Mass Communication and Society, 14*(4), 407–430. doi:10.1080/15205436.2010.496135

Kaid, L. L., McKinney, M. S., & Tedesco, J. C. (2007). Introduction: Political information efficacy and young voters. *American Behavioral Scientist, 50*(9), 1093–1111. doi:10.1177/0002764207300040

Katz, J., Barris, M., & Jain, A. (2013). *The social media president: Barack Obama and the politics of digital engagement.* New York, NY: Palgrave Macmillan.

Kenski, K., & Stroud, N. J. (2006). Connections between Internet use and political efficacy, knowledge, and participation. *Journal of Broadcasting & Electronic Media, 50*(2), 173–192. doi:10.1207/s15506878jobem5002_1

Kim, Y., Chen, H., & Gil de Zúñiga, H. (2013). Stumbling upon news on the Internet: Effects of incidental news exposure and relative entertainment use on political participation. *Computers in Human Behavior, 29*, 2607–2614. doi:10.1016/j.chb.2013.06.005

Kim, Y., & Khang, H. (2014). Revisiting civic voluntarism predictors of college students' political participation in the context of social media. *Computers in Human Behavior, 36*, 114–121. doi:10.1016/j.chb.2014.03.044

Kushin, M. J., & Yamamoto, M. (2010). Did social media really matter? College students' use of online media and political decision making in the 2008 election. *Mass Communication & Society, 13*, 608–630. doi:10.1080/15205436.2010.516863

Lee, K. M. (2006). Effects of Internet use on college students' political efficacy. *Cyber-Psychology and Behavior, 9*, 415–422. doi:10.1089/cpb.2006.9.415

Lin, M., Haridakis, P. M., & Hanson, G. (2016). The role of political identity and media selection on perceptions of hostile media bias during the 2012 presidential campaign. *Journal of Broadcasting & Electronic Media, 60*(3), 425–447. doi:10.1080/0883815/2016.120331

Little, T. D. (2013). *Longitudinal structural equation modeling.* New York, NY: Guilford Press.

McKinney, M. S., & Warner, B. R. (2013). Do Presidential debates matter? Examining a decade of campaign debate effects. *Argumentation and Advocacy, 49*, 238–258. Retrieved from www.americanforensics.org/aa/aa_info.html

Miller, A. H. (1974). Political issues and trust in government: 1964–1970. *The American Political Science Review, 68*, 951–972.

Mou, Y., Atkin, D., & Fu, H. (2011). Predicting political discussion in a censored virtual environment. *Political Communication, 28*(3), 341–356. doi:10.1080/10584609.2011.572466

Moy, P., &. Pfau, M. (2000). *With malice toward all? The media and public confidence in democratic institutions.* Westport, CT: Praeger.

Norris, P. (1999). *Who surfs Café Europa? Virtual democracy in the U.S. and western Europe.* Cambridge, MA: Harvard University, JFK School of Government.

Painter, D. L., Fernandes, J., Mahone, J., & Nashmi, E. A. (2015). Social network sites and interactivity: Differential expression effects in campaign 2012. In J. A. Hendricks & D. Schill (Eds.), *Presidential campaigning and social media: An analysis of the 2012 campaign* (pp. 185–195). New York, NY: Oxford University Press.

Pinkleton, B. E., & Austin, E. W. (2001). Individual motivations, perceived media importance, and political disaffection. *Political Communication, 18*(3), 321–334. doi:10.1080/10584600152400365

Pinkleton, B. E., Austin, E. W., & Fortman, K.K.J. (1998). Relationship of media use and political disaffection to political efficacy and voting behavior. *Journal of Broadcasting & Electronic Media, 42*(1), 34–50.

President Obama's farewell address: Full video and text. (2017, January 10). *New York Times.* Retrieved from www.nytimes.com/2017/01/10/us/politics/obama-farewell-address-speech.html

Rosseel, Y. (2012). Lavaan: An R package for structural equation modeling. *Journal of Statistical Software, 48*, 1–36. Retrieved from www.jstatsoft.org/v48/i02/

Saldaña, M., McGregror, S., & Gil de Zúñiga, H. (2015). Social media as a public space for politics: Cross-national comparison of news consumption and participatory behaviors in the United States and the United Kingdom. *International Journal of Communication, 9*, 3304–3326.

Slater, M. D. (2007). Reinforcing spirals: The mutual influence of media selectivity and media effects and their impact on individual behavior and social identity. *Communication Theory, 17*(3), 281–303. doi:10.1111/j.1468-2885.2007.00296.x

Small, T. A. (2011). What the hashtag? A content analysis of Canadian politics on Twitter. *Information, Communication & Society, 14*(6), 872–895. doi:10.1080/1369118X.2011.554572

Warner, B. R., Turner McGowen, S., & Hawthorne, J. (2012). Limbaugh's social media nightmare: Facebook and Twitter as spaces for political action. *Journal of Radio & Audio Media, 19*(2), 257–275. doi:10.1080/19376529.2012.722479

Weeks, B., Ardévol-Abreu, A., & Gil de Zúñiga, H. (2016). Online influence? Social media use, opinion leadership, and political persuasion. *International Journal of Public Opinion Research, 29*(2), 214–239. doi:10.1093/ijpor/edv050

Xenos, M., Vromen, A., & Loader, B. D. (2014). The great equalizer? Patterns of social media use and youth political engagement in three advanced democracies. *Information, Communication & Society, 17*(2), 151–167. doi:10.1080/1369118X.2013.871318

7

STREAMING ENTERTAINMENT AND TALKING POLITICS

Social Television in the Shaping of Online and Offline Political Talk During the 2016 Campaign

Sarah Krongard and Jacob Groshek

Streaming television has become a global phenomenon; Netflix currently reports 86 million members in 190 countries (Netflix, 2016), altogether streaming upward of 42.5 billion hours of media in 2015 (McAlone, 2016). Hulu has grown to 12 million members (Perez, 2016), and Amazon Prime's rise to 63 million members in 2016 suggests massive potential for their streaming viewership (Shi, 2016). New digital television applications are continuously emerging, offering niche content, such as NBC Universal's new streaming comedy TV platform Seeso (NBC Universal, 2016) and HBO Now, which offers access to HBO content without a traditional cable package (HBO, 2016). Nielsen Corporation (2016b) reports that traditional television still leads as the most frequently used medium, but time-adjusted, connected television is on the rise.

However, social video applications have complicated the contemporary definition of "television." According to YouTube's global reach statistics (YouTube, 2017), through mobile alone, YouTube reaches more adults aged 18–49 than any cable network in the U.S. Popular social media applications such as Facebook, SnapChat, and Instagram each offer video-sharing capabilities. For example, Facebook Live allows users to stream live video with friends; the function is increasingly popular with celebrities, brands, and media companies (Julian, 2016). According to Nielsen Corporation (2016a), 50% of heavy social media users reported watching video content through a social platform during the previous 30 days. The consuming and sharing of video content is ubiquitous, whereas the line between social media and television becomes increasingly blurred. This chapter examines how the increased use of digital streaming television shaped both the frequency and tenor of political talk during the 2016 campaign, specifically investigating the role of social trust as a moderating variable. This area of focus offers a distinct contribution to the body of literature on media and political engagement due to the emergent nature of the medium; streaming television offers unique affordances, including on-demand, algorithmically determined personalized content, representing both a departure from and convergence of social media and traditional television (Groshek & Krongard, 2016).

Several prior research studies illustrate the generally positive relationship between the use of social-networking sites (SNSs) and political participation, both online and off, among citizens (i.e., Bode, Vraga, Borah, & Shah, 2014; Boulianne, 2015; Gil de Zúñiga, Jung, & Valenzuela, 2012; Rainie & Smith, 2012; Vitak et al., 2011). Similarly, a litany of research has examined traditional television's relationship with social trust (Moy, Scheufele, & Holbert, 1999; Putnam, 1995, 2000; Uslaner, 1998) and civic engagement (Drew & Weaver, 2006; Moy, Xenos, & Hess, 2005; Shah, 1998; Street, Inthorn, & Scott, 2012; Weaver & Drew, 2001). However, whereas streaming television is informed by social media logic (van Dijck & Poell, 2013) and offers content created for traditional TV, the distinct combination of features requires a unique investigation of its political implications. Therefore, this specific study expands upon prior work and addresses this gap in the literature to more fully understand today's convergent and on-demand television landscape, extending beyond SNSs or television alone.

Additionally, this chapter shifts away from a general conception of civic participation and focuses rather on political talk exclusively to understand the extent to which streaming television consumption may contribute to the body of literature on media's intersection with and contribution to engagement with the public sphere (Dahlgren, 1995, 2009; Habermas, 1989; Papacharissi, 2002). Political talk is critical for the health of an active democracy and serves as a means for individuals to make sense of a political landscape; Walsh (2004) highlights the importance of exploring informal political talk as a vehicle for developing understanding and crafting social identity. Similarly, McCoy and Scully (2002) maintain that the health of civic life depends on citizens engaging in the process of informed dialogue and deliberation. Klofstad's (2011) study of college-aged students demonstrates that, although political talk is not a magic bullet, when people are exposed to political discussion within their daily environments, they are more likely to become more civically engaged. From the perspective of the virtual public sphere, social media environments can serve as a space to engage in politically oriented conversation (Papacharissi, 2002; Kirk & Schill, 2011), complicating distinctions between private and public life (Papacharissi, 2009). For example, Kirk and Schill (2011) suggest that during the 2008 presidential election, media outlets became a communication source for not only pundits and candidates but also private citizens; spaces such as YouTube were converted into vehicles that inspired civic participation. These findings demonstrate the blending of social and civic worlds, as well as the intermingling of entertainment and information within the digital realm.

Talking Media, Civic Engagement, and Social Trust

Since the emergence of television, researchers have examined the relationship between television consumption and political engagement with mixed findings. Early research explored voter turnout and TV viewership, particularly in comparison to newspaper readership. Glaser (1965), for example, found that those who watched and owned a television voted at higher rates than nonowners, and newspaper readers voted at higher rates than nonreaders, demonstrating that access to media in general facilitated voter participation, as opposed to one medium superseding another as a political motivator. However, in an historical analysis, Gentzkow (2006) found that as television entered the marketplace, consumption of newspapers and radio programming dropped, along with a drop in political knowledge.

During the cable era of television, Simon (1996) found that voter turnout was positively related to newspaper readership and negatively to television viewing. Famously, Putnam (1995, 2000) identified television as one factor to blame for the decline in civic engagement and social capital in his *Bowling Alone* argument, due largely to the displacement of time, suggesting that time spent watching television takes the place of moments that could be dedicated to civic pursuits, and potential cultivation for "mean world syndrome" (Gerbner & Gross, 1976). Emerging from cultivation research, the "mean world syndrome" suggests that those who spend more time consuming television tend to perceive the outside world as an unkind place (Gerbner & Gross, 1976). Several authors refuted Putnam's claims regarding television's role in the decline of social capital and civic engagement; Uslaner (1998) identified no support for Putnam's findings, and Shah (1998) added nuance to the relationship between television, civic engagement, and interpersonal trust, identifying genre of the content consumed as a critical factor.

To complicate the debate further, an empirical analysis by Moy et al. (1999) refuted Putnam's time displacement hypothesis, illustrating that time viewing television did not necessarily take the place of civic activities, but simultaneously supported Putnam, finding a negative relationship between time spent consuming television and civic engagement. Questions regarding television's relationship with political engagement persisted as the medium evolved. More recently, van Zoonen (2004) offered an analysis of the ways in which television fandom behaviors reflect democratic engagement; findings demonstrate that entertainment television may engender the affective intelligence that can be transferred to political involvement. In other words, the habits, behaviors, and ways of being exhibited within television fandom cultures, such as participation, imagination, and active discussion, may actually translate into real-world civic engagement (van Zoonen, 2004).

The research described thus far considers the relationships among both traditional television and social media engagement in political participation and discourse. However, the emerging technological affordances (Gaver, 1991) of Internet-enabled, algorithmically informed television require a reconceptualization of the medium's defining qualities (Groshek & Krongard, 2016).

During the network era of television, the viewing experience was synchronous, linear, and culturally shared (Lotz, 2007); the rise of cable television packages and home recording represented a shift toward increased viewer control and agency (Lotz, 2007). But today's post-network era of television represents a fundamentally altered landscape, where viewer choice, agency, and personalization dictate the television experience. Consumption practices have shifted along with the technology; for example, using multiple devices at once, a practice known as second-screening, is increasingly frequent. Mann et al. (2015) share that 87% of consumers surveyed use more than one device at a time. Gil de Zúñiga, Garcia-Perdomo, and McGregor (2015) report that second-screening to access news content serves as a significant predictor of online political participation. Moreover, in a recent study, Groshek and Krongard (2016) found a positive relationship between streaming television and political engagement; these findings necessitate that researchers in the field of media and politics examine the implications of digital TV consumption.

The Social Media Logic of Streaming Television

Streaming television integrates elements of social media logic (van Dijck & Poell, 2013) into its design and user experience. Van Dijck and Poell (2013) outline the principles of social media logic: programmability, popularity, connectivity, and datafication (p. 2). Television is now programmable in the sense that the technology can both direct and be directed by its users. Streaming services such as Netflix, Apple TV, and Hulu offer recommended content to the user based on viewer data; however, viewers ultimately choose what and when they watch. The interaction is a dynamic process of giving and receiving on the part of both the user and the tool. Similarly, television viewing is informed by popularity, manifested through user recommendations, ratings, and feedback. Netflix, for example, consistently prompts users to rate the programs viewed in order to gather data on preference, which subsequently informs the algorithms that generate recommendation systems (van Dijck & Poell, 2013). Television is connected across and throughout the user's media ecosystem, permeating sundry devices. Experiences are shareable across platforms; Hulu provides users with the ability to share their current viewing via Twitter or Facebook with the click of a button. Viewing patterns, preferences, and habits are transformed into data and used to improve the platform's efficacy and responsiveness (van Dijck & Poell, 2013).

With increased choice and personalization, viewing behavior has shifted accordingly. Access to on-demand content has resulted in an increase in binge-watching, which is defined as watching three or more episodes of one series in a day. TiVo's 2015 binge-viewing survey found that 92% of respondents have participated in binge-viewing at some point, and 32% indicated that they will wait for a full season to become available before watching to ensure their ability to binge (Spangler, 2015). Netflix recently released a "binge-scale" that indicates the relationship between genre of program and type of binge-behavior, ranging from "shows to savor" to "shows to devour" (Dwyer, 2016).

Therefore, the technological landscape of television has shifted to a more personally tailored, nonlinear experience, adopting the logic of social media environments and demonstrating a significant departure from broadcast and mass media. In order to better understand implications of this television environment, this research study explores the extent to which this marriage of traditional television and social media facilitates political talk in both on and offline settings. Building on previous work on streaming television, particularly that of Groshek and Krongard (2016), we expect that individuals who stream television more frequently will also engage with others more often, in this case in talking about politics, thus:

> H1: Greater frequency of streaming television online will relate positively to higher levels of a) online and b) offline political talk.

Additional research has examined social media as a space for engaging in political discourse. For example, Himelboim et al. (2014) examined the emotional valence of casual political talk via Twitter, suggesting that valence-based homophily explained interactions among users on Twitter; in other words, when it comes to controversial political topics, Twitter users tend to engage with those who express similar feelings toward the issue. Choi (2014) analyzed the effectiveness of cognitive versus affective conversation regarding politics in social media settings; findings revealed that participants tend to refer to messages shared by like-minded users and that political discourse tends to be more emotional than cognitive. However, according to Choi (2014), the cognitive discussions are more influential than emotional conversations. Papacharissi (2015) extended research on the virtual public sphere by specifically examining the ways in which affective publics use SNSs to participate to engage with political movements through storytelling. Wright (2012) highlighted the potential for political talk to emerge among everyday citizens within apolitical online spaces; Wright (2012) likens these informal online spaces to Oldenburg's (1999) concept of a "third space," a socially constructed environment outside of the home or workplace where people can engage informally. Selva (2016) found through an empirical study that social television, defined as engaging with Twitter in real time while consuming broadcast television, may offer a new conception of audiencehood and foster political engagement due to social television's encouragement of active participation among viewers.

Bridging the gap between television and online engagement, Graham and Hajru (2011) and Graham (2012) suggest that engaging in dialogue about apolitical, reality television programming can facilitate political talk in online forums.

Similarly, Street et al. (2012) built upon the work of Graham and Hajru (2011) and discovered that among young people in the U.K., popular culture served as a means to consider the world and their own social connections through discourse, thus potentially facilitating political reflection. Based on this body of work, and on similar findings by Groshek and Krongard (2016) that found content type barely registered as a moderating effect on political participation, we continue to build on this growing body of emerging media scholarship and pose the following:

H2: Viewing apolitical and political content interacts with the frequency of streaming television online and relative levels of a) online and b) offline political talk.

Methods

We collected nationally representative data using a generalizable online panel provided by Qualtrics. In total, 1,105 respondents completed questionnaires between November 16 and December 3, 2015, which was a relatively early period in the U.S. presidential campaign, before voting in primaries or caucuses began. As such, this time frame provides a valuable window into the campaign cycle that is understudied but nonetheless crucial to the eventual outcome.

Sample

This sample was well matched to the larger U.S. population and, although the sample may present obstacles to perfect generalizability, this sort of data collection is routinely used to make inferences in the field (cf., Baker et al., 2010; Gil de Zúñiga et al., 2015). Specifically, 516 respondents were male (46.7%) and 589 female (53.3%), with a median age of 44 years (M = 45.19, SD = 17.14). In terms of income, 26.2% earned $24,999 or less, 27.1% made between $25,000 and $49,999 as a household, 30.3% were in the $50,000 to $99,999 income bracket, and 16.4% reported earning $100,000 or more annually. Regarding ethnicity, 74.1% respondents indicating being Caucasian, 11.0% and 7.2% identifying as African American and Hispanic/Latino, respectively, with another 5.2% indicating being Asian, 1.3% Native American, 0.3% Pacific Islander, and 0.9% self-identifying as "other."

Measures

Frequency of Talking Politics Online and Offline

We used two scales of talking politics, one for online and the other for face-to-face using factor analysis processes with varimax rotation as our two key dependent variables. For both forms of talking politics, scales included eight items from "never" (0) to "always" (4) talking politics with a range of individuals that were more and less intimate and personal, or that were more distant, strangers, or that held differing opinions. More specifically, these questions began with "How often do you talk about politics or public affairs with" others, where conditions of being face-to-face or online were set as separate items. Here, we included options such as, "People you know well, like family members or close friends," "Strangers, or people that you have only met online," "People whose political views are different from yours and generally disagree with you," "People from a different race or ethnicity," and "People from a different social class," among other similar items. When looking at the indexes of talking politics online (α = .968; M = 0.94, SD = 1.02) and offline (α = .949; M = .16, SD = .94), there was a strong, positive bivariate correlation (Pearson's r = 0.82, $p < .01$).

Political Antecedents

In keeping with conventions in the field, we accounted for germane political beliefs among this sample as controls. Here, 27.7% of respondents self-reported as Republicans, 35.4% were Democrats, 33.1% were Independents, 6.8% indicated "other" or "don't know." Political ideology (M = 3.98, SD = 1.83) ranged from very liberal (1) to very conservative (7). Political knowledge (M = 2.49, SD = 1.28) had a possible range of zero to four correct answers to four general questions and followed roughly normal distribution with a relatively low level of knowledge, with 71.1% of the sample answering three or fewer questions correctly.

Political Efficacy and Voting Behavior

To operationalize internal (three items, α = .781; M = 3.27, SD = 0.94) and external (two items; α = .769; M = 3.39, SD = 1.13) political efficacy, scales ranged from very low (1) to very high (5). Voting in local and state elections (two items, α = .948; M = 2.20, SD = (1.61) had a possible range of never (0) to always (4).

Psychological Characteristics

This block was form by measures of trust in others (two items, α = .761; M = 3.26, SD = 0.85), personal feelings of connectedness and belonging (three items, α = .735; M = 3.73, SD = 0.78), and life satisfaction (two items, α = .839; M = 3.28, SD = 1.05). All these items are previously validated measures (cf., McCroskey, 1982).

General Use of Media for Politics

All traditional media scales were collected on a scale of never (0) to always (4). This block included both a combined measure of radio and newspapers in print (four items, α = .725; M = 1.21, SD = 0.91) as well as a measure of viewing local, network, and cable news (three items, $\alpha = .747$; $M = 2.38$, $SD = 0.97$) through broadcast or cable television.

Social Media and Streaming Television

Frequency of using social network sites for politics (seven items, $\alpha = .933$) was also set on the same never (0) to always (4) scale and had a mean of 0.84 ($SD = 0.93$). The metric for streaming television on laptops, desktops, Internet-enabled television, mobile phones, or tablets (five items; $\alpha = .870$) likewise ranged from zero to four ($M = 1.28$, $SD = 1.23$), but the range for this scale was unique. Here, no streaming television use at all was zero (0), one was less than 1 hour on average per day (1), with incremental increases for between 1 and 2 hours (2), 2 and 3 hours daily (3), and 3 hours or more (4).

To determine content that respondents watched, they indicated which programs they had binge-watched through streaming television. Six shows that were most frequently streamed in our sample were categorized into political (namely, *House of Cards, Orange Is the New Black*, and *Homeland*) and apolitical (*The Unbreakable Kimmy Schmidt, The Walking Dead*, and *Game of Thrones*) groupings. Programs were categorized as "political" if the content were directly, rather than allegorically, focused on political subject matters. Although it is, of course, possible to categorize almost any media content as having some sort of possible political implications or themes, our goal here was to identify programs that were explicitly political in a real-world contemporary context, as opposed to those that were fantasies. This resulted in having respondents who binge-watched only political (12.7%; $N = 140$), only apolitical (17.8%; $N = 197$), and both apolitical and political content (15.2%; $N = 168$). A remaining 54.3% ($N = 600$) of this sample reported not streaming any of these shows.

Findings

We began by testing the first hypothesis, that greater frequency of streaming television online will relate positively to higher levels of a) online and b) offline political talk with a straightforward pair of hierarchical regression models. Both of these analytic specifications control for a host of independent variables that are fairly commonplace to the existing literature (cf., Gil de Zúñiga, Molyneux, & Zheng, 2014), and provide insights to the largely still unexplored domain of streaming television and its relationship to political communication.

To begin, when online political talk was set as the dependent variable, there were statistically significant relationships to a number of factors, all of which are summarized in Table 7.1. Of specific interest to H1, it was observed that more frequent streaming of television was positively associated with more regular political talk online ($B = 0.063$, $p < .001$).

TABLE 7.1 Regression Model of Talking Politics Online Frequency

	Coef. (B)	*Std. Err.*	*Beta(β)*
Step 1—*Demographics*			
Gender (being female)	–0.147***	0.038	–0.072
Age in cohorts	–0.020	0.023	–0.018
Income	–0.016	0.020	–0.016
Education	0.023	0.015	0.031
ΔR^2	0.076***		
Step 2—*Political Antecedents*			
Republican	–0.018	0.048	–0.008
Democrat	–0.017	0.045	–0.008
Political ideology (very liberal—very conservative)	–0.018	0.012	–0.032
Political knowledge	–0.003	0.015	0.004
ΔR^2	0.037***		
Step 3—*Political Efficacy and Voting Behavior*			
Vote in local/state elections	0.001**	0.013	0.002
Internal efficacy	0.068**	0.025	0.059
External efficacy	0.016	0.017	0.018
ΔR^2	0.141***		
Step 4—*Psychological Characteristics*			
Trust in others	0.041#	0.024	0.034
Connectedness and belonging	0.078**	0.028	0.058
Life satisfaction	–0.025	0.020	–0.026
ΔR^2	0.024***		
Step 5—*General Use of Media for Politics*			
Radio and newspaper	0.054*	0.027	0.048
Traditional television	–0.010	0.0202	–0.009
ΔR^2	0.121***		
Step 6—*Social Media and Streaming TV*			
SNS political purposes	0.777***	0.026	0.720
Streaming television across devices	0.063***	0.017	0.076
ΔR^2	0.303***		

Notes: N = 1024, listwise deletion; overall Adjusted R^2 = 0.698.

#$p < .10$
*$p < .05$
**$p < .10$
***$p < .001$

With the fairly comprehensive model specification entered here, each hourly increase in streaming any type of streaming television (on a daily basis) was related to a 0.063 unit increase in online political talk (on a scale where 0 = "never" and 4 = "always"). In addition, when looking at standardized Betas in this model, more frequent streaming of television was the second-largest statistically significant predictor (β = 0.076). This coefficient was behind only increased use of social-networking sites for politics (β = 0.720), and followed by being female (β = -0.072), internal efficacy (β = 0.059), connectedness and belonging (β = 0.058), radio and newspaper use (β = 0.048), trust in others (β = 0.034), and voting in local or state elections (β = 0.002) as statistically significant factors. Given these results, it is clear that there is obvious support for H1a and the proposition that more frequent use of streaming television relates positively to talking politics online.

In other words, the empirical results reported here indicate that those individuals who streamed television more frequently were far more involved in talking about politics with others.

Perhaps just as importantly, this factor was the second-most influential factor that explained talking about politics, which has been shown elsewhere to be vital activity for healthy democratic participation.

When transitioning to H1b and the extent to which the greater use of streaming television online relates positively to higher levels of offline participation, another hierarchical regression was modeled. In this instance, the frequency of political talk offline was set as the dependent variable, and nearly identical positive relationships were observed.

In particular, even when again taking into account a wide range of controls, more frequent use of streaming television was a statistically significant predictor of offline political talk ($B = 0.069$, $p < .001$) to an extent that is just barely greater than that of its relationship to online political talk reported in the previous model. The relative effect of streaming television in this model was somewhat more modest (β = 0.090) when compared to other standardized Betas. Here, more frequent streaming of television was the fourth-largest statistically significant predictor behind using social media for politics (β = 0.556), internal efficacy (β = 0.126), and general feelings of connectedness and belonging (β = 0.108). This ranking nonetheless situated hours spent streaming as having more of an effect on talking politics than combined radio and newspaper use (β = 0.084), being more educated (β = 0.050) or in older age cohorts (β = -0.050), voting in local or state elections (β = 0.042), or being female (β = -0.039) as statistically significant factors. In other words, our findings suggest that time spent streaming television actually serves as a better predictor of whether individuals will engage in political discourse than these other variables that may seem, at first glance, to be more related to civic engagement, such as education or voting behaviors.

These findings are summarized in Table 7.2 and illustrate that there was relatively robust support for H1b. Adding to that support, it is worthwhile to

TABLE 7.2 Regression Model of Talking Politics Offline Frequency

	Coef. (B)	*Std. Err.*	*Beta(β)*
Step 1—*Demographics*			
Gender (being female)	–0.073#	0.040	–0.039
Age in cohorts	–0.051*	0.024	–0.050
Income	0.015	0.021	0.016
Education	0.034*	0.015	0.050
ΔR^2	0.087***		
Step 2—*Political Antecedents*			
Republican	0.042	0.051	0.021
Democrat	–0.019	0.047	–0.010
Political ideology (very liberal—very conservative)	–0.007	0.012	–0.014
Political knowledge	0.016	0.016	0.022
ΔR^2	0.029***		
Step 3—*Political Efficacy and Voting Behavior*			
Vote in local/state elections	0.025#	0.014	0.042
Internal efficacy	0.132***	0.026	0.126
External efficacy	–0.021	0.018	–0.025
ΔR^2	0.173***		
Step 4—*Psychological Characteristics*			
Trust in others	0.018	0.025	0.017
Connectedness and belonging	0.132***	0.029	0.108
Life satisfaction	–0.020	0.021	–0.022
ΔR^2	0.029***		
Step 5—*General Use of Media for Politics*			
Radio and newspaper	0.087**	0.029	0.084
Traditional television	–0.002	0.023	–0.002
ΔR^2	0.104***		
Step 6—*Social Media and Streaming TV*			
SNS political purposes	0.551***	0.028	0.556
Streaming television across devices	0.069***	0.018	0.090
ΔR^2	0.191***		

Notes: N = 1024, listwise deletion; overall Adjusted R^2 = 0.606.

#$p < .10$
*$p < .05$
**$p < .10$
***$p < .001$

also observe that though using social media for politics and streaming television were the only variables entered in the last block of the regression models, the adjusted R^2 change figures were not only significant for both models, they easily accounted for the most variance of any block for each respective model. Importantly, these statistical models control for the influence of various factors to gauge the relative impact of each individual factor, as well as groups of factors that are measured together as blocks. These results highlight the importance of identifying which content is being viewed, rather than simply focusing on the number of hours spent consuming online television.

Next, we report our findings on Hypothesis 2, and the extent to which viewing political or apolitical content interacts with the frequency of streaming television and the relative levels of a) online and b) offline political talk. The factors of content type (political, apolitical, or both) and average hours spent streaming per day (0–1 hours, 1–2, 2–3, and 3+ hours) were thus modeled jointly in two separate factorial ANOVAs that set online and offline political talk as the respective dependent variables.

Support for H2a was evidenced by a statistically significant interaction ($F(6, 423) = 2.28$, $p < .05$, partial $\eta^2 = .032$) with talking politics online. Though the interaction term for talking politics offline was not significant ($F(6, 423) = 1.08$, $p = 0.373$, partial $\eta^2 = .015$), the pattern was similar to, but less exaggerated than, online political talk. This is to say that respondents who streamed both apolitical and political video content—in other words the heaviest and most diverse streamers of television—talked politics the most in online and offline settings, and more frequent streaming of apolitical content was associated with more frequently talking about politics online and offline than streaming political content, except at 3 hours or more of streaming per day.

These results are visually presented in Figures 7.1 and 7.2, and also demonstrate statistically significant main effects for content type *and* hours streaming in each model. Taking these results as a whole suggests that the type of content streamed may be less crucial than the activity of streaming itself. As these results indicate, viewing apolitical content and, especially in conjunction with a blend of political content, relates strongly and positively to talking about politics more often in both online and offline settings.

Perhaps most interestingly, the frequency of streaming political-only video content consistently related *least* of the content conditions to the frequency of talking about politics online or offline, except at 3+ hours of average viewing per day, when it increased to an estimated level more than apolitical content alone. This means that apolitical content, or a combination of apolitical and political content, more effectively encourages political talk than the preference for streaming only political content. In other words, streaming entertainment content more effectively generates political talk than streaming political content alone.

Although support for H2b was not uniformly observed in terms of a statistically significant interaction, it was nonetheless clear that in all content viewing

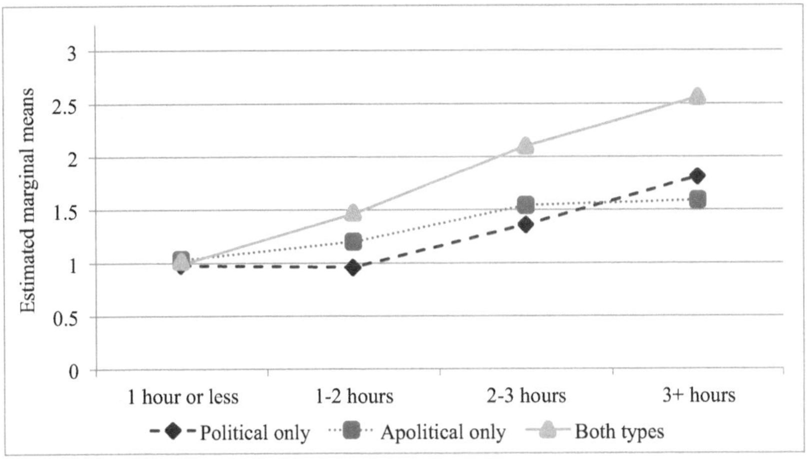

FIGURE 7.1 Relationships Between Types of Content Binge-Watched, Hours Spent Streaming Television, and Frequency of Talking Politics Online

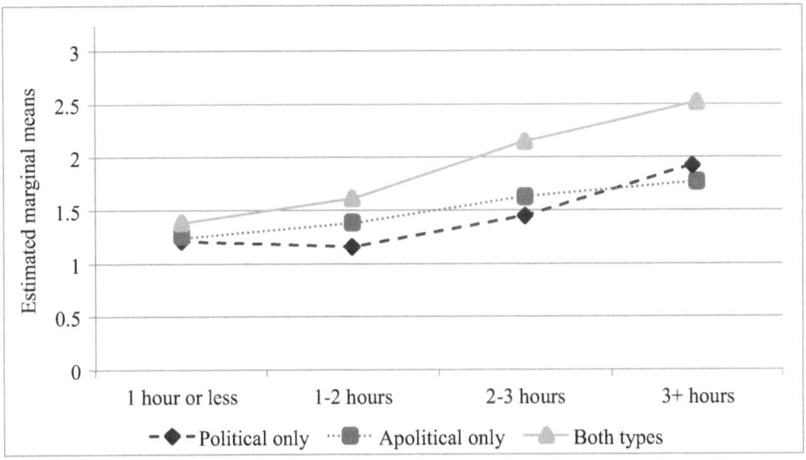

FIGURE 7.2 Relationships Between Types of Content Binge-Watched, Hours Spent Streaming Television, and Frequency of Talking Politics Offline

conditions, average levels for both online and offline political talk increased for each additional hour of television streamed. As reported by Groshek and Krongard (2016, p. 13), "these analyses also identify how engagement with differing types of streaming television content has largely positive but still differential effects," in this case on political talk. Put simply, those who stream television more, regardless of content but especially those with a mixed-content diet that includes entertainment, are those who talk more—not less—about politics in online and offline settings.

Discussion and Conclusion

In 1985, Neil Postman published *Amusing Ourselves to Death*, arguing that the rise of television was detrimental to the intellectual development of Americans. Postman maintained that television contributes to the dumbing-down of American culture, particularly when television content purports to be educational, academic, or generally more substantial than meaningless entertainment. Due to a bias for visual stimuli, television's educational content, such as *Sesame Street* or *60 Minutes*, is often incomplete and superficial, according to Postman, and therefore harmful to public discourse. That said, our findings suggest otherwise; contrary to Postman's assertions, results of this study demonstrate a positive relationship between time spent consuming streaming television and engaging in political talk, both on and offline. Of course, Postman's work referred to traditional television, whereas we are examining streaming TV. However, as we explore television's present and future, it is necessary to engage with its past. Perhaps streaming television presents an opportunity to shift the reputation of a TV consumer from "couch potato" to active and engaged citizen. Moreover, our results illustrate significant interactions with increased online and offline political talk that continues to amplify with more time spent streaming, regardless of content type viewed. Instead of serving as detrimental to high-minded engagement, streaming television may instead serve as a facilitator of political discourse.

Although perhaps counterintuitive, viewing apolitical programming (such as *The Unbreakable Kimmy Schmidt*) is more strongly related with online and offline political talk than consuming political content (such as *House of Cards*); this relationship shifts after 3 hours of television consumption, when political content is more strongly related with online and offline political talk. Thus, apolitical content may ultimately serve as a trigger for engaging in political discourse; these findings most directly build upon the work of Graham and Hajru (2011) as well as Graham (2012) and Street et al. (2012); despite (or perhaps even due to) the consumption of apolitical stories, the act of engaging with content through an interactive medium supports the participation in political discourse.

Longer-term consumption of television seems to necessitate greater alignment with the subject matter presented within the programming. As illustrated in the analyses summarized in the tables reported here, there are many interesting and statistically significant relationships that will be important to explore further. At this stage, what we can suggest is that the largely positive findings reported here may be due to the increased passivity experienced by viewers during lengthy consumption; perhaps the auto-play feature, which automatically presents viewers with the next episode within a series via online streaming platforms, decreases viewers' agency.

This positive relationship between streaming television and political talk necessitates a reconceptualization of television, both as a technological apparatus and a social force. As suggested by theorists such as Gerbner (1998) and Bandura (1986), television serves as a powerful storytelling machine that crafts and perpetuates cultural myths, priorities, and values. However, as the technology evolves, perhaps power dynamics shift accordingly. As mentioned previously, the body of literature on television's relationship with political engagement has yet to examine the post-network era; for example, Postman's (1985) and Putnam's (1995, 2000) seminal pieces emerged during the broadcast and cable era, when the television experience was generally synchronous, linear, and culturally shared, although viewer agency was increasingly due to access to new channels and the advent of the VCR (Lotz, 2007). Today, web-enabled streaming television pivots away from the unidirectional storytelling experience of yesteryear toward a more dynamic, interactive dialogue, offering power to the consumer. Television viewers can individually determine the unique content, device, and time for viewing, rather than passively waiting to receive the programming dictated by networks. Based on our findings, perhaps these responsive, bidirectional affordances of the emerging technology may actually support the development of agency within viewers. Therefore, the functionality of the apparatus, rather than the messages communicated, might help to stimulate dialogic communication patterns and thus support engagement in today's networked public sphere.

There are limitations to this study that can be addressed and further developed through future research. First, causality must be questioned; could it be possible that those viewers who generally prefer and are drawn to opportunities for active engagement choose streaming television as well as political participation? Future research ought to examine this possibility. Additionally, this study examined the quantity of time spent consuming six different commonly binge-watched television programming; in order to develop a more nuanced understanding of role of genre, a more representative sample of commonly binge-watched programs ought to be considered. For example, *The Unbreakable Kimmy Schmidt* is the only comedy within the sample; a more systemic sample could offer greater insights into differences among genres.

Second, future studies, particularly a detailed content analysis, could assess the level of political themes present within the series, rather than using a binary of *political* versus *apolitical*; current television programming is often complex and politically allegorical. In this study, programs were identified as *political* if the content of the program is directly political in nature. However, programs *The Walking Dead* and *Game of Thrones* offer political commentary on a more metaphorical level, although the storylines are set in fantasy worlds. Additionally, future qualitative research could complement this study to better understand the perspectives of streaming television users; audience research could offer insights regarding motivations for viewing and interpretations of programs.

Thus, streaming television, informed by its dynamic and interactive affordances, may very well serve as a means for empowerment; perhaps then this sense of agency transfers to our social realities. The technology asks audiences to redefine the TV experience and rethink the role of consumers, placing control and power into the hands of the viewer. The findings shared above reveal an exciting opportunity for future research; it is imperative for media scholars to explore the ways in which our ever-evolving media landscape can serve as a vehicle for prosocial behavior and civic health.

References

Baker, R., Blumberg, S. J., Brick, J. M., Couper, M., Courtright, M., Dennis, J. M., Dillman, D., Frankel, M., Garland, P., & Groves, R. M. (2010). AAPOR report on online panels. Retrieved from https://pprg.stanford.edu/wp-content/uploads/2010-AAPOR-Report-on-Online-Panels.pdf

Bandura, A. (1986). *Social foundations of thought and action: A social cognitive theory*. Upper Saddle River, NJ: Prentice Hall.

Bode, L., Vraga, E. K., Borah, P., & Shah, D. V. (2014). A new space for political behavior: Political social networking and its democratic consequences. *Journal of Computer-Mediated Communication, 19*(3), 414–429.

Boulianne, S. (2015). Social media use and participation: A meta-analysis of current research. *Information, Communication & Society, 18*(5), 524–538. doi:10.1080/1369118x.2015.1008542

Choi, S. (2014). Flow, diversity, form, and influence of political talk in social-media-based public forums. *Human Communication Research, 40*(2), 209–237. doi:10.1111/hcre.12023

Dahlgren, P. (1995). *Television and the public sphere: Citizenship, democracy and the media*. London: Sage.

Dahlgren, P. (2009). *Media and political engagement*. New York, NY: Cambridge University Press.

Drew, D., & Weaver, D. (2006). Voter learning in the 2004 presidential election: Did the media matter? *Journalism & Mass Communication Quarterly, 83*(1), 25–42. doi:10.1177/107769900608300103

Dwyer, E. (2016). Netflix & binge: New binge scale reveals TV series we devour and those we savor. *Netflix Media Center*. Retrieved from https://media.netflix.com/en/press-releases/netflix-binge-new-binge-scale-reveals-tv-series-we-devour-and-those-we-savor-1

Gaver, W. (1991). Technology affordances. *Proceedings of the SIGCHI Conference on Human Factors in Computing Systems*, New Orleans, LA, US.

Gentzkow, M. (2006). Television and voter turnout. *The Quarterly Journal of Economics, 121*(3), 931–972. doi:10.1162/qjec.121.3.931

Gerbner, G. (1998). Cultivation analysis: An overview. *Mass Communication and Society, 1*(3/4), 175–14. doi:10.1080/15205436.1998.9677855

Gerbner, G., & Gross, L. (1976). Living with television: The violence profile. *Journal of Communication, 26*(2), 172–194. doi:10.1111/j.1460–2466.1976.tb01397

Gil de Zúñiga, H., Garcia-Perdomo, V., & McGregor, S. C. (2015). What is second screening? Exploring motivations of second screen use and its effect on online political participation. *Journal of Communication, 65*(5), 793–815. doi:10.1111/jcom.12174

Gil de Zúñiga, H., Jung, N., & Valenzuela, S. (2012). Social media use for news and individuals' social capital, civic engagement and political participation. *Journal of Computer Mediated Communication, 17*(3), 319–336. doi:10.1111/j.1083–6101.2012.01574.x

Gil de Zúñiga, H., Molyneux, L., & Zheng, P. (2014). Social media, political expression, and political participation: Panel analysis of lagged and concurrent relationships. *Journal of Communication, 64*(4), 612–634. doi:10.1111/jcom.12103

Glaser, W. A. (1965). Television and voting turnout. *Public Opinion Quarterly, 29*(1), 71–86. doi:10.1086/267298

Graham, T. (2012). Beyond 'political' communicative spaces: Talking politics on the wife swap discussion forum. *Journal of Information Technology & Politics*, *9*(1), 31–45. doi:10.1080/19331681.2012.635961

Graham, T., & Hajru, A. (2011). Reality TV as a trigger of everyday political talk in the net based public sphere. *European Journal of Communication*, *26*(1), 18–32. doi:10.1177/0267323110394858

Groshek, J., & Krongard, S. (2016). Netflix and engage? Implications for streaming television on political participation during the 2016 US presidential campaign. *Social Sciences*, *5*(4), 65–74. doi:10.3390/socsci5040065

Habermas, J. (1962/1989). *The structural transformation of the public sphere*. (T. Burger, Trans.). Cambridge, MA: MIT Press.

HBO. (2016). HBO Now. Retrieved from https://order.hbonow.com/

Himelboim, I., Sweetser, K., Tinkham, S., Cameron, K., Danelo, M., & West, K. (2014). Valence-based homophily on Twitter: Network analysis of emotions and political talk in the 2012 presidential election. *New Media & Society*, *18*(7), 1382–1400. Retrieved from http://dx.doi.org/10.1177/1461444814555096

Julian, J. (2016). Facebook live and Periscope: Live streaming by the numbers. *Socialbakers.com*. Retrieved from www.socialbakers.com/blog/2642-facebook-live-and-periscope-live-streaming-by-the-numbers

Kirk, R., & Schill, D. (2011). A digital agora: Citizen participation in the 2008 presidential debates. *American Behavioral Scientist*, *55*(3), 325–347. doi:10.1177/0002764210392167

Klofstad, C. (2011). *Civic talk: Peers, politics, and the future of democracy*. Philadelphia, PA: Temple University Press.

Lotz, A. (2007). *The TV will be revolutionized*. New York, NY: New York University Press.

Mann, G., Venturini, F., Murdoch, R., Mishra, B., Moorby, G., & Carlier, B. (2015). Digital video and the connected consumer. *Accenture Report*. Retrieved from www.accenture.com/t20150914T152334__w__/us-en/_acnmedia/Accenture/Conversion-Assets/DotCom/Documents/Global/PDF/Dualpub_20/Accenture-Digital-Video-Connected-Consumer.pdf#zoom=50

McAlone, N. (2016). People became even more addicted to Netflix in 2015, according to Goldman Sachs. *Business Insider*. Retrieved from http://uk.businessinsider.com/subscribers-spent-more-time-per-person-watching-netflixin-2015-2016-1

McCoy, M. L., & Scully, P. L. (2002). Deliberative dialogue to expand civic engagement: What kind of talk does democracy need? *National Civic Review*, *91*(2), 117–135.

McCroskey, J. C. (1982). *An introduction to rhetorical communication* (4th ed.). Englewood Cliffs, NJ: Prentice-Hall.

Moy, P., Scheufele, D. A., & Holbert, R. L. (1999). Television use and social capital: Testing Putnam's time displacement hypothesis. *Mass Communication and Society*, *2*(1/2), 27–45. doi:10.1080/15205436.1999.9677860

Moy, P., Xenos, M. A., & Hess, V. K. (2005). Communication and citizenship: Mapping the political effects of infotainment. *Mass Communication & Society*, *8*(2), 111–131. doi:10.1207/s15327825mcs0802_3

NBC Universal. (2016). Seeso. Retrieved from www.nbcuniversal.com/business/seeso

Netflix. (2016). Overview. *Ir.netflix.com*. Retrieved from https://ir.netflix.com/

Nielsen Corporation. (2016a). The 2016 social media report. Retrieved from www.nielsen.com/us/en/insights/reports/2017/2016-nielsen-social-media-report.html

Nielsen Corporation. (2016b). The total audience report: Q1 2016. Retrieved from www.nielsen.com/us/en/insights/reports/2016/the-total-audience-report-q1-2016.html

Oldenburg, R. (1999). *The great good place: Cafes, coffee shops, bookstores, bars, hair salons, and other hangouts at the heart of a community*. Philadelphia, PA: Da Capo Press.

Papacharissi, Z. (2002). The virtual sphere: The Internet as a public sphere. *New Media & Society*, *4*(1), 9–27. doi:10.1177/14614440222226244

Papacharissi, Z. (2009). The virtual sphere 2.0: The Internet, the public sphere, and beyond. In A. Chadwick & P. N. Howard (Eds.), *Routledge handbook of internet politics* (pp. 230–245). New York, NY: Routledge.

Papacharissi, Z. (2015). *Affective publics: Sentiment, technology, and politics.* New York, NY: Oxford University Press.

Perez, S. (2016). Hulu grows to 12 million subscribers, prepares new interactive ads for living room TVs. *TechCrunch.* Retrieved from https://techcrunch.com/2016/05/04/hulu-grows-to-12-million-subscribers-prepares-new-interactive-ads-for-living-room-tvs/

Postman, N. (1985). *Amusing ourselves to death: Public discourse in the age of television.* New York, NY: Viking.

Putnam, R. D. (1995). Bowling alone: America's declining social capital. *Journal of Democracy*, *6*(1), 65–78. doi:10.1353/jod.1995.0002

Putnam, R. D. (2000). *Bowling alone: The collapse and revival of American community.* New York, NY: Simon and Schuster.

Rainie, L., & Smith, A. (2012). Social networking sites and politics. *Pew Research Center.* Retrieved from www.pewinternet.org/files/oldmedia/Files/Reports/2012/PIP_PoliticalLifeonSocialNetworkingSites.pdf

Selva, D. (2016). Social television audience and political engagement. *Television & New Media*, *17*(2), 159–173. doi:10.1177/1527476415616192

Shah, D. V. (1998). Civic engagement, interpersonal trust, and television use: An individual level assessment of social capital. *Political Psychology*, *19*(3), 469–496. doi:10.1111/0162–895X.00114

Shi, A. (2016). Amazon Prime members now outnumber non-prime customers. *Fortune.* Retrieved from http://fortune.com/2016/07/11/amazon-primecustomers/

Simon, J. (1996). Media use and voter turnout in a presidential election. *Newspaper Research Journal*, *17*(1/2), 25–34.

Spangler, T. (2015, June 30). Binge-viewing is becoming a less shameful activity: Survey. *Variety.* Retrieved from http://variety.com/2015/digital/news/binge-viewing-tivo-survey-1201531441/

Street, J., Inthorn, S., & Scott, M. (2012). Playing at politics? Popular culture as political engagement. *Parliamentary Affairs*, *65*(2), 338–358. doi:10.1093/pa/gsr037

Uslaner, E. (1998). Social capital, television, and the 'mean world': Trust, optimism, and civic participation. *Political Psychology*, *19*(3), 441–467. doi:10.1111/0162–895x.00113

van Dijck, J., & Poell, T. (2013). Understanding social media logic. *Media and Communication*, *1*(1), 2–14. Retrieved from https://ssrn.com/abstract=2309065

van Zoonen, L. (2004). Imagining the fan democracy. *European Journal of Communication*, *19*(1), 39–52. doi:10.1177/0267323104040693

Vitak, J., Zube, P., Smock, A., Carr, C. T., Ellison, N., & Lampe, C. (2011). It's complicated: Facebook users' political participation in the 2008 election. *CyberPsychology, Behavior, and Social Networking*, *14*(3), 107–114. doi:10.1089/cyber.2009.0226

Walsh, K. (2004). *Talking about politics.* Chicago, IL: University of Chicago Press.

Weaver, D., & Drew, D. (2001). Voter learning and interest in the 2000 presidential election: Did the media matter? *Journalism & Mass Communication Quarterly*, *78*(4), 787–798. doi:10.1177/107769900107800411

Wright, S. (2012). From 'third place' to 'third space': Everyday political talk in non-political online spaces. *Javnost: The Public*, *19*(3), 5–20. doi:10.1080/13183222.2012.11009088

YouTube. (2017). Statistics—YouTube. Retrieved from www.youtube.com/yt/press/statistics.html

PART 3

Candidate Discourse in Social Media

Image, Tone, and Rhetoric

8

THE VERBAL TONE OF THE 2016 PRESIDENTIAL PRIMARIES

Candidate Twitter, Debate, and Campaign Speech Rhetoric

David Lynn Painter and Katherine Rizzo

U.S. presidential candidates have been using campaign websites since 1996 and social-networking sites since 2004, but little research has compared the content of these candidates' online messages to the content of their messages on other channels. Although the relatively recent development and rapid adoption of Internet technologies and social media may explain this lack of analyses, the power of social media to set the agenda for both other media outlets and the public continues to increase (Conway, Kenski, & Wang, 2015; Kiousis, Mitrook, Wu, & Seltzer, 2006; Meraz, 2009; Pallotta, 2016). Similarly, political communication researchers have also generally overlooked primary contests (but see Benoit et al., 2013; Pollard, Chesebro, & Studinski, 2009), focusing instead on general-election presidential campaigns. This lack of research on primary campaign rhetoric persists despite the lengthening of the electoral cycle and the attendant growth in campaign budgets and debate schedules. In addition to determining the major party nominees, U.S. presidential primary contests may also shape voters' perceptions of and attitudes toward those candidates (Painter, 2013). Moreover, U.S. presidential primaries are intra-party contests wherein the candidates' rhetoric targets partisan audiences, unlike general-election campaign rhetoric generally designed to appeal to the median voter, creating the optimal context for exploring differences between Republican and Democratic candidates' rhetoric across a variety of communication channels. Thus, this investigation finds its place in the literature by using DICTION®, a computer-assisted text analysis software, to analyze the main and interaction effects of candidate partisanship (Republican and Democratic) and media channel (Twitter, televised debates, and speeches) on the 2016 U.S. presidential primary candidates' verbal tone.

Verbal Tone of Political Campaign Rhetoric: Partisanship Effects

Traditionally, political communication scholars have analyzed campaign messages in speeches, debates, ads, and online content by categorizing their tone as either positive, negative, or mixed/contrast, and by categorizing their content as focused on either issues (policies) or image (character) traits. Similarly, most analyses of social media and user-generated online content center on the valence of the sentiment expressed in the posts, failing to provide more than the messages' directionality or relevance to a particular aspect of a brand, product, or service (Cambria, Schuller, Xia, & Havasi, 2013; Gayo-Avello, Metaxas, & Mustafaraj, 2011). Although some content analyses used Videostyle and Webstyle protocols that provided more robust and nuanced findings than previous studies or sentiment analyses, they still relied on human coders with their attendant limitations (Banwart, 2002; Bystrom, Robertson, Banwart, & Kaid, 2004; Johnston & Kaid, 2002; Kaid & Davidson, 1986; Kaid & Johnston, 2001).

Alternately, Hart and colleagues (Hart, 2000; Hart & Childers, 2004; Hart, Childers, & Lind, 2013) created DICTION® software to describe the verbal tone of 30,000 political communication documents with a particular focus on general-election presidential campaigns from 1960 to 2008. DICTION® searches texts for 10,000 terms, sorts them into 33 dictionaries or categories, calculates Insistence, or word repetition, Variety, or the number of different words divided by the total number of words, and Complexity, or the average number of characters per word (see Table 8.1). DICTION® also calculates five master variables

TABLE 8.1 DICTION® Dictionary Classifications and Descriptions

Verbal Variable	*Description (Hart, 2000)*
Numerical Terms	Dates, integers, quantitative topics, numerical operations
Ambivalence	Uncertainty, restraint, hedges, inexactness
Self-Reference	All first-person references
Tenacity	All uses of the verb "to be" and its variants
Leveling Terms	Totalizing (everyone), permanence (always), and absolute terms
Collectives	Social (crowd), task (army), and geographical (world) group terms
Praise	Affirmations of social, physical, intellectual, or other positive qualities
Satisfaction	Positive affective states, joy, pleasure, and diversions
Inspiration	Positive, moral, attractive, physical, and idealistic political terms
Blame	Social inappropriateness, evil, unfortunate circumstances (bankrupt)
Hardship	Natural disasters, hostility, immoral behavior, fears, and incapacities
Aggression	Physical energy, social domination, triumph, and resistance (defend)
Communication	Social interactions, participants, purposes (rebuke), and media (television)

Verbal Variable	*Description (Hart, 2000)*
Cognition	Discovery modes (learn), studies (biology), reasoning, and calculating terms
Passivity	Compliance, docility, cessation, inertness, and tranquility terms
Spatial Terms	Geographical entities, physical distances, and modes of measurement
Familiarity	Prepositions (across), demonstrative & interrogative pronouns (that, what)
Temporal Terms	Literal (minute) and metaphorical (seniority) time references
Present Concern	Physical activity (take), social operations (govern), and task (make) terms
Human Interest	Personal pronouns (them), family relations, and generic (baby) terms
Concreteness	Sociological groups, physical structures, material and tangible terms
Past Concern	Past tense form of words in Present Concern dictionary
Centrality	Agreement on substantive values (decorum, reliable, conformity)
Rapport	Attitudinal similarities, affinity, assent, deference, and identity (consensus)
Cooperation	Associations (union, friend), sharing, exchange, and altruistic terms
Diversity	Terms denoting heterogeneity (nonconformist, unique, dispersed)
Exclusion	Sources and effects of social isolation (displaced, private, lonely)
Liberation	Maximizing individual choice and rejecting social conventions
Denial	Negative contractions (won't), function words (not), and null sets (none)
Motion	Movement, journeys, speed, and modes of transport terms
Accomplishment	Task completion (finish) and organized behavior (manage) terms
Embellishment	Score = ratio of adjectives to verbs devised by Broder (1940)
Variety	Score = number of different words used divided by total number of words
Complexity	Score = average number of characters per word in input text
Insistence	Score = number of words repeated 3 or more times divided by 0

(see Figure 8.1) to estimate the text's verbal tone. The five master variables include: Certainty, or words indicating resoluteness, inflexibility, and completeness, and a tendency to speak ex-cathedra. Activity is language featuring movement, change, the implementation of ideas, and the avoidance of inertia. Optimism refers to language endorsing some person, group, concept, or event, or highlighting their positive entailments. Realism denotes language describing tangible, immediate, recognizable matters that affect people's everyday lives. Commonality refers to language emphasizing the agreed-upon values of a group and rejecting idiosyncratic modes of engagement. Based on the works of semanticists, linguists, rhetorical critics, political scientists, philosophy and psychology scholars, these master variables were chosen because they answer the five most informative questions one may ask about any text (Hart, Childers, & Lind, 2013). Although there are other text analysis computational tools available, none employs such

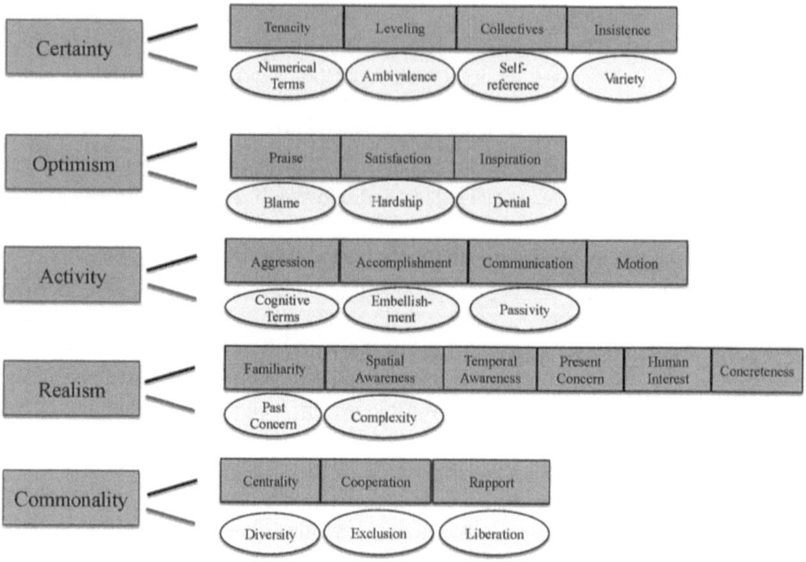

FIGURE 8.1 DICTION® Variable Structure

Source: Adapted from Hart (2000). Oval variable scores are subtracted from rectangular variable scores to construct master variable scores.

exhaustive lists of search terms or is more informative or efficient than DICTION®, which analyzes texts in mere seconds that would take human coders months to complete. Finally, not only will DICTION® track things that the human brain cannot consistently detect, such as frequencies and patterns of word choices, but it also will categorize language patterns in terms signifying their cultural significance (Hart, 2000).

Hart et al. (2013) suggest "tone is the product of (1) individual word choices that (2) cumulatively build up (3) to produce patterned expectations (4) telling an audience something important (5) about the author's outlook on things" (p. 12). They assert that verbal tone is "a tool people use (sometimes unwittingly) to create distinct social impressions via word choice" (p. 9), and that words and patterns of word choice are important and meaningful areas of study. Moreover, Hart and Childers (2004) contend:

> (1) people have scant ability to monitor their individual language decisions; (2) people have no ability to monitor their patterns of word choice; (3) people think they have considerable control over such matters; and therefore, (4) they invite the enterprising researcher to study that which they deem unworthy of study.
>
> *(p. 35)*

This approach is particularly relevant in political communication cases, where campaign communication operatives practice their wordsmith craft whereas journalists and voters parse every statement uttered. Last, Hart and Childers (2004) argue election campaigns serve renewal, centripetal, immediacy, and dialectic functions in U.S. society. These functions re-engage incumbents with the voters, spin rhetorical outliers out of the race, make candidates' thoughts and words "crisper and more pungent" (p. 79), and sharpen the differences between the political parties. No prior research has analyzed the verbal tone of Republican and Democratic presidential primary candidates' rhetoric, but scholars have found partisan differences in verbal tone among general-election candidates (Ballotti & Kaid, 2000; Hart, 2000; Hart & Childers, 2004; Hart et al., 2013). Thus, our first research question asks:

RQ1: How does candidate partisanship influence the verbal tone of the 2016 presidential candidates' rhetoric?

Social Media and Channel Effects

Previous research analyzed political campaigns' uses of websites and blogs (Baker & Stromer-Galley, 2006; Kruikemeier, Aparaschivei, Boomgaarden, Van Noort, & Vliegenthart, 2015; Stromer-Galley, 2000), Facebook (Sweetser & Lariscy, 2008; Williams & Gulati, 2012), Twitter (Adams & McCorkindale, 2013; Graham, Broersma, Hazelhoff, & van't Haar, 2013; Kruikemeier, 2014), and YouTube (Lev-On, 2012). This investigation, on the other hand, compares the verbal tone of the 2016 U.S. presidential primary candidates' tweets, debate comments, and speeches. Based on McLuhan's (1964) famous assertion that the "medium is the message," prior research suggests identical information presented on different media channels may exert different effects on viewers and receivers (Kaid, 2002; McKinnon, Tedesco, & Kaid, 1993). These studies focused on the effects of identical information presented on television or the Internet, but little research has compared the content or verbal tone of political messages across media channels, and none has focused on social media. Grounded in Hart et al.'s (2013) contention that institutional factors, personal characteristics, and contextual forces shape verbal tone, this investigation expects to find significant differences across media channels.

When considering the nature of the media in this study, it is clear that the structure, format, and capabilities of each platform will shape the message. First, the debates are live television events requiring candidates to formulate their responses in a more immediate manner than their tweets or campaign speeches, which may be written by campaign operatives and undergo a formal review process. Second, campaign speeches are more scripted than debates and are generally presented to largely supportive, face-to-face audiences, or they are focused on specific issues or events designed for the candidates to present their views. Third, Twitter is a micro-blogging social network site that limits content to 140-character tweets and, as with other social network sites, the posts are public, but are usually directed at followers, who are typically supporters or at least interested in the candidates' campaign. Additionally, much of the news media's coverage of the 2016 presidential primary campaign news focused on the candidates' tweets and interactions as well as user-generated Twitter content and trending topics. Although not all of the candidates may have created all the content posted on their Twitter accounts, it is important to remember that presidential campaigns employ a broad range of professionals to craft their branding messages by writing speeches, preparing and rehearsing debate comments, and posting social media content. Because contemporary presidential campaigns are largely engaged in branding operations, not interpersonal communications, all their messages are strategically planned to achieve specific outcomes (Levenshus, 2010).

Beyond the structure, format, and capabilities of each platform, televised debates were chosen for comparison to Twitter messages and campaign speeches because debates represent moments when the public is actively paying attention to politics (Delli Carpini & Keeter, 1996; O'Connor, 2016). Indeed, interest in the 2016 primary debates was evident in the increased viewership during the current cycle: the most popular Democratic primary debate in 2015 had 50% more viewers than the most watched Democratic primary debate in 2008 (CNN, 2015; Slack, 2016). Alternately, the Republican primary debates attracted up to 24 million viewers and are some of the most watched primary debates in history (Slack, 2016). The increased salience and influence of the debates make them an important topic for analysis, allowing us to compare the language of social media to a debate where all leading candidates have the opportunity to present their views and differentiate themselves from each other in a live, immediate setting. In contrast to televised debates or tweets, campaign speeches represent the most traditional form of political campaign communication. Historically, presidential candidates have traveled the country and given speeches at political rallies and other events to crowds of citizen supporters. Traditionally, most of the content of these speeches remained unmediated because the news media only provided soundbites or quotes of the candidates' rhetoric. Today, however, some cable television channels and online platforms broadcast or publish these speeches to wider audiences. Nevertheless, the context and setting for these speeches are much different from those of Twitter and televised debates because the candidates are addressing a live, face-to-face (versus social media or television) audience that provides powerful and immediate feedback, and they are not sharing the stage with their opponents. Thus, our second research question asks:

> RQ2: How does the communication channel influence the verbal tone of the 2016 presidential primary candidates' rhetoric?

Finally, based on the theories underpinning the expectations of main effects from the candidates' partisanship and the media channel on the verbal tone of the 2016 presidential primary candidates' rhetoric, we ask:

> RQ3: How do the interactions between candidate partisanship and communication channel influence the verbal tone of the 2016 presidential primary candidates' rhetoric?

Method

Sample

To answer the research questions, we used DICTION® software to conduct a quantitative content analysis of the verbal tone of the 2016 U.S. presidential primary candidates' tweets, debate comments, and speeches. Although there were 17 Republican and six Democratic candidates at the beginning of the 2016 primaries, many of these candidates appeared in under-card or a limited number of debates, suspended their campaigns early, and/or failed to post content to Twitter or make speeches at rates comparable to the other candidates. Thus, we limited our analysis to the top Republican and Democratic Party candidates based on popular vote totals and campaign longevity to include: Hillary Clinton (D), Bernie Sanders (D), Donald Trump (R), Ted Cruz (R), John Kasich (R), and Marco Rubio (R).

Data

Twitter

To access the tweets, we used the Twitter Data Collection and Analysis tool on the Data-driven Computational Social Science (DD-CSS) website to download the candidates' Twitter posts over the course of the primary campaign. The candidates' tweets were aggregated from the date of their official announcement to the date they suspended their campaign, or through June 7, the date of the last 2016 primary for Clinton, Sanders, and Trump. Once the tweets were downloaded, they were edited to remove the Uniform Resource Locators (URLs) and prepared for DICTION® software analysis by month and candidate.

Debates

Transcripts of the 12 Republican and nine Democratic debates were retrieved from The American Presidency Project website, separated by candidate and debate.

Speeches

The transcripts of the candidates' speeches at the Iowa caucuses, the New Hampshire, Super Tuesday, and the Southeastern Super Tuesday primaries, as well as their official foreign policy, economic, and AIPAC remarks were accessed from either the candidates' websites, *TIME*'s website, or the Council on Foreign Relations website.

Coding Process

Categories

Once the Twitter, debate, and speech transcripts were gathered and prepared, they were analyzed by DICTION® software, a computer-assisted text analysis (CATA) program that searches for more than 10,000 words, sorts them into 35 categories (see Table 8.1), and calculates five master variables (see Figure 8.1). Hart (2000) explicates the theoretical and rhetorical underpinnings for each variable and demonstrated by analyzing a 20,000-item sample of contemporary discourse that there is no statistical relationship or repetition among any of the dictionaries, classifications, or master variables.

Units of Analysis

DICTION® calculates mean scores on each dictionary, category, and variable from 500-word segments of each text: the candidate's monthly tweets, comments in each debate, and speeches. There was a total of 7,793 units of analysis: 4,322 in the candidates' tweets, 2,587 in their debate comments, and 884 in their speeches; 5,350 for Republican candidates and 2,443 for Democratic candidates.

Results

The first research question asked: How does candidate partisanship influence the verbal tone of the 2016 presidential candidates' rhetoric? To answer this question, we performed an analysis of variance (ANOVA) test with DICTION®'s five master variables as dependent variables and political party as the independent variable. As shown in Table 8.2, the results indicated there was a main effect of partisanship because Republican candidates' rhetoric (M = 51.63, SD = 2.54) contained significantly more terms denoting Optimism than did the Democratic candidates' rhetoric (M = 50.12, SD = 2.08), $F(1, 186) = 15.78$, $p < .001$, $\eta^2 = .078$.

The second research question asked: How does the communication channel influence the verbal tone of the 2016 presidential primary candidates' rhetoric? To answer this question, we performed an ANOVA test with DICTION®'s

TABLE 8.2 Mean Verbal Tone Scores by Political Party

	GOP (n = *5350)*	*DEM* (n = *2443)*	F	p	ηp^2
Certainty	48.44 (3.19)	48.37 (2.87)	.736	.114	.001
Optimism	51.63 (2.54)	50.12 (2.08)	17.66	.000	.088
Realism	49.53 (3.62)	50.38 (2.09)	3.43	.066	.018
Commonality	50.20 (1.84)	50.48 (1.67)	1.45	.230	.008
Activity	50.10 (3.74)	50.43 (2.13)	0.032	.857	.000

Notes: Values in parentheses represent standard deviations.

TABLE 8.3 Mean Verbal Tone Scores by Channel

	TWITTER (n = *4322)*	*DEBATES* (n = *2587)*	*SPEECHES* (n = *884)*	F	p	ηp^2
Certainty[a]	46.34 (2.61)	50.57 (2.34)	48.66 (2.55)	38.62	.000	.298
Optimism[b,d]	52.03 (2.77)	50.11 (2.02)	51.28 (2.15)	4.34	.014	.046
Realism[b,c]	47.50[b] (2.84)	50.94 (2.07)	51.76 (3.03)	33.10	.000	.267
Commonality[a,b]	50.85 (1.67)	49.82 (1.76)	50.05 (1.80)	3.68	.027	.039
Activity	50.06 (4.45)	50.21 (2.26)	50.40 (2.48)	0.82	.921	.001

Notes: Values in parentheses represent standard deviations.
Adjustment for multiple comparisons: Bonferroni.
[a] Twitter, Debate, and Speech values are significantly different from each other, $p < .01$
[b] Twitter and Debate values are significantly different, $p < .01$
[c] Twitter and Speech values are significantly different, $p < .01$
[d] Debate and Speech values are significantly different, $p < .01$

five master variables as dependent variables and communication channel as the independent variable. As shown in Table 8.3, the results indicated there was a main effect of channel on Optimism, $F(2, 185) = 11.54$, $p < .05$, $\eta^2 = .046$; Realism, $F(2, 185) = 33.01$, $p < .01$, $\eta^2 = .267$; Certainty, F (2, 185) = 38.62, $p < .01$, $\eta^2 = .298$; and Commonality, F (2, 185) = 3.68, $p < .05$, $\eta^2 = .039$; but not on Activity, $p > .05$. Not only were the mean scores on these variables significantly different across all three outlets, but the results of post-hoc testing using Bonferroni's adjustment revealed there were significant differences between specific media as well. First, the candidates' tweets (*M* = 52.03, *SD* = 2.77) contained more Optimism than their debate comments (*M* = 50.11, *SD* = 2.02) or speeches (*M* = 51.28, *SD* = 2.15). Second, the candidates' tweets (*M* = 50.85, *SD* = 1.67) contained significantly less Realism than did their debate comments (*M* = 49.82, *SD* = 1.76) or speeches (*M* = 50.70, *SD* = 1.80). Third, the candidates' tweets (*M* = 46.35, *SD* = 2.61) contained significantly fewer words denoting Certainty than did their debate comments (*M* = 50.57, *SD* = 2.34) or speeches (*M* = 48.66, *SD* = 2.54). Fourth, the candidates' debate comments contained significantly more Certainty than did their speeches. And fifth, the candidates' tweets (*M* = 50.85, *SD* = 1.67) contained significantly more words denoting Commonality than did their debate comments (*M* = 49.82, *SD* = 1.76) or speeches (*M* = 50.05, *SD* = 1.80).

The third research question asked: How do the interactions between candidate partisanship and communication channel influence the verbal tone of the 2016 presidential primary candidates' rhetoric? As shown in Table 8.4, the results of a Multivariate Analysis of Variance (MANOVA) revealed a significant interaction effect on Optimism, $F(2, 182) = 19.29$, $p < .01$, $\eta^2 = .175$, and Realism, $F(2, 182) = 10.40$, $p < .01$, $\eta^2 = .10$. The interaction effect on Optimism indicated that whereas Twitter is generally more optimistic than debates, the Republican candidates' tweets were significantly more optimistic than the Democratic candidates' tweets. When examining the differences in Optimism among the candidates' tweets, the results of an analysis of variance test using Bonferroni's

TABLE 8.4 Mean Verbal Tone Variable Scores by Medium and Political Party

	Twitter		*Debates*		*Speeches*	
	GOP (n =*2940)*	*DEM* (n =*1382)*	*GOP* (n = *1824)*	*DEM* (n = *763)*	*GOP* (n = *586)*	*DEM* (n = *298)*
Certainty	46.17	46.69	50.66	50.32	48.59	48.82
	(2.77)	(2.28)	(2.32)	(2.43)	(2.50)	(2.72)
Optimism*	53.34**	49.47	49.89	50.70	51.64	50.50
	(1.97)	(2.28)	(1.99)	(2.02)	(2.30)	(1.57)
Realism*	46.43**	49.60	51.08	50.56	51.89	51.74
	(2.44)	(2.40)	(2.22)	(1.63)	(3.52)	(1.52)
Commonality	50.10	50.56	49.69	50.18	49.75	50.70
	(1.65)	(1.69)	(1.67)	(1.99)	(1.96)	(1.17)
Activity	49.43	51.28	50.31	49.94	50.77	49.58
	(5.23)	(1.79)	(2.28)	(2.14)	(2.53)	(2.23)

Notes: Values in parentheses represent standard deviations.

*Interaction effect significant, $p < .01$

**Simple effects tests indicate score is significantly different from others in row, $p < .01$

adjustment in a post-hoc test indicated that Sanders's tweets (M = 47.69, SD = 1.56) were significantly less optimistic than Clinton's (M = 51.41, SD = 0.94), Trump's (M = 54.07, SD = 2.08), Cruz's (M = 52.72, SD = 0.56), Kasich's (M = 52.05, SD = 1.95), or Rubio's (M = 54.27, SD = 2.33) tweets, largely driving this interaction effect, $F(5, 68) = 27.11, p < .01, \eta^2 = .642$.

The interaction effect on Realism, on the other hand, indicated that whereas Twitter generally contained significantly less Realism than debates or speeches, the Republican candidates' tweets contained significantly less Realism than the Democratic candidates' tweets and were responsible for this interaction effect. The results of an analysis of variance test using Bonferroni's adjustment in a post-hoc test indicated that Trump's tweets (M = 45.48, SD = 3.31) contained significantly fewer words denoting Realism than did Clinton's (M = 48.49, SD = 1.33), Sander's (M = 50.63, SD = 2.75), or Rubio's (M = 48.76, SD = 1.60), but not Cruz's (M = 45.31, SD = 0.88) or Kasich's (M = 46.17, SD = 1.67) tweets, largely driving this effect $F(5, 68) = 13.67, p < .01, \eta^2 = .465$.

Discussion

Based on the premise that words have meanings that can be classified into rhetorical dictionaries, the results of this computer-assisted text analysis provide a compelling, quantitative basis for describing, comparing, and drawing inferences about the verbal tone and rhetorical style of the 2016 U.S. presidential primary candidates. Additionally, this investigation is the first data-driven attempt to describe the verbal style of any social media content or that of U.S. presidential primary campaigns, analyzing 3.9 million words, or more than 15,500 pages of text using DICTION® software. Finally, this analysis allows us to describe the main and interaction effects of candidate partisanship and communication channel on the 2016 U.S. presidential primary candidates' verbal tone.

Specifically, the results suggest candidate partisanship and communication channel significantly influenced the content and tone of the rhetoric in the 2016 U.S. presidential primaries. The results of this analysis indicate there was a main effect of partisanship on the candidates' verbal tone because Republican candidates' rhetoric contained significantly more Optimism than the Democratic candidates' rhetoric, accounting for 8.8% of the variance. The results also suggest there was a main effect of communication channel on the candidates' verbal tone because their tweets contained significantly more words denoting Optimism and Commonality, but significantly fewer words denoting Realism and Certainty than did their debate comments or speeches. In fact, the analysis indicated that communication channel accounted for 4.6% of the variance in Optimism, 26.7% of the variance in Realism, 29.8% of the variance in Certainty, and 3.9% of the variance in Commonality. Finally, the results indicated the interaction between candidate partisanship and communication channel significantly influenced two aspects of the candidates' verbal tone. First, whereas Twitter generally contains more Optimism than debates or speeches, the Republican candidates' tweets contained significantly more Optimism than the Democratic candidates' tweets, mainly due to the pessimism of Bernie Sanders's (D) tweets. Second, whereas Twitter generally contained significantly less Realism than debates or speeches, the Republican candidates' tweets, and especially Donald Trump's tweets, contained significantly less Realism than did the Democratic candidates' tweets, largely driving this effect. Specifically, the interaction between candidate partisanship and communication channel accounted for 17.5% of the variance in Optimism and 10.3% of the variance in Realism.

When examining the influence of candidate partisanship on the verbal tone of the 2016 U.S. presidential primaries, the finding that the Republican candidates' rhetoric contained more Optimism than did that of the Democratic candidates runs counter to previous research suggesting the rhetoric from challenging party candidates generally contains more Optimism than does that from candidates in the incumbent party (Hart & Childers, 2004). That said, the effects of the interaction between candidate partisanship and communication channel indicate the difference in Optimism scores between the political parties was largely due to lack of Optimism in Bernie Sanders's rhetoric. Indeed, as a Democratic Socialist, Sanders repeatedly called for a revolution due to his dire view of the current system, and his campaign may have functioned as a social movement as much as a campaign for the U.S. presidency during the 2016 primaries (Horsey, 2016). When Sanders's campaign is considered more of an insurgent social movement, the lack of Optimism in his rhetoric is in line with previous research indicating social activists' rhetoric generally contains much less Optimism than does that of politicians (Hart & Childers, 2004).

When exploring the influence of communication channel on the candidates' verbal tone, it is intuitive that their tweets contained more Optimism than their debate comments or speeches because Optimism refers to language endorsing some person, group, concept, or event, or highlighting their positive entailments. That is, much Twitter content is purposely crafted to endorse, retweet, or highlight one's own or another's action, or words. Although some Twitter rhetoric is extremely adversarial, most candidates' tweets are directed at their followers or supporters and are designed to promote their common cause. Similarly, it is also not surprising that the candidates' tweets contained more Commonality and less Realism or Certainty than did their debate comments or speeches because much of their Twitter content focuses on promoting themselves, their supporters, and their shared values, goals, and bonds, not on the tangible, immediate, recognizable matters that affect people's everyday lives. Finally, the finding that the interaction between candidate partisanship and communication channel resulted in the Republican candidates' tweets, and especially those of Donald Trump, containing much less Realism than the Democratic candidates' tweets, is in line with previous research suggesting that Republicans' rhetoric generally focuses more on principles and ideals, not on particularities (Hart & Childers, 2004).

Hart and Childers (2004) extend Weaver's (1948, 1953) contention that conservatives argue from definition and that liberals argue from circumstance. The results of Hart's and Childers's (2004) analysis indicates Republican rhetoric is idealistic and "emboldened by some grand vision, some grand adventure, some grand idea" (p. 162); whereas "Democrats produce a rhetoric of narrative, a rhetoric grounded in the lived moment, in people's experiences" (p. 164). More specifically, Donald Trump's rhetoric was especially vague in terms of policy details, and it was fueled by his use of hyperbole. Although these types of emotional appeals may lack Realism, Aristotle explained in *Rhetoric* (trans. 1954, III) that hyperboles are effective because they "show vehemence of character. And besides, an emotional speaker always makes his audience feel with him, even when there is nothing in his arguments; which is why many speakers try to overwhelm their audience by mere noise" (p. 141). Moreover, the effects of fact-checkers or analysts who identity the lack of substance or the fallacies in the rhetoric are nullified among those with whom Trump's rhetoric resonates because the hyperbole, by definition, is an exaggeration not meant to be taken literally.

Finally, in theoretical terms, these findings provide compelling evidence that the 2016 presidential primary campaigns served immediacy and dialectic functions, sharpening differences between the political parties and bringing a sense of urgency to the elections. Regarding the centripetal function, however, the 2016 U.S. presidential primaries rewarded one of the outliers in verbal style, as Donald Trump's rhetoric was exceptionally low on Realism, yet he won the Republican nomination and eventually the U.S. presidency. Indeed, a large segment of the U.S. electorate appeared to be in open rebellion against "politics as usual" as well as political correctness and its more moderate tone, which may have been key factors in Trump's win (Tumulty & Johnson, 2016).

References

Adams, A., & McCorkindale, T. (2013). Dialogue and transparency: A content analysis of how the 2012 presidential candidates used Twitter. *Public Relations Review*, *39*, 357–359. doi:10.1016/j.pubrev.2013.07.016

Baker, A., & Stromer-Galley, J. (2006). Joy and sorrow on interactivity on the campaign trail: Blogs in the primary campaign of Howard Dean. In A. Williams & J. Tedesco (Eds.), *Internet election* (pp. 111–131). Lanham, MD: Rowman and Littlefield.

Ballotti, J., & Kaid, L. L. (2000). Examining verbal style in presidential campaign spots. *Communication Studies*, *51*(3), 258–273. doi:10.1080/10510970009388523

Banwart, M. C. (2002). *Videostyle and webstyle in 2000: Comparing the gender differences of candidate presentations in political advertising and on the Internet* (Unpublished doctoral dissertation). Retrieved from https://shareok.org/handle/11244/464

Benoit, W. L., Henson, J., Davis, C., Glantz, M., Phillips, A., & Rill, L. (2013). Stumping on the Internet: 2008 presidential primary candidate campaign webpages. *Human Communication*, *16*, 1–12.

Bystrom, D. G., Robertson, T., Banwart, M. C., & Kaid, L. L. (Eds.). (2004). *Gender and candidate communication: Videostyle, webstyle, newstyle.* New York, NY: Routledge.
Cambria, E., Schuller, B., Xia, Y., & Havasi, C. (2013). New avenues in opinion mining and sentiment analysis. *IEEE Intelligent Systems, 28*(2), 15–21. doi:10.1109/mis.2013.30
CNN. (2015, December 16). CNN Debate was third most watched debate ever. *CNN.* Retrieved from http://cnnpressroom.blogs.cnn.com/2015/12/16/cnn-debate-was-third-most-watched-debate-ever/
Conway, B. A., Kenski, K., & Wang, D. (2015). The rise of Twitter in the political campaign: Searching for intermedia agenda-setting effects in the presidential primary. *Journal of Computer-Mediated Communication, 20,* 363–380. doi:10.1111/jcc4.12124
Delli Carpini, M. X., & Keeter, S. (1996). *What Americans know about politics and why it matters.* New Haven, CT: Yale University Press.
Gayo-Avello, D., Metaxas, P. T., & Mustafaraj, E. (2011). Limits of electoral predictions using Twitter. *Proceedings of the Fifth International AAAI Conference on Weblogs and Social Media.* Retrieved from www.aaai.org/ocs/index.php/ICWSM/ICWSM11/paper/view/2862
Graham, T., Broersma, M., Hazelhoff, K., & van't Haar, G. (2013). Between broadcasting political messages and interacting with voters. *Information, Communication, & Society, 16*(5), 692–716. doi:10.1080/1369118x.2013.785581
Hart, R. (2000). *Campaign talk: Why elections are good for us.* Princeton, NJ: Princeton University Press.
Hart, R., & Childers, J. P. (2004). Verbal certainty in American politics: An overview and extension. *Presidential Studies Quarterly, 34*(3), 516–535.
Hart, R., Childers, J. P., & Lind, C. J. (2013). *Political tone: How leaders talk and why.* Chicago, IL: University of Chicago Press.
Horsey, D. (2016, May 31). Bernie Sanders' sober social activism wins him fans in California. *Los Angeles Times.* Retrieved from www.latimes.com/opinion/topoftheticket/la-na-tt-bernie-activism-20160531-snap-story.html
Johnston, A., & Kaid, L. L. (2002). Image ads and issue ads in US presidential advertising: Using videostyle to explore stylistic differences in televised political ads from 1952 to 2000. *Journal of Communication, 52*(2), 281–300. doi:10.1093/joc/52.2.281
Kaid, L. L. (2002). Political advertising and information seeking: Comparing the exposure via traditional and Internet media channels. *Journal of Advertising, 31,* 27–35. doi:10.1080/00913367.2002.10673658
Kaid, L. L., & Davidson, D. K. (1986). Elements of videostyle: Candidate presentation through television advertising. In L. L. Kaid, D. Nimmo & K. R. Sanders (Eds.), *New perspectives on political advertising* (pp. 184–209). Carbondale, IL: Southern Illinois University Press.
Kaid, L. L., & Johnston, A. (2001). *Videostyle in presidential campaigns: Style and content of televised political advertising.* New York, NY: Greenwood Publishing Group.
Kiousis, S., Mitrook, M., Wu, X., & Seltzer, T. (2006). First- and second-level agenda-building and agenda-setting effects: Exploring the linkages among candidate news releases, media coverage, and public opinion during the 2002 Florida gubernatorial election. *Journal of Public Relations Research, 18,* 265–285. doi:10.1207/s1532754xjprr1803_4
Kruikemeier, S. (2014). How political candidates use Twitter and the impact on votes. *Computers in Human Behavior, 34,* 131–139. doi:10.1016/j.chb.2014.01.025
Kruikemeier, S., Aparaschivei, A. P., Boomgaarden, H. G., van Noort, G., & Vliegenthart, R. (2015). Party and candidate websites: A comparative explanatory analysis. *Mass Communication & Society, 18*(6), 821–850.

Levenshus, A. (2010). Online relationship management in a presidential campaign: A case study of the Obama campaign's management of its Internet-integrated grassroots effort. *Journal of Public Relations Research, 22*(3), 313–335.

Lev-On, A. (2012). YouTube usage in low-visibility political campaigns. *Journal of Information Technology & Politics, 9*(2), 205–216. doi:10.1080/19331681.2011.645360

McKinnon, L. M., Tedesco, J. C., & Kaid, L. L. (1993). The third 1992 presidential debate: Channel and commentary effects. *Argumentation and Advocacy, 30*, 106–118.

McLuhan, M. (1964). *Understanding media.* New York, NY: New American Library.

Meraz, S. (2009). Is there an elite hold? Traditional media to social media agenda setting influence in blog networks. *Journal of Computer-Mediated Communication, 14*, 682–707.

O'Connor, P. (2016, January 20). Republican race gets more attention than democratic primary. *Wall Street Journal.* Retrieved from www.wsj.com/articles/republican-race-gets-more-attention-than-democratic-primary-1453159834

Painter, D. L. (2013). Collateral damage: Involvement and the effects of negative super PAC advertising. *American Behavioral Scientist, 58*(4), 510–523. doi:10.1177/0002764213506210

Pallotta, F. (2016, January 28). Donald Trump vs. Fox News: Timeline of a war of words. *CNN Money.* Retrieved from http://money.cnn.com/2016/01/28/media/donald-trump-fox-news-war-timeline/

Pollard, T. D., Chesebro, J. W., & Studinski, D. P. (2009). The role of the Internet in presidential campaigns. *Communication Studies, 60*(5), 574–588. doi:10.1080/10510970903260418

Slack, D. (2016, January 1). Presidential debates, ranked by viewership. *USA Today.* Retrieved from www.usatoday.com/story/news/politics/onpolitics/2016/01/15/presidential-debates-ranked-viewership/78867956/

Stromer-Galley, J. (2000). On-line interaction and why candidates avoid it. *Journal of Communication, 50*(4), 111–132. doi:10.1093/joc/50.4.111

Sweetser, K. D., & Lariscy, R. W. (2008). Candidates make good friends: An analysis of candidates' uses of Facebook. *International Journal of Strategic Communication, 2*(3), 175–198. doi:10.1080/15531180802178687

Tumulty, K., & Johnson, J. (2016, January 4). Why Trump may be winning the war on 'political correctness'. *The Washington Post.* Retrieved from http://wapo.st/1ZKLMAY

Weaver, R. (1948). *Ideas have consequences.* Chicago, IL: University of Chicago Press.

Weaver, R. (1953). *The ethics of rhetoric.* Chicago, IL: Henry Regnery Company.

Williams, C. B., & Gulati, G. J. (2012). Social networks in political campaigns: Facebook and the congressional elections of 2006 and 2008. *New Media & Society, 15*(1), 52–71. doi:10.1177/1461444812457332

9

THEMES IN CANDIDATE MESSAGING ON TWITTER DURING THE "INVISIBLE" PRESIDENTIAL PRIMARY

Kate Kenski and Christine R. Filer

Presidential candidates promise voters that they will improve the U.S. either by building upon previous administration successes if the economy is strong or by leaving their own marks of distinction upon the country by departing from the current administration when things are not going well for particular segments of the public or the country overall. Rather than simply keeping the status quo, presidential candidates are compelled to promise change one way or another. The public expects leaders to make the country a better place through change and improvements. In this chapter, we explore thematic commonalities and differences in the tweets of the major party candidates who ran for their parties' nominations during the so-called invisible primary, also known as the surfacing phase or preprimary campaign, paying particular attention to themes of change versus experience as candidates established themselves in the races in 2015. We consider whether candidates' calls for change differed by party and the extent to which experience was emphasized by the candidates.

The Invisible Primary

The extent to which campaigns have had influence over the nomination phase outcomes through voters has transformed over time. Aldrich (2009, p. 35) contends that "outsiders could run as unknowns and convince people to vote for them—and win the nomination" in the 1970s but, since then, the spiraling cost of campaigns and frontloading of state caucuses and primaries have led to a decrease in the role that voters have played in the process. Frontloading refers to the packing of state primaries and caucuses close together near the Iowa caucuses and New Hampshire primary. To have greater influence in presidential candidate selection, many state parties have moved their nominating events toward the front of the schedule as early contest results appear to have an impact on media coverage and subsequent contests. This has disrupted the logic of a spread out primary and caucus season that allowed for the momentum of candidates to evolve across the primary period. Aldrich (2009) observes that Carter's 1976 run led to the momentum model, whereas Bill Clinton's "advance preparations led to the first sustained study of the importance of the pre-primary season—what came to be called the "invisible primary" (p. 34) in 1992.

Presidential campaigns now begin long before primary and caucuses take place. The groundwork for presidential runs is often laid well before a candidate has announced his or her candidacy. It is during the preprimary or surfacing phase that many candidates start their runs and also end them (Christenson & Smidt, 2012). The preprimary is the unveiling period for the candidates when they must increase their name recognition and frame their priorities. It is also an understudied period of the campaign, despite the fact that it is arguably the time when media are most influential in affecting voter opinion because voters often do not have preconceived notions about many of the candidates running.

Early campaigning has become a prerequisite for a presidential run. Preprimary campaigns are important because fundraising during that time period matters. According to Adkins and Dowdle, "while many factors influence the outcome of presidential nominations, early fundraising activity is among the most important" (2002, p. 257). The fundraising matters not only for the candidate's success in securing the nomination but also lays the groundwork for their general election success as well. Accordingly, the invisible primary deserves more scholarly attention.

The 2016 Major Party Presidential Preprimary Candidates

The Democratic and Republican presidential preprimary season was crowded in 2015. The preprimary period was defined as the date on which a major candidate first officially announced his candidacy, which happened to be Republican Mark Everson on March 5, 2015, through December 31, 2015. There were many individuals who announced their candidacies but were not invited to participate in the televised debates and forums during the preprimary season. Coming up with a hard figure on the number of candidates depends on how one chooses to define a candidate and whether viability matters.

Three debates and two candidate forums were held for the Democratic candidates during the preprimary season. The first Democratic debate was held on October 13, 2015 in Las Vegas, Nevada. Democratic aspirants Hillary Clinton, Bernie Sanders, Jim Webb, Martin O'Malley, and Lincoln Chafee participated. To be included in the debate, the candidates had to capture at least 1% of the vote in three national polls. In our study, we focused on these five candidates and political outsider Lawrence Lessig as the main Democratic candidates during the surfacing phase. Lessig was excluded from the debate and forum events, but received some modest news media attention. Of these six candidates, three dropped out before the primary season began (i.e., Chafee, Lessig, and Webb).

The Republicans held three debates and three forums during the preprimary period with 17 candidates participating in at least one of them during that time period. The candidates were Jeb Bush, Ben Carson, Chris Christie, Ted Cruz, Carly Fiorina, Jim Gilmore, Lindsey Graham, Mike Huckabee, Bobby Jindal, John Kasich, George Pataki, Rand Paul, Rick Perry, Marco Rubio, Rick Santorum, Donald Trump, and Scott Walker. The first Republican forum was held on August 3, 2015 in Goffstown, New Hampshire. Mark Everson was included in our main Republican candidate list because he was the first Republican to announce his candidacy, but he did not participate in the debates and forums. Of these 18 candidates, six dropped out before the surfacing phase had ended (i.e., Everson, Graham, Jindal, Pataki, Perry, and Walker).

Tweets as Campaign Theme Indicators

The Internet has contributed to the way that campaigns raise money and reach voters with their messages. Just as television advertising became an integral part of campaigns after television was widely adopted in American homes, as social media use has expanded among U.S. adults, candidate use of social media has become a fundamental part of campaigns as well (Adams & McCorkindale, 2013; Conway, Kenski, & Wang, 2013; Golbeck, Grimes, & Rogers, 2010; Graham, Broersma, Hazelhoff, & van't Haar, 2013; Gueorguieva, 2008; Johnson & Perlmutter, 2010).

Given that Conway et al. (2013) had found that candidate Twitter presence was not uniform during the 2012 primary season, we felt that documenting candidate presence during the 2016 preprimary was a worthy endeavor, but one that should be left as an open research question. We had no a priori expectations about which candidates would tweet the most. We, therefore, asked the question: To what extent did the candidates tweet during the invisible primary? (RQ1)

How the Internet affects preprimary and primary campaigns in the long term as new technologies provide novel ways to reach and utilize voters in the process is still being discovered. It is reasonable, however, to assume that campaigns must be active on social media, but social media use alone is not a sufficient condition for success. Although candidate social media use is expected, social media are still relatively young in their development, and the norms surrounding social media use by candidates, consequently, have not yet become routinized, meriting continued examination. Nevertheless, a study of the 2012 presidential campaign tweets suggested that whereas issue themes in tweets were not synonymous with the priorities in candidate television advertising, there was significant overlap such that social media can be as a proxy for campaign themes (Kenski, Conway, & Filer, 2015). As an exploratory research question, we asked: What words appeared most frequently in candidate tweets, and did these patterns differ by party? (RQ2)

In this study, we examine tweets of the preprimary candidates to uncover campaign themes and explore how the words "change" and "experience" were used by those running for president. Trent, Short-Thompson, Mongeau, Metzler, & Trent (2005) observed that voters have preconceived beliefs about the characteristics that presidential candidates should possess that affect a candidate's success. Experience in office and forceful public speaking are often two of those characteristics. "In the low-information environment of the pre-primary stage at least in terms of candidate information," writes Parmelee, focus group "participants drew from preexisting sources, such as ideal candidate characteristics, in order to judge the attractiveness and legitimacy of the candidate" (2008, p. 75). Experience, therefore, is a theme that we would expect to be emphasized in campaign messages.

For opponents to a presidential administration during times of economic crisis or perceived sluggishness, security threats, and/or political unrest, priming thoughts about a presumably more stable, nostalgic time can be powerful as a foundation for calls for change. One of the ways in which people decide for whom to vote is retrospective voting. "The central tenet of retrospective voting is that voters make simple assessments about current conditions, broadly defined, and then support or oppose the incumbent administration based on those assessments" (Holbrook, Clouse, & Weinschenk, 2012, p. 263). For example, when Ronald Reagan ran for the presidency in 1980, he invoked retrospective voting by asking the audience during a debate with incumbent president Jimmy Carter,

> Are you better off now than you were four years ago? . . . If you don't think that this course that we've been on for the last four years is what you would like to see us follow for the next four, then I could suggest another choice that you have.
>
> *(October 28, 1980, Debate Transcript (n.d.))*

Given the poor economy and international crises during the Carter administration, many felt that the U.S. generally and they as individuals specifically were not better off than they had been four years earlier. Consequently, the change candidate won the 1980 election.

Levine, Clark, Haygood, and Muenchen (2011) observed that when the incumbent president has low public approval ratings, "the party that is not in the White House may be able to make a stronger case for change" (p. 480). Whereas most candidates make the case that they are the agents of change, the theme appears to have greater fidelity and resonance for the opposition party to the White House when things are not going well for the country.

Presidential candidates play particular roles when running for office depending on their backgrounds. Candidates are either incumbents, challengers, or successors (Popkin, 2012). Their success depends, in part, on understanding their roles and how campaign themes fit into those roles. Popkin explained, "Whereas challengers offer hope and change, the incumbent has no alternative but to" offer "more of the same" (2012, p. 137). In 2008, change was a theme in Senator Barack Obama's presidential campaign (Coe & Reitzes, 2010). The Obama campaign was able to convince voters that voting for Senator John McCain, who had long been vocal in his opposition to a few Republican positions, would be the same as voting for a Bush third term. "Throughout the campaign, the incantation 'yes we can' and 'yes you can' invited Obama supporters to participate in the process of altering the country's course," observed Kenski, Hardy, and Jamieson (2010, p. 34). "In Oregon in May [2008], Obama said in an ad, 'Some people say we can't change Washington. I'm Barack Obama and I approve this message to say that this time we can.'" Obama embraced the role of challenger, whereas McCain was forced into the position of successor, which meant being saddled with some of the burdens of the then-current administration.

In 2016, like in 2008, there was no incumbent running for either party, but former Secretary of State Hillary Clinton essentially was President Barack Obama's successor, having served in his administration. Democratic candidates running against Clinton had the option to argue that Clinton was part of a wide Washington problem, but as Democrats, calls for change had to be made carefully so as not to alienate the nearly four-fifths of Democrats who approved of Obama's job performance during his sixth year in office (Jones, 2015). The extent to which the economy was doing poorly was a matter of interpretation. Some segments of the country felt economic pressures more than other parts of the country. In contrast to the Democrats, less than 10% of Republicans approved of Obama's performance (Jones, 2015), opening up the possibility that the Republican candidates would call for change. We hypothesized that calls for change would be more prevalent in the Republican candidate and campaign tweets during the surfacing phase than they would be in the Democratic tweets (H1). We also suspected that of the Democrats, Clinton would be the one least likely to make use of calls for change (H2a) and would instead focus on her political leadership experience (H2b).

Methods

Computer-assisted content analysis was used to examine word selections in the U.S. major party preprimary candidates' and campaigns' Twitter feeds. In addition to examining the presence of words in an exploratory fashion, the use of words connoting "change" versus "experience" was observed. Tweets were analyzed employing a dictionary approach. Word indices reflecting the concepts were created, and then tweets were scanned for those words.

Dataset

All tweets on verified major party candidate Twitter feeds and candidate campaign feeds were collected from March 5, 2015 through December 31, 2015 ($N = 66{,}463$). Although many eventual candidates posted frequently to Twitter prior to the start of this collection, March 5, 2015 marked the date when Republican Mark Everson became the first official entrant in the presidential race. As mentioned earlier, the collection of candidate tweets included six Democrats and 18 Republicans. The frequencies by candidate/campaign tweets can be found in Table 9.1. When candidates dropped out from the race, their tweet collection was discontinued.

TABLE 9.1 Preprimary Tweet Frequency

Candidates	*Handle*	*Campaign Announcement*	*Campaign Withdrawal*	*Party Outsider*	*Preprimary Tweet Frequency*
Democrats					
Lincoln Chafee	@LincolnChafee	6/3/15	10/23/15	Yes*	421
Hillary Clinton	@HillaryClinton @TheBriefing2016 @HFA	4/12/15	—	No	4,203
Lawrence Lessig	@lessig @Lessig2016	9/6/15	11/2/15	Yes	3,549
Martin O'Malley	@MartinOMalley	2/1/16	2/1/16	No	2,312
Bernie Sanders	@BernieSanders @SenSanders	5/26/15	—	Yes*	5,949
Jim Webb	@JimWebbUSA	7/2/15	10/20/15	No	1,443
Republicans					
Jeb Bush	@JebBush	6/15/15	2/20/16	No	2,080
Ben Carson	@RealBenCarson	5/4/15	3/4/16	Yes	1,438
Chris Christie	@ChrisChristie @GovChristie	6/30/15	2/10/16	No	2,371
Ted Cruz	@SenTedCruz @tedcruz @TeamTedCruz	3/23/15	5/3/16	No	5,377
Mark Everson	@MarkForAmerica	3/5/15	11/5/15	Yes*	1,100
Carly Fiorina	@CarlyFiorina	5/4/15	2/10/16	Yes	1,302
Jim Gilmore	@gov_gilmore	7/30/15	2/12/16	No	971
Lindsey Graham	@GrahamBlog @LindseyGrahamSC	6/1/15	12/21/15	No	3,203
Mike Huckabee	@GovMikeHuckabee	5/5/15	2/1/16	No	1,778
Bobby Jindal	@BobbyJindal	6/24/15	11/17/15	No	1,371
John Kasich	@JohnKasich @TeamJohnKasich	7/21/15	5/4/16	No	1,929
George Pataki	@GovernorPataki	5/28/15	12/29/15	No	1,678
Rand Paul	@RandPaul	4/7/15	2/3/16	No	4,674
Rick Perry	@GovernorPerry @TeamRickPerry	6/4/15	9/11/15	No	1,571
Marco Rubio	@marcorubio @TeamMarco	4/13/15	3/15/16	No	5,171
Rick Santorum	@RickSantorum @TeamSantorum	5/27/15	2/3/16	No	3,439
Donald Trump	@realDonaldTrump	6/16/15		Yes	6,778
Scott Walker	@ScottWalker @GovWalker	7/13/15	9/21/15	No	2,355

Note: *Chafee and Sanders were elected officials but did not have long histories with their party. Mark Everson was an administration insider but had not served in an elective capacity.

Tweets were downloaded using the "twitteR" package in R and Twitter's API. Twitter data for each tweet consist of the user who posted the tweet, the date and time it was posted, and the tweet's content. Original tweets contained up to 140 characters. Retweets contained up to 140 characters in the scraping but that included the identification of the source of the retweets, resulting in a few words at the very end of the material retweeted occasionally cut off to make room for the source's handle.

Coding

QDA Miner and WordStat were used to identify word mention frequencies across tweets. QDA Miner is a computer-assisted qualitative coding program. WordStat is its quantitative component that allows researchers to search for words, word strings, and complex word combinations. We used this text-mining software to compose change and experience dictionaries to examine the candidate/campaign tweets. Jang and Pasek (2015) acknowledge that automated keyword analysis is not without its limitations, but that keywords can "have strong face validity in signifying the presence of the key real-word issues" (p. 586). We maintain that, in our study, such a keyword approach also has face validity in identifying the presence of themes during the campaign.

WordStat identified the most common words used in the tweets, excluding prepositions and articles of speech. The common words were examined by the candidates to determine whether patterns and uses differed by candidates taking into account their party affiliations as well.

Dictionaries were created for change and experience labels and candidate names. Whereas synonyms of *change* and *experience* were considered, we decided to use the words *change*, *experience*, and their plural or slightly modified forms exclusively for the analyses because some of the synonyms have slightly different connotations than what we were trying to capture in this study. Specifically, *change* was captured using the words *change*, *changes*, and *changing*, but not *shortchange* (or derivations of it), *exchange*, or *climate change*. *Experience* was captured using the words *experience*, *experiences*, and *experienced*. The candidates were identified by their Twitter handles.

Analysis

WordStat was used to identify the most common words in the candidate/campaign tweets by candidates to answer the exploratory question about themes in tweets. Then, the tweets were assessed for the containment of change and experience words, disaggregated by candidate. We examined both raw numbers and frequency by percentage of inclusion in candidate tweets. We had predicted that Clinton would use fewer calls for change in her tweets than her Democratic competitors and that the Republicans would use more calls for change than Clinton and the other Democrats overall. We also investigated the extent to which the word *experience* was used.

Because the dataset contained the entirety of the candidate and campaign tweets during the time period under investigation, inferential statistics were not generated, as such statistics are only useful for making inferences about a population. As Gorard (2013) explains, "Significance tests are relevant only to making a judgement about sampling variation produced by the random selection of cases for a sample, and whether this variation is a good explanation of any manifested difference between the groups" (p. 54). Here, no inference needed to be made about the population, as the entire population was captured; any observed differences are the real differences. The extent to which differences, when they appear, are important is a matter of interpretation.

Results

Our first research question asked about the prevalence of social media use during the preprimary season (RQ1). Social media use was prevalent during the invisible primary. As shown in Table 9.1, the six major Democratic candidates in the preprimary phase tweeted 17,877 times and the 18 major Republican candidates tweeted 48,586 in that same period. Recalibrating those figures, taking into account that there were three times as many major Republican candidates as Democratic ones, Democrats tweeted more on average (2,980 Democratic tweets on average compared to 2,699 Republican tweets) during the invisible primary. Candidates differed greatly in how much they tweeted. For the Democrats, Lincoln Chafee tweeted the least (N = 421) and Bernie Sanders tweeted the most (N = 5,949; 19.7 tweets per day). Front-runner Hillary Clinton tweeted 4,203 times, which resulted in approximately 13.9 tweets per day over the 302 days analyzed. For the Republicans, John Gilmore tweeted the least (N = 971) and Donald Trump tweeted the most (N = 6,778). Trump tweeted approximately 22.4 times per day over the preprimary period. It is noteworthy that the eventual Republican nominee tweeted 1.6 times more than the eventual Democratic nominee. This may, however, be attributed in part to Clinton's relatively secure feelings about winning the Democratic nomination, whereas Trump, a front-runner during most of the Republican campaign season, was considered a long shot by the media given his lack of political and/or military experience, among other things.

It is worth noting that outsider versus insider candidate status did not predict volume of tweets consistently. Whereas highest volume tweeters in both parties were party outsiders (i.e., Sanders and Trump), Democrat Lincoln Chafee tweeted the least out of his party's candidates, and Republican outsiders Mark Everson and Carly Fiorina were second and third from the bottom on Republican candidate tweet frequency.

The second research question inquired about common words in the tweets. Common words give a sense of how tweets were used. The words that appeared in the largest percentage of tweets were *http* (38.0%), *https* (29.0%), *RT* (30.4%), *today* (6.1%), and *great* (4.9%). Instead of connoting a specific issue or trait theme, the top words convey the purpose of content sharing: the sharing of links and retweeting someone else's tweet content.

Putting aside these general functions, we examined the five most frequent words found in the Twitter feeds. When disaggregated by candidates, a common theme across tweets was that candidates mentioned their own names frequently, as shown in Table 9.2. For example, Hillary Clinton's Twitter handle @TheBriefing2016 retweeted content from @HillaryClinton: "RT @ HillaryClinton: Are you ready for the first woman president? #DemDebate #Hillary2016" (November 15, 2015). Donald Trump's handle @RealDonaldTrump tweeted: "@alphainparis: @seanhannity DonaldTrump is the 21st

TABLE 9.2 Top Five Most Frequent Words in Candidate/Campaign Tweets

Candidate	*Most Frequent Words*				
Democrats	#1	#2	#3	#4	#5
Chafee	NH	NHpolitics	good	today	tonight
Clinton	Hillary	HillaryClinton	ed	plan	Clinton
Lessig	Lessig	campaign	democracy	debate	support
O'Malley	MartinOMalley	Iacaucus	NHpolitics	today	governor
Sanders	Sanders	Bernie	people	BernieSanders	Sen
Webb	JimWebbUSA	Webb	Jim	candidate	DemDebate
Republicans					
Bush	today	Obama	Jeb	HillaryClinton	plan
Carson	RealBenCarson	Carson	DC	BC	people
Christie	ChrisChristie	Christie	live	today	town
Cruz	TedCruz	Cruz	CruzCrew	join	Ted
Everson	pjnet	GOP	tcot	Mark	time
Fiorina	Carly	Tune	today	joining	join
Gilmore	Gilmore	gov	Jim	GOP	today
Graham	LindseyGrahamSC	FITN	Graham	ISIL	live
Huckabee	ImwithHuck	GovMikeHuckabee	GT	GOPDebate	president
Jindal	today	Live	great	America	president
Kasich	JohnKasich	Kasich	gov	John	today
Pataki	GovernorPataki	FITN	NH	GOP	great
Paul	RandPaul	StandWithRand	Rand	today	GT
Perry	GovernorPerry	Perry	Rick	GT	tcot
Rubio	MarcoRubio	Ed	Marco	TeamMarco	Rubio
Santorum	RickSantorum	Rick	Santorum	GOPDebate	today
Trump	RealDonaldTrump	Trump	great	Donald	America
Walker	Walker	SW	SKW	Scott	today

Note: The words "http," "https," and "RT" are excluded.

century Ronald Reagan. Intelligent. Bold. Surrounded by good people. Gets the job done" (May 29, 2015).

Democrat Lincoln Chafee and Republican Bobby Jindal were outliers insofar as they did not mention themselves in their tweets frequently. All other candidates used some form of their names as one of the top words. Given that the purpose of the preprimary campaign is to boost name recognition and a measure of a tweet's success is the extent to which the tweet is passed along to others through the retweet function, it makes sense that candidates would prioritize their names as a theme in their tweets.

The word "today" appeared in 11 of the candidates' top words. Surprisingly, only two candidates had "America" as one of their top words (i.e., Jindal and Trump), and two candidates used the word "president" as one of their top words (i.e., Huckabee and Jindal). Issues were not prevalent as top words. Only two issues made the top word lists: "ISIL" and "ed." Graham tweeted about ISIL, and Clinton and Rubio tweeted about education ("ed"). For example, Marco Rubio retweeted an issue-laden tweet on August 10, 2015, "RT @AlexConant: NEW: Marco discusses violence in Ferguson, Clinton's outdated higher ed ideas & Schumer's opposition to Iran deal: http:// . . . ." That only three candidates had issues as top words is telling about the preprimary campaign.

The hypotheses investigated pertained to the use of change and experience words. Overall, 581 tweets (0.9%) contained some form of the word *change* and 262 tweets (0.4%) used the word *experience.* In other words, these words were not used frequently during the surfacing phase of the campaign.

As shown in Table 9.3, both in terms of average frequency and percentage of tweets, the Democratic candidates were more likely to use change words than were the Republican candidates. The average number of tweets mentioning change made by a Democratic candidate was 40.5, and the percentage of Democratic candidate tweets mentioning change was 1.4%. Republican candidates tweeted about change less than half as frequently as the Democratic candidates did on average. The average number of tweets mentioning change made by a Republican candidate was 18.8, and the percentage of Republican candidate tweets mentioning change was 0.7%. Our first hypothesis that the Republicans would mention *change* more than the Democrats was not supported.

When it came to mentioning experience, Republican candidates mentioned *experience* more than the Democratic candidates did on average in terms of frequency; Republicans also had the edge on the percentage of their tweets but, in terms of substantive significance, the percentages were nearly at parity. The average number of tweets mentioning experience made by a Democratic candidate was 7.7, and the percentage of Democratic candidate tweets mentioning experience was 0.3%. The average number of tweets mentioning *experience* made by a Republican candidate was 12, and the percentage of Republican candidate tweets mentioning *experience* was 0.4%.

TABLE 9.3 Frequency of Tweets/Percentage of Candidate Tweets Mentioning *Change* and *Experience*

Candidate	*Change*		*Experience*	
	N	%	*N*	%
Democrats				
Chafee	1	0.24	2	0.48
Clinton	43	1.02	19	0.45
Lessig	76	2.14	1	0.03
O'Malley	8	0.35	10	0.43
Sanders	105	1.77	3	0.05
Webb	10	0.69	11	0.76
Republicans				
Bush	12	0.58	4	0.19
Carson	5	0.35	6	0.42
Christie	15	0.63	13	0.55
Cruz	21	0.39	8	0.15
Everson	67	6.09	10	0.91
Fiorina	12	0.92	5	0.38
Gilmore	2	0.21	12	1.24
Graham	7	0.22	22	0.69
Huckabee	7	0.39	5	0.28
Jindal	15	1.09	3	0.22
Kasich	10	0.52	35	1.81
Pataki	12	0.72	3	0.18
Paul	31	0.66	1	0.02
Perry	9	0.57	18	1.15
Rubio	23	0.44	6	0.12
Santorum	21	0.61	40	1.16
Trump	57	0.84	22	0.32
Walker	12	0.51	3	0.13

We had hypothesized that Clinton would be the candidate least likely to mention *change* (H2a) and most likely to mention *experience* (H2b). These hypotheses were not supported overall by the data and require explanation. As noted previously, the Republican candidates simply did not embrace the language of "*change*" in its direct form in the way that the Democratic candidates did. Among Democrats, Clinton did not mention *change* nearly as much as her most viable internal party competitor Bernie Sanders. Sanders mentioned *change* in 105 of his tweets in comparison to Clinton's 43. In terms of Democratic percentages, Clinton ranked third out of the six candidates in calls for change. She was the Democratic candidate who mentioned *experience* the most, with 19 mentions, but, to contextualize that finding, it is important to remember that this composed a very small percentage of tweets overall. There were a few Republican candidates who mentioned *experience* more than did Clinton. Graham mentioned it 22 times, Kasich 35, Santorum 40, and Trump 22.

There were qualitative differences in how *experience* was invoked by the candidates. For example, TheBriefing2016 tweeted on November 19: "Great, comprehensive speech from @HillaryClinton. Demonstrated experience, command of issues, and plan to deal with threats we face.—LMR." TeamSantorum referred to Santorum's experience as "insider experience" with a December 24, 2015 tweet that read, "Next President Needs 'Very Bold Plan To Shake Up Washington' @RickSantorum-outsider with right insider experience https://t.co/3vlJYohoUa." On December 29, 2015, TeamSantorum tweeted a similar message, "There is no candidate with stronger foreign policy experience than @RickSantorum #ISIS #tcot #Rick2016 #iacaucus https://t.co/qg4UhjxE3N."

Political outsider Donald Trump tweeted about experience, but not political experience. His tweets often used the word *experience* to mean an *event* rather than personal background characteristic. On March 11, 2015, he retweeted: "RT @Alexcrter: Getting to see Trump Tower after reading #ArtOfTheDeal was an awesome experience. @realDonaldTrump http://t.co/s5tZ73jlTt." In the same vein on March 16, he retweeted: "RT @TrumpCollection: Enhance your travel experience. Become a TRUMP CARD member today: http://t.co/feKNoLNvsI." In some tweets, he emphasized his business experience, such as in a March 23 missive contending: "'In N.H., Trump says his business experience would play well in government' http://t.co/UbiLFwmcyK via @ConMonitorNews by @AP" and a May 6 tweet stating: "'@atmaxh: Please run @realDonaldTrump! With your toughness and business experience you can put this country back on track!' Very true."

Discussion

During the surfacing phase of the campaign, the candidates' top priorities are getting name recognition and fundraising. Twitter is one social media venue that allows candidates to put forth messages in a relatively less expensive outlet than television advertising. It has the limitation, however, of requiring users to pay attention to one's Twitter feed. If one does not have followers, then the messages will not be seen. The candidates hope that members of the news media will pick up and disseminate the content and that followers will share the candidates' messages through retweets, which will lead to further interest and expand the candidates' networks. The candidate tweet frequencies demonstrate that social media use by candidates was prevalent, but there was variation across candidates as well. The top candidates in each party tweeted the most. Although frequent tweeting did not assure performance in the race, those candidates who did not tweet as often did not perform as well as their competitors.

The exploratory word analyses of the candidate tweets indicated that, across the board, regardless of party, candidates were using Twitter to share links to more elaborate forms of content, which was evident in the frequent appearance of the https and http words. All candidates had link sharing among their most frequent words. Retweeting signified by RT was on almost everyone's initial top five list as well, save for a few candidates.

After excluding basic functions such as link sharing and retweeting from our analysis of frequently used words, the most prevalent theme that came across the Twitter feeds was self-references, as shown in Table 9.2. Only candidates Democrat Lincoln Chafee and Republican Bobby Jindal did not have self-references as at least one of their top five tweet words. It is worth noting that these candidates also did not do well in their respective races. This suggests that the self-promotion theme is a key part of successful surfacing phase candidacies.

In addition to wording, candidates make a series of decisions prior to publishing tweets. One important choice is how to draw in one's audience. Several candidates attempted to inspire engagement by encouraging viewers to join them at various campaign events or watch them live (as evidenced by the frequent use of the words "join" and "live"). Retweeting was also a common occurrence. In addition to retweeting, Trump tried to engage potential voters by broadcasting their words (quoting them to all his followers), sometimes appending his own comments. In so doing, Trump capitalized on the interactive nature of social media. Rather than trot out a professionally created and focus group-tested message, he often simply repeated individuals who had tweeted positive messages about him. It is plausible that this implied to potential voters that Trump was both of the masses and had widespread support. Further research should test variations of tweets to explore the effects they may have.

The themes of change and experience are common in media discussions about the meaning of campaigns and candidacies. Based on retrospective voting, we expected that the party not in the White House would embrace calls for change more than party members affiliated with the current administration, particularly when the opposition party sees the economy weak or public sentiment as negative toward the current president. Although the vice president is generally considered the heir apparent as a successor, in 2016 Joe Biden was not in the race. Hillary Clinton was linked to Obama, however, through her time as secretary of state in his administration and was therefore considered the successor of sorts. Consequently, we hypothesized that she would emphasize her experience over change, which was not borne out in the data. As a female candidate running for the presidency, Clinton reached out to females with messages about female empowerment that mentioned change, such as, "Change can come—sometimes, even in the form of a $10 bill. #TheNew10 http://t.co/Zyk7oHojJ8" (Clinton, 2015b) and, "Too many women still earn less than men on the job—and women of color often lose out the most. This needs to change. #WomensEqualityDay" (Clinton, 2015d). Her messages of change included tweets such as, "RT @HillaryClinton: We can't harness change and solve problems if we go back to the top-down economic policies that failed us before" (Clinton, 2015a) and, "'As President, I will work with every possible partner to turn the tide—to make these currents of change start working for us'" (Clinton, 2015c). She also used change words in reference to policy warnings about changes that could come if she wasn't elected: "(6) Hillary Clinton believes tax policy changes that favor the wealthy are misguided https://t.co/FzaaaZoMcG" (The Briefing, 2015).

Despite the fact that a Democrat had held the presidency for nearly two terms during the surfacing phase, Democratic candidates made more frequent references to change than did the Republican candidates. Change has to be cast against a moment in time, and it is sometimes unclear where that moment in time should be anchored. Retrospective voting suggests that calls for change should pivot against what has happened the past four years. When it comes to the rhetoric of change, it may be the case that ideological positioning constrains the extent to which candidates can frame their candidacies in that language. Hayes (2005) has suggested that candidate trait perceptions are influenced by partisanship, such that Republicans tend to have an edge on perceptions of strong leadership and morality, but Democrats have an edge on compassion and empathy. One possible explanation for the findings in the current study is that parties may also have ownership over orientations toward change versus stability. In this case, Democrats tended to focus on "change," because "change" is consistent with their more progressive, liberal ideology. Yet, in the context of an election in which the more liberal party has been in the White House for the previous eight years, such calls for change may appear somewhat ironic or paradoxical. By the same token, Republicans are rooted in stability and leadership, which are kin to the concept of experience. So even when the other side has arguably more political experience, the Republican candidates emphasize experience and do not use the rhetoric of change more so than do the Democrats.

This study is not without its limitations. The findings of the study are limited to the 2015 surfacing phase of the presidential campaign. The approach examined keywords found in the census of tweets made by the major party presidential candidates. The keyword approach identifies important elements of how tweets are used. It is limited, however, to interpretations of manifest content at the expense of subtle messaging conveyed through latent content. One possible explanation for the finding that Republicans did not mention "change" more than did the Democrats is that Republicans frame change in ways that invite inference about change without using the word "change" directly. Nevertheless, that the direct use of the word "change" was not more prevalent is noteworthy, particularly in a highly polarized context in which the two parties are so intent on differentiating themselves from the other.

Although social media use generally and Twitter use specifically are expected of presidential candidates running for office, and the 2016 campaigns were run with some understanding of social media's benefits and limitations from the previous presidential election cycle, the various tweeting frequencies across presidential candidates suggests that social media use by candidates is still not uniform. What is consistent, however, is the focus on the self as the major theme of the preprimary campaign tweets.

References

Adams, A., & McCorkindale, T. (2013). Dialogue and transparency: A content analysis of how the 2012 presidential candidates used Twitter. *Public Relations Review*, *39*(4), 357–359. doi:10.1016/j.pubrev.2013.07.016

Adkins, R. E., & Dowdle, A. J. (2002). The money primary: What influences the outcome of pre-primary presidential nomination fundraising? *Presidential Studies Quarterly*, *32*, 256–275. doi:10.1111/j.0360–4918.2002.00220.x

Aldrich, J. (2009). The invisible primary and its effects on democratic choice. *PS: Political Science and Politics*, *42*, 33–38. doi:10.1017/S1049096509090027

The Briefing. [TheBriefing2016]. (2015, July 12). (6) Hillary Clinton believes tax policy changes that favor the wealthy are misguided [Tweet]. Retrieved from https://twitter.com/TheBriefing2016/status/620256934625693696

Christenson, D. P., & Smidt, C. D. (2012). Still part of the conversation: Iowa and New Hampshire's say within the invisible primary. *Presidential Studies Quarterly*, *42*, 597–621. doi:10.1111/j.1741–5705.2012.03994.x

Clinton, H. [HillaryClinton]. (2015a, June 13). We can't harness change and solve problems if we go back to the top-down economic policies that failed us before [Tweet]. Retrieved from https://twitter.com/HillaryClinton/status/609753504014536705

Clinton, H. [HillaryClinton]. (2015b, June 19). Change can come—sometimes, even in the form of a $10 bill. #TheNew10 http://t.co/Zyk7oHojJ8 [Tweet]. Retrieved from https://twitter.com/hillaryclinton/status/612020140662747136

Clinton, H. [HillaryClinton]. (2015c, July 13). "As President, I will work with every possible partner to turn the tide—to make these currents of change start working for us" [Tweet]. Retrieved from https://twitter.com/HillaryClinton/status/620597490895622144

Clinton, H. [HillaryClinton]. (2015d, August 27). Too many women still earn less than men on the job—and women of color often lose out the most. This needs to change. #WomensEqualityDay [Tweet]. Retrieved from https://twitter.com/hillaryclinton/status/636690910206644226

Coe, K., & Reitzes, M. (2010). Obama on the stump: Features and determinants of a rhetorical approach. *Presidential Studies Quarterly*, *40*, 391–413. doi:10.1111/j.1741-5705.2010.03777.x

Conway, B. A., Kenski, K., & Wang, D. (2013). Twitter use by presidential primary candidates during the 2012 campaign. *American Behavioral Scientist*, *57*(11), 1596–1610. doi:10.1177/0002764213489014

Golbeck, J., Grimes, J. M., & Rogers, A. (2010). Twitter use by the U.S. Congress. *Journal of the American Society for Information Science and Technology*, *61*(8), 1612–1621. doi:10.1002/asi.21344

Gorard, S. (2013). *Research design: Creating robust approaches for the social sciences*. Los Angeles, CA: Sage.

Graham, T., Broersma, M., Hazelhoff, K., & van't Haar, G. (2013). Between broadcasting political messages and interacting with voters: The use of Twitter during the 2010 UK general election campaign. *Information, Communication & Society, 16*(5), 692–716. doi:10.1080/1369118X.2013.785581

Gueorguieva, V. (2008). Voters, MySpace, and YouTube: The impact of alternative communication channels on the 2006 election cycle and beyond. *Social Science Computer Review, 26*(3), 288–300. doi:10.1177/0894439307305636

Hayes, D. (2005). Candidate qualities through a partisan lens: A theory of trait ownership. *American Journal of Political Science, 49*, 908–923. doi:10.2307/3647705

Holbrook, T. M., Clouse, C., & Weinschenk, A. C. (2012). Bringing the president back in: The collapse of Lehman Brothers and the evolution of retrospective voting in the 2008 presidential election. *Political Research Quarterly, 65*, 263–274. doi:10.1177/1065912911398051

Jang, S. M., & Pasek, J. (2015). Assessing the carrying capacity of Twitter and online news. *Mass Communication and Society, 18*, 577–598. doi:10.1080/15205436.2015.1035397

Johnson, T. J., & Perlmutter, D. D. (2010). Introduction: The Facebook election. *Mass Communication and Society, 13*(5), 554–559. doi:10.1080/15205436.2010.517490

Jones, J. M. (2015, February 6). Obama approval ratings still historically polarized. *Gallup*. Retrieved from www.gallup.com/poll/181490/obama-approval-ratings-historically-polarized.aspx

Kenski, K. M., Conway, B. A., & Filer, C. R. (2015). Campaign media congruence: Issues in 2012 presidential election tweets and ads. *Paper Presented at the annual meeting of the American Political Science Association*, San Francisco, CA, September 3–6, 2015.

Kenski, K. M., Hardy, B. W., & Jamieson, K. H. (2010). *The Obama victory: How media, money, and message shaped the 2008 election*. New York, NY: Oxford University Press.

Levine, K. J., Clark, N., Haygood, D. M., & Muenchen, R. A. (2011). Change: How young voters interpreted the messages sent during the 2008 presidential election season. *American Behavioral Scientist, 55*, 479–501. doi:10.1177/0002764211398075

October 28, 1980 Debate Transcript. (n.d.). Commission on Presidential Debates. Retrieved from http://debates.org/index.php?page=october-28-1980-debate-transcript

Parmelee, J. H. (2008). Meet the (ideal) candidate: How viewers interpret political advertising during the 'invisible primary'. *Communication Studies, 59*, 68–83. doi:10.1080/10510970701849404

Popkin, S. L. (2012). *The candidate: What it takes to win—and hold—the White House*. New York, NY: Oxford University Press.

Trent, J. S., Short-Thompson, C., Mongeau, P. A., Metzler, M. M., & Trent, J. D. (2005). The idealized presidential candidate: A vision over time. *American Behavioral Scientist, 49*, 130–156. doi:10.1177/0002764205279437

10

RHETORIC IN A TRANSMEDIA STORYTELLING CAMPAIGN

How Trump Deployed the Paranoid Style in 2016

Zac Gershberg

The "kaleidoscope of conservative doctrines" that align the Republican Party cohere around three main themes: social conservatism, promoting religious and traditional values in American culture; fiscal conservatism, emphasizing a reduction in the size of the federal government, lowering taxes, and supporting global capitalism; and neo-conservatism, a robust foreign policy opposing communism and encouraging military spending and interventions to project American power (Lee, 2012, p. 2). Yet in the 2016 primary and general presidential election campaigns, Donald J. Trump distanced himself from these pillars of conservativism. As the *National Review*, the conservative publication founded by William F. Buckley, reported following the Trump victory in the November 2016 presidential election, "Trump's ideology is disjointed at best and his core philosophy on the appropriate role of government is anyone's guess" (Alberta, 2016, para. 11). Trump did not just eschew conservative orthodoxy in his campaign, he also ignored more traditional methods of campaigning, which includes paying special attention to "metrics and advances in market research and data collection" (Johnson, 2016, p. 10). Trump did not adhere to political norms from an ideological or campaign perspective, then, but still managed to claim victory in both the Republican primary campaign, culminating in his nomination, and in the electoral college, elevating him to the presidency.

Providing a definitive causal account that explains Trump's victory is beyond the scope of this or any essay, as many factors—both political and structural—were at play. By drawing attention to two particular facets of the Trump campaign interrelated among mediated and rhetorical strategies, though, this study hopes to identify and assess political efficacies unique to him as a candidate. First, Trump elevated a historically marginalized rhetorical genre—that of the paranoid style—to the political mainstream. As articulated by Hofstadter (1996), who first coined the term in a 1964 magazine article, the paranoid style appeals to right-wing Americans who feel dispossessed, emphasizes conspiracies in apocalyptic terms, and assumes an anti-cosmopolitan attitude. Trump is not the first politician to deploy the paranoid style, but, considering Hofstadter observed that it has historically been a "minority movement" that does not translate to "effective two-way communication with the world outside [the] group" (pp. 7, 38), it is fair to conclude Trump is certainly the most successful to do so. Second, Trump facilitated what can be considered a comprehensive transmedia branding and storytelling campaign—a concept that encapsulates creative corporate synergies between mass entertainment and fandom. Relying on the work of unpaid prosumers, or everyday people such as fans, transmedia storytelling solicits creative contributions across news media platforms such as online message boards, Facebook, and Twitter to publicize a corporate brand. As Jenkins (2010) writes, transmedia storytelling "represents a process where integral elements of a fiction get dispersed systematically across multiple delivery channels for the purpose of creating a unified and coordinated entertainment experience" (p. 944). Though transmedia storytelling has traditionally been understood in the context of corporate media entertainment with publicity surrounding movies or video games, the Trump campaign expanded its scope to include politics. Inspiring a constellation of multiplatform entertainments that generated publicity in variously effective ways across traditional, online, and social media, Trump benefited from this process and understanding political transmedia storytelling helps contextualize the role of all forms of media in the 2016 presidential election.

The two prongs of this chapter are intertwined insofar as transmedia storytelling afforded Trump and his supporters in the alt-right movement the ability to increase the salience and legitimacy of the paranoid style. Again, there is no claim that the combined forces of a paranoid rhetorical style and transmedia storytelling inevitably translated to Trump's election as president. I simply wish to highlight these aspects of the Trump campaign that diverge from the norms of political communication. In doing so, it is claimed the paranoid style, effectively harnessed through a transmedia storytelling campaign, collapsed the policies of conservative ideology and distinguished Trump's candidacy as entertaining and novel. An understanding of Trump and his campaign should not be limited to the populist rhetorical frame, either (White, 2016); it was an all-encompassing communications strategy with contributions, as this chapter will show, from across the globe. Regardless of how he governs as president, Donald J. Trump fostered two distinct changes in how we assess political communication and media: one, ideology can be transcended rhetorically—even with a rather extreme style—and two, political campaigns can effectively inspire transmedia storytelling from prosumers who complement the traditional functions of a candidate and his or her surrogates.

The Paranoid Style

In articulating the paranoid style and following its rise and fall throughout American history, Hofstadter (1996) observes that its dynamism "may be traced to the effects of the mass media" (p. 24). He does not explore this thought or provide a thorough accounting of the media infrastructure in each epoch, but we can identify how Hofstadter's historical markers of the paranoid style align with changes to mass media. His essay, for instance, charts it as beginning with the anti-Masonic and anti-Illuminati movements of the late eighteenth century, moving on to the anti-Catholic surge of the 1830s, conspiracies about global finance in the late nineteenth century, and then, finally, the anti-Communist and anti-intellectual frames that began in response to the New Deal, which reached a crescendo with McCarthyism and the John Birch Society. More research could explore the aligning of this phenomena, but suffice to say the above instances of the paranoid style correlate with newer forms of media of the time, including the partisan press, the penny press, yellow journalism, and radio and magazines, respectively. More recently, research has demonstrated the contemporary rise in anti-establishment discourses as well as conspiracy theories in response to a fragmented media infrastructure defined by cable news, the Internet, and social media (Oliver & Wood, 2014; Serazio, 2016). As such, there were ripe opportunities for a re-imagination of the paranoid style and Trump, it can be concluded, exploited this opening.

To review, the paranoid style, regardless of when it appears, traffics in conspiratorial fantasies that allege "vast and sinister" plots exist to harm the independence and security of the U.S. (Hofstadter, 1996, p. 29). Trump, using his notoriety as a celebrity game show host and real estate mogul, began a public campaign challenging the authenticity of President Barack Obama's birth certificate in 2011. The birther movement, as it was called, implied the sitting president did not meet the constitutional eligibility for the presidency. As an African American born in Hawaii to a father from Kenya, it is difficult not to consider the racist underpinnings of these false charges against President Obama, who has always been, in fact, an American citizen. Yet the Trump-led birther movement was but the opening gambit in unleashing a new paranoid style of political communication replete with participatory narratives of conspiratorial fantasy. Even after the president publicly released his long-form birth certificate, Trump, in 2013, raised doubts about it an interview with ABC News: "Was it a birth certificate? You tell me. Some people say that was not his birth certificate. Maybe it was, maybe it wasn't. I'm saying I don't know. Nobody knows" (quoted in Karl, 2016, para. 12). Whereas Trump may appear evasive or non-committal, his framing the birther debate as a question, followed by ruminating on the ambiguity of its authenticity, emboldened Trump's skeptics and followers to sustain the conspiratorial fantasy. Such a strategy also keeps the narrative of paranoia alive—both as the mainstream media reports on these sensationalist charges and the online margins of blogs and social media traffic in them.

There is a precedent for influencing the media like this. As Streitmatter (2012) recounts, Senator Joseph McCarthy had an "uncanny ability to manipulate the press" through making unfounded claims about communist saboteurs in American government (p. 143). Specifically, McCarthy knew that if he released his charges at wire service deadlines for newspapers, there would be no time for fact-checking (p. 144). Though McCarthy's career in politics fizzled due to the news media figuring out his methods and then exposing them, Trump inhabits a different, more fragmented media infrastructure with cable news networks and online platforms giving credence to his claims. His career in the media spotlight, from running beauty pageants to hosting a reality television show and appearing in televised wrestling events, suggests he can negotiate the mass media with aplomb.

This was particularly apparent when Trump first announced his bid for the presidency in June 2015. Once again, charges of racism appeared as Trump asserted that immigrants from Mexico were "bringing crime" and "[t]hey're rapists" (Trump, 2015, para. 9). However, such racial animus obscured the larger conspiratorial fantasies Trump offered in the speech that align with the paranoid style. "The U.S.," Trump said just prior to his comments on Mexican immigrants, "has become a dumping ground for everyone else's problems" (para. 8). Trump would move on to note how China is taking away American jobs because our politicians are stupid and letting it happen. We should not deny the racist, provocative language emanating from Trump, but such commentary can be subsumed under the umbrella of the paranoid style in general, which, as Hofstadter (1996) observed, proceeds in "apocalyptic terms" (p. 29).

For the paranoid style to achieve such a prominent platform, it took a dynamic media persona to deploy it and then required a fragmented, sensationalist media infrastructure to help sustain it. As *The New York Times* reported during the primary campaign, Trump amassed close to $2 billion in free media coverage from national and cable television network whereas no other candidate marshalled so much as $750 million (Confessore & Yourish, 2016). The sheer amount of publicity generated from this paranoid style of rhetoric permitted Trump to consistently violate conservative orthodoxy from the very beginning of the campaign. In his June 2015 announcement speech, Trump claimed to be against the Iraq War, which was championed by neo-conservative thinking about American power, and railed against free trade deals with China, which are part of the global capitalist order promoted by free-market conservatives. In another twist on conservatism, the Trump campaign was able to change the language on Russia and Ukraine for the party platform of the 2016 Republican National Convention, which represents a dramatic shift in foreign policy (Rogin, 2016).

In each of these instances, it is clear that ideology operates in a subordinate role to the mediatized ethos of the candidate. These concerns troubled Postman (1985), who remonstrated against President Ronald Reagan for conflating politics with show business (p. 125). Yet Reagan consistently promoted a conservative vision highlighting religious values, smaller government, and a strong national defense. The rhetorical staging of the former movie star complemented Reagan's conservativism, from his time as an American Medical Association spokesman opposing Medicare to serving as California governor and on to the presidency. With Trump, whose politics are fluid, improvisational, and conspiratorial, that is not the case.

Moreover, Trump's general-election opponent, Hillary Clinton, fed into the paranoid style he sought to promote on the campaign trail. Ethical questions regarding the Clinton Foundation, an international charitable organization, and her behind-closed-door speeches to members of the banking industry; the private email server she used in her time as secretary of state; and the investigations into her alleged role in the alleged cover-up of the tragic death of four Americans at the Benghazi consulate, in Libya, facilitated Trump's desire to run against a corrupt Washington establishment in apocalyptic terms. What is more, Trump often called her "Crooked Hillary," presided over audiences who chanted "Lock her up" at his rallies, and threatened to put her in jail once becoming president at the second presidential debate. Given that Trump trailed in many national and state-wide polls leading up to the November election, he also suggested the election was rigged against him and, in the third presidential debate, refused to say whether he would accept the results if he lost. His final slogan of the campaign, "Drain the Swamp," referred to a corrupt elite in government that he would displace. Trump not only embraced the paranoid style, then, but established it as the core message and narrative of his campaign. Whereas Trump shifted the rhetorical frame from consistent party ideology to the paranoid style to distinguish himself from other Republicans in the primary process, he wielded the style in the general-election campaign in an effort to fully discredit his opponent.

In addition to traditional rhetorical exercises in political communication including speeches, debate performances, and television advertisements, Trump relied heavily on the social media platform of Twitter to communicate with public audiences. His provocative tweets often became the subject of news and invited criticism. Regardless, it allowed for generating more publicity and another rhetorical platform to reinforce the tenets of the paranoid style. On October 24, 2016—mere weeks before the election—Trump tweeted: "Wow, just came out on secret tape that Crooked Hillary wants to take in as many Syrians as possible. We cannot let this happen—ISIS!" (Trump, 2016c). It is unclear what specific Clinton policy—or what "secret tape"—Trump is referring to, but the suggestion that his opponent plans to allow terrorists to enter the U.S. is in keeping with the paranoid style. Another tweet, from October 18, demonstrates this conspiratorial fantasy as well: "If we let Crooked [Hillary] run the govt [*sic*], history will remember 2017 as the year America lost its independence. #DrainTheSwamp" (Trump, 2016a). These comments are just a sampling as reviewing over 34,000 tweets from Trump would surpass the scope of this chapter; needless to say, they demonstrate Trump's commitment to sustaining the paranoid style as a rhetorical narrative. He, as a candidate, not only sought to establish that the U.S. was under apocalyptic threats, but that those conspiracies are actively facilitated by those working in, and hoping to serve, the American government. Importantly, it is he, candidate Trump, who can drain the swamp and eliminate the internal and external threats that render American independence, security, and way of life vulnerable. Beyond his own comments, Trump continually retweeted other news stories and visual Internet memes that questioned Clinton's fitness for office with provocative allegations. On October 19, for example, Trump tweeted: "#CrookedHillary is nothing more than a Wall Street PUPPET! #BigLeagueTruth #Debate" (Trump, 2016b). The text of the tweet was accompanied by an animated image of Clinton as a marionette with strings controlled by a street sign of Wall Street. Twitter, taken as a whole, provided Trump a rhetorical platform to stretch and even exaggerate the paranoid style he was promulgating in his more traditional campaign oratory.

The November 2016 election is notable not only in that Trump achieved an electoral victory but how his presidency will be ushered in with a Republican-controlled Senate and House of Representatives. As most congressional Republicans adhere more consistently to the ideological principles of conservatism, President Trump will have to choose between adopting their policies or maintaining the conspiratorial mien he assumed as a public celebrity and candidate. It is unclear, as of this writing, which path he will take, but such questions are muddled because, as Hofstadter (1996) points out, the paranoid style has never been elevated into power on so grand a scale as the presidency. If President Trump does pass a significant amount of conservative legislation, it suggests political campaigns need not articulate any consistent positions to achieve their goals, but simply rely on conspiratorial fantasy. The paranoid style—and that of apocalyptic conspiracies in general—should not be dismissed as a simple minority movement. Afforded a broad enough platform to consistently be reinforced, the paranoid style emerges as an ongoing rhetorical narrative that activates user participation. Only time will tell whether the paranoid style completely eclipses conservatism as a set of governing policies or is but a front to shield its more unpopular attributes.

The Transmedia Branding of Candidate Trump

Trump's political rhetoric did not occur in a vacuum. It was supported by a transmedia storytelling campaign that dominated a profuse platform of discursive channels. The paranoid style is not strong enough to stand oratorically on its own through traditional political communication formats such as rallies and television but requires a comprehensive communications strategy to disseminate its messages. As such, Trump's campaign benefited from not only its own digital and social media platforms but by encouraging non-professionals to create and share content in service of the political brand of Trump. This process can be best understood, then, as a marketing exercise in transmedia storytelling. One solitary, dominant medium is not simply the message—at least not in 2016. Rather, as Madianou and Miller (2012) write, the "emerging environment of communicative opportunities function as an 'integrated structure' within which each individual medium is defined in relational terms in the context of all other media" (p. 170). Trump and his surrogates thus exploited different facets of the media in different ways. In addition to traditional rhetorical exercises in political communication including speeches, debate performances, and television advertisements, Trump, as detailed above, tweeted profusely, which made for a highly interactive, intimate campaign. And beyond Trump's own rhetorical activity, his surrogates in traditional media—such as former campaign manager Corey Lewandowski, who served as a paid commenter for CNN—meshed with the online platform of the alt-right movement through websites such as Breitbart News. Stephen Bannon, the chairman of Breitbart, was appointed in August 2016 to serve as the Trump campaign's chief executive; Kellyanne Conway, meanwhile, was named campaign manager at the same time. The interplay between Bannon and Conway is important to pay attention to: whereas Bannon, who identifies as a nationalist and often defies Republican Party norms, was not visible as a spokesperson on television, Conway, who is telegenic and a more traditional Republican in her past leanings and work in politics, became a prominent surrogate for Trump across both network and cable television. Splitting the campaign leadership like this was highly effective, from a transmedia branding standpoint. Bannon directed the efforts of arousing online support from alt-right nationalists who oppose certain tenets of conservative orthodoxy whereas Conway served as a traditional spokesperson for the conservative rank-and-file on legacy media platforms such as newspapers and television.

The strategic influence of Bannon, both from a media and political standpoint, should not be discounted. After the November 2016 election, Trump announced Bannon was being appointed to the role of senior counselor and chief White House strategist. Bannon broke his media silence by giving an interview to *The Hollywood Reporter*: "Like [Andrew] Jackson's populism, we're going to build an entirely new political movement," he said, adding, "The conservatives are going to go crazy" (quoted in Wolff, 2016, para. 14). Not only does this demonstrate the degree to which President Trump may countervail the forces of conservative ideology, it evinces the next logical step for the paranoid style to be transformed into a plan for governance. Bannon understands how transmedia branding and storytelling operates on a multiplatform level: beyond serving the Trump campaign, the incoming presidential administration, and Breitbart News, he is the founding chairman of the Government Accountability Institute (GAI), a non-profit organization "that builds rigorous, fact-based indictments against major politicians, then partners with mainstream media outlets conservatives typically despise to disseminate those findings to the broadest audience" (Green, 2015, para. 8). The president of GAI, Peter Schweitzer, published a 2015 book, *Clinton Cash*, which challenged the ethics of Hillary Clinton and received publicity from conventional news organizations. In an interview with *Bloomberg*, Bannon said: "What you realize hanging out with investigative reporters is that, while they may be personally liberal, they don't let that get in the way of a good story" (quoted in Green, 2015, para. 16). Just as the Trump campaign sought to elevate Kellyanne Conway in the mainstream media during election season, Bannon distinguished his own transmedia storytelling: a traditional, fact-based public relations campaign from a nonprofit to generate mainstream investigative stories against the opponent, and then provocative opinion pieces about nationalism on alt-right websites such as Breitbart News.

The structure of campaign messaging was thus integrated across various contexts. First, Trump himself, in speeches and on Twitter, would draw attention advancing the paranoid style. Second, surrogates on television, such as Lewandowski and Conway, would perform traditional punditry roles in supporting their preferred candidate. Third, nonprofits such as GAI would marshal information to convince mainstream media outlets to run stories critical of the opponent. And fourth, alt-right websites would traffic in conspiracy theories and provocative, if not racially motivated, opinions about the election and the meaning of Trump's candidacy. The elements of transmedia storytelling are here, but that is not all.

Encouraging fans to generate user content on message boards, blogs, and fan-fiction sites represents another staple of promoting corporate entertainment in transmedia storytelling. Though the transmedia paradigm of research often focuses on feature films, video games, and television shows (Scolari, 2013; Fast & Örnebring, 2015; Freeman, 2015), it is appropriate, given the creative and pervasive uses of media harnessed by Trump and his supporters, to consider transmedia branding and storytelling from a political perspective. As Jansson and Lindell (2015) point out, this method of communication crosses geographic boundaries in an "interconnected and open-ended circulation of media content between various platforms, where social agents are increasingly involved in the production of flows" (p. 82). Trump benefited from crowdsourcing user content across international borders to influence the American electorate. First, Trump publicly encouraged and solicited the help of Russian espionage and WikiLeaks to secure and disseminate negative information on the Democratic National Committee and Hillary Clinton and her campaign. Second, Trump supporters created online fake-news propaganda that was promoted on Facebook with likes and shares. Third, the conspiratorial fantasies from both the candidate and his supporters were developed and indulged on web platforms such as Alex Jones's Infowars webcast as well as the messaging boards of Reddit, its sub-Reddit The_Donald, and Pizzagate, in particular. These include not just wild allegations but the creation and distribution of playful memes such as self-identifying as "deplorables" and highlighting "Pepe the frog." For Trump supporters, transmedia storytelling served as a useful tool to promote the brand in the digital realm across social media.

Trump was, if nothing else, open about this complicity. "Russia, if you're listening, I hope you're able to find the 30,000 emails that are missing," he said during a July 2016 campaign speech referring to Hillary Clinton's private email server, adding, "I think you will probably be rewarded mightily by our press" (quoted in Parker & Sanger, 2016, para. 2). Whether influenced by this open invitation or not, WikiLeaks, the media organization devoted to publicizing leaked government documents, began releasing internal communications from the Democratic National Committee and the Clinton campaign from August through early November of 2016, leading up to the presidential election. Subsequently, American intelligence agencies have alleged that WikiLeaks came into possession of the communications from hacking by Russian espionage in an effort to influence the election in favor of Trump (Sanger & Shane, 2016). Debates over who obtained the hacked information and to what degree it persuaded voters for Trump may persist for some time. Whether or not it was a coordinated conspiracy at the behest of Russian espionage, though, we should recognize the hacking and leaking of information for how it contributed to a transmedia storytelling campaign. As reporting in *The New York Times* illustrates, "Every major publication, including *The Times*, published multiple stories citing the D.N.C. and Podesta emails posted by WikiLeaks, becoming a de facto instrument of Russian intelligence" (Lipton, Sanger, & Shane, 2016, para. 129). As a branding and licensing guru in his business practice, transmedia storytelling campaigns appear to come natural for Trump. Though we may never be able to pinpoint how closely aligned Trump was with these outside forces that contributed to the transmediated practices of generating politically discursive content during the campaign, it is clear he inspired—in fact, lobbied for—collaborative content from outside the norms of traditional campaigning.

Still, the user-generated content of transmedia storytelling in the 2016 election goes beyond the Ecuadorian embassy in London, where WikiLeaks founder Julian Assange resides, and Russian intelligence, whether or not President Vladimir Putin played a personal role in directing such espionage. The rise of fake news and its diffuse spread across social media demonstrates the global reach of transmedia storytelling and its impact on the 2016 election. Though hoaxes and fabrications are not new to American journalism (Henry, 2007), the news-aggregation potential of social media, with sites such as Facebook and Twitter—combined with the decrease in salience of legacy media such as newspapers, magazines, and television networks—played an outsized role in shaping what information the public absorbed. This (mis-)information was both user generated and shared with and by the public, speaking to a velocity of mediated communication with a global reach. As Smith and Banic (2016) reported for NBC News, "The articles, sensationalist and often baseless, were posted to Facebook, drawing in armies of readers and earning fake-news writers money from penny-per-click advertising" (para. 4). The fake-news author interviewed for this particular story, meanwhile, came from a village in Macedonia, and he generated revenue from articles with headlines such as, "JUST IN: Obama Illegally Transferred DOJ Money To Clinton Campaign!." "Nothing can beat Trump's supporters when it comes to social media engagement," the author told Smith and Banic (para. 7). The transmedia prosumers in support of Trump were not just from Macedonia, however, as *The New York Times* reported how a British citizen, James Dowson, created "a constellation of websites" such as The Patriot News Agency to influence American voters with "pro-Trump hoaxes tying his opponent Hillary Clinton to Satanism, pedophilia and other conspiracies" (McIntire, 2016, paras. 4, 2). Whereas propaganda, traditionally understood, functions in a top-down manner seeking to persuade and gain compliance from a passive audience, political transmedia storytelling relies on interactive publics who create, disseminate, and share distorted information. Fake news and other user-generated content serves as transmedia storytelling that contributes to a comprehensive communications strategy surrounding a brand—in this case, Trump.

If transmedia storytelling is different from traditional propaganda, it owes to operating in a more engaged fashion with respect to conspiracy theories. One particular fake-news story, Pizzagate, is as illustrative as it is troubling. The conspiracy cropped up in October 2016 in response to the WikiLeaks release of documents that supplied hacked emails from Clinton's campaign chair, John Podesta. Though untrue, social media platforms such as the Pizzagate sub-Reddit established and circulated "the belief that code words and satanic symbols point[ed] to a sordid" child-sex ring of pedophilia at the behest of Hillary Clinton and her campaign, and that a pizzeria in Washington, D.C., was the operation's headquarters (Fisher, Cox, & Hermann, 2016, para. 5). As a result, Trump supporter and talk-show host Alex Jones, of Infowars, stated, in a YouTube video, "When I think about all the children Hillary Clinton has personally murdered and chopped up and raped, I have zero fear standing up against her" (quoted in Fisher, Cox, & Hermann, 2016, para. 10). One North Carolina man grew so agitated about the alleged Pizzagate child-sex ring that he drove to Washington in order to personally investigate the restaurant. In the process, he fired rounds from an assault-like rifle and was arrested, though no one was reported injured. Nothing about the story was true, but social media allows for conspiratorial fantasies to sustain themselves. As Kang and Goldman (2016) concluded in *The New York Times*, "Debunking false news articles can sometimes stoke the outrage of the believers, leading fake news purveyors to feed that appetite with more misinformation" (para. 9). When, for instance, the CEO of Reddit stepped in to ban the Pizzagate sub-Reddit, where the conspiracy incubated, the *Washington Post* reported how the redditors in charge of the sub-forum adapted by moving the discussion to an alternative online platform (Ohlheiser, 2016).

Transmedia storytelling is thus not limited to an exercise in branding corporate entertainment. Adapted to the political sphere and given the contemporary global infrastructure of online and social media, it is a world-building enterprise that seeks to activate audiences as participants. Ideology is subordinate to the entertaining narratives created and shared among like-minded people. The veracity or appropriateness of such user-generated content does not matter and may even, as suggested in *The New York Times*, cement beliefs in that which is false. The fragmented mainstream news media—which dropped in public trust to an all-time low of 32% in 2016, according to Gallup (Swift, 2016)—cannot redress the paranoia as it, too, is seen as biased. Between the creative, chaotic new media forces of the digital realm and a traditional mass media facing structural challenges and a lack of trust, the 2016 election campaign was ripe to be exploited by a transmedia storytelling campaign in the service of a brand. Considering Trump's business practices center on the licensing of his name and celebrity as a brand, it is little wonder that he, as a political candidate in the age of social media, would be able to galvanize an effective transmedia storytelling campaign.

Conclusion

It is neither appropriate nor possible to conclude definitively whether it was Trump's paranoid rhetorical style, enmeshed within a transmedia storytelling campaign, that secured an electoral victory in 2016. Trump, after all, lost the popular vote by more than two-and-a-half million votes nationwide. However, we can state the dynamic qualities of Trump's communications strategy as sui generis. Both he and his closest strategic advisor, Bannon, openly defied the norms of conservative ideology and modern political campaigning, yet they still achieved a victory for the Republican Party in capturing the presidency. Two significant conclusions may be drawn from this analysis, then. First, the rhetoric of the paranoid style is not limited to minority conspiracy theory movements on the margins of society and can displace the traditional tenets of party policies in a national campaign. Specifically, the paranoid style may be activated as an ongoing rhetorical narrative that invites participation. Second, transmedia storytelling, often understood as part of user-generated content and world-building in corporate entertainment, can flourish in political campaigns as part of a comprehensive communication strategy with a global reach. Trump dominated the media through his rhetoric in speeches and on Twitter, the pervasive earned coverage generated by the reporting on his provocative behavior, and the user-generated content by his international following across the digital spaces of websites, message boards, and social media. Though Hillary Clinton delivered polished performances in the traditional media spaces of political communication, such as the convention speech and the debates, the media ecosystem of politics had changed. In the absence (but also shattering) of political norms, an entirely different playing field in American politics emerged. Trump, his campaign, and his prosumer-supporters exploited these new media spaces in politics by enacting an all-out blitz replete with conspiracies, provocations, and propaganda. The creators and purveyors of fake news on Facebook, Twitter, and Reddit recognized the lack of a public trust in traditional news sources. The misinformation that ensued in the 2016 presidential campaign is a product of determined propaganda but also, it should be said, the inability of the fragmented media ecosystem of American journalism to play its traditional gatekeeping role. Ideally, the traditional news media of newspapers and television would officiate the behavior and ideas of political candidates; in 2016, though, they were left as spectators while the game was played online.

The startling profusion of conspiracy narratives offered in apocalyptic terms across different mediated channels of information overwhelmed the contemporary media infrastructure. If ideology, in the end, did not matter—conservative ideology, in particular—partisanship still did. Politics in 2016 was not a debate about ideas but a game to be won with the help of a home-field advantage through transmedia storytelling. Perhaps, in the future, social media websites such as Facebook will begin to regulate the dissemination of fake news. Even so, transmedia storytelling traverses both the geographic borders of place as well as the virtual thresholds of online space. It is a powerful branding tool that invites the creation of content on a global scale and, as witnessed in the 2016 presidential election, has the power to upend political norms and influence elections.

Further research adapting transmedia storytelling to political discourses is needed, both situating transmedia strategies theoretically within the public sphere as well as examining previous campaigns that sought to generate content from social and online media. The 2004 presidential campaign of Howard Dean, for instance, is known as one of the first to energize online supporters, but Dean ultimately failed to win a single state in the primary elections of that year. The 2008 candidacy of Barack Obama may also warrant interest as his campaign drew user-generated content in the form of inspiring posters and YouTube videos to win the primaries as an underdog and then comfortably achieve victory in the general election. As the Dean campaign suggests, though, transmedia storytelling is not, in and of itself, a guarantee for political success. However, it represents an important strategic force when enfolded into a broader communications plan. In the case of Trump and Obama, it appears that political transmedia storytelling works most effectively when tied, like corporate entertainment, to that of a brand. Though their political differences run deep, both Obama and Trump possess clearly established, recognizable brands of ethos that can be operationalized by others to contribute to an ongoing political narrative. Just as Obama offered a narrative of hope that became rhetorically operational through mediated content, Trump offered the apocalyptic fervor of paranoia. Hillary Clinton and her surrogates were certainly critical of Trump as a candidate, but there is little evidence of her candidacy inspiring a global level of user-generated content in the digital realm. In terms of branding, Clinton relied on her experience as a former First Lady, senator, and secretary of state. Yet this tied her to the political establishment against which Trump founded his campaign. Worse, claiming Trump was unfit for office energized those who supported Trump precisely because he was unfit as a political outsider. Clinton's campaign thus failed to generate a narrative for her and her supporters while feeding fuel to the transmedia storytelling campaign Trump and his supporters were burning across the digital media environment.

Fisher (1987) argued how narratives function as the chief communication device among humans to share and understand information as well as be persuaded. Though the narrative paradigm focuses exclusively on rhetorical strategies, the 2016 campaign demonstrated, if it was not clear beforehand, that rhetoric is not only mass mediated but that mass media, as an intertwining of technological channels and content, are rhetorical. There is no daylight between media studies and rhetorical practices; within the transmedia storytelling paradigm, there are not even strict geographical boundaries in place to control the velocity of communication. Digital media spaces are thus simultaneously global and rhetorical. As such, Trump's narrative of the paranoid style, which was disseminated through a transmedia storytelling campaign worthy of corporate-branded entertainment, collapsed not just the ideological principles of conservatism, then, but any distinction between media and rhetoric. There is not one medium that functions as the message; rather, the message is diffusely spread across media.

References

Alberta, T. (2016, December 21). Conservatism in the era of Trump. *National Review*. Retrieved from www.nationalreview.com/article/443236/donald-trump-conservatism-right-wing-future

Confessore, N., & Yourish, K. (2016, March 15). $2 billion worth of free media for Donald Trump. *New York Times*. Retrieved from www.nytimes.com/2016/03/16/upshot/measuring-donald-trumps-mammoth-advantage-in-free-media.html

Fast, K., & Örnebring, H. (2015). Transmedia world-building: *The Shadow* (1931-present) and *Transformers* (1984-present). *International Journal of Cultural Studies*, 1–17. doi:10.1177/1367877915605887

Fisher, M., Cox, J. W., & Hermann, P. (2016, December 6). Pizzagate: From rumor, to hashtag, to gunfire in D.C. *Washington Post*. Retrieved from www.washingtonpost.com/local/pizzagate-from-rumor-to-hashtag-to-gunfire-in-dc/2016/12/06/4c7def50-bbd4-11e6-94ac-3d324840106c_story.html

Fisher, W. R. (1987). *Human communication as narration: Toward a philosophy of reason, value, and action*. Columbia, SC: University of South Carolina Press.

Freeman, M. (2015). Up, up and across: Superman, the Second World War and the historical development of transmedia storytelling. *Historical Journal of Film, Radio & Television, 35*(2), 215–239.

Green, J. (2015, October 8). This man is the most dangerous political operative in America. *Bloomberg Businessweek*. Retrieved from www.bloomberg.com/politics/graphics/2015-steve-bannon/

Henry, N. (2007). *American carnival: Journalism under siege in an age of new media*. Berkeley, CA: University of California Press.

Hofstadter, R. (1996). *The paranoid style in American politics and other essays*. Cambridge, MA: Harvard University Press.
Jansson, A., & Lindell, J. (2015). News media consumption in the transmedia age: Amalgamations, orientations, and geo-social structuration. *Journalism Studies, 16*(1), 79–96.
Jenkins, H. (2010). Transmedia storytelling and entertainment: An annotated syllabus. *Continuum: Journal of Media and Cultural Studies, 24*(6), 943–958.
Johnson, D. W. (2016). *Campaigning in the twenty-first century: Activism, big data, and dark money* (2nd ed.). New York, NY: Routledge.
Kang, C., & Goldman, A. (2016, December 5). In Washington pizzeria attack, fake news brought real guns. *New York Times*. Retrieved from www.nytimes.com/2016/12/05/business/media/comet-ping-pong-pizza-shooting-fake-news-consequences.html
Karl, J. (2016, September 7). The last time Donald Trump talked about 'Birtherism'. *ABC News*. Retrieved from http://abcnews.go.com/Politics/time-donald-trump-talked-birtherism/story
Lee, M. J. (2012). The conservative canon and its uses. *Rhetoric & Public Affairs, 15*(1), 1–40.
Lipton, E., Sanger, D. E., & Shane, S. (2016, December 13). The perfect weapon: How Russian cyberpower invaded the U.S. *The New York Times*. Retrieved from www.nytimes.com/2016/12/13/us/politics/russia-hack-election-dnc.html
Madianou, M., & Miller, D. (2012). Polymedia: Towards a new theory of digital media in interpersonal communication. *International Journal of Cultural Studies, 16*(2), 169–187.
McIntire, M. (2016, December 17). How a Putin fan overseas pushed pro-Trump propaganda to Americans. *New York Times*. Retrieved from www.nytimes.com/2016/12/17/world/europe/russia-propaganda-elections.html
Ohlheiser, A. (2016, November 24). Fearing yet another witch hunt, Reddit bans 'Pizzagate'. *Washington Post*. Retrieved from www.washingtonpost.com/news/the-intersect/wp/2016/11/23/fearing-yet-another-witch-hunt-reddit-bans-pizzagate/
Oliver, J. E., & Wood, T. J. (2014). Conspiracy theories and the paranoid style(s) of mass opinion. *American Journal of Political Science, 58*(4), 952–966.
Parker, A., & Sanger, D. E. (2016, July 27). Donald Trump calls on Russia to find Hillary Clinton's missing emails. *New York Times*. Retrieved from www.nytimes.com/2016/07/28/us/politics/donald-trump-russia-clinton-emails.html
Postman, N. (1985). *Amusing ourselves to death: Public discourse in the age of show-business*. New York, NY: Penguin Books.
Rogin, J. (2016, July 18). Trump campaign guts GOP's anti-Russia stance on Ukraine. *Washington Post*. Retrieved from www.washingtonpost.com/opinions/global-opinions/trump-campaign-guts-gops-anti-russia-stance-on-ukraine/2016/07/18/98adb3b0-4cf3-11e6-a7d8-13d06b37f256_story.html
Sanger, D. E., & Shane, S. (2016, December 9). Russian hackers acted to aid Trump in election, U.S. says. *New York Times*. Retrieved from www.nytimes.com/2016/12/09/us/obama-russia-election-hack.html
Scolari, C. A. (2013). Lostology: Transmedia storytelling and expansion/compression strategies. *Semiotica, 195*, 45–68.
Serazio, M. (2016). Encoding the paranoid style in American politics: 'Anti-establishment' discourse and power in contemporary spin. *Critical Studies in Media Communication, 33*(2), 181–194.
Smith, A., & Banic, V. (2016, December 9). Fake news: How a partying Macedonian teen earns thousands publishing lies. *NBC News*. Retrieved from www.nbcnews.com/news/world/fake-news-how-partying-macedonian-teen-earns-thousands-publishing-lies-n692451

Streitmatter, R. (2012). *Mightier than the sword: How the news media have shaped American history* (3rd ed.). Boulder, CO: Westview Press.

Swift, A. (2016, September 24). Americans' trust in mass media sinks to new low. *Gallup*. Retrieved from www.gallup.com/poll/195542/americans-trust-mass-media-sinks-new-low.aspx

Trump, D. J. (2015, June 16). Donald Trump presidential announcement speech. New York, NY. Retrieved from http://time.com/3923128/donald-trump-announcement-speech/

Trump, D. J. [@realdonaldtrump]. (2016a, October 18). If we let crooked run the govt. *Twitter*. Retrieved from https://twitter.com/realDonaldTrump/status/788403448593002496

Trump, D. J. [@realdonaldtrump]. (2016b, October 19). #CrookedHillary. *Twitter*. Retrieved from https://twitter.com/realDonaldTrump/status/788921683629400064

Trump, D. J. [@realdonaldtrump]. (2016c, October 24). Wow, just came out on secret tape. *Twitter*. Retrieved from https://twitter.com/realDonaldTrump/status/790523240351498241

White, K. (2016). Donald Trump and the scourge of populism. *Forum*, *14*(3), 265–279.

Wolff, M. (2016, November 18). Ringside with Steve Bannon at Trump Tower as the president-elect's strategist plots 'an entirely new political movement'. *Hollywood Reporter*. Retrieved from www.hollywoodreporter.com/news/steve-bannon-trump-tower-interview-trumps-strategist-plots-new-political-movement-948747

11

HUMOR USE AND POLICY MENTIONS IN CANDIDATE INTERVIEWS ACROSS TALK-SHOW SUB-GENRES IN THE 2016 PRESIDENTIAL ELECTION

Dannagal G. Young and Johanna M. Lukk

In a fragmented media environment in which politically disinterested citizens can tune out from political life altogether, political candidates struggle to reach all of their political constituents (Prior, 2007). This mediated landscape has given presidential candidates cause to look to other venues to present an unfiltered presentation of themselves, instead of an edited snapshot of their views (Hallin, 1992). In addition to reaching voters directly through social media such as Twitter and Facebook, one solution candidates have adopted is to appear on daytime, prime-time, and late-night talk-shows. In a digital media environment, such interview segments enjoy a life that extends beyond the airing of the shows themselves, as they are shared as short video segments through Facebook and Twitter. During the 2016 campaign, voters were treated to memorable (and sometimes criticized) candidate appearances across daytime, late-night and satire talk-shows. From Secretary Hillary Clinton on *Ellen* to Governor Jeb Bush on Colbert's *Late Show* to Donald Trump on *Jimmy Fallon*, these talk-show interviews establish a tone of "regular" people discussing political topics in accessible and informal ways (Baym, 2010). Talk-shows such as late-night comedy programs or daytime talk-shows are generally considered to offer a supportive environment for politicians where they can expect few difficult or hard-hitting questions (Baum, 2005). Overall, the entertainment talk-show genre is a broad one that encompasses several sub-genres, each with its own appeal, philosophy, and audience. With those distinctions come notable differences in the nature of the candidate interviews and conversations we might expect to see on such shows.

Data show that the number of candidate interviews on talk-shows increased from 20 in 2000 to 27 in 2004, 101 appearances in 2008, and 48 (the drop attributable to Obama's incumbent status) in 2012 (Parkin, 2014). Research indicates that both parties use this tactic equally. These "new political television" programs offer novel ways of talking about politics using a combination of information and entertainment-based appeals (Jones, 2009). The producers of these shows present political and current events content in a way that follows the production norms and ethos of fictional entertainment programming (Jones & Baym, 2010). Most importantly, these programs were not created with politics at the center. A publicist for *The Tonight Show* stated, "Of course ratings are top priority . . . If people get anything out of it, that's fine, but that's not why we are doing this. We're not 'Hardball'" (Baum, 2005, p. 273). The producers have found that focusing on personal qualities of candidates over policy platforms is widely received and more engaging for their audiences (Baum, 2003). This kind of attitude toward political content on the part of producers strengthens the motives for candidates to seek = these venues as quasi-apolitical forums to connect with voters on matters of personality and biography.

Personalization of Politics

The increase of candidate appearances on these types of programs has been linked to various causes, including media fragmentation and advancements in media innovations (Jones, 2009). In addition, due to changes in the party nominating processes, which include voter-centered primary campaigns, we have witnessed a shift away from the power of political parties towards individual politicians (Dalton & Wattenberg, 2002; Garzia, 2011; Mazzoleni, 2000). Voters are increasingly disconnected from political parties, with increasing numbers of Americans reporting being politically "independent" (Dalton & Wattenberg, 2002; Garzia, 2011). Citizens' perceptions of politics today are based less on ideology and party, and more on evaluations of individual politicians. In fact, Kaase (1994) found when respondents were asked to discuss positive or negative aspects of political parties, citizens framed their responses in terms of individual politicians instead. Today's citizens evaluate presidential candidates with the same criteria they use to evaluate friends and peers (Sullivan, Aldrich, Borgida, & Rahn, 1990). Rahat and Sheafer (2007) defined personalization as the "change in the presentation of politics in the media, as expressed in a heightened focus on individual politicians and a diminished focus on parties' organizations and institutions" (p. 67). This shift puts more emphasis on politicians as individual people, rather than as representatives of their party or ideological leaning. This trend towards "candidate-centered politics" has come to dominate how campaigns are conducted and covered (Swanson & Mancini, 1996). Because of this, candidates are increasingly invested in the image they present to the public (Newman, 1999).

Entertainment talk-show appearances offer candidates a way to connect with citizens, not as politicians but as human beings with interests and concerns that mirror those of the audience. As candidate personality emerges as an increasingly important criteria upon which citizens evaluate candidates (Jones & Hudson, 1996), cultivating a familiar and accessible persona becomes crucial to a campaign's success. Candidate appearances on talk-show programs allow candidates to show a personal, private side of themselves, while appearing separate from their political party as a whole. One specific rhetorical device that we see used by political candidates across their talk-show appearances is humor. Humor can be used strategically to reduce tension, foster connection, and promote understanding.

Humor and Politics: Self- vs. Other-Deprecation

Humor is often used by politicians to make themselves more relatable to the audience or to undermine the credibility of their opponents (Stewart, 2011). Through the strategic use of self-deprecating humor and other-deprecating humor, candidates are able to define themselves and make their opponents appear less qualified or acceptable (Sloane, 2001). Self-deprecating humor allows a speaker to present and acknowledge personal flaws and mistakes by addressing them in a playful way. It is typically self-directed and invites the audience to laugh at the faults or short-comings of the speaker, hence putting the audience and the speaker on equal footing (Meyer, 2000). Through these exchanges, speakers are perceived as more accessible to the audience, which can lead to increases in overall likability (Stewart, 2011). Research on the perceived effectiveness of self- and other-deprecating humor used by candidates in a debate context indicates that self-deprecation is perceived as most effective (Bippus, 2007).

In contrast to self-deprecating humor is other-deprecating humor. Other-deprecating humor highlights a key distinction between the speaker and the target of the joke (Meyer, 2000). The humor targets an opposing individual, group, or concept, and tries to reduce support for that entity through ridicule and insult (Lorenz, 2002; Zillmann, 1983). According to work by Stewart (2012), in the 2008 primaries, other-deprecation was the most frequently used type of humor by candidates, with two-thirds of all laughter resulting from these other-deprecating interactions (Stewart, 2012). When laughter is evoked through the use of other-deprecating humor, it signals a bond between the speaker and the audience, and differentiates them *all* from the target of the joke, creating an "us versus them" scenario (Stewart, 2012).

Talk-Show Sub-Genres

As we think about the unique genres of programming on which political candidates make appearances, it becomes clear that a brief exploration of each is warranted. In this section, we highlight the key defining features of the production norms and atmosphere across traditional news programming, daytime talk, late-night comedy programming, and satire programs.

Traditional News Interviews

Primetime news programs are often the home of the traditional political interview. These interviews might focus on policies, but are often dominated by conversations about polls—so-called "horse-race" coverage—and questions of candidate strategy and outreach (Patterson, 2011). Often, such interviews are the home to "gotcha journalism" (Baym, 2007; Jones, 2009), in which the interviewer attempts to catch a guest in a discrepancy between current and prior statements they have made on a topic. This type of interview is exemplified by programs such as *The O'Reilly Factor* (on Fox News), *CBS Evening News*, and *60 Minutes* (on CBS). According to Clayman and Heritage (2002), the functions of presidential candidate interviews on traditional news programs include sharing concrete statements of official policy, holding officials accountable, and making public debate available to citizens. Cable news channels such as CNN, Fox, and MSNBC, although varied in their partisan leanings, all offer candidate interviews featuring a mix of current events, policy, and strategy discussion between the candidate and a journalist or pundit. The conversations typically center on the campaign dynamics and policy positions (occasionally), but less on the personal biography or personality of the candidate (Parkin, 2014).

Daytime Talk

Daytime talk-show programs, such as *Oprah*, *Ellen*, and *The View*, are entertainment oriented and often include a humorous and relaxed atmosphere. Most episodes feature a guest who engages with the host in a question-response sequence (Ilie, 2001). According to Fairclough, daytime talk serves as an extension of a casual interaction; the exchange allows viewers to feel included in the content being discussed (Fairclough, 1995). The cadence and tone of these interactions tends to mirror that of casual conversation with the topics discussed ranging from personal conflicts to larger issues affecting society as a whole. Daytime talk-shows employ primarily female hosts, have females in positions of creative control, and address issues central to females and minorities (Villalobos, 2012).

Baum's work (2003) suggests that when interviewing politicians and candidates, shows such as Oprah's rarely mention political parties or partisan themes. Instead, appearances on her show present an opportunity to connect with a less politically engaged segment of the population on matters of human interest such as family and biographic information (Baum, 2003). Addressing struggles and vulnerabilities in the context of daytime talk is not only acceptable but encouraged as a way to connect with the female audience (who make up 78% of the daytime talk audience). These direct appeals have been found to increase engagement, efficacy, and political discussion among female audiences (Villalobos, 2012).

One of the beneficial consequences of exposure to daytime talk appears to be the "gateway effect" (Baum, 2003) through which politically inattentive viewers are incidentally exposed to politically relevant information in an apolitical programming environment. As Baum notes, "personality driven political entertainment appearances on TV talk-shows afford the candidates their best opportunity to communicate with a substantial niche of the electorate" (Baum, 2003, p. 213). Baum and Jamison (2011) explain that the "piggybacking" of politically relevant information on top of entertainment programming makes political information accessible and can encourage otherwise politically disinterested viewers to then seek more information on the topic.

Late-Night Comedy

Programs classified as network late-night comedy present some political humor in the context of monologues, headlines, and celebrity interviews. Examples of the late-night comedy genre include *The Late Show* on CBS, *The Tonight Show* on NBC, and *Jimmy Kimmel! Live!* on ABC. These programs serve as a way for presidential candidates to gain exposure to a more diverse audience than daytime talk (Feldman & Young, 2008). The hosts of programs such as *The Tonight Show* and *The Late Show* portray themselves as the "average" citizen. This portrayal allows the programs to present easy-to-understand interviews with high-profile guests. Hosts deliver pre-scripted questions using vernacular that is simplified, leaving out the wonky political speak typical of news programming (Baym, 2013). The audience of late-night comedy is the most diverse of talk-show programs in terms of gender, age, and political party affiliation (Parkin, 2014). This diverse audience combined with the opportunities for strategic use of humor provide unique advantages to presidential candidates interested in mocking themselves or others in a public forum that is playful and accessible.

In terms of issue coverage in a late-night comedy context, Young and Tisinger (2006) found that viewers of late-night programs such as those hosted by Jay Leno and David Letterman were associated with higher levels of political knowledge and news attention than was found among non-viewers of the shows. Similar to the "gateway" effect articulated by Baum (2003) in the context of daytime talk-show programming, late-night comedy programming has been found to encourage subsequent information seeking (Feldman & Young, 2008). These findings suggest that, although not its main focus, late-night comedy shows do "piggyback" political issues and information on top of their entertainment fare (Baum, 2003).

Political Satire Programming

We define the "political satire program" as that which is entertainment and comedy oriented, but with a strict focus on politics and current events. This includes programming akin to *The Daily Show* (with Jon Stewart or Trevor Noah) or *The Colbert Report*, *Last Week Tonight with John Oliver* (on HBO), *Full*

Frontal with Samantha Bee (on TBS), and *The Larry Wilmore Show* (on Comedy Central). Previous research has found that watching political satire programming such as this is associated with higher levels of political knowledge, higher political participation, and increased levels of interpersonal discussion involving politics (Cao & Brewer, 2008; Young & Tisinger, 2006; Young & Esralew, 2011; Young & Hoffman, 2012).

These programs highlight inconsistencies in political rhetoric and use satire to draw attention to the dysfunction of the "norms" governing typical news media (Young, 2008). The programs explore this contrast with clips or references to traditional news outlets from earlier in the day or week. This hybrid form of satire and news is a combination of investigative reporting, punditry, and comedy show. These shows contextualize and mash up reports and footage from other news outlets, while the hosts present themselves as the common citizen, discussing politics in casual, often-humorous, and above-all accessible terms (Baym, 2010). Interviews on these programs vary in frequency, with Jon Stewart engaging in several candidate interviews over his years on *The Daily Show* to hosts such as John Oliver airing very few, if any. What is important to note, however, is that when they do occur, political interviews on these programs are substantive, discursive, and policy oriented (Baym, 2010). Although they have moments of light-hearted play, they also offer a serious discussion of political ideology, current events, and issues. Some content analyses indicate comparable rates of substantive policy discussions on shows such as *The Daily Show* as we would find on traditional news programming (Fox, Koloen, & Sahin, 2007), hence making it unsurprising that the policy-related content in candidate interviews on these programs is salient as well.

Research Questions

When the media environment is as full of hybridity as the current one, it is important to understand, through formal analysis, how politicians are using various programs and what role those programs may be playing in terms of personalizing candidates and offering policy discussions. Our goal is to better understand the kinds of exchanges that occur between candidates in such interviews—specifically with regards to the quantity and nature of humor employed, as well as the extent of policy discussions that take place.

RQ1: Which form of humor (self- or other-deprecating) is most commonly used by presidential candidates?

RQ2: How does the prevalence of humor vary across talk-show sub-genres?

RQ3: How do candidates vary in their use of self- and other-deprecating humor?

RQ4: How does the prevalence of policy discussion vary across talk-show sub-genre?

Methods

The formal quantitative content analysis was completed during the 2016 presidential primaries (December 1, 2015 to March 1, 2016). With a larger number of candidates looking to connect with voters in the primaries compared to the general election, we imagined that the primaries would be an appropriate context in which to content analyze a sizable sample of candidate interviews. The programs included in the analysis were obtained through two different collection methods: standard television DVR and online resources from the cable providers. Programs examined include three programs of each type: traditional news-oriented broadcasts (*NBC Nightly News, The O'Reilly Factor, Rachel Maddow*), daytime talk-shows (*Ellen, The View, The Talk*), late-night comedy shows (*The Late Show with Stephen Colbert, The Tonight Show with Jimmy Fallon, Jimmy Kimmel Live*), and political satire shows (*The Daily Show with Trevor Noah, Last Week Tonight with John Oliver, and The Nightly Show with Larry Wilmore*). The coding scheme captured the air date, title of the program, program length, and each candidate's name, gender, and party. The coding scheme also captured the following key constructs:

> **Total number of policy or issue mentions** was coded and mentions were broken down into categories of foreign policy, education, environment, health, economy, and other.
>
> **Self-deprecating humor** included any time the candidate made a joke in which the target of the joke was him- or herself. When a candidate made multiple self-deprecating comments in succession, each of the comments was coded as an individual instance of self-deprecation. When a candidate made a joke that targeted themselves as well as another individual, this was coded separately as one instance of self-deprecation and one instance of other-deprecation.
>
> **Other-deprecating humor** was coded when the speaker made a joke in which the target of the joke was anyone other than him/herself. It could be an individual, group, or institution. If a candidate's joke targeted more than one party or individual within a single joke, each individual target of the joke was coded as a separate instance of other-deprecation.

The principal investigator and a second graduate student coder engaged in independent coding of a subsample of 20 of the interviews from the dataset. Krippendorff's Alpha of .70 or above was attained for all main constructs of interest, including: a) total instances of humor, b) self-deprecating humor, c) other-deprecating humor, and d) references to policies and issues.

Results

Frequency of candidate appearances across talk-show sub-genres is shown in Table 11.1. Overall, traditional public affairs/news programs saw the most candidate interviews compared to the three entertainment-oriented talk-show

TABLE 11.1 Frequency of Appearances by Candidates Within Talk-Show Sub-Genre

Candidate	*Traditional News*	*Daytime Talk*	*Political Satire*	*Late-Night Comedy*	*Total Interviews*
Donald Trump	7	0	0	2	9
Bernie Sanders	3	1	1	2	7
Hillary Clinton	4	1	0	1	6
Marco Rubio	1	0	1	1	3
Rand Paul	1	0	1	1	3
Ben Carson	2	0	0	0	2
Ted Cruz	1	0	0	0	1
Mike Huckabee	0	1	0	0	1
Chris Christie	1	0	0	0	1
Total	20	3	3	7	33

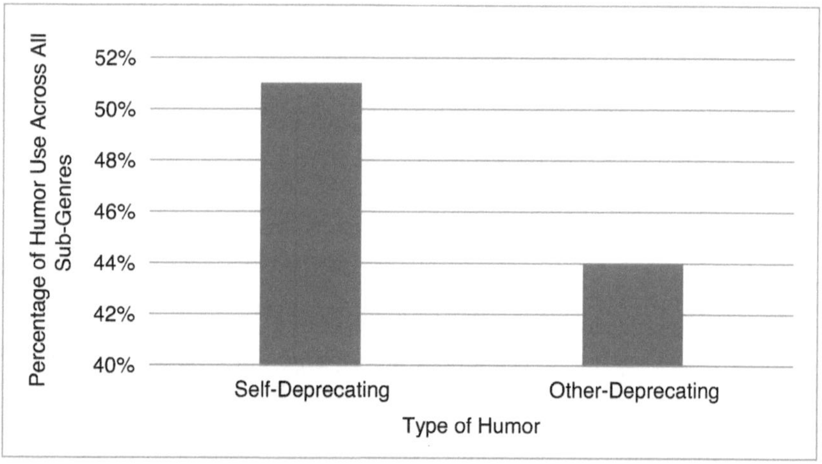

FIGURE 11.1 Percentage of Type of Humor Used Across All Talk-Show Sub-Genres

sub-genres. Trump, Sanders, and Clinton had the most appearances on the programs coded here, compared to Rubio, Cruz, Carson, and others.

RQ1 examined the relative frequency of self-deprecating humor versus other-deprecating humor used by political candidates across all talk-show programs. As indicated in Figure 11.1, although both self- and other-deprecating humor were used by candidates, self-deprecation was employed most frequently.

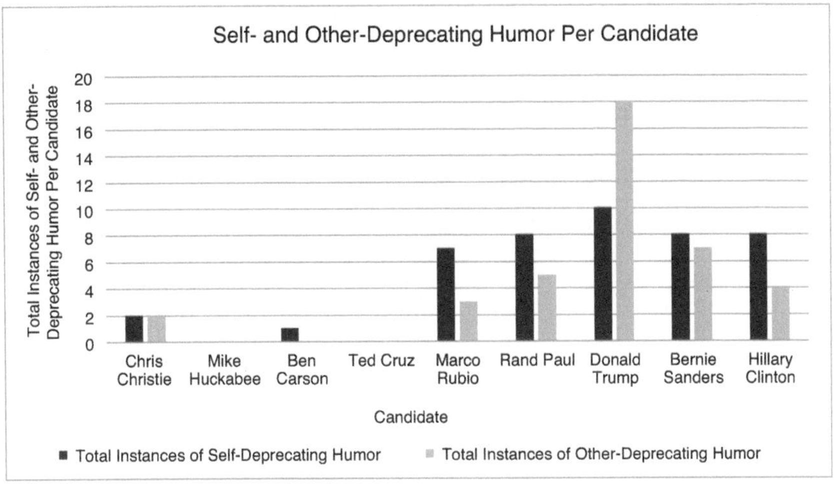

FIGURE 11.2 Self- and Other-Deprecating Humor Used by Candidates

Self-deprecating humor comprised 51%, or 44 out of 86 of the total instances of humor coded across all programs. Other-deprecating humor comprised 44%, or 38 out of 86 total instances.

To better understand differences in the use of self- and other-deprecating humor across the various candidates (RQ3), we explored the prevalence of these forms of humor across all interviews per candidate. Results are shown in Figure 11.2.

As illustrated in Figure 11.2, eventual Democratic nominee, Hillary Clinton, rarely used other-deprecating humor, in spite of the fact that she (along with Trump and Sanders) had the highest number of interviews captured in our analysis. Instead, Clinton appeared to be more comfortable using self-deprecating humor, often to diffuse criticism.

Another striking finding (see Figure 11.2) is the significant number of other-deprecating humorous comments from eventual GOP nominee Donald Trump. The spirit and function of these comments stands in stark contrast to the self-deprecating humor of Clinton. For example, in an appearance on *The Tonight Show with Jimmy Fallon*, Trump used the opportunity to criticize both Clinton and her Democratic opponent, Bernie Sanders, in the same response. Fallon asked, "Let's talk about Hillary Clinton. How do you think she's doing?" Trump responds,

> Well it's tough. I think she's having a tough time. She's got some guy [Sanders], I mean, he should be easy to beat! I mean how can you lose like this! He really isn't even a Democrat; I mean he said he's a socialist!

RQ2, concerning the frequency of candidate humor across talk-show sub-genres, is explored in Figure 11.3. Instances of humor were most frequent in late-night comedy interviews (6.7 instances per interview), followed by political satire (5.5 instances per interview) and daytime talk (2 instances per interview).

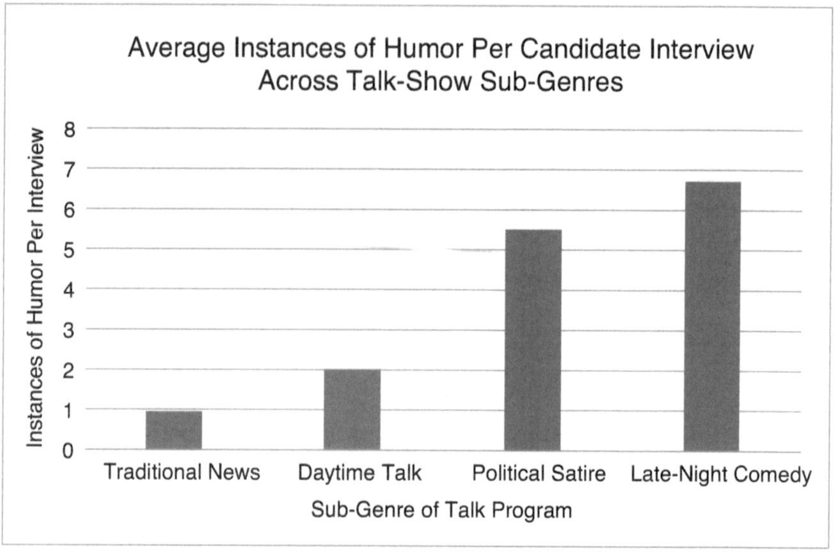

FIGURE 11.3 Average Instances of Humor Per Candidate Interview Across Talk-Show Sub-Genres

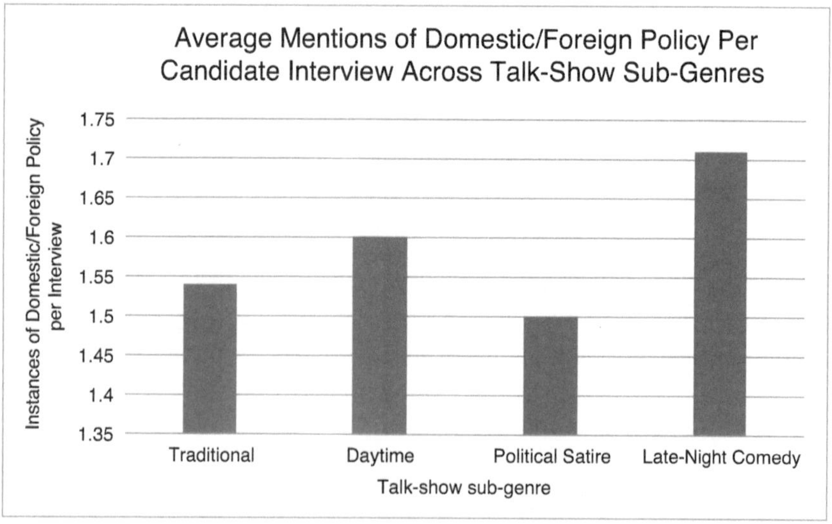

FIGURE 11.4 Average Policy Mentions Per Interview Across Talk-Show Sub-Genres

Humor was least prevalent in the traditional news interview context (less than one instance per interview).

Turning now to RQ4 concerning references to foreign and domestic policy, the data are striking. Although one might anticipate references to foreign and domestic policy to be most frequent in traditional public affairs/news interviews compared to the entertainment talk-show genres, this did not prove to be true. With seven candidate appearances and 12 domestic/foreign policy mentions, late-night comedy programs had the most total policy mentions per candidate interview, with 1.71 mentions per candidate appearance. Traditional news had 1.54 mentions per candidate appearance, daytime talk had 1.6 mentions per candidate appearance, and political satire had 1.5 mentions per candidate appearance.

It seems that although late-night comedy programs served as a place for humor, they also served as a forum to at least make mention of policies and issues. Take, for example, the January interview with Trump on *The Tonight Show with Jimmy Fallon* (January 11, 2016); Fallon asked Trump about his recent statements regarding the banning of Muslims from the country, stating,

> I don't know what you're going to do or say next, I don't think anyone does. It's kind of exciting to watch the debates and everything. But you say things sometimes and I go, "That's a little controversial." The Muslim thing—not allowing any Muslims into the country.

Although the question was framed in a gentle, non-confrontational way, Fallon was essentially bringing the issue of Trump's proposed "Muslim-ban" to a wide network audience. Meanwhile, the lack of issue mentions in candidate interviews on traditional news programming was startling (and disheartening). It seems that when given the chance to talk directly with candidates on news programs, journalists and their producers opted to focus on recent polls, strategy, scandal, and campaign dynamics over issues. This particular finding will be explored further in the discussion.

The General Election

Whereas the formal quantitative content analysis from the primaries provided a robust sample size, the follow-up examination of candidate interviews during the general election (defined as July 1 through November 8, 2016) only included 11 total appearances. Given the small sample size (six interviews on traditional news shows, two on daytime talk, and three on late-night comedy), a quantitative content analysis would be inappropriate, so we instead offer a qualitative assessment. In traditional news programs, Trump appeared on the *O'Reilly Factor* four different times throughout the summer and fall, engaging in conversations heavy on strategy and campaign choices, light on policy discussions, and almost completely devoid of humor. Clinton appeared once via telephone on *O'Reilly* on the topic of terrorism and did a sit-down interview with Lester Holt on NBC News. The two candidate appearances on daytime talk-shows during this time featured Hillary Clinton on *Ellen* (once in July and again in October), with light-hearted banter, some policy mentions by Clinton, and self-deprecating and other-deprecating humor aimed at Trump. Clinton also appeared on the late-night show, *Jimmy Kimmel Live!*, in August, in which she jokingly opened a pickle jar as a way of both making fun of her own health and mocking Trump's fascination with it. In mid-September, both Trump and Clinton appeared on *The Tonight Show with Jimmy Fallon* just days apart.

The Fallon interviews deserve special attention, if for no other reason than the blowback Fallon received from liberals, journalists, and other comics. For example, Samantha Bee, host of TBS's *Full Frontal*, criticized NBC and called the Fallon interview the "continued normalization of deplorable" (Bauder, 2016). *Vulture's* Mark Harris (2016) tweeted, "I don't fault Jimmy Fallon for not being a journalist. I do fault him for his willingness to serve as hell's court jester" (@MarkHarrisNYC, 2016). What troubled liberal critics was the fact that Fallon approached the Trump interview in the same way he approached all candidate interviews, as a light-hearted, playful exchange designed to humanize the candidate. Fallon mussed Trump's hair (which *Slate's* Willa Paskin called "The Point of No Return"), asked Trump about his childhood home, and encouraged Trump to get nostalgic over childhood memories. When Clinton appeared on the show a few days later, Fallon jokingly handed her a paper bag filled with items Trump had "left behind" in the dressing room. The items included a picture of Trump and Putin in a heart-shaped frame and a bunch of "softballs," which Fallon vowed he would be giving to Clinton later in the interview.

The overall feel of candidate appearances on the entertainment-oriented shows heading into the fall was that things were more serious and the stakes were higher. The instances of humor were few, particularly when it came to Clinton, and there was more of a sense that her time was running out to highlight the enormity of the decision that Americans would be making in November. Even on *Fallon* and *Ellen*, Clinton moved quickly from playful introductions from the hosts back into policy mode, discussing what was at stake and how viewers needed to take this election seriously.

Discussion

This study offers a preliminary examination of the use of humor and extent of policy discussions in candidate interviews across various sub-genres of political talk-shows. Although scholars have explored general patterns in daytime talk and late-night talk-show content, less attention has been paid to the kind of conversations that happens with political candidates when they appear on these different kinds of programs.

This examination has resulted in several noteworthy findings. First is the frequent appearances of candidates across late-night comedy programs and their extensive use of humor within those interviews. Within just seven candidate appearances during the primaries, late-night comedy dominated in terms of candidates' use of humor, with 47 instances of humor for an average of 6.71 instances of humor per interview. Late-night comedy was also home to a significant proportion of the self-deprecating humor we found in the shows coded here. Overall, within the late-night comedy interviews, candidates used an average of 4.3 self-deprecating jokes per interview, suggesting that for most candidates (except Trump), interviews within entertainment talk-shows provide an opportunity to humanize one's self and to bring one's self down to the level of a regular fallible person.

Then-candidate Trump is an outlier in these analyses (as is likely the case across myriad analyses of political campaigns). Contrary to common practice and historical trends, Trump did not use humor mainly as a way to humanize himself or render himself more accessible or fallible. Instead, he was far more likely to use humor to target "others": other people, other candidates, other institutions, and other policies. Given the Trump campaign's focus on Trump as the "only one" who could fix problems ranging from the economy to immigration and foreign policy, this strongman persona would be logically inconsistent with self-deprecation. Trump's campaign emphasized strength, status, and consolidated power in the presidency. Although most candidates employ self-deprecation as a way to be human and accessible, for a candidate such as Trump, self-deprecation would signify weakness.

Although the extensive use of humor in the late-night comedy candidate interview is unsurprising, what is surprising is the frequent mentions of foreign and domestic policy in the late-night comedy interview—exceeding even the policy mentions in traditional news interviews. The presence of substantial issue content, combined with the high frequency of humor, suggests that these late-night programs are reaching their wide audiences with substantial policy information "piggybacked" onto entertainment fare. This presents an opportunity for scholars to look at the unique impact that these late-night candidate interviews may have on viewers' understanding of issues, and the extent to which such appearances fuel the so-called "gateway effect" (Baum, 2003; Feldman & Young, 2008), leading viewers to seek additional information on these topics from other media sources.

Next, when looking at the extent of policy discussion on traditional news interviews with the candidates, this study found interviews on public affairs programs fell short compared to late-night comedy interviews. The reasons for this are likely varied. From casual observations made throughout the completion of the content analysis, it seems much of the focus of the traditional news interview was on campaign strategy; that is: a) who is ahead and who is behind, b) why a candidate is taking certain steps to reach certain groups, and c) how they are going to bring up their polling numbers. It has long been noted that television news treats politics, and elections in particular, as a game (Patterson, 2011). Journalists frame elections as battles to defeat competitors (Cappella & Jamieson, 1997). In candidate interviews on traditional news shows, the candidates were treated less as individuals with platforms and concerns, and more as cogs in the machinery of the wider political apparatus. Questions regarding other candidates, attack ads, and poll numbers were far more frequent than questions about platforms or stances.

In an appearance on *The O'Reilly Factor*, following Trump's victory in the New Hampshire primary, O'Reilly asked, "So after some reflection on your victory last night, who do you think your main competition is among Republicans right now?" O'Reilly followed up by asking about the upcoming South Carolina primaries, saying, "South Carolina looks to be a battle between you and Cruz—so don't you consider Cruz to be your main competitor in South Carolina?" This led to more discussion of upcoming debates and potential outcomes of those debates. The center of the conversation focused on competition within the party, primary results, and the spectacle of the election coverage. Yet, the conversation never once explored details of policy or platform.

One of the biggest limitations of this study is the lack of comparative data. Many of the trends observed here may be unique to this specific campaign at this time with these particular candidates. Without additional elections to serve as comparisons, it is difficult to know which findings illustrate broader trends and which are merely anomalies, unique to this campaign. In addition, with only 12 programs examined, these analyses might not adequately capture the complexity and hybridity of the information environment we live in. During the primaries, Trump appeared on the online/radio talk-show "Infowars" hosted by conspiracy theorist Alex Jones. Clinton appeared on the viral comedy web series "Between Two Ferns" with Zack Galifianakis in September. These types of programming rest outside the sub-genres carefully articulated here, hence raising the question of how we deal with the content and effects of such unique specialized programs across digital platforms.

This project provides a preliminary analysis to help us understand the strategic use of news and talk-show interviews among political candidates and how the nature of the interviews varies across talk-show sub-genre. These results provide a framework upon which media effects researchers may build as they articulate possible effects mechanisms to account for the likely consequences of exposure to such programming. Researchers may begin exploring how self-versus other-deprecating humor shape not only viewer attitudes, but also the cognitive processing of candidates' messages. Perhaps self- and other-deprecating humor operate in unique ways as they are received and processed in the brain, which might render audiences more or less likely to recall or elaborate upon subsequent information. Finally, the notion that the late-night comedy interviews featured more policy mentions than did the traditional news interviews is concerning from a democratic standpoint. Future research ought to address the question of what is supplanting the issue coverage on the news. Although our cursory investigation suggests horse-race and strategy coverage are replacing issue discussions, a formal examination is warranted.

Overall, these results speak to the politicization of entertainment programming—particularly in the election context. Obviously these programs have notably different orientations and goals: Late-night comedy programs are generally focused on the candidate not just as a political instrument, but as a person. The focus of late-night comedy interviews (with politicians and celebrities) tends to center on individuals' personality traits and personal lives. For many political candidates, what is *most* salient in their day-to-day lives during the primaries are policies and issue positions, hence making it likely that these topics will come up in casual conversation in a late-night context. In the past, the label of entertainment has caused many to dismiss these programs as "fluffy" or irrelevant in terms of substantive policy information, yet, given our findings, this assumption needs to be reassessed.

References

@MarkHarrisNYC (2016, September 16). I don't fault Jimmy Fallon for not being a journalist. I do fault him for his willingness to serve as hell's court jester. Retrieved from https://twitter.com/MarkHarrisNYC/status/776648998824316928?ref_src=twsrc%5Etfw&ref_url=http%3A%2F%2Fwww.telegraph.co.uk%2Fnews%2F2016%2F09%2F16%2Fjimmy-fallon-criticised-for-joking-with-donald-trump-and-rufflin%2F

Bauder, D. (2016, September 21). Bee says she likes Fallon, but couldn't take Trump interview. *Associated Press*. Retrieved from http://bigstory.ap.org/article/102a94020fe2494b8e00f7f8e787cbac/bee-says-she-likes-fallon-couldnt-take-trump-interview

Baum, M. A. (2003). Soft news and political knowledge: Evidence of absence or absence of evidence? *Political Communication, 20*(2), 173–190.

Baum, M. A. (2005). Talking the vote: Why presidential candidates hit the talk show circuit. *American Journal of Political Science, 49*(2), 213–234.

Baum, M. A., & Jamison, A. (2011). Soft news and the four Oprah effects. In L. Jacobs & R. Shapiro (Eds.), *Oxford handbook of American public opinion and the media* (pp. 121–137). Oxford: Oxford University Press.

Baym, G. (2007). Representation and the politics of play: Stephen Colbert's better know a district. *Political Communication, 24*(4), 359–376.

Baym, G. (2010). *From Cronkite to Colbert: The evolution of broadcast news*. New York, NY: Oxford University Press.

Baym, G. (2013). Political media as discursive modes: A comparative analysis of interviews with Ron Paul from *Meet the Press, Tonight, The Daily Show*, and *Hannity. International Journal of Communication*, 7(19), 489–507.

Bippus, A. (2007). Factors predicting the perceived effectiveness of politicians' use of humor during a debate. *Humor: International Journal of Humor Research, 20*(2), 105–121.

Cao, X., & Brewer, P. R. (2008). Political comedy shows and public participation in politics. *International Journal of Public Opinion Research, 20*(1), 90–99.

Cappella, J. N., & Jamieson, K. H. (1997). *Spiral of cynicism: The press and the public good.* Oxford: Oxford University Press.

Clayman, S. E., & Heritage, J. (2002). Questioning presidents: Journalistic deference and adversarialness in the press conferences of US presidents Eisenhower and Reagan. *Journal of Communication, 52*(4), 749–775.

Dalton, R. J., & Wattenberg, M. P. (2002). *Parties without partisans: Political change in advanced industrial democracies.* Oxford: Oxford University Press.

Fairclough, N. (1995). *Critical discourse analysis.* London and New York, NY: Longman.

Feldman, L., & Young, D. G. (2008). Late-night comedy as a gateway to traditional news: An analysis of time trends in news attention among late-night comedy viewers during the 2004 presidential primaries. *Political Communication, 25*(4), 401–422.

Fox, J. R., Koloen, G., & Sahin, V. (2007). No joke: A comparison of substance in *The Daily Show with Jon Stewart* and broadcast network television coverage of the 2004 presidential election campaign. *Journal of Broadcasting & Electronic Media, 51*(2), 213–227.

Garzia, D. (2011). The personalization of politics in western democracies: Causes and consequences on leader-follower relationships. *The Leadership Quarterly, 22*, 697–709.

Hallin, D. C. (1992). Sound bite news: Television coverage of elections, 1968–1988. *Journal of Communications, 42*, 5–24.

Ilie, C. (2001). Semi-institutional discourse: The case of talk shows. *Journal of Pragmatics, 33*(2), 209–254.

Jones, J. P., & Baym, G. (2010). A dialogue on satire news and the crisis of truth in postmodern political television. *Journal of Communication Inquiry, 34*(3), 278–294.

Jones, P., & Hudson, J. (1996). The quality of political leadership: A case study of John Major. *British Journal of Political Science, 26*(2), 229–244.

Jones, R. A. (2009). Media subpoenas: Impact, perception, and legal protection in the changing world of American journalism. *Washington Law Review, 84*, 317.

Kaase, M. (1994). Is there personalization in politics? Candidates and voting behavior in Germany. *International Political Science Review, 15*(3), 211–230.

Lorenz, K. (2002). *On aggression.* New York: Routledge.

Mazzoleni, G. (2000). A return to civic and political engagement prompted by personalized political leadership? *Political Communication, 17*(4), 325–328.

Meyer, J. C. (2000). Humor as a double-edged sword: Four functions of humor in communication. *Communication Theory, 10*(3), 310–331.

Newman, B. I. (1999). *The mass marketing of politics: Democracy in an age of manufactured images.* Thousand Oaks, CA: Sage.

Parkin, M. (2014). *Talk show campaigns: Presidential candidates on daytime and late night television.* New York, NY: Routledge.

Patterson, T. E. (2011). *Out of order.* New York, NY: Vintage.

Prior, M. (2007). *Post-broadcast democracy: How media choice increases inequality in political involvement and polarizes elections.* Cambridge, UK: Cambridge University Press.

Rahat, G., & Sheafer, T. (2007). The personalization(s) of politics: Israel, 1949–2003. *Political Communication, 24*(1), 65–80.

Sloane, A. A. (2001). *Humor in the White House: The wit of five American presidents.* Jefferson, NC: McFarland.

Stewart, P. A. (2011). The influence of self- and other-deprecatory humor on presidential candidate evaluation during the 2008 US election. *Social Science Information, 50*(2), 201–222.

Stewart, P. A. (2012). Laughter on the 2008 campaign trail: How presidential candidates used humor during primary debates. *Humor, 25*(3), 233–262.

Sullivan, J. L., Aldrich, J. H., Borgida, E., & Rahn, W. (1990). Candidate appraisal and human nature: Man and superman in the 1984 election. *Political Psychology, 11*(3), 459–484.

Swanson, D. L., & Mancini, P. (1996). *Politics, media, and modern democracy: An international study of innovations in electoral campaigning and their consequences.* Santa Barbara, CA: Greenwood Publishing Group.

Villalobos, J. D. (2012). Sitting with Oprah, dancing with Ellen: Presidents, daytime television, and soft news. In J. Vaughn & L. Goren (Eds.), *Women and the White House: Gender, popular culture, and presidential politics* (pp. 163–179). Lexington, KY: University Press of Kentucky.

Young, D. G. (2008). The daily show as new journalism: In their own words. In J. S. Morris & J. C. Baumgartner (Eds.), *Laughing matters: Humor and American politics in the media age* (pp. 241–259). New York, NY: Routledge.

Young, D. G., & Esralew, S. (2011). Jon Stewart a heretic? Surely you jest: Political participation and discussion among viewers of late-night comedy programming. In A. Amarasingam (Ed.), *The Stewart/Colbert effect: Essays on the real impact of fake news* (pp. 99–116). Jefferson, NC: McFarland.

Young, D. G., & Hoffman, L. (2012). Acquisition of current-events knowledge from political satire programming: An experimental approach. *Atlantic Journal of Communication, 20*(5), 290–304.

Young, D. G., & Tisinger, R. M. (2006). Dispelling late-night myths news consumption among late-night comedy viewers and the predictors of exposure to various late-night shows. *The Harvard International Journal of Press/Politics, 11*(3), 113–134.

Zillmann, D. (1983). Disparagement humor. In P. E. McGhee & J. H. Goldstein (Eds.), *Handbook of humor research* (pp. 85–107). New York, NY: Springer.

PART 4

Social Media Messaging

Candidate Branding and Agenda Setting

12

DONALD TRUMP AND THE "OXYGEN OF PUBLICITY"

Branding, Social Media, and Traditional Media

Sarah Oates and Wendy W. Moe

This chapter places social media within the broader context of media systems in order to detect and analyze the effect of political messaging that resonated among candidate, media, and citizens in the 2016 U.S. presidential elections. By conceptualizing candidates as political brands that parallel business brands, our research sought to leverage marketing research on social media intelligence into political communication, with a particular emphasis on tracking and measuring the response to the candidate "brand" in both traditional and social media. This research proved especially useful in explaining a Donald Trump victory that was generally unexpected by most analysts. Evidence from both the primary and general election showed that traditional mass media was consistently giving Trump a greater volume of coverage, which was also reflected in social media. We argue that the traditional media in particular gave Trump the "oxygen of publicity," a term that originates from the idea that extremist views should not be publicized as they will gain legitimacy.

In this chapter, we mine the intersection of social media intelligence in business branding and political communication to suggest a Campaign Message Flow Model. We analyzed messages created by Trump and Hillary Clinton, using Twitter as a proxy for campaign statements and focusing on messages that were linked to key issues and personality traits. We tracked the same issues in the traditional mass media, using three national newspapers as proxies for legacy media. Finally, we looked at how these messages linked to specific concepts and keywords circulated in social media, again using Twitter.

Using the Campaign Message Flow Model, we focused on the relationship among different elements of attempts to create candidate brands—from how candidates broadcast their messages, to how they were covered in the traditional mass media, to how messages were circulated in social media. The unexpected finding in the research was that Trump failed to follow traditional political campaigning either by establishing policy positions or even an ideology as a political "brand." Rather, Trump created a storm of publicity about his outrageous statements or scandals. This led us to a broader study of the media ecosystem and brands in election campaigns, finding that traditional media outlets continue to play a large role in amplifying and spreading particular political "brand" elements (e.g., Trump's immigration stance). This overwhelmed attempts by other candidates to attract voter attention in a crowded race in the primaries and against a seasoned campaigner in the general election. Given his victory, it is important to consider why and how this strategy led to success and what this means for the future of election campaigning in our current media ecology.

Intersections: Corporate and Political Branding

Commercial brands have increasingly monitored social media activity in recent years to gain insights into their customers. Several studies have linked the volume of social media activity to sales performance (Dellarocas & Narayan, 2006; Dellarocas, Zhang, & Awad, 2007; Moe & Trusov, 2011; Tirunillai & Tellis, 2012). Analyzing the text content of social media activity has aided in prediction, competitive benchmarking, and strategy design (Bollen, Mao, & Zeng, 2011; Netzer, Feldman, Goldenberg, & Fresko, 2012; Schweidel & Moe, 2014). However, studies also have shown that many metrics collected by social media listening platforms are superficial and often suffer from bias (Schweidel & Moe, 2014), emphasizing the importance of having a more complete contextual understanding of the users underlying social media data and metrics.

Social media intelligence developed for businesses suggests that you need to observe and analyze brands within social media ecosystems, particularly given that consumers tend to comment in different ways on a range of social media platforms. So merely looking at volume or even sentiment of tweets (even if that sentiment measure can be made significantly more robust than its current state) is giving partial or even misleading signals to businesses. As a result, commercial brands need to consider mentions on Twitter, Facebook, and key blogs, as well as group those messages into how they relate to key brand perceptions and preferences. For example, it is not enough to know that people are mentioning your product on social media; it is important to know how they are talking about key aspects of your brand such as specific features, preference, price, support, reputation, etc.

Many of the developments in the study of social media for business applications have been paralleled in political communication, in particular with a strong interest in how citizens consume, share, and react to information in the digital age. Communication scholars have been hopeful that affordances of digital technology would empower citizens through a range of features, including the ability of citizens to post content, the ties created by social-networking platforms, the vastly augmented ability to collect information through search engines, as well as instantaneous horizontal communication among citizens. In particular, hopes were raised as barriers to online access were lowered as inexpensive smartphones became ubiquitous in the U.S. Although studies have shown a variety of ways in which ICTs bring benefits to citizens, particularly during election campaigns (Gainous & Wagner, 2013; Karpf, 2012; for a meta-analysis of user-engagement research, see Boulianne, 2009), evidence that this has created significant change in the relationship between elites (candidates) and the masses (voters) so far is not strong. Indeed, Stromer-Galley (2014) argues that online communication technology has been used to promote the goals of campaigns rather than the needs of citizens, making it a "means to an end, rather than an opportunity for in-depth citizen engagement and empowerment" (p. 2). There is significant evidence that campaigns are able to leverage online information to better identify potential supporters, in particular for Democrats to get a larger number of small campaign donations (Magleby, Goodliffe, & Olsen, 2014). However, this success at more effective fundraising rather underlines Stromer-Galley's point that campaigns are using online data for an extension of marketing rather than as an augmentation of citizen engagement.

If there is relatively little evidence of the use of citizen feedback and engagement to influence U.S. election campaigns, what can social media content tell us about the thoughts and feelings of potential voters during the campaign? Understandably, much of the focus on social media research in political communication is on the ability to predict election outcomes (Lampos, Preoţiuc-Pietro, & Cohn, 2013). Moving forward, it would be illuminating to use social media data more intensively to understand more about reactions to particular campaign statements, events, appearances, scandals, and news stories. Ultimately elections are about winners and losers, but a focus on the process, rather than the outcome, could strengthen the understanding of political communication (Patterson, 1994).

Both businesses and political campaigns ultimately live or die by the final results—sales or votes—but as Moe and Schweidel (2014) point out, the correlation between social media volume and gross outcomes often falls short of providing reliable predictions. Rather, organizations should use social media data to get specific and targeted response to various aspects of their brands. How can we define "brands" in the context of political communication? In attempting to make academic synergy between business and political science studies of online brands, a useful vector is the consideration of nuanced sub-elements of a campaign and how ideas surrounding these sub-elements travel through media ecologies. For example, how can one define the different specific elements of the "brands" of the Trump campaign or the Clinton campaign? In order to do this, we studied a) the emphasis that the two candidates gave key issues in the campaign on social media; b) how the mass media covered these issues; and c) how the audience responded on social media.

Brand and Media Ecology

Traditionally, there have been many metrics that measure the amount of media coverage in a political campaign, such as how much money is spent on advertising, which types of ad content are most effective, as well as how successful candidates are at garnering editorial coverage. There is a wide range of studies on editorial coverage as well, with a particular emphasis on detecting bias or unfairness. For example, work on the 2008 election found that reporting on Clinton in the Democratic primary employed genderized coverage to treat her more critically than Barack Obama (Parry-Giles, 2014). In recent years, there has been a rising interest not just in campaign messages, traditional news coverage, and online attention, but also in understanding the relationship among the three. In particular, Chadwick's hybrid media theory (2013) points out that there is no longer "offline" or "online" news but that traditional media, online media, citizen journalists, interest groups, activists, and attentive users online have created a dynamic news environment that is no longer defined by the traditional gatekeepers of journalists and politicians.

If candidate statements, traditional media coverage, and campaign messages no longer essentially define the media environment, how can we define and track a brand in a political campaign in the new digital age? Taking elements of the model developed by Moe and Schweidel to measure social media intelligence, we expanded this to develop a Campaign Message Flow Model that shows how specific issues within a campaign circulate among candidate messages, traditional media, and social media (see Figure 12.1).

In Figure 12.1, we have operationalized the flow of messages in a campaign with the traditional mass media as the main source through which candidate messages flow and the central messaging platform to which the public respond. In creating this model, we are attempting to show how messages can take dynamic and differing paths. For example, a candidate could tweet a message about immigration and this message could then be redistributed and commented upon on social media with no coverage from traditional mass media. This is

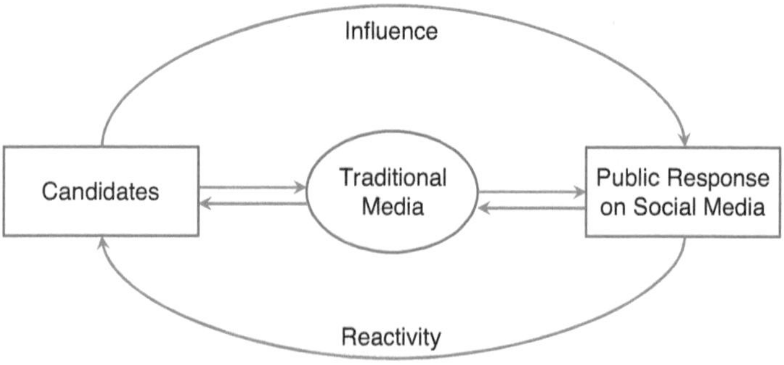

FIGURE 12.1 Campaign Message Flow Model

represented by the top arrow (labeled influence) and the bottom arrow (labeled reactivity). In addition, the model acknowledges the feedback loops between candidates and the media that may have nothing to do with the public—candidates often speak directly to news organizations both on and off the record, media outlets often use their influence to get information out of campaigns, and campaigns often attempt to shape traditional media coverage through use of influence, persuasion, threats, etc. The arrows linking candidates and the traditional media represent this relationship. By the same token, journalists generally are concerned with how their audience is receiving news—and the audience is often complimentary or critical of news coverage on social media. That flow of influence is represented by the arrows between traditional mass media and public response on social media.

Methods

This project looked at two specific time periods in the U.S. 2016 presidential campaign. For the primary campaign, we examined data from July 1 to September 24, 2015, as this part of the primary campaign included a range of interesting events, including two Republican debates; the release of a statement on the economy by Clinton in July; as well as Clinton turning over her private computer records to the U.S. Justice Department. Trump received a lot of attention during this time period for his comments on immigration, including his repeated calls to "build a wall" on the southern U.S. border. For the general election, we looked at the final month of the campaign, stopping the day before Election Day on November 8, 2016 (October 7 to November 7, 2016).

We quickly found that the very different approach by Trump to online communication did not fit neatly into traditional ways of studying political messages. For example, political scientists traditionally measure how candidates and parties stand on political issues by examining their websites. During the period studied for the primary campaign, Trump did not post clear issue statements on his website, although Clinton did. This meant it was not possible to replicate methods from earlier studies, such as by Gibson, Margolis, Resnick, and Ward (2003).

Nor could one draw a parallel between classic ideas of party identification and "brand"—the Democrats and Republicans both offer a deeply historic political "product." There is a wealth of study and analysis, much of it linked to the American National Election Studies, which has looked at how Americans have identified with these parties since 1948. However, this was problematic when thinking about how to mine brand opinions from social media for this study of the 2016 campaign. Although it was relatively easy to identify whether people are supporters of Republicans or Democrats from their social media content, online networks, and/or traditional media consumption habits, this did not tell us much about how citizens were reacting to the sub-attributes of a brand of a specific candidate. It also drew us into the ongoing debate about the shifting meaning of what it is to be Republican or Democrat. In addition, given the somewhat loose affiliation between party organization and presidential campaigns in the U.S., we decided the individual campaigns of candidates were more useful as definitions of "brands" within the presidential election. Thus, this study focused on individual campaigns rather than political parties, while acknowledging that party brands might be much more relevant in party-based systems that are more prevalent in most democracies.

We chose to look at how candidates were linked to key political issues important to both Democrats and Republicans as defined by a survey by the Pew Research Center in late 2014 (Pew Research Center, September 12, 2014). In the primary campaign, we focused on the economy, healthcare, immigration, and Iran (due to the controversy over its nuclear program that was being discussed at the time). For the general election, we added keywords to measure a range of issues that arose prominently by fall 2016, including the Clinton email scandal, sexual-assault comments regarding Trump, and Trump's tax returns. We slightly amended the keywords for two issue categories when moving from the primary to the general election to try to continue to capture the issue discussion (see full list in Appendix 12.1). For both periods, we used positive and negative keywords to try to capture the discussion about personality traits (an important part of political branding).

Results

Candidate Tweets

We gathered all tweets authored by the official Twitter accounts of the candidates (@realDonaldTrump and @HillaryClinton) from July 1 to September 24, 2015 using Brandwatch and from early October through Election Day in 2016 via Twitter's API. We acknowledge that Clinton has a separate "elections" account (@VoteHillary2016) but we decided to focus on one central account for each candidate. In the primary period studied, daily tweet volume ranged considerably, from 0 to 57 tweets daily for Clinton (average of 11 daily) and 0 to 68 for Trump (average of 21 daily). Although Clinton tweeted less, she was more likely to tweet in a way that was easier to identify with specific issues. However, this analysis made it clear that the candidate tweets were not "politics as usual"—despite searching for an array of search terms relating to the election in the tweets, the majority of the tweets for both candidates did not fit into our issue or even personality categories. Rather, most tweets we collected were essentially devoid of meaning in the traditional political sense, often expressing just vague thanks or support to followers. For Clinton, we could see evidence of Twitter acting as a "megaphone" for campaign communication, such as her July 13 announcement of her "Growth and Fairness" economic platform when 17 out of the 31 campaign tweets for the day were focused on the economy (see Figure 12.2).

Of all the tweets relating to the issues we measured (economy, healthcare, immigration, and Iran), Trump unsurprisingly had the largest volume of tweets

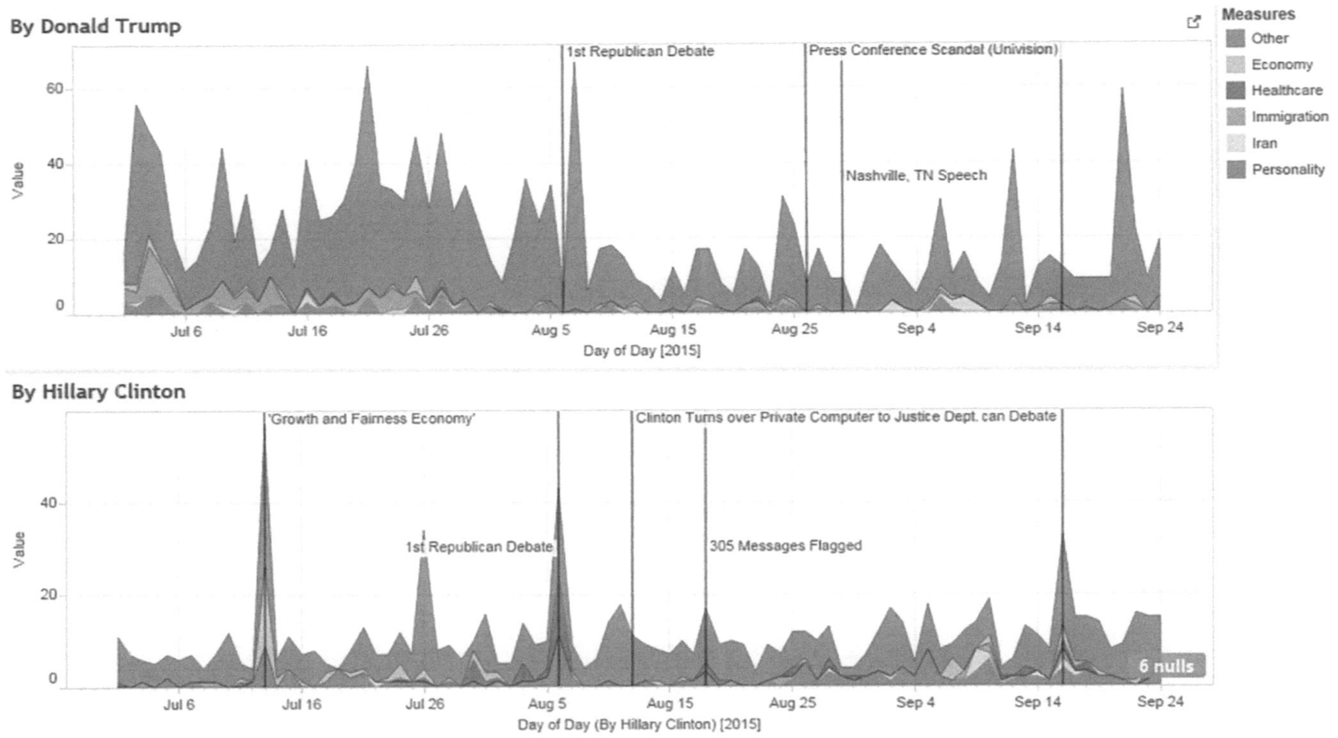

FIGURE 12.2A Tweets Authored by Trump and Clinton Mentioning Issue/Personality Keywords, July 1 to September 24, 2015

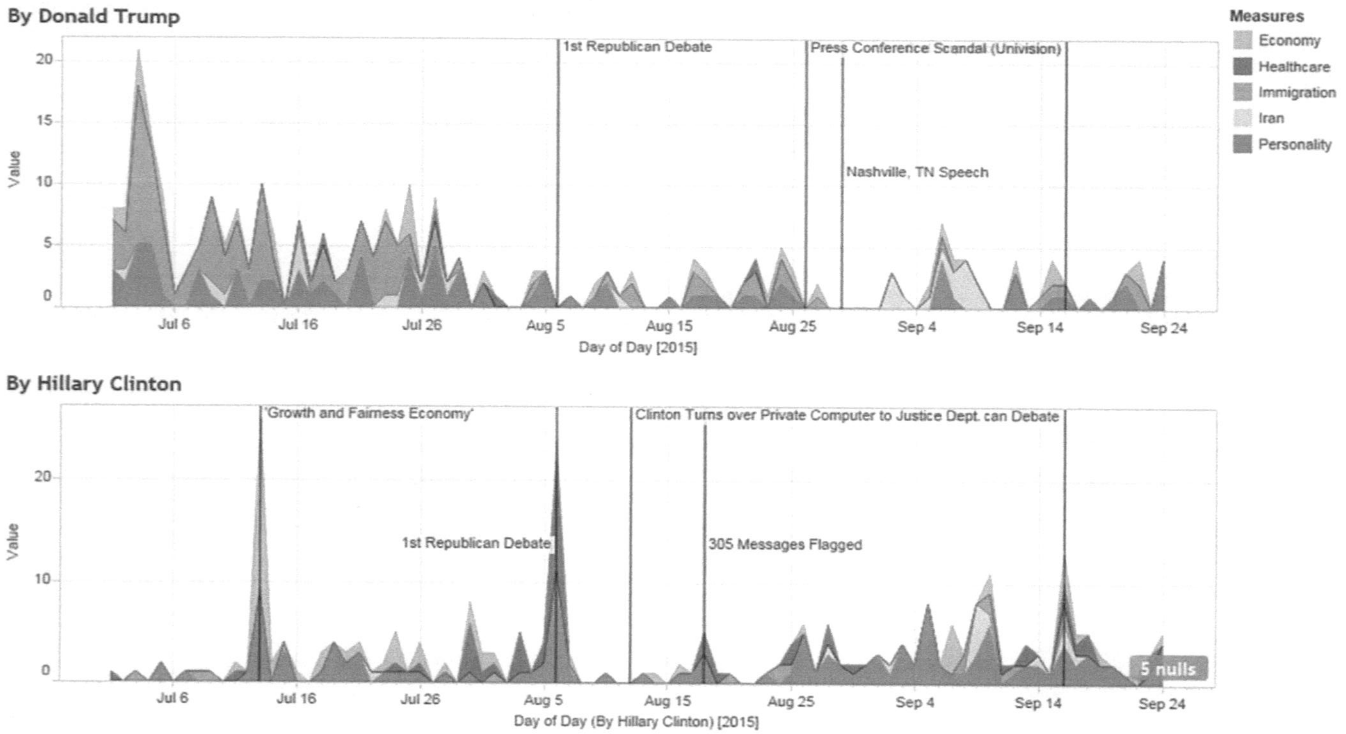

FIGURE 12.2B (Continued)

relating to immigration. However, these tweets were never a major proportion of his tweets and the number of immigration-themed tweets faded over time in this primary period (see Figure 12.2). Aside from immigration, there was little political content (as measured by our keywords) in Trump's tweets. It's interesting to note that, after immigration, the second most visible issue in his tweets during this period concerned Iran. This fits his pattern of attacking Clinton's record, as she was involved with the Iranian negotiations.

In the general election, Clinton and Trump continued a similar pattern—Trump tweeted more and the peaks in tweets correlated with significant campaign events (see Figure 12.3). Both Trump and Clinton tweeted the most on

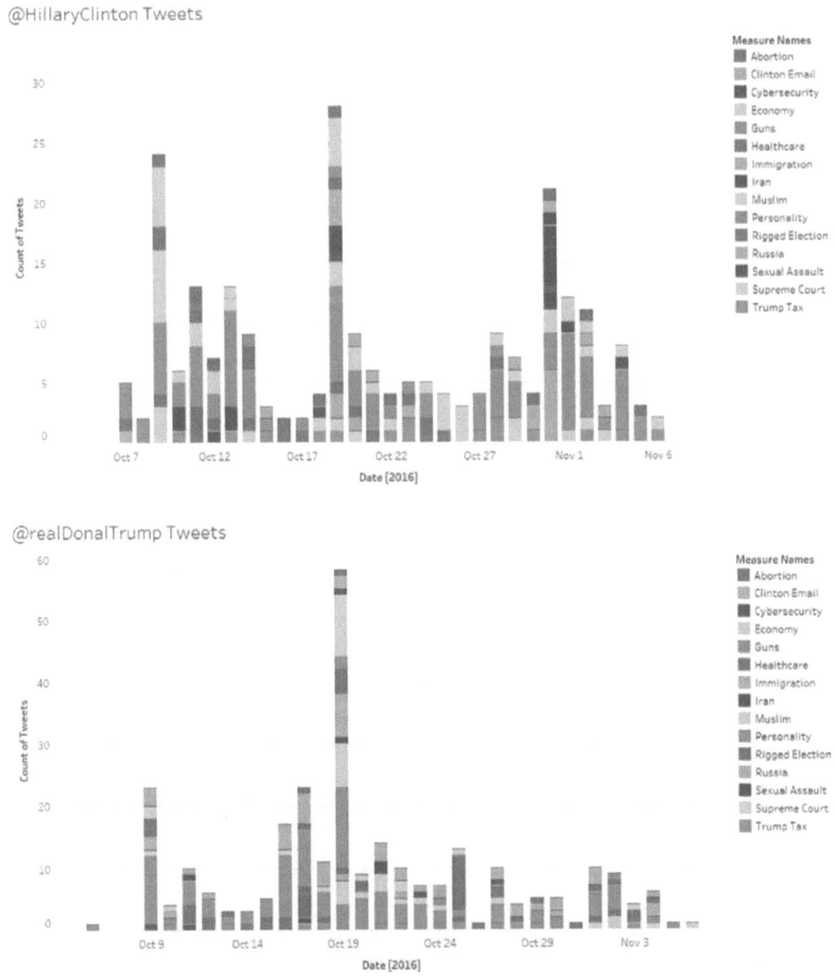

FIGURE 12.3 Trump and Clinton Tweets General Election

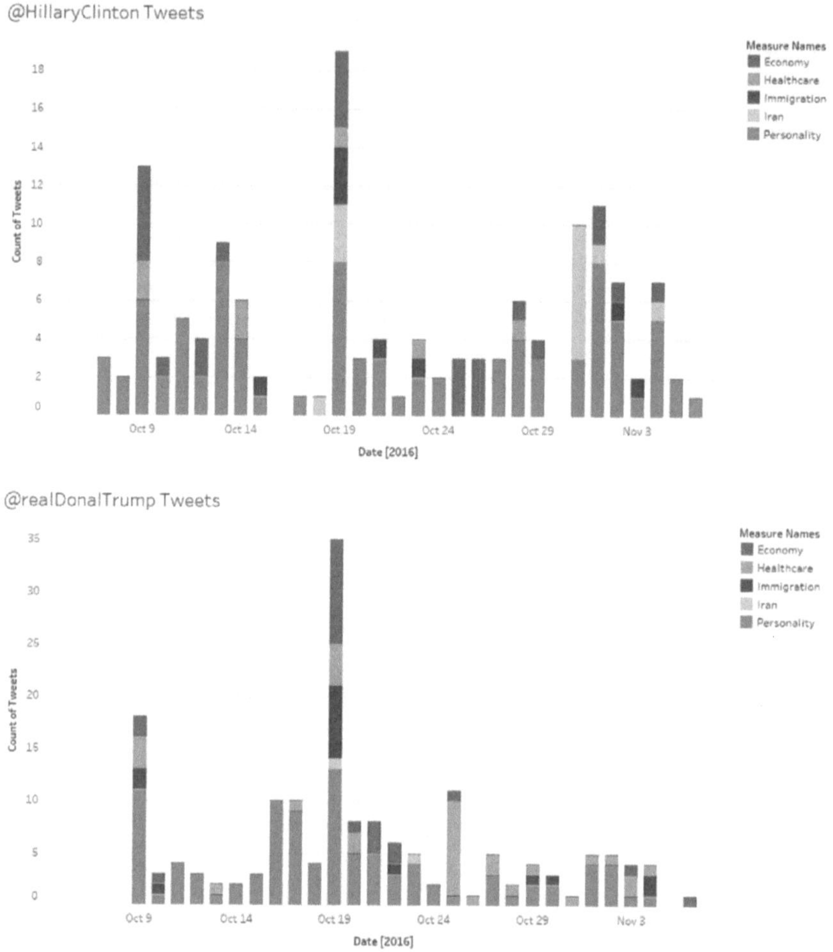

FIGURE 12.3 (Continued)

October 19, the day of the final presidential candidate debate. In looking at the same categories as in the primary elections, we note that Clinton continued to tweet consistently on issues such as economics and healthcare, although her focus on healthcare was less in the general election. On the other hand, Trump tweeted less about immigration in the general election, suggesting that aspect of his "brand" was less visible. For both candidates, however, most tweets were not specifically on core issues: even by targeting only tweets with our keywords, their tweets were more typically identified with "personality" keywords than "issue" keywords. New threads entered into their Twitter feeds for the general election, in particular as both candidates tweeted about rigged elections (Trump to raise concerns, Clinton to dismiss them), the Clinton email scandal, Muslims, and Trump's income tax returns. Unsurprisingly, Clinton tweeted consistently about Trump's sexual-assault remarks while Trump himself did not.

Analysis of Traditional Media

There is no question that Trump dominated media coverage throughout the election. *The New York Times* reported in March 2016 that Trump had amassed an unprecedented $2 billion worth of unearned (i.e., not paid) media coverage, making him "far better than any other candidate—maybe than any candidate ever—at earning media" (Confessore & Yourish, 2016). Given that we were a) studying a relatively short period; b) testing an idea rather than attempting to capture an entire universe of traditional media coverage; and c) felt that three national newspapers would be a relevant sample for our study, we used search terms to manually download articles from LexisNexis Academic (see Appendix 12.1 for details). For the primary period we studied, we downloaded 756 items from the *Washington Post*, *The New York Times*, and *USA Today* that were published between July 1 and September 24, 2015. We identified 475 relevant articles (200 from the *Washington Post*, 229 from *The New York Times*, and 46 from *USA Today*) for the primary period. For the general-election period, we analyzed a sample of 674 stories, 382 from the *Times*, 220 from the *Post*, and 72 from *USA Today*. We used a coding scheme to identify which articles mentioned one or both candidates and which issues were mentioned, along with a date and place of publication. Coding was performed by one author (Oates) and two research assistants.

For the primary period under review, both Trump and immigration dominated in the coverage coded in the three newspapers (see Figure 12.4). Our coding found that 208 of the 475 articles (43.8%) in our sample were focused on Trump, whereas only 90 (18.9%) were focused on Clinton. As this was prior to a surge in popularity for Democratic primary contender Bernie Sanders, it

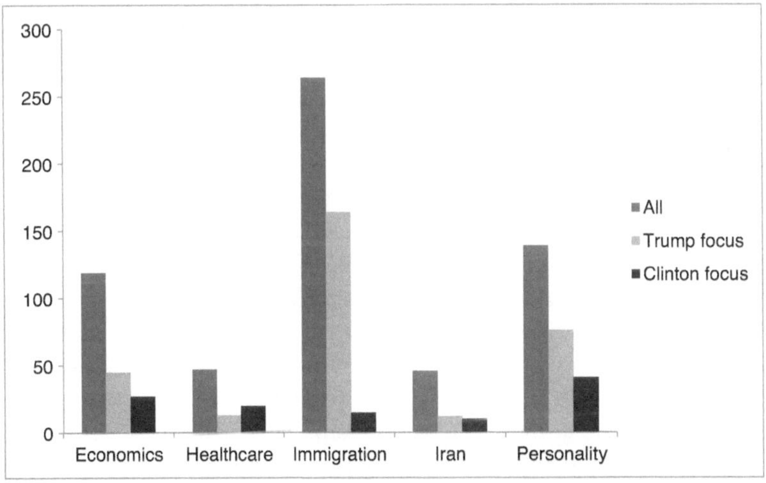

FIGURE 12.4 Candidates Linked With Issues or Personality Keywords in Newspaper Articles, July 1 to September 24, 2015

Source: Coding of 475 articles from *The New York Times*, *The Washington Post*, and *USA Today*.

could be argued that there was less news value in Clinton because there was less contestation of her as the Democratic nominee. In addition, we searched for and retrieved only articles that mentioned *both* a candidate and specific issues. This meant that articles about Clinton, who has been in politics for decades, which did not relate directly to our search terms were not included in our study (nor were articles that only discussed Trump business issues). However, given that the research was designed to compare candidate coverage, it is still surprising that one candidate was covered so much more than the other.

The topic of immigration dominated stories that mentioned Trump, Clinton, or both—whether in substance or merely with a minor reference. Immigration was mentioned in 264 out of the 475 stories or almost 56% of the stories analyzed for the primary period. This is compelling evidence that Trump was able to dominate the traditional media with his anti-immigration messages, despite the fact that immigration was only one of an array of issues that concerned voters. Nor were the mentions of immigration—which almost all directly referenced Trump's hard-right policies—limited to only stories about the campaign. Rather, the reaction to Trump's views dominated a range of stories about other candidates and even other issues in the campaign. It would seem that a mention of Trump almost always elicited a mention of his views on immigration. In addition, Trump's stand on immigration bled into stories that were relatively far from the traditional politics "beat," including stories on golf events being canceled on Trump properties, a network dropping a Trump-backed beauty pageant after his remarks about Mexicans, and even a school that wanted to move its prom out of a Trump property due to the controversy (see Protestors call to remove Trump, or at least his name, from project, *The Washington Post*, July 10, 2015, B1; Trump Gets Earful in Spanish as Latino Outlets Air Disdain, *The New York Times*, August 27, 2015, p. A1; Trump's Remarks on Mexican Immigrants Prompt Call to Move a Prom, *The New York Times*, August 20, 2015, p. A18). Thus, Trump's comments on immigration not only dominated the traditional coverage of a presidential primary in the three newspapers, it is also made its way into other sectors of the news. As a brand element, this was very effective. There was almost no coverage of Clinton that was not found in traditional political stories that followed the events of the primary (debates, policy speeches, ongoing political scandals, etc.).

We did find significant evidence that other issues were discussed as well. In our list of stories that mentioned either or both candidates, economics was mentioned in 119 out of 475 stories (25%), Iran in 46 (9.7%), and healthcare in 47 (9.9%). The search for stories with our personality terms yielded almost as much as these three issues combined—personality aspects were found in 139 (41%) of the stories (totals add up to more than 100 because some stories had more than one issue and/or a personality trait mentioned). It was most common to encounter a story that focused on just one of the issues under review. There were 273 articles that mentioned one category, 86 that mentioned two, 40 that mentioned three, 10 that mentioned four, and two stories that mentioned all five categories (economics, healthcare, immigration, Iran, or personality terms). There were 64 stories (13% of the articles) that mentioned one or both candidates that had no mention of either the four issue areas or personality trait keywords. For example, our set of articles included stories that mentioned Clinton's plans for student debt (which we did not include in general economics) or stories that profiled other Republican candidates and mentioned Trump as a strong contender, etc.

For the general election, we decided not to repeat the broad personality category used in the primary news analysis but rather focus on three issues that were linked to candidate character in the general election: a) the Clinton email scandal, b) Trump's comments advocating sexual assault, and c) Trump's refusal to release his own tax returns (including the partial leaking of tax returns to *The New York Times*). We did this in part because these narratives emerged so strongly and we felt they would better capture the election coverage in general. We also did it because we found, in coding the primary content, that it was relatively difficult to ascertain what constituted a comment on personality or what was really just background description in a news story. We coded each story to determine if one or the other candidate was the focus of the story or whether it focused on both—or neither, as in a story that merely mentioned the presidential campaign. The numbers add up to more than 674 because, as with the news analysis for the primary period, some articles mentioned more than one topic being coded.

The most important finding from the primaries—that one Trump-linked news area dominated—was also true in the month before the general election (see Figure 12.5). In this case, the largest volume of news was about a recording of remarks made by Trump about sexually assaulting women. These comments were the subject of 246 (36.5%) of all the articles in the general-election sample. The coverage of economic issues was 202 articles (30%), followed by immigration (161 articles or 23.9%). Healthcare was rarely mentioned (10.4%) and Iran was barely on the map at 3.6%. Indeed, the Iran scandal had essentially disappeared, although there was some coverage as it was often linked to concerns about Syria or nuclear safety in general because "Assad" and "nuclear" were keywords. Clinton did get her "own" scandal, as coverage of the investigation into her email security continued, especially with last-minute claims by the FBI that the investigation would be re-opened (160 stories or 23.7%). The email scandal is the only category in which Clinton had the spotlight, with more stories focusing on her than on Trump. In every other category, Trump drew more focus. The overall news focus was more evenly split between the two candidates than in the primary period studied, but there was still a disparity: 38.7% (261 articles) focused on Trump, whereas only 15.9% (107) focused on Clinton. In terms of classic campaigning, the month was a disaster for Trump, as his twin scandals of sexual-assault comments and his taxes were the focus of enormous attention. In terms of branding, it appeared once again that his visibility, rather than his actual behavior, framed him as a powerful persona. Overall, scandals rather than issues dominated the news, leaving readers with scant information with which to make informed decisions on key policies such as the economy or healthcare.

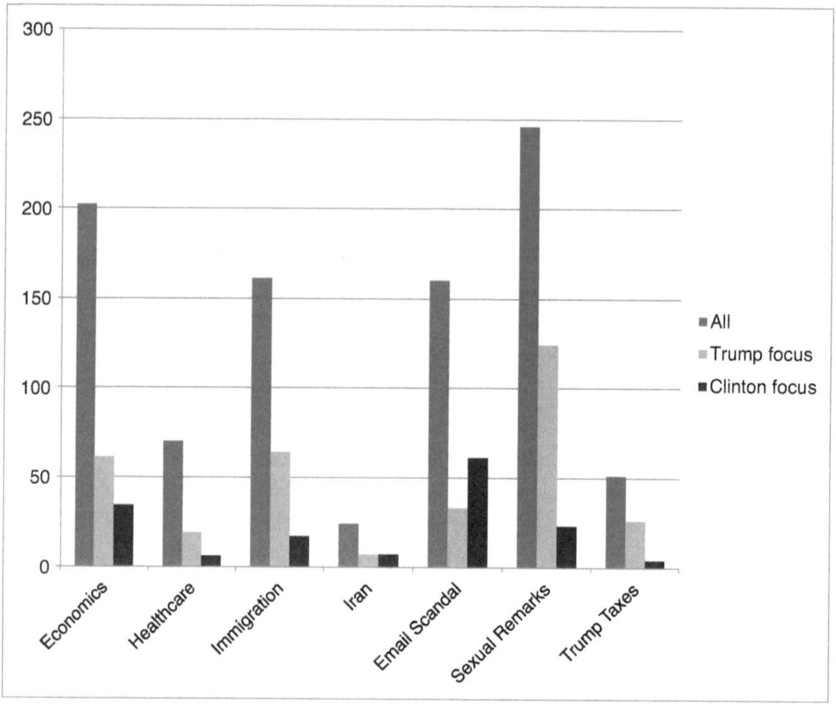

FIGURE 12.5 Candidates Linked With Issues or Scandal Keywords in Newspaper Articles, October 7 to November 7, 2016

Source: Coding of 674 articles from *The New York Times*, *The Washington Post*, and *USA Today*.

Citizen Tweets

For the primary election, we retrieved 955,193 tweets that named Trump and one of our keywords, again using Brandwatch data. We retrieved 272,579 tweets for Clinton with the same keywords. There was some overlap, as occasionally people mentioned both candidates in a tweet in a comparative way. There were also a significant number of retweets, with some items being retweeted thousands of times. An analysis (counting the number of downloaded tweets that were labeled RT) showed that 59% of the Trump tweet volume for this period was retweets while 51% of the Clinton tweets were retweets. In the analysis for this paper, we considered all tweets equally and did not code retweets differently. This analysis could benefit from further qualitative investigation into the content of tweets—and especially how often they link to traditional media content of newspapers, television networks, radio, etc.—but this was beyond the scope of this chapter.

An overview of the tweets that related to the candidates in this primary period does not show a high level of political engagement at work, particularly for Trump (see Figure 12.6). Many of the tweets were critical, angry, or called

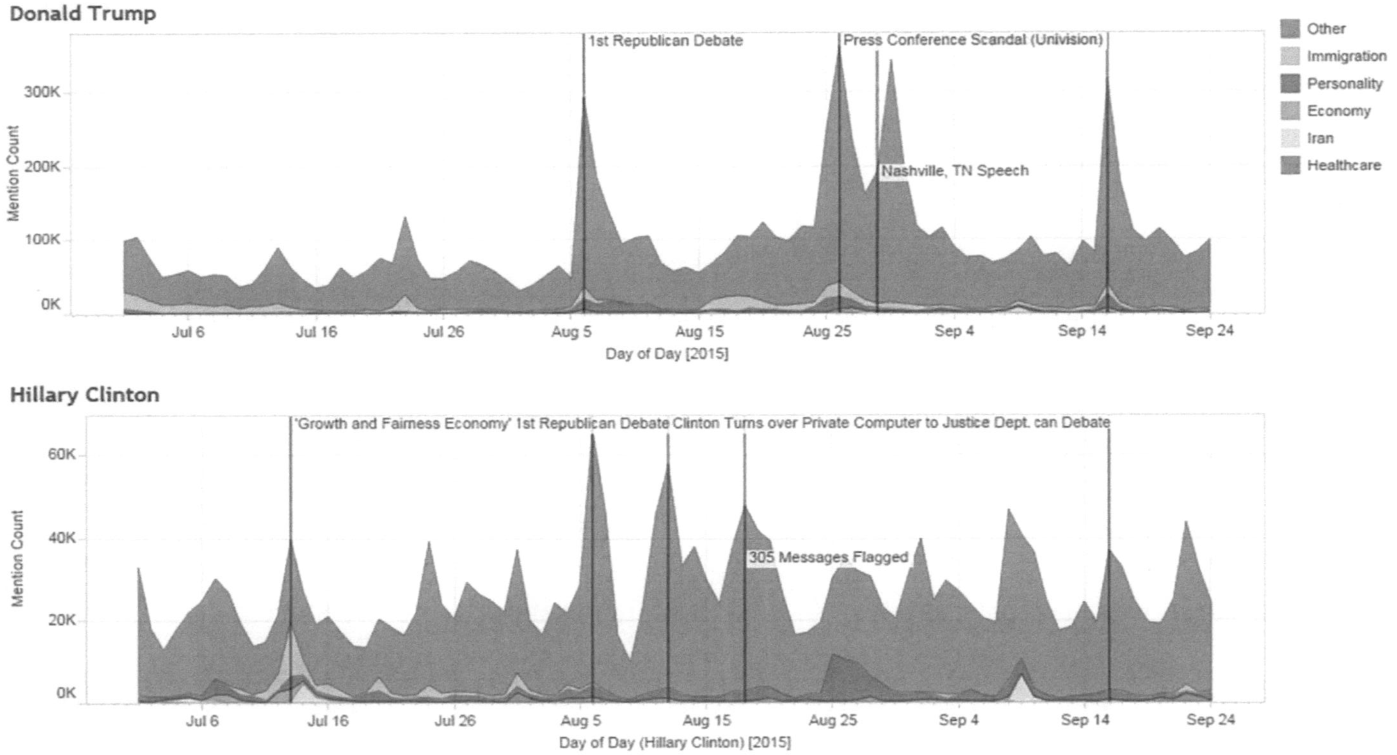

FIGURE 12.6A Tweets Mentioning Donald Trump and Hillary Clinton by Issue/Personality Terms, July 1 to September 24, 2015

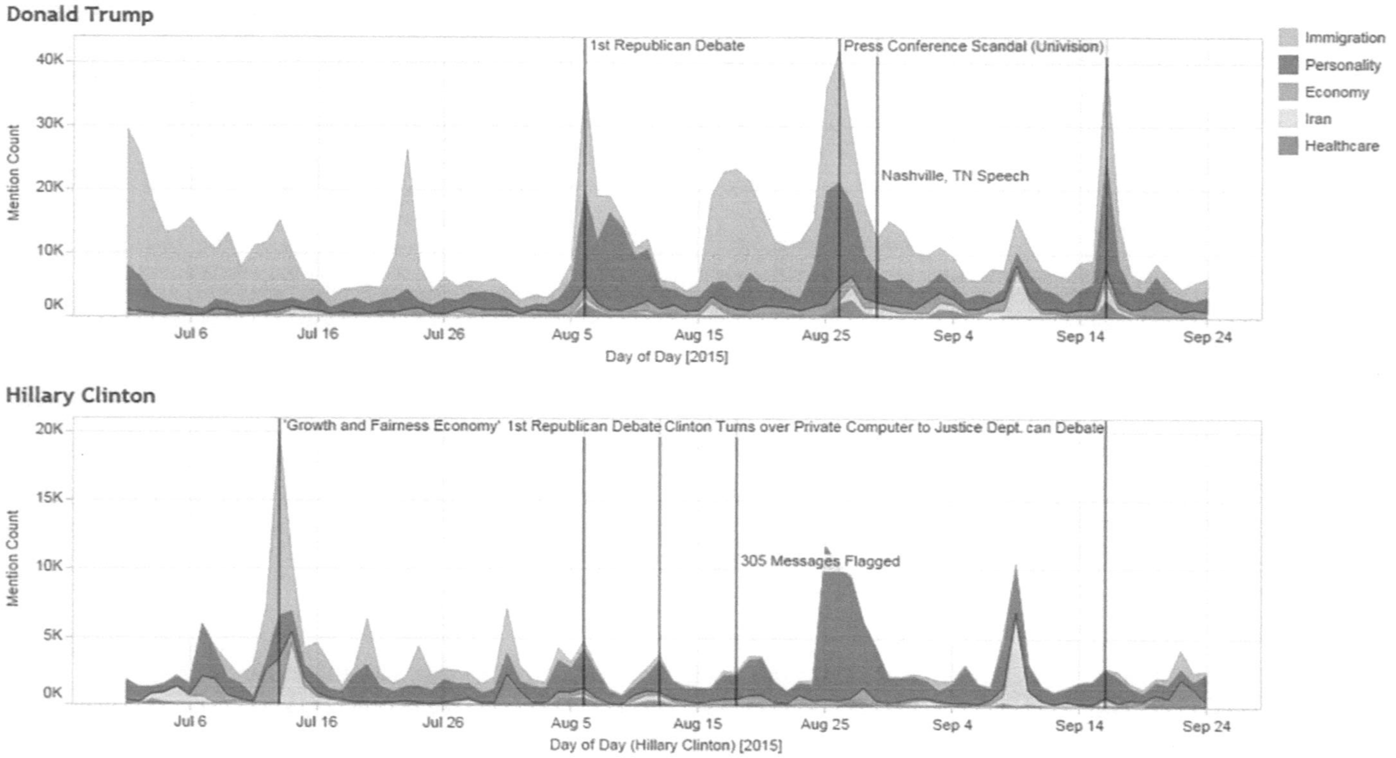

FIGURE 12.6B (Continued)

the candidates names (although there was not as much profanity as in other parts of the online sphere). A large number of links referred to media coverage, typically without any comment. Occasionally (particularly with Clinton), tweets praised the issues raised by the candidates.

The only consistent link between our keywords and the Trump-related (as opposed to the Trump-generated) tweets were mentions of immigration and personality terms. In this primary period, the volume of tweets mirrored significant campaign events such as debates, scandals, speeches, etc., quite closely (see Figure 12.6). Perhaps what is most interesting is the sheer volume of the tweets, climbing close to or past 300,000 daily on four separate days. This was more than five times the volume of people tweeting about Clinton in the same time period, according to our data. If you look specifically at the tweets that are linked to particular issues, there is still both a reasonable volume and link to campaign events. Immigration dominated the Twitter traffic in this primary period, although there is issue content in other tweets. The fact that large peaks of Twitter activity take place during or just after significant campaign events that make the news reinforces the idea that social media activity follows the regular news/news-reporting cycle in U.S. politics. We also show the pattern of tweets for Clinton in Figure 12.6.

Our analysis could not determine whether those who were tweeting or retweeting messages with issue or personality content were supporting or opposing the candidates. Attempts to use automated sentiment detection were abandoned, as hand coding showed that tweets that were being deemed negative or positive did not fit with our interpretation of the terms and there was far too much volume to code by hand. This is unsurprising, in that determining affect (even in the confines of a single tweet) is very difficult only using keywords. Yet, although we could not determine sentiment, the broader point is that this tweet volume is impressive in terms of share of audience. Whether people were supporting, opposing, or even vilifying Trump, he was getting much more attention on social media than Clinton during the primary campaign.

For the general election, we retrieved all tweets mentioning Clinton or Trump from early October through Election Day by using the Twitter API (due to technical difficulties, October 28 is missing from the dataset for the general public tweets). The volume was so large that we refined this dataset with the categories used for analysis in the primary election (economy, healthcare, immigration, Iran, personality) and added in categories (defined by keywords) that were relevant to the general election: abortion, Clinton email, cybersecurity, guns, Muslims, rigged elections, Russia, Supreme Court, and Trump's income taxes (see Appendix 12.1 for details). Our categories created a volume of up to 500,000 tweets a day (see Figure 12.7). Looking first at the broader range of categories, we can see that our "personality" category continued to dominate within even this filtered measure. Within the tweets the Clinton email scandal had a large and persistent presence on Twitter, which is unsurprising given the last-minute allegations by

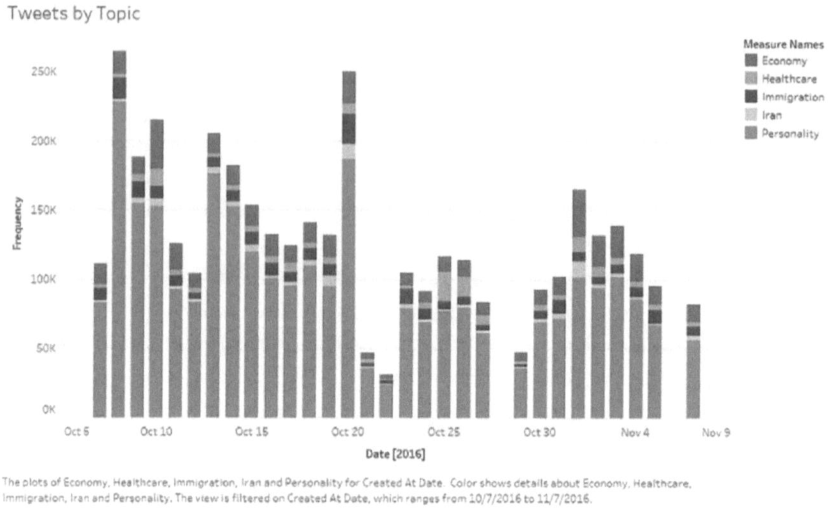

FIGURE 12.7 Tweets Mentioning Donald Trump and Hillary Clinton by Issue/Personality Terms, General Election

FBI Director James Comey on October 28 that there were additional emails to investigate. Unlike other issues or scandals, it is noteworthy that the volume of tweets about Clinton's email was clearly reinvigorated by that announcement. This continued interest is in direct contrast to tweets about Trump's comments on sexual assault from more than a decade ago (released on October 6, so we started the Twitter chart two days before our October 7 window) peaked on October 6, then steadily declined while retaining a persistent presence over the last month of the campaign. Trump's taxes were a consistent presence as well. In addition, the specter of rigged elections peaked on October 18 after Trump raised the issue in a speech on October 17. The rigged-election issue continued to resonate through the Twitter comments throughout the campaign.

What is the lesson for social media intelligence from this pattern of tweets linked to candidates and issues in the general election? First of all, it is interesting how persistent Clinton's email issues continued to be throughout the election period. Our research has not yet determined if this was significantly augmented by a concerted campaign to amplify this negative news about Clinton or whether this was a genuine grassroots concern. Nor do we know if these tweets were supportive or disparaging, although we suspect the latter. However, there is no question that the volume remained high, far higher than the tweets related to either the sexual-assault comments by Trump or Trump's tax issues. In addition—unlike immigration in the primary period we studied—newspaper articles were focusing more on Trump's sexual-assault comments than on Clinton's email controversy, although the renewed attention from the FBI clearly spurred a significant amount of coverage. Why then (unlike in the primary period) did the Twitter traffic fail to resonate the same attention as the mainstream media? We need additional research, but we are particularly interested in whether the email scandal was augmented by a concerted campaign against Clinton in the online sphere—in particular given that Trump's sexual-assault comments did not reach the same volume of interest. Overall, we should note that public tweets about key issues such as the economy or healthcare were dwarfed by tweets about scandals. You could say here that the Clinton email "branding" failed to translate into political capital—unlike Trump, who was able to parlay extremist statements on immigration into populist appeal, attention for Clinton mired her in past problems and appeared to alienate voters. Twitter logic appears to work for campaign brands that have shallow roots in traditional politics.

Are people on Twitter merely echoing and re-distributing snippets of news or opinion around campaign events or are there grassroot networks of discussion that arise from social media? Our data would strongly suggest the former on Twitter. The way in which the volume of tweets parallel significant campaign events suggests that social media traffic follows events rather than having a separate genesis. We acknowledge that we only analyzed Twitter as a proxy for social media. However, these visualizations of tweets remind us of the strong link among political events, traditional reporting to publicize those events, and social media activity. In particular, social media comments served to augment and extend the traditional media coverage of Trump's views on immigration, views that were at odds with mainstream U.S. media narratives about immigration.

It would be useful to say much more about the nature of that augmentation—were the tweets contesting the candidates' statements, agreeing with them, or perhaps merely echoing them? We could not say this based on our analysis, but it points to the need for a more comprehensive approach to analyzing social media comments with computational linguistic analysis so that the nature (as well as the volume) of the discourse can be evaluated with some degree of validity and reliability. We know that people were engaged with Trump's views on immigration in social media (or at least on Twitter) during the primary elections. We know that they tweeted a great deal about Clinton's email investigation as well as Trump's sexual-assault comments (although less on the latter). However, we don't know the nature or depth of that engagement, although we can draw some conclusions from our study. Namely, as noted above, engagement tended to follow candidate behavior, strongly suggesting that social media would generally augment, rather than contest, candidate narratives. For example, if Trump's extremist statements were going to spark an interest in response by other candidates, we would expect to see a surge in tweets about immigration that mentioned Clinton (such as her response or different approach to the issue) but we did not find this in the data. We can surmise that Trump enjoyed strong ownership of the immigration discourse as a sub-element of his political brand. Yet, this social media logic of "ownership" did not appear to help Clinton as she battled an ongoing fight about her transparency during her time as secretary of state with her email issues.

We also do not know how much of the attention surrounding Clinton's email was driven by a deliberate campaign of influence, such as by the Russian government. This would require a different approach that would both map the origin of particular comments and measure their spread among specific Twitter users (with a particular emphasis on looking for automated or human influencers). Although this is beyond the scope of this chapter, there is evidence that suggests that propaganda warfare was taking place in the 2016 U.S. election. This chapter presents the overall landscape of Twitter content as it related to the candidates, but future studies should look into the construction of that landscape in more detail. This is an element of broader concerns over the general amount of misinformation either deliberately or mistakenly circulated among voters in 2016, an important part of the current debate about "fake" news and the problem of media literacy in America.

Conclusions

We launched this project in an attempt to apply social media marketing theory, particularly social media intelligence (Moe & Schweidel, 2014), to political communication. At the same time, we were interested in whether we could augment theories and understanding of business brands via a consideration of the study of social media in political campaigns.

In the primary campaign, we found both social and traditional media dominated by Trump's remarks about immigration, to the point that discussion about other candidates and issues was drowned out by the media furor. Thus, any attempts to carefully build political "brands" by other Republicans or Democrats were overwhelmed by the attention Trump and the media directed to a single issue. Either Trump put forth these views due to his nature, which could be described as reflexively aggressive, or he did it as part of a carefully concerted campaign to disrupt "politics as usual" by suggesting ideas that were (apparently in almost equal measure) either deeply offensive or deeply attractive to almost everyone in the country. Whether by accident or design, the Trump anti-immigrant narrative was firmly established and one could argue that the brand had credibility, given the candidate's widely covered disparaging remarks on many individuals and groups over the course of the campaign. This continued into the general election, where in the month before Election Day, Trump's scandals continued to garner more coverage than key political issues (so did Clinton's main scandal, but it did not appear to help). Trump was the "bad boy" of American politics, breaking the rules, but winning the game. The immigration "brand" did not dominate in the final month of the campaign, but by then it did not really matter. By this point, the dynamic was established—Trump was outrageous, the media was outraged, and people were paying attention and drawing their own conclusions (with remarkably few details about policy or its implementation). Once this logic was established, the showman, rather than the politician, was far better placed to win the campaign.

This brings us to the idea of the "oxygen of publicity," a phrase made famous by former British Prime Minister Margaret Thatcher, who first used it in a speech to the American Bar Association in July 1985 to describe how terrorists could use the media to gain legitimacy. Her government was concerned about how British media coverage could give popularity and political credibility to groups it considered allied with terrorists in Northern Ireland. The historical parallel is interesting with the coverage of Trump and his views on immigration and treatment of women that sit well outside the accepted political norms of the U.S. media. On the one hand, Trump would be unable to propagate these views without the heavy coverage by the media (often expressing outrage through the framing of the story or by one-sided quotes, although finding people willing to openly support Trump's views publicly was perhaps a bit challenging). In this way, his remarks came to dominate both the traditional and social media. U.S. media were facing the same challenge as the British media in covering Northern Ireland: How do you cover a divided country? How do you write "news" about something that could be considered provocation or even hate speech by some, but not all, of the audience? The response in *The New York Times* and *The Washington Post* was to provide a lot of attention, although ironically attempts to illuminate how far out of step Trump's views were with one part of the audience may have given these views greater attention and legitimacy with another part of the media audience.

This emphasis on Trump's remarks on immigration had a range of effects on the campaign. In terms of this study, it demonstrates how anti-immigration became a key element of the Trump brand, giving him a significant advantage in a crowded Republican primary field. It even dominated over news coverage of the Democratic front-runner in the primaries. It allowed one "noisy" issue to overshadow a range of policy issues, ones in which arguably Trump would have had a harder time using soundbites and outrage to establish a dominant position. In their rush to cover Trump's extreme rhetoric, the traditional media gave visibility and, arguably, credence to these remarks. It also shows how, although it was not the only thing that people were talking about in the primary campaign, it became the touchstone around which that part of the campaign was structured. Our analysis of Twitter shows that social media discussion tended to follow main events and issues of the campaign, again demonstrating that the traditional nature of the campaign was intact: politicians led, media covered, and the public followed. In reflecting on our Campaign Message Flow Model, analysis for this chapter suggests that messages are more likely to flow from the candidate via a traditional campaign event (such as a speech or debate), be covered in the traditional media, and then messages from this traditional media content will be shared and discussed on social media.

Looking back at our study of political brands in the 2016 U.S. elections, our insights for business brands are to consider more carefully the way in which brands travel through a media ecology. In particular, elements of a brand that can disrupt normal media coverage or attention would appear to have a corresponding depth of attention on social media and can attract an irrationally large amount of attention. This goes beyond the idea of a single social media post going viral or a particular ad campaign. This suggests that an understanding of how and why a brand holds a particular place in a media ecology is a useful evolution in thinking about the relationship among brands, traditional media, new media, and citizens.

Acknowledgements

The authors gratefully acknowledge both funding for this project from the ADVANCE program at the University of Maryland and the graduate students who worked with us: Paul Cranford, Justin Hudson, Carole Lee, Jun Rossetti, and Stephen Witkowski. The authors would like to also thank Brandwatch, an international social media analytics company based in the U.K., for giving us access to tweets for our analysis.

APPENDIX 12.1

We used the following search terms to download tweets from twitter.com relating to our five categories:

Primary election time period: July 1 to September 24, 2015
General election time period: October 7 to November 7, 2016 (we downloaded additional times around these dates, but generally confined our analysis to one month)
Author: @realDonaldTrump
Author: @HillaryClinton

For the traditional mass media, we used the same dates and terms to search for articles on LexisNexis Academic in *The New York Times, the Washington Post,* and *USA Today* with "Trump" and "Clinton." Any story identified as not news (including editorials, letters, opinion pieces, analysis, etc.) was excluded from the study. We coded each story for the presence of our categories, which candidates were mentioned, and whether one candidate was the focus of the story.

Words/word stems used in searches (*indicates a word stem):

Category: Economy

Economy* OR jobs OR wage* OR tax* OR trade OR outsource* OR unemploy* OR prices

Category: Iran

Iran OR nuclear OR Assad OR Tehran

Category: Immigration

immigration OR immigrants OR mexico* OR border OR citizen* OR deport* OR visa OR amnesty

Category: Healthcare

Healthcare OR health* OR medical OR obamacare OR medicare OR insurance OR socialized OR doctors OR malpractice
Add for general election: Medicaid

Category: Personality

strong OR leader OR woman OR women OR boring OR powerful OR dishonest OR honest OR liar OR conservative OR idiot OR tough OR smart OR corrupt OR liberal OR "big mouth" OR "Bill Clinton" OR businessman OR competitive OR trust* OR distrust
Add for general election: crooked

The following categories were added for the general election:

Category: Clinton Email

Email, server, Comey, FBI, indictment*, WikiLeaks, "attorney general"

Category: Rigged Election

rigged, fraud, register*, "double voting," "ballot stuffing"

Category: Sexual Assault Comments

pussy, locker room, "Billy Bush," "Arianne Zucker," grop* [for groper, groping]

Category: Trump Tax Return

"tax return," audit, deduction, $916 million, IRS

Category: Cybersecurity

cybersecurity, hack*, cyberattack*

Category: Russia

Russia, Putin, Moscow, Kremlin

Category: Gun Rights/Second Amendment

gun*, NRA, "2nd amendment," "Second Amendment," "bill of rights," "felons," "bear arms," "background check"

Category: Middle East

ISIS, Syria, Afghanistan, Iraq, "Extremist Muslim," Islam, Aleppo, Mosul

Category: Abortion Rights

"right to life," "abortion rights," "Roe" [as in Roe v. Wade], "right to choose," "planned parenthood," "partial birth"

Category: Supreme Court

"Supreme Court," Scalia, Garland

References

Bollen, J., Mao, H., & Zeng, X. (2011). Twitter mood predicts the stock market. *Journal of Computational Science, 2*(1), 1–8. Retrieved from https://doi.org/10.1016/j.jocs.2010.12.007

Boulianne, S. (2009). Does Internet use affect engagement? A meta-analysis of research. *Political Communication, 26*, 193–211. Retrieved from https://doi.org/10.1080/10584600902854363

Chadwick, A. (2013). *The hybrid media system: Politics and power.* New York, NY: Oxford University Press. Retrieved from https://doi.org/10.1093/acprof:oso/9780199759477.001.0001

Confessore, N., & Yourish, K. (2016, March 15). $2 billion worth of free media for Donald Trump. *The New York Times.* Retrieved from www.nytimes.com/2016/03/16/upshot/measuring-donald-trumps-mammoth-advantage-in-free-media.html

Dellarocas, C., & Narayan, R. (2006). *What motivates consumers to review a product online? A study of product-specific antecedents of online movie reviews.* Chicago, IL: Workshop on Information Systems and Economics. Retrieved from http://digital.mit.edu/wise2006/papers/2b-3_finalwise2006abstract-dell-narayan.pdf

Dellarocas, C., Zhang, X., & Awad, N. F. (2007). Exploring the value of online product reviews in forecasting sales: The case of motion pictures. *Journal of Interactive Marketing, 21*(4), 23–45. Retrieved from https://doi.org/10.1002/dir.20087

Gainous, J., & Wagner, K. M. (2013). *Tweeting to power: The social media revolution in American politics.* New York, NY: Oxford University Press. Retrieved from https://doi.org/10.1093/acprof:oso/9780199965076.001.0001

Gibson, R. K., Margolis, M., Resnick, D., & Ward, S. J. (2003). Election campaigning on the WWW in the USA and UK: A comparative analysis. *Party Politics, 9*(1), 470–475. Retrieved from https://doi.org/10.1177/135406880391004

Karpf, D. (2012). *The MoveOn effect: The unexpected transformation of American political advocacy.* New York, NY: Oxford University Press. Retrieved from https://doi.org/10.1093/acprof:oso/9780199898367.001.0001

Lampos, V., Preoţiuc-Pietro, D., & Cohn, T. (2013). A user-centric model of voting intention from social media. *Proceedings of the 51st Annual Meeting of the Association for Computational Linguistics*, Sofia, Bulgaria. Retrieved from www.aclweb.org/website/old_anthology/P/P13/P13-1098.pdf

Magleby, D., Goodliffe, J., & Olsen, J. (2014). How the Internet, BCRA, and Super PACs have affected donor attitudes, behavior, and campaigns. Paper presented at American Political Science Assocation annual meeting. Retrieved from https://ssrn.com/abstract=2454301

Moe, W. W., & Schweidel, D. A. (2014). *Social media intelligence.* New York, NY: Cambridge University Press. Retrieved from https://doi.org/10.1017/CBO9781139381338

Moe, W. W., & Trusov, M. (2011). The value of social dynamics in online product ratings forums. *Journal of Marketing Research, 48*(3), 444–456. Retrieved from https://doi.org/10.1509/jmkr.48.3.444

Netzer, O., Feldman, R., Goldenberg, J., & Fresko, M. (2012). Mine our own business: Market-structure surveillance through text mining. *Marketing Science, 31*(3), 521–543. Retrieved from https://doi.org/10.1287/mksc.1120.0713

Parry-Giles, S. (2014). *Hillary Clinton in the news: Gender and authenticity in American politics.* Chicago, IL: University of Illinois Press.

Patterson, T. E. (1994). *Out of order.* New York, NY: First Vintage Books Edition.

Pew Research Center. (2014, September 12). *Wide partisan differences over the issues that matter in 2014: GOP continues to hold engagement advantage.* Washington, DC: Pew

Research Center. Retrieved from www.people-press.org/2014/09/12/wide-partisan-differences-over-the-issues-that-matter-in-2014/

Schweidel, D. A., & Moe, W. W. (2014). Listening in on social media: A joint model of sentiment and venue format choice. *Journal of Marketing Research, 51*(4), 387–402. Retrieved from https://doi.org/10.1509/jmr.12.0424

Stromer-Galley, J. (2014). *Presidential campaigning in the Internet age.* New York, NY: Oxford University Press. Retrieved from https://doi.org/10.1093/acprof:oso/9780199731930.001.0001

Tirunillai, S., & Tellis, G. J. (2012). Does chatter really matter?: Dynamics of user-generated content and stock performance. *Marketing Science, 31*(2), 198–215. Retrieved from https://doi.org/10.1287/mksc.1110.0682

13

THE INFOGRAPHIC ELECTION

The Role of Visual Content on Social Media in the 2016 Presidential Campaign

Terri L. Towner

In the last 50 years, the popular format of communication has shifted from text to visuals. As a result, mass media coverage, particularly television news, have become an important determinant of a presidential candidate's electoral success (Bartels, 1993; Patterson & McClure, 1976; Rosenberg, Bohan, McCafferty, & Harris, 1986), with coverage influencing citizens' candidate perceptions and ultimately their vote choice. Beyond television news, other research has examined the impact of different visual forms of communication on candidate evaluations, such as televised debates (Benoit, Hansen, & Verser, 2003; Chaffee & Choe, 1980; Davis, 1979), televised campaign advertising (Ansolabehere & Iyengar, 1995; Just et al., 1996; Kaid, 2004; Wattenberg & Brians, 1999), television talk-shows and late-night comedy shows (Baumgartner & Morris, 2006; Moy, Xenos, & Hess, 2006; Pfau, Cho, & Chong, 2001), and the Internet, blogs, and websites (Johnson, Braima, & Sothirajah, 1999; Johnson & Kaye, 2004). Indeed, the importance of images and visuals in campaigning is not new; however, what is relatively new is the prominent use of social media.

Since 2008, political candidates have considered social media a key campaign tool (Mitchell, Holcomb, & Weisel, 2016; Shearer, 2016). As the consumption of political news and information on social media increased, visuals became king—with impressive results. For example, a photo of President Obama embracing his wife after winning the 2012 presidential election was the most-liked and most-retweeted post in social media history (Harding, 2012). Social media users are now communicating more with visuals and less words (Walter, 2012). The 2016 presidential candidates also engaged in visual marketing, employing the standard social media—Facebook, Twitter, and YouTube—along with newer forms, such as Snapchat, Instagram, Pinterest, and Flickr, for advertising and outreach (Crist, 2016; Mitchell et al., 2016). On these social networks, candidates post a variety of textual and visual content, including issue stance statements, hyperlinks to their campaign website, snapshots with family members, informative infographics, and videos of stump speeches. Digital content is certainly not unseen. Sixty-five percent of citizens learned about the 2016 presidential election from online sources, with Facebook, YouTube, Twitter, Instagram, and Snapchat indicated as top digital platforms for election news (Gottfried, Barthel, Shearer, & Mitchell, 2016).

The empirical impact of attention to social media for campaign information has been well documented, linking social media to offline political participation (Bode, 2012; Chen, Ping, & Chen, 2015; Dimitrova, Shehata, Stromack, & Nord, 2014; Gil de Zúñiga, Jung, & Valenzuala, 2012; Gil de Zúñiga, Molyneux, & Zhang, 2014; Theocharis & Lowe, 2016; Towner, 2013; Towner & Dulio, 2011a, 2011b; Towner & Munoz, 2017; Wells & Thorson, 2015; Zhang, Setlzer, & Bichard, 2013), political efficacy (Ha et al., 2013; Towner, 2016; Towner & Dulio, 2011a), and political knowledge (Baumgartner & Morris, 2010; Dimitrova et al., 2014; Groshek & Dimitrova, 2011; Towner & Dulio, 2011c; Towner & Dulio, 2015). Previous research also indicates that attention to campaign information on social media influences candidate evaluations as well as vote choice (Dimitrova & Bystrom, 2013; Towner, 2016; Towner & Dulio, 2015; Towner & Dulio, 2011a, 2011b; Towner & Munoz, 2016). Less is known, however, about how specific content, visuals versus text, posted on social media influence citizens' candidate evaluations. This is important because social media allows candidates and campaigns to directly communicate with social media users, without the mainstream media filter (Gainous & Wagner, 2013). Therefore, this study's purpose is to examine the effects of attention to campaign content in the form of photos, infographics, and videos posted on social media on citizens' evaluations of the presidential candidates.

Media and Candidate Evaluations

Newspapers and Newsmagazines

It is widely known that photographs in print newspapers and newsmagazines play an important role in candidates' image-making. Existing literature focuses primarily on how candidate images are presented by the mass media. Early work conducted during the presidential elections in the 1980s determined that the candidates' image established how candidates depicted themselves and, most important, how the media represents the candidate (Moriarty & Garramone, 1986). To determine whether certain presidential candidates received more favorable pictorial coverage than other candidates, Moriarty and co-authors examined photographs of 1984, 1988, and 1992 presidential candidates published in prominent newsmagazines (Moriarty & Garramone, 1986; Moriarty & Popovich, 1991; Popovich, Moriarty, & Pitts, 1993). The authors found evidence that some candidates received better pictorial treatment: Reagan was covered more favorably than Mondale (Moriarty & Garramone, 1986). In the 1988 election, George H. W. Bush garnered more favorable visual coverage than Michael Dukakis (Moriarty & Popovich, 1991). More recently, Goodnow (2010) reported bias in *Time* magazine's photo essays on the Democratic candidates Barack Obama and Hillary Clinton during the 2008 presidential election, concluding that the *Time* pictorial favored Obama over Clinton.

Newspapers and its use of photographs during presidential campaigns has also been frequently examined. During the 1996 presidential election, Waldman and Dewitt (1998) content analyzed newspaper photographs of Bill Clinton and Bob Dole, finding little pictorial favoritism. Only Bill Clinton received a bit more favorable pictorial coverage. In the George W. Bush versus Al Gore battle in 2000, German (2010) examined photographs in *The New York Times*, finding that Bush garnered more photographic attention than Gore. Bush was more likely to appear "above the fold" and received more "close ups" than Gore. After a systemic examination of candidate photography across seven newspapers and different races during the 1998 and 2002 general elections, Barrett and Barrington (2005) concluded that images published matched the newspapers' "political atmosphere," meaning that newspapers are indeed biased toward certain candidates. Examining front-page newspaper photos of Barack Obama and Mitt Romney in the 2012 presidential election, Dahmen (2016a) did not find overwhelming overall differences in the candidates' pictorial presentation. Some differences included dress, as Obama appeared more often in stiff suits and ties whereas Romney was photographed in more relatable casual dress. Obama was also pictured shaking hands and waving (favorable coverage) while Romney was often shown with his arms folded (unfavorable coverage). Overall, studies show that photographs and images in newsmagazines and newspapers can vary in important ways, ultimately influencing a voter's perceptions of the candidates (e.g., Barrett & Barrington, 2005; Boomgaarden, Boukes, & Iorgoveanu, 2016; Rosenberg et al., 1986; Rosenberg & McCafferty, 1987; Todorov, Mandisodza, Goren, & Hall, 2005).

Television

Television fundamentally altered the relationship between voters and candidates by using moving pictures and sound, rather than the printed image and word, to communicate campaign information (Patterson & McClure, 1976). To inform and entertain, television news coverage focuses viewers' attention on the personalities of candidates and, thus, the standards of evaluating political candidates have shifted to candidates' personalities, traits, and characteristics (Bartels, 1993). In fact, prior research suggests that voters dependent on television for political news have been more focused on a candidate's traits, unlike those who gather news from newspapers (Keeter, 1987).

Television has also changed the style of campaigning, with campaign strategists focusing on carefully crafted "photo ops," "soundbites," and "video style" (Schill, 2009). Similar to newspaper and newsmagazine coverage, television news portrays candidates in images and sound very differently. For example, an examination of 1984 presidential television news coverage found that television offered generous coverage of candidate traits, but candidate trait coverage varied (Graber, 1987). In a more recent study of television news coverage of the 2000 presidential campaign, Coleman and Banning (2006) found that news coverage included more negative nonverbal behavior of George W. Bush whereas coverage of Al Gore included more positive nonverbal expressions. Most important, the authors offered evidence that citizens' candidate evaluations corresponded with the news coverage—citizens felt significantly more positively about Gore than about Bush (Kiousis, Bantimaroudis, & Ban, 1999). Candidates' facial expressions, appearance, and other body language broadcast by television also influenced viewers (e.g., Coleman & Banning, 2006; Coleman & Wu, 2015; Lanzetta, Sullivan, Masters, & McHugo, 1985).

Beyond news coverage, scholars have also examined the influence of televised debates (Benoit et al., 2003; Chaffee & Choe, 1980; Davis, 1979), televised campaign advertising (Ansolabehere & Iyengar, 1995; Just et al., 1996; Kaid, 2004; Wattenberg & Brians, 1999), and entertainment television (Baumgartner & Morris, 2006; Moy et al., 2006; Pfau et al., 2001) on citizens' candidate perceptions. Much of the research on presidential debates asserts that debates influence viewer perceptions of candidates (Benoit, McKinney, & Holbert, 2001; Benoit et al., 2003; McKinney & Carlin, 2004; McKinney, Dudash, & Hodgkinson, 2003; Scheufele, Kim, & Brossard, 2007; Zhu, Milavsky, & Biswas, 1994). The visual aspect of televised presidential debates allows viewers to evaluate candidates' personal qualities and characteristics, such as competence and warmth (Lanoue & Schrott, 1991). Even nonverbal behavior seen during debates is important to viewers (Goethals, 2005). Regarding political advertising, visual images in political television ads from the candidates themselves can be very persuasive (Brader, 2005) and, most notably, can even affect the public's knowledge on candidates' issue positions (Brians & Wattenberg, 1996). Along with traditional television news, citizens also consume "soft news" or "infotainment" shows that often touch on politics (Baum, 2002, 2003; Patterson, 2000). These "soft" shows, particularly late-night comedy, employ satire and humor, often negatively framing presidential candidates (Hess, 2001; Jones, 2005; Niven, Lichter, & Amundson, 2003). Not surprisingly, attention to soft television news can also impact citizens' perceptions and evaluations of candidates (Baum, 2005; Baumgartner & Morris, 2006; Pfau et al., 2001; Young, 2004).

Internet

The rise of the Internet as a campaign communication tool added another form of media offering photos, videos, and text to potential voters. In the early Internet years, campaigns commonly employed campaign websites to directly communicate with citizens. This direct digital link allowed candidates to carefully craft a positive image with photos, videos, and additional information without the mainstream media filter (Bimber & Davis, 2003; Kaid & Johnston, 2001). Hansen and Benoit (2005) found that viewing Al Gore and George W. Bush's websites in the 2000 election altered perceptions of candidate character, policy positions, leadership, and global feelings (see also Bimber & Davis, 2003). Examining visual content on Gore and Bush's websites, Verser and Wicks (2006) reported that Gore posted significantly more photos on his website than Bush. Specifically, Gore included photos that portrayed him as interactive with voters, casual, cheerful, and caring whereas Bush posted photos that presented him as less active, giving speeches to large audiences, and in suits and ties. The authors concluded that Gore sought to create positive impressions with pictures—much more so than Bush (see also Grabe & Bucy, 2009).

Social Media

Today, political visual rhetoric has spread from campaign websites to social media platforms: Facebook, Twitter, YouTube, and Instagram. Several scholars have found a connection between social media use and candidate evaluations, but results differ by platform, candidate, and campaign. For instance, during the 2008 presidential campaign, Kaye (2013) found that reliance on social-networking sites, online newspapers and newsmagazines, political blogs, and candidate websites positively predicted support for Barack Obama, but negatively predicted support for John McCain. Similarly, Towner and Dulio (2011c) reported evidence that young adults paying attention to campaign information on video-sharing sites and social networks was positively associated with Obama likeability, but there was no link to McCain likeability. In contrast, however, an experiment exposing young adults to campaign information on YouTube'08 and ABCNews.com revealed no effect on evaluations of Obama and McCain (Towner & Dulio, 2011b).

Studies conducted during the 2012 election reveal a similar mix of findings. During the 2012 Iowa caucuses, Dimitrova and Bystrom (2013) found that social media use was related to Iowa voters' evaluations, but each online platform had differing effects on candidate evaluations. For example, watching YouTube videos had a negative influence on candidate evaluations whereas following candidates on Facebook had a positive impact on candidates' intelligence and leadership ratings. During the 2012 presidential campaign, Towner and Dulio (2015) concluded that young adults' attention to campaign information on social media outlets rarely influenced their evaluations of Barack Obama and Mitt Romney (see also Towner & Munoz, 2016).

A similar line of research also reveals that social media use—commenting, liking, scrolling—during campaign events, such as presidential debates, has notable effects on candidate perceptions. Examining social media communication on Facebook and Twitter about the first 2012 presidential debate, Hawthorne and Warner (2015) found a significant link between how much an individual communicated on social media and Obama and Romney evaluations. Similarly, live tweeting while watching the 2012 primary and presidential debates is significantly linked to tweeters' candidate perceptions and attitudes toward the debate itself (Houston, Hawthorne, Spialek, Greenwood, & McKinney, 2013; McKinney, Houston, & Hawthorne, 2014). Live tweeting did not have the same impact on all candidate evaluations, however. Specifically, during the 2012 presidential debate, live debate tweeting was related to more favorable views of Obama, but not for Romney (Houston et al., 2013).

Text, Photos, Video, and Infographics on Social Media

The above research confirms that attention to some forms of social media can influence candidate evaluations; however, there is still little understanding of exactly what content on these social media sites matters the most. A labyrinth of social media research examines textual messages posted by presidential candidates in their Facebook and Twitter feeds, such as references to challengers, policies discussed, calls to action, personal posts, and solicitations for donations, along with other social media characteristics, such as the frequency of posts, likes, comments, shares, and hyperlinks (e.g., Ancu, 2011; Borah, 2016; Gueorguieva, 2008; Robertson, Vatrapu, & Medina, 2010; Rosenstiel & Mitchell, 2012; Svensson, Kiousis, & Strömbäck, 2015; Towner, 2016). In general, this research suggests that candidates employ social media to craft favorable campaign narratives, communicate with and mobilize voters, and build a credible reputation. In a systematic study of Mitt Romney's Twitter feed, for example, Johnson (2012b) concluded that Romney's textual tweets strengthened his credibility, expressed his reasoning, and created connections with users. Svensson et al. (2015) found some evidence that Obama and Romney sought to cultivate relationships with voters, largely through collaboration strategies, using email, Facebook updates, and tweets (see also Svensson, 2012). Clearly, candidates who seek to build and sustain relationships with voters may be viewed as more credible as well as more highly evaluated.

More recently, scholars have begun to examine photos and images posted on candidates' social media platforms. Tracking visual images posted on the 2012 Republican presidential primary candidates' Twitter and Facebook feeds, Page and Duffy (2016) find that visual social media strategies differed greatly across four remaining candidates (i.e., Santorum, Gingrich, Paul, and Romney), but all sought to communicate credibility concepts of trustworthiness and expertise with visual storytelling. Interestingly, the authors deemed Santorum's social media imagery as most credible, as he offered a well-rounded visual narrative, emphasizing a plot, character, and setting. In a similar study, Goodnow (2013) examines Obama's and Romney's Facebook timeline images (i.e., photos of the candidate only) during the 2012 presidential campaign, asserting that both candidates sought to fulfill the "ideal candidate" image (see also, Grabe & Bucy, 2009). Indeed, candidate-controlled social media images should present candidates in a favorable manner, emphasizing leadership, honesty, and so forth. Yet, Dahmen (2016b) suggests that this is not always the case. An in-depth analysis of Twitter profiles among 2014 senatorial candidates finds that candidates surprisingly offered visuals that depicted them unfavorably, regarding behavior, context, and perspective.

YouTube, the most popular video-sharing site, has also proved to be a powerful campaign tool. During the 2008 campaign, will.i.am's "Yes, We Can" music video, which was viewed over 20 million times, cemented 2008 as the "YouTube election" (Wallsten, 2010). Since 2008, scholars have documented presidential candidates' YouTube content, focusing on interactivity and campaign strategies (Church, 2010; Davisson, 2009; Duman & Locher, 2008; Powell, 2010; Ricke, 2015). Examining leadership discourse in YouTube videos, Church (2010) found that the 2008 presidential primary candidates were more likely to mention civic advocacy, virtue, courage, and unification in YouTube videos, promoting themselves as champions for democracy. Other research specifically examines campaign ads posted on YouTube by both candidates and general users (Groshek & Brookes, 2015; Ridout, Fowler, & Branstetter, 2010). Today, candidates frequently employ YouTube in their campaign, but with different goals in mind. Ricke (2015), for example, noted that Obama's YouTube channel in the 2012 campaign contained mostly campaign ads (54%) along with video focused on policy and agenda information (30%), as well as video directed at encouraging voter engagement (17%). In contrast, Romney's YouTube channel predominately posted campaign ads (90%). As online video begins to rival television for viewership, one questions the ability of digital video to influence candidate evaluations.

There is little scholarly research on the role of infographics or graphics posted on social media sites during election campaigns. The latter is likely because infographics first gained popularity during the 2012 Obama and Romney presidential race. Infographics are unique in that they offer a visual portrayal of information with intriguing facts and eye-catching images. Most important, infographics seek to simplify and package information that may be difficult to understand. On her blog, Johnson (2012a, para. 5) anecdotally compared Obama and Romney's infographics, stating: "The candidate's web site show striking visual content that break down numbers, policies, and issues. The importance of how visual communication can affect the electorate's understanding of the campaign is crucial to the end result—a vote." Currently, however, it is unclear if infographics posted on social media influence citizens.

Expectations

Does visual campaign content influence candidate evaluations more so than textual content posted on social media? In general, a link between attention to visual content and evaluations is expected for two main reasons. First, psychology literature has long since established that images have greater impact on the public's memory and attitudes than text. This latter is known as the "picture superiority effect" (e.g., Curran & Doyle, 2011; Defetyer, Russo, & McPartlin, 2009; Hockley, 2008; McBride & Dosher, 2002; Nelson, Reed, & Walling, 1976; Paivio, 1971; Shepard, 1967; Whitehouse, Maybery, & Durkin, 2006). Unlike images, textual information is more difficult to remember, as it is more logically and rationally processed in one's mind. Visuals are more memorable, easily recalled, and easily recognized than words (Berry & Brosius, 1991; Edwards, 2004; Hockley, 2008; Paivio, 1979; Stenberg, 2006). Moreover, visuals are purported to have a more powerful emotional force than text (Barry, 1997; Hill & Helmers, 2004; Joffe, 2008). In addition, the combination of text and images, rather than text alone, is more likely to be remembered (Childers & Houston, 1984; Edell & Staelin, 1983; Miniard, Bhatla, Lord, Dickson, & Unnava, 1991). Verbal information is processed linearly and systematically (Barry, 2005; Elkins, 2003; Schneider & Maasen, 1998), which makes it difficult for citizens to access and recall (Messaris, 1997). Even when verbal and visuals are combined, images are more easily remembered than verbal. Individuals are simply more likely to remember what they see rather than what the read or hear (Grimes, 1991; Lang, 1995; Noller, 1985; Schweiger & Adami, 1999; Shea & Burton, 2001).

Second, social media has become much more visually based, bombarding users with a continuous stream of photos, infographics, and videos—many of which are reposted and shared over and over. Recent data suggest that photos and online video receive the most engagement on sites such as Facebook and Twitter (Rogers, 2014; Ross, 2014a, 2014b, 2016). This shift to visual social media increases the importance and impact of photos, video, and infographics posted by candidates, campaigns, and other users, further encouraging the "personalization" of politics (Bennett, 2012; Boyd & Ellison, 2007; Lawrence, McGregor, Cardona, & Mourão, 2016). For example, Hillary Clinton posted numerous photos on social media of her as a young schoolgirl, as a college student at Wellesley, as a new mother, and vintage family photos. Donald Trump shared pictures of his children and grandchildren and snapshots of him eating at McDonald's on various social platforms. This type of visual content personalizes candidates. By using social media to share images or videos with citizens, political candidates can offer a feeling of authenticity, something more raw or personal, and "a first-person view" of the campaign, which may influence candidate credibility and overall evaluations (see

Housholder & LaMarre, 2014; Lee & Oh, 2012; Powell, Richmond, & Williams, 2011). Given the known impact of visuals coupled with the increasing use of photos, video, and infographics on social media, this research argues:

H1: Attention to visual campaign content—photos or images—posted on social networks will more significantly predict candidate evaluations than textual campaign content posted on social networks.

H2: Attention to visual campaign content—infographics or graphics—posted on social networks will more significantly predict candidate evaluations than textual campaign content posted on social networks.

H3: Attention to visual campaign content—video—posted on social networks will more significantly predict candidate evaluations than textual campaign content posted on social networks.

Method

Survey Data

Two surveys were conducted. The first survey was fielded during the presidential primary: between April 1, 2016, and June 14, 2016. The logic for this time period was that the primary period was well underway, with about 50 primaries and caucuses completed and 24 remaining. In addition, the candidate field had narrowed to Republican candidates Ted Cruz, Donald Trump, and John Kasich and Democratic candidates Hillary Clinton and Bernie Sanders. To survey respondents, U.S. residents over the age of 18 were recruited to participate in an online survey through Amazon.com's Mechanical Turk (MTurk) platform. MTurk is a website that allows the public to earn money for completing online work, including participating in survey research. Presently, many scholars are employing Mechanical Turk to obtain a more representative sample of the population in experimental and survey research (Berinsky, Huber, & Lenz, 2012; Chandler, Mueller, & Paolacci, 2014; Huff & Tingley, 2015). Each respondent was paid $0.10 for completing the survey. After removing non-completions, a total of 519 respondents completed the survey. Respondent demographics for the primary-period survey were: 52% women, over 50% have a college degree or higher, average age was 34.36 years old (SD = 12.38), 78% identified as Caucasian, 46% identified themselves as either a strong Democrat or a Democrat, and 26% indicated that they were either a strong Republican or a Republican. Twenty-seven percent identified themselves as independent.

A second online survey was also fielded during the fall, general-election period with the same target audience. This survey was conducted in order to compare the primary-period results to the general-election period results. The second online survey, which was largely identical in structure and questions asked, was also administered through the MTurk online platform two weeks before Election Day, from October 22, 2016 to November 7, 2016. The second survey was fielded at the campaign's peak, asking respondents about the party's nominees: Hillary Clinton and Donald Trump. Respondents were paid $0.10 for completing the survey. A total of 732 respondents completed the second survey. Respondent demographics for the general-election survey were: 57% women, over 50% have a college degree or higher, average age was 34.22 years old (SD = 14.97), 78% identified as Caucasian, 40% identified themselves as either a strong Democrat or a Democrat, and 40% indicated that they were either a strong Republican or a Republican. Nineteen percent identified themselves as independent.

Dependent Variables

Candidate Evaluations

Citizens' evaluations of a political candidate, including traits such as viability, competence, and trustworthiness, can ultimately influence a candidate's electoral success (e.g., Bishin, Stevens, & Wilson, 2006; Elis, Hillygus, & Nie, 2010; Funk, 1999, 1996; Goren, 2002; Goren, Federico, & Kittilson, 2009; Hayes, 2005; Kinder, Peters, Abelson, & Fiske, 1980; Rosenberg et al., 1986). Identifying the most important candidate traits has been long debated, particularly with the rise of candidate-centered campaigning (e.g., Funk, 1999, 1996, 1997; Kinder et al., 1980; Kinder, 1983, 1986; Miller, Wattenberg, & Malanchuk, 1986). Although there is still some disagreement regarding which candidate traits matter most, scholars would agree that 1) citizens hold multidimensional views of a candidate; 2) the structure of candidate traits remains rather stable over time with some variations across candidates and elections (see Wattenberg, 1991); and 3) the measurement should include traits focusing on the profession (e.g., competence and leadership) and interpersonal abilities (e.g., charisma, integrity, empathy). Considering this research, this analysis included both personal and professional candidate attributes. Specifically, in the primary-period survey, respondents were asked about the five remaining candidates: "Based on your opinion, how well or not well do the following attributes describe presidential candidate: [Hillary Clinton, Bernie Sanders, Donald Trump, Ted Cruz, or John Kasich]," where: 1 = not well at all; 2 = not too well; 3 = neutral; 4 = quite well; and 5 = extremely well. In the general-election survey, respondents were only asked about Hillary Clinton and Donald Trump. The candidate attributes were (a) "experienced," (b) "knowledgeable," (c) "qualified," (d) "dependable," (e) "honest," and (f) "trustworthy." These items were then combined to measure the respondents' overall evaluation of each candidate, with a higher number indicating more favorability. The reliability coefficients for the candidate evaluation indices are reported in Table 13.1.

TABLE 13.1 Descriptive Statistics for Candidate Evaluations, Attention to Visuals and Text on Social Media, Political Predispositions, and Demographics

	Primary-Election Survey			*General-Election Survey*		
Measure	*Mean*	SD	*Cronbach's Alpha*	*Mean*	SD	*Cronbach's Alpha*
Candidate Evaluations						
Clinton Evaluation Index	17.5	6.46	.913	16.68	6.72	.93
Sanders Evaluation Index	21.8	6.62	.947	—	—	—
Trump Evaluation Index	12.8	7.82	.963	14.02	7.42	.96
Cruz Evaluation Index	14.5	6.10	.925	—	—	—
Kasich Evaluation Index	17.9	5.53	.925	—	—	—
Attention to Visuals and Text						
Photos or Images	3.13	1.24	—	3.25	1.20	—
Infographics or Graphics	3.04	1.16	—	3.06	1.21	—
Videos	3.08	1.20	—	3.24	1.24	—
Text-Only Posts/Comments	2.95	1.09	—	2.87	1.21	—
Hyperlinks or Hashtags	2.51	1.15	—	2.54	1.17	—
Political Predispositions			—			—
Party Identification (1 = Strong Republican; 5 = Strong Democrat)	3.35	1.15	—	3.01	1.23	—
Political Interest (1 = Not Interested; 5 = Extremely Interested)	3.78	1.09	—	3.62	1.20	—
Demographics						
Age	34.36	12.38	—	34.22	14.97	—
Male (1 = Male; 0 = Female)	.48	.501	—	1.43	.495	—
Race (1 = White; 0 = Non-White)	.79	.411	—	.78	.411	—
Education (1 = Less than HS; 8 = Professional JD, MD)	4.30	1.34	—	3.89	1.32	—
		N = 519			*N* = 732	

Independent Variables

Attention to Visuals and Text on Social Media

The main independent variables are attention to visuals, such as photos, infographics, and videos, as well as attention to text, such as comments, about the campaign for president on social-networking sites. Respondents were asked five questions with the following format: "How much attention did you pay to '*photos or images, such as GIFs, memes, of selfies*,' about the campaign for president on social networking sites?" (1 = none; 3 = some, 5 = a great deal). In subsequent questions, the phrase in italics was replaced with the phrases "infographics or graphics," "videos," "text only posts or comments," and "text only posts or comments with hyperlinks or hashtags." These questions were operationalized with references to social-networking sites, particularly Facebook, Instagram, Twitter, Snapchat, YouTube, and Flickr.

Control Variables

Based on previous research (McLeod, Glynn, & McDonald, 1983; Verba, Schlozman, & Brady, 1995), two categories of control measures are included. Key demographic variables—such as age, gender (1 = male, 0 = female), education level (1 = less than high school, 2 = high school/GED, 3 = Some college, 4 = Associate's degree, 5 = Bachelor's degree, 6 = Master's degree, 7 = Doctoral degree, 8 = Professional degree), and race (1 = White, 0 = non-White) —were introduced into the analysis. Also, two political predispositions, political interest and party identification, were included. For political interest, the survey asked: "Some people don't pay much attention to political campaigns. How about you? Would you say that you have been very much interested, somewhat interested or not much interested in the political campaigns so far this year?" (1 = not at all interested, 3 = moderately interested, 5 = very interested). To measure partisan attachment, the survey asked: (1) "Generally speaking, do you usually think of yourself as a Republican, a Democrat, an Independent, or something else?" (1 = strong Republican, 2 = Republican, 3 = Independent, 4 = Democrat, 5 = strong Democrat). Descriptive statistics are reported in Table 13.1.

Results

Primary Period

To test Hypotheses 1–3, ordinary least squares models were estimated by regressing candidate evaluations on attention to visual and textual campaign content (see Table 13.2). The first hypothesis predicted that attention to visual campaign content, particularly photos and images, posted on social networks will more significantly predict candidate evaluations than textual campaign content posted on social networks (H1). The results in Table 13.2 show some variation in effects across the five primary candidates. In Row 1 in Table 13.2, attention to campaign content in the form of photos and images on social media was positively linked to Sanders and Trump evaluations (columns 2 and 3). However, attention to photos and images did not significantly predict evaluations for any other presidential primary candidate. Although this finding does not offer strong support for H1, it does provide evidence that photos and images on social media are better predictors of candidate evaluations than textual campaign content, as

TABLE 13.2 Primary Election Candidate Evaluations by Attention to Visual and Textual Campaign Content on Social Media

	Candidate Evaluation Index				
	Clinton	*Sanders*	*Trump*	*Cruz*	*Kasich*
Attention to ____ about the campaign for president on social-networking sites					
Photos or Images	−.148 (−.029)	.832* (.120)	.857* (.134)	−.249 (−.051)	−.558 (−.127)
Infographics or Graphics	.992** (.178)	.743* (.132)	−.093 (−.014)	.064 (.012)	.931** (.196)
Videos	−.170 (−.032)	−.213 (−.039)	.322 (.049)	.564 (.113)	−.176 (−.039)
Text-Only Posts/ Comments	−.026 (−.004)	−.047 (−.008)	.373 (.051)	−.479 (−.087)	.371 (.074)
Text-Only Hyperlinks or Hashtags	.760* (.136)	−.266 (−.046)	.151 (.022)	.503 (.096)	.046 (.010)
Political Predispositions					
Party ID (1 = Strong Republican)	3.46*** (.614)	2.70*** (.564)	−4.17*** (−.596)	−1.68*** (−.318)	−.067 (−.014)
Political Interest	−.664* (−.106)	1.17*** (.183)	.331 (.043)	−.421 (−.072)	−.085 (−.016)
Demographics					
Age	−.004 (−.007)	.074* (.137)	−.119*** (−.184)	−.029 (−.059)	−.114*** (−.260)
Male	−.442 (−.034)	.906 (.067)	2.68*** (.166)	−.171 (−.014)	1.65** (.147)
Race (1 = White)	−2.29*** (−.146)	.173 (.011)	−.219 (−.011)	−1.71 (−.079)	−.570 (−.043)
Education	.468 (.095)	−.355 (−.070)	.014 (.002)	−.317 (−.068)	−.480 (−.115)
Constant	18.38	−136.66*	254.50***	81.22	245.72***
R^2	.40	.24	.42	.07	.04
N	491	494	493	492	490

Note: Cell entries are unstandardized ordinary least squares coefficients with standardized coefficients in parentheses.

**p* < .10. ***p* < .05. ****p* < .01 (one-tailed)

attention to text-only posts/comments and text-only hyperlinks/hashtags are not significantly linked to Sanders and Trump evaluations.

Row 2 in Table 13.2 reports more consistent findings across the primary candidates. Campaign content in the form of infographics and graphics was a positive predictor of Clinton, Sanders, and Kasich evaluations (H2). The latter, however, was not the case for Trump and Cruz evaluations. Nonetheless, Hypothesis 2 is largely supported, as attention to infographics is a stronger predictor of Clinton, Sanders, and Kasich evaluations than attention to textual campaign content. Indeed, column 1 shows that attention to campaign content in "text-only hyperlink/hashtags" posted on social media significantly predicted Clinton evaluations. Yet, Clinton's evaluations were more strongly predicted by attention to campaign infographics/graphics on social media ($\beta = .992$, $p < .05$) than textual content with hyperlinks/hashtags ($\beta = .760$, $p < .10$), offering further evidence for Hypothesis 2. Beyond Clinton, neither attention to campaign content in "text-only posts/comment" nor "text-only hyperlinks/hashtags" was linked to any other candidate evaluations. Last, contrary to Hypothesis 3, attention to campaign content posted on social media in the form of online video was not significantly associated with any candidate evaluations (row 3).

General-Election Period

Hypotheses 1–3 were retested during the fall general-election period. Replicating the methodology conducted during the primary period, ordinary least squares models were estimated by regressing citizens' evaluations of Clinton and Trump on their attention to visual and textual campaign content (see Table 13.3). In contrast to the primary period results, the findings in Table 13.3 offer no support for Hypothesis 1, which asserted that attention to photos and images posted on social networks would more significantly predict candidate evaluations than textual campaign content posted on social networks. There is again some evidence for Hypothesis 2 during the general-election period, which is consistent with the primary period findings. Attention to campaign content in the form of infographics and graphics was more significantly linked to evaluations of Clinton than textual content (Table 13.3, row 2). Similar to the primary period findings, attention to infographics was not linked to evaluations of Trump (row 2, column 2). In addition, attention to campaign content in the form of online video was not more significantly linked to Clinton or Trump evaluations than text or hyperlinks (H3).

Discussion and Conclusion

The rise of social media platforms, such as Facebook, YouTube, Twitter, and Instagram, have ushered in a new era of visual campaigning. During the "Web 2.0 campaign" in 2008 (Towner & Dulio, 2011a, 2011c), content was king, but now text is quickly being replaced with photos and images of the campaign. Quite literally, in the 2016 presidential primary campaign, "a picture really is worth a thousand words." Digital photos, images, and videos are a short way of

TABLE 13.3 General Election Candidate Evaluations by Attention to Visual and Textual Campaign Content on Social Media

	Candidate Evaluation Index	
	Clinton	*Trump*
Attention to ____ about the campaign for president on social-networking sites		
Photos or Images	–.396 (–.068)	.320 (.051)
Infographics or Graphics	.535* (.096)	–.178 (–.028)
Videos	–.119 (–.021)	.108 (.017)
Text-Only Posts/Comments	–.027 (–.005)	.317 (.051)
Text-Only Hyperlinks or Hashtags	.312 (.053)	.314 (.049)
Political Predispositions		
Party ID (1 = Strong Republican)	3.88*** (.685)	–4.00*** (–.647)
Political Interest	.739*** (.123)	.031 (.005)
Demographics		
Age	.012 (.027)	–.048*** (–.098)
Male	–.201 (.419)	.478 (.031)
Race (1 = White)	–1.19** (–.071)	–.794 (–.044)
Education	.321** (.062)	–.338 (–.060)
Constant	–21.48	120.9***
R^2	.53	.45
N	663	667

Note: Cell entries are unstandardized ordinary least squares coefficients with standardized coefficients in parentheses.

*$p < .10$. **$p < .05$. ***$p < .01$ (one-tailed)

communicating a large amount of information quickly and succinctly. What does this visual stimulation mean for political campaigns? It means that candidates and campaigns will use digital imagery more than ever before. In fact, much of the content on presidential primary candidates' social media sites are visual

(Brousell, 2015; Mitchell et al., 2016; Peters & Parker, 2016). For instance, a Pew Research Study conducted in May 2016, found that Hillary Clinton posted more videos on Facebook and Twitter than both Trump and Sanders (Mitchell et al., 2016). In addition to video, Donald Trump posted screenshots of polls, Hillary Clinton posted text-heavy infographics, and Sanders posted infographics about rallies and voting. What does this visual stimulation mean for voters? Most likely this means that voters are encountering digital visual information about the campaign to a much greater extent. But to what effect? Do visuals about the campaign posted on social networks affect candidate trait evaluations?

This project sought to answer the above question by exploring the effects of citizens' attention to visual and textual campaign content posted on social-networking sites on their evaluations of the 2016 presidential candidates. During both the primary and general-election periods, two surveys asked respondents how much attention they paid to photos/images, infographics/graphics, videos, text-only posts/comments, text-only hyperlinks, or hashtags about the campaign for president on social-networking sites. Building on the phenomenon of the "picture superiority effect" and the apparent rise of visual social media employed in political campaigns, it was expected that visual campaign content would be linked to candidate evaluations. The results in Tables 13.2 and 13.3 show that there were significant relationships between citizens' attention to photos and infographics about the campaign and their evaluations of the presidential candidates. In other words, visuals on social media matter, having greater influence on how users feel about the candidates (see Barry, 1997; Hill & Helmers, 2004; Joffe, 2008). For instance, photos posted on Facebook of a candidate at a campaign rally grabs users' attention. Colorful campaign infographics uploaded to Instagram help social media users learn and understand tough issues. Attention to videos, text-only posts/comments, and text-only hyperlinks or hashtags had little to no relationship to candidate evaluations. As previously noted, citizens are better able to recall still images than something they are reading, hearing, and watching (see Grimes, 1991; Schweiger & Adami, 1999; Shea & Burton, 2001). When users see a picture or infographic on Facebook, Twitter, or Instagram, it can be processed in a shorter amount of time, with users understanding the meaning immediately.

These results suggest two major findings relevant to campaign strategists, candidates, and voters: first, infographics and photos posted on social media matter more than text and video. The most consistent finding was that attention to photos and infographics about the campaign were significantly and positively linked to candidate evaluations. It is important to note that these data do not indicate that attention to infographics and photos caused candidate evaluations, as it may be the case that an individual's candidate perceptions influenced the likelihood of paying attention to infographics and photos about the campaign. Nevertheless, the results suggest the possibility of a causal relationship between attention to digital photos and infographics and candidate evaluations. This relationship is notable because it suggests that photos and infographics about the campaign are indeed more stimulating, comprehensible, persuasive, and memorable to social media users, which is consistent with the notion of the picture superiority effect as well as the importance of personalized politics. Online videos, however, with moving images and sound, simply take more time for users to watch, process, and absorb than a simple still image.

It is perhaps not surprising that attention to infographics was consistently linked to candidate evaluations. In an age of information overload, campaign-related infographics quickly capture attention with fancy graphics and font, report complicated data in an accessible manner, convey more information in less time, and spread the message more quickly. For example, Hillary Clinton posted an infographic on Facebook comparing her challengers' stances on women's health with pictures of Trump, Cruz, and Kasich's heads along with a check list (Clinton, 2016). This infographic provided quick, easy-to-understand, and negative information about each candidate's challengers. Photos and images can be just as powerful. Bernie Sanders posted a photo on Instagram of him as a young elected official exuberantly taking on Wall Street and big banks (Sanders, 2016). This image personalizes the candidate, portraying him as a lifelong politician protecting the less fortunate. As the research findings suggest, these infographics and photos can be persuasive, significantly influencing candidate evaluations. It can be concluded that images and infographics are the most important content for political campaigns to post on social media platforms. Perhaps candidates who can win the infographic and photo social media battle can win the White House.

The second major finding of interest is that one visual medium on social media—video—did not significantly influence citizens' candidate evaluations. This finding is surprising, as it is inconsistent with research that shows that political advertising (Ansolabehere & Iyengar, 1995; Just et al., 1996; Kaid, 2004; Wattenberg & Brians, 1999), presidential debates (Benoit et al., 2003; Chaffee & Choe, 1980; Davis, 1979), and television news coverage (Bartels, 1993) impact candidate perceptions. This result seems to point out that static campaign images, such as photos, infographics, and graphics, posted on social media, are more powerful than digital ads or videos of stump speeches. Photos and infographics allow for greater emphasis on fewer topics and may have less distracting elements. In addition, photos and infographics posted on social media usually take less time to consume than video. For example, digital videos posted on Hillary Clinton's Facebook page range from 20 seconds to an hour long. A cursory glance at the number of views for each of Hillary Clinton's videos on Facebook suggests that shorter videos garner more views than longer videos. Thus, it is reasonable to conclude that static campaign images on social media play a more important role in shaping candidate perceptions than campaign video. This may be a startlingly finding to campaign strategists, particularly when the 2016 presidential candidates dedicated a significant portion of their posts and tweets to video (Mitchell et al., 2016).

Limitations and Future Research Directions

Although this research adds to the understanding of the influence of visual campaign information on candidate evaluations, there are limitations that require discussion. First, this survey research employs two convenience samples of adults. Due to the latter, this research cannot infer causality. That is, one cannot determine whether attention to visuals about the campaign caused the relationship observed or whether those who supported the candidates were more likely to pay attention to visuals. This convenience sample was also gathered via the online platform MTurk, which has documented limitations regarding participant demographics and data quality (see Berinsky et al., 2012; Chandler et al., 2014). For example, those adults who are not online are not represented in this sample. Future research should seek to confirm causality through experimental or longitudinal studies that are able to isolate the direction of the relationship. Second, the overall statistical impact of attention to photos and infographics on candidate evaluations was small, often outweighed by the impact of party identification. It is likely that the effect of visual campaign content is dependent on an individual's political party affiliation or existing feelings toward the candidates. Social media offer citizens greater control over the political messages received and sources used (Prior, 2007); therefore, citizens are likely to seek visuals and text on social media that reinforce how they already perceive the candidates (Holbert, Garrett, & Gleason, 2010). Third, this research does not examine the impact of the exact visual and textual content respondents consumed on social networks during the primary period. It is not known if respondents were viewing campaign content posted on social media by the campaigns or other users. It is also unknown if respondents are consuming positive or negative visual content about the campaign. One could speculate that satirical candidate memes versus a candidate's sentimental family photo would influence candidate evaluations very differently. An experimental study exposing subjects to favorable and unfavorable visual content posted on social media would be an interesting endeavor. Notwithstanding these limitations, this research is an important step into furthering the study of social media effects, as it offers some evidence that visual campaign content on social media influences candidate evaluations.

References

Ancu, M. (2011). From soundbite to textbite: Election 2008 comments on Twitter. In J. A. Hendricks & L. L. Kaid (Eds.), *Techno politics in presidential campaigning: New voices, new technologies, and new voters* (pp. 11–21). New York, NY: Routledge.

Ansolabehere, S., & Iyengar, S. (1995). *Going negative: How political advertising shrinks and polarizes the electorate.* New York, NY: Free Press.

Barrett, A. W., & Barrington, L. W. (2005). Is a picture worth a thousand words? Newspaper photographs and candidate evaluations of political candidates. *Press/Politics, 10*(4), 98–113.

Barry, A. M. (1997). *Visual intelligence: Perceptions, image, and manipulation in visual communication.* Albany, NY: SUNY Press.

Barry, A. M. (2005). Perception theory. In K. Smith, S. Moriarty, G. Barbatsis & K. Kenney (Eds.), *Handbook of visual communication* (pp. 45–62). Mahwah, NJ: Lawrence Earlbaum.

Bartels, L. (1993). Messages received: The political impact of media exposure. *American Political Science Review, 87*(2), 267–285.

Baum, M. A. (2002). Sex, lies, and war: How soft news brings foreign policy to the inattentive public. *American Political Science Review, 96*, 91–109.

Baum, M. A. (2003). Soft news and political knowledge: Evidence of absence or absence of evidence? *Political Communication, 20*, 73–190.

Baum, M. A. (2005). Talking the vote: Why presidential candidates hit the talk show circuit. *American Journal of Political Science, 49*, 213–234.

Baumgartner, J., & Morris, J. (2006). The *Daily Show* effect: Candidate evaluations, efficacy, and American youth. *American Politics Research, 34*(3), 341–367.

Baumgartner, J., & Morris, J. (2010). MyFaceTube politics: Social networking websites and political engagement of young adults. *Social Science Computer Review, 28*(1), 24–44.

Bennett, W. L. (2012). The personalization of politics: Political identity, social media, and changing patterns of participation. *The ANNALS of the American Academy of Political and Social Science, 644*(1), 20–39.

Benoit, W. L., Hansen, G. J., & Verser, R. (2003). A meta-analysis of the effects of viewing U.S. presidential debates. *Communication Monographs, 70*(4), 335–350.

Benoit, W. L., McKinney, M. S., & Holbert, R. L. (2001). Beyond learning and persona: Extending the scope of presidential debate effects. *Communication Monographs, 68*, 259–273.

Berinsky, A. J., Huber, G. A., & Lenz, G. S. (2012). Evaluating online labor markets for experimental research: Amazon.com's Mechanical Turk. *Political Analysis, 20*, 351–368.

Berry, C., & Brosius, H. B. (1991). Multiple effects of visual format on TV news learning. *Applied Cognitive Psychology, 5*, 519–528.

Bimber, B., & Davis, R. (2003). *Campaigning online: The Internet in U.S. elections.* New York, NY: Oxford University Press.

Bishin, B. G., Stevens, D., & Wilson, C. (2006). Character counts? Honesty and fairness in election 2000. *Public Opinion Quarterly, 70*(2), 235–248.

Bode, L. (2012). Facebooking it to the polls: A study in online social networking and political behavior. *Journal of Information Technology & Politics, 9*, 352–369.

Boomgaarden, H. G., Boukes, M., & Iorgoveanu, A. (2016). Image versus text: How newspaper reports affect evaluations of political candidates. *International Journal of Communication, 10*, 2529–2555.

Borah, P. (2016). Political Facebook use: Campaign strategies used in the 2008 and 2012 presidential elections. *Journal of Information Technology & Politics, 13*(4), 326–338.

Boyd, D., & Ellison, N. (2007). Social network sites: Definition, history, and scholarship. *Journal of Computer Mediated Communication, 13*(1), 210–230.

Brader, T. (2005). Striking a responsive chord: How political ads motivate and persuade voters by appealing to emotions. *American Journal of Political Science, 49*(2), 388–405.

Brians, C. L., & Wattenberg, M. P. (1996). Campaign issue knowledge and salience: Comparing reception from TV commercials, TV news, and newspapers. *American Journal of Political Science, 40*, 173–193.

Brousell, L. (2015). Why social media could swing the 2016 presidential election. *CIO*. Retrieved from www.cio.com/article/2976083/social-networking/why-social-media-could-swing-the-2016-presidential-election.html

Chaffee, S. H., & Choe, S. Y. (1980). Time of decision and media use during the Ford-Carter campaign. *Public Opinion Quarterly, 44*, 53–69.

Chandler, J., Mueller, P., & Paolacci, G. (2014). Nonnaïveté among Amazon Mechanical Turk workers: Consequences and solutions for behavioral researchers. *Behavior Research Methods, 46*, 112–130.

Chen, H., Ping, S., & Chen, G. (2015). Far from reach but near at hand: The role of social media for cross-national mobilization. *Computers in Human Behavior, 53*, 443–451.

Childers, J. L., & Houston, M. J. (1984). Conditions for a picture superiority effect on consumer memory. *Journal of Consumer Research, 11*(September), 643–654.

Church, S. H. (2010). YouTube politics: YouChoose and leadership rhetoric during the 2008 campaign. *Journal of Information Technology & Politics*, 7, 124–142.

Clinton, H. (2016). Infographic. Retrieved from www.facebook.com/hillaryclinton/photos/a.889773484412515.1073741828.889307941125736/1114645158592012/

Coleman, R., & Banning, S. (2006). Networked TV news' affective framing of the presidential candidate: Evidence for second-level agenda-setting effect through visual framing. *Journalism & Mass Communication Quarterly, 83*(2), 313–328.

Coleman, R., & Wu, D. (2015). *Image and emotion in voter decisions: The affect agenda*. Lanham, MD: Lexington Books.

Crist, R. (2016). How the 2016 presidential candidates measure up on social media. *Tech Culture*. Retrieved from www.cnet.com/news/2016-elections-comparing-presidential-candidates-on-social-media/

Curran, T., & Doyle, J. (2011). Picture superiority doubly dissociates the ERP correlates of recollection and familiarity. *Journal of Cognitive Neuroscience, 23*(5), 1247–1262.

Dahmen, N. S. (2016a). Obama and Romney photos receive equal treatment. *Newspaper Research Journal, 37*(1), 21–33.

Dahmen, N. S. (2016b). Picturing the senate candidate: Image building in the Twitterverse. In J. A. Hendricks & D. Schill (Eds.), *Communication and midterm elections: Media, message, and mobilization* (pp. 169–190). New York, NY: Palgrave Macmillan.

Davis, D. K. (1979). Influence on vote decisions. In S. S. Kraus (Ed.), *The great debates: Carter vs. Ford, 1976* (pp. 331–347). Bloomington, IL: Indiana University Press.

Davisson, A. (2009). 'I'm in!': Hillary Clinton's 2008 democratic primary campaign on YouTube. *Journal of Visual Literacy, 28*(1), 70–91.

Defetyer, M. A., Russo, R., & McPartlin, P. L. (2009). The picture superiority effect in recognition memory: A developmental study using the response signal procedure. *Cognitive Development, 24*, 265–273.

Dimitrova, D. V., & Bystrom, D. (2013). The effects of social media on political participation and candidate image evaluations in the 2012 Iowa caucuses. *American Behavioral Scientist, 57*(11), 1568–1583.

Dimitrova, D. V., Shehata, A., Stromack, J., & Nord, L. (2014). The effects of digital media on political knowledge and participation in election campaigns: Evidence from panel data. *Communication Research*, *41*, 95–118.
Duman, S., & Locher, M. (2008). 'So let's talk. let's chat. let's start a dialog.': An analysis of the conversation metaphor employed in Clinton's and Obama's YouTube campaign clips. *Multilingua*, *27*, 193–230.
Edell, J. A., & Staelin, R. (1983). The information processing of pictures in print advertisements. *Journal of Consumer Research*, *10*(June), 41–61.
Edwards, J. L. (2004). Echoes of camelot: How images construct cultural memory through rhetorical framing. In C. A. Hill & M. Helmers (Eds.), *Defining visual rhetorics* (pp. 179–194). New York, NY: Routledge.
Elis, R., Hillygus, D. S., & Nie, N. (2010). The dynamics of candidate evaluations and vote choice in 2008: Looking to the past of future? *Electoral Studies*, *29*(4), 582–593.
Elkins, J. (2003). *Visual studies: A skeptical introduction*. New York, NY: Routledge.
Funk, C. (1996). The impact of scandal on candidate evaluations: An experimental test of the role of candidate traits. *Political Behavior*, *18*(1), 1–24.
Funk, C. (1997). Implications of political expertise in candidate trait evaluations. *Political Research Quarterly*, *50*(3), 675–697.
Funk, C. L. (1999). Bringing the candidate into models of candidate evaluation. *The Journal of Politics*, *61*, 700–720.
Gainous, J., & Wagner, K. M. (2013). *Tweeting to power: The social media revolution in American politics*. New York, NY: Oxford University Press.
German, K. (2010). Bush/Gore photos reveal different styles, strategies. *Newspaper Research Journal*, *31*(4), 48–61.
Gil de Zúñiga, H., Jung, N., & Valenzuala, S. (2012). Social media use for news and individuals' social capital, civic engagement and political participation. *Journal of Computer Mediated Communication*, *17*(3), 319–336.
Gil de Zúñiga, H., Molyneux, L., & Zhang, P. (2014). Social media, political expression and political participation: Panel analysis of lagged and concurrent relationships. *Journal of Communication*, *64*(4), 612–634.
Goethals, G. R. (2005). Nonverbal behavior and political leadership. In R. E. Riggio & R. S. Feldman (Eds.), *Applications of nonverbal communication* (pp. 95–115). Mahwah, NJ: Lawrence Erlbaum Associates.
Goodnow, T. (2010). Visual bias in *Time's* 'the great divide': A semiotic analysis of Clinton and Obama photographs. *American Behavioral Scientist*, *54*(4), 406–416.
Goodnow, T. (2013). Facing off: A comparative analysis of Obama and Romney Facebook timeline photographs. *American Behavioral Scientist*, *57*(11), 1584–1595.
Goren, P. (2002). Character weakness, partisan bias, and presidential evaluation. *American Journal of Political Science*, *46*(3), 627–641.
Goren, P., Federico, C., & Kittilson, M. C. (2009). Source cues, partisan identities, and political value expression. *American Journal of Political Science*, *53*(4), 805–820.
Gottfried, J., Barthel, M., Shearer, E., & Mitchell, A. (2016). The 2016 presidential campaign: A news event that's hard to miss. *Pew Research Center*. Retrieved from www.journalism.org/2016/02/04/the-2016-presidential-campaign-a-news-event-thats-hard-to-miss/
Grabe, M. E., & Bucy, E. P. (2009). *Image bite politics: News and the visual framing of elections*. Oxford, UK: Oxford University Press.
Graber, D. A. (1987). Kind pictures and harsh words: How television presents the candidates. In K. L. Schlozman (Ed.), *Elections in America* (pp. 115–141). Winchester, MA: Allen & Unwin.

Grimes, T. (1991). Mild auditory-visual dissonance in television news may exceed viewer attentional capacity. *Human Communication Research, 18*, 268–298.

Groshek, J., & Brookes, S. (2015). YouTube/OurTube/TheirTube: Official and unofficial online campaign advertising, negativity, and popularity. In J. A. Hendricks & D. Schill (Eds.), *Presidential campaigning and social media: An analysis of the 2012 campaign* (pp. 140–153). New York, NY: Oxford University Press.

Groshek, J., & Dimitrova, D. (2011). A cross-section of voter learning, campaign interest and intention to vote in the 2008 American election: Did web 2.0 matter? *Studies in Communications, 9*, 355–375.

Gueorguieva, V. (2008). Voters, MySpace, and YouTube: The impact of alternative communication channels on the 2006 election cycle and beyond. *Social Science Computer Review, 26*(3), 288–300.

Ha, L. S., Wang, F., Fang, L., Yang, C., Hu, X., Yang, L., Yang, F., Xu, Y., & Morin, D. (2013). Political efficacy and the use of local and national new media among undecided voters in a swing state: A study of general population voters and first-time college student voters. *Electronic News*, 7(4), 204–222.

Hansen, G. J., & Benoit, W. (2005). Presidential campaigning on the web: The influence of candidate world wide web sites in the 2000 general election. *Southern Communication Journal, 70*(3), 219–229.

Harding, L. (2012). U.S. election 2012: Hug photo makes social media history. *The Guardian*. Retrieved from www.theguardian.com/media/2012/nov/07/us-election-2012-hug-photo

Hawthorne, J., & Warner, B. (2015). The influence of user controlled messages on candidate evaluations. In V. Farrar-Myers & J. Vaughn (Eds.), *Controlling the message: New media in American political campaigns* (pp. 161–187). New York: New York University.

Hayes, D. (2005). Candidate qualities through a partisan lens: A theory of trait ownership. *American Journal of Political Science, 49*(4), 908–923.

Hess, V. (2001). The role of political comedy during the 2000 election campaign: Examining content and third-person effects. *Paper Presented at the annual meeting of the American Political Science Association*, San Francisco.

Hill, C. A., & Helmers, M. (2004). The psychology of rhetorical images. In C. A. Hill & M. Helmers (Eds.), *Defining visual rhetorics* (pp. 25–40). Mahwah, NJ: Lawrence Erlbaum Associates.

Hockley, W. E. (2008). The picture superiority effect in associative recognition. *Memory & Cognition, 36*(7), 1351–1359.

Holbert, R. L., Garrett, R. K., & Gleason, L. S. (2010). A new era of minimal effects? A response to Bennett and Iyengar. *Journal of Communication, 60*, 15–34.

Housholder, E. E., & LaMarre, H. L. (2014). Facebook politics: Toward a process model for achieving political source credibility through social media. *Journal of Information Technology & Politics, 11*(4), 368–382.

Houston, J. B., Hawthorne, J., Spialek, M. L., Greenwood, M., & McKinney, M. S. (2013). Tweeting during presidential debates: Effect on candidate evaluations and debate evaluations. *Argumentation and Advocacy, 49*, 301–311.

Huff, C., & Tingley, D. (2015). 'Who are these people?': Evaluating the demographic characteristics and political preferences of MTurk survey respondents. *Research and Politics, 2*(3), 1–15.

Joffe, H. (2008). The power of visual material: Persuasion, emotion, and identification. *Diogenes, 217*, 84–93.

Johnson, J. (2012a). The infographic and the 2012 presidential campaign. Retrieved from www.mediarhetoric.com/blog/the-infographic-2012-u-s-presidential-campaign

Johnson, J. (2012b). Twitter bites and Romney: Examining the rhetorical situation of the 2012 presidential election in 140 characters. *Journal of Contemporary Rhetoric, 2*(3/4), 54–64.

Johnson, T. J., Braima, M.A.M., & Sothirajah, J. (1999). Doing the traditional media sidestep: Comparing the effects of the internet and other nontraditional media with traditional media in the 1996 presidential campaign. *Journalism & Mass Communication Quarterly, 76*(1), 99–123.

Johnson, T. J., & Kaye, B. (2004). Wag the blog: How reliance on traditional media and the internet influence credibility perceptions of weblogs among blog users. *Journalism & Mass Communication Quarterly, 81*(3), 622–642.

Jones, J. P. (2005). *Entertaining politics: News political television and civic culture.* Lanham, MD: Rowman & Littlefield.

Just, M. R., Crigler, A. N., Alger, D. E., Cook, T. E., Kern, M. & West, D. M. (1996). *Crosstalk: Citizens, candidates, and the media in a presidential campaign.* Chicago, IL: University of Chicago Press.

Kaid, L. L. (2004). Videostyle in the 2004 presidential advertising. In R. E. Denton Jr. (Ed.), *The 2004 presidential campaign* (pp. 283–299). Lanham, MD: Rowman & Littlefield.

Kaid, L. L., & Johnston, A. (2001). *Videostyle in presidential campaigns.* Westport, CT: Praeger.

Kaye, B. K. (2013). I can choose clearly now: The influence of online source reliance on candidate preference during the 2008 presidential election. *Atlantic Journal of Communication, 21*(5), 294–311.

Keeter, S. (1987). The illusion of intimacy: Television and the role of candidate personal qualities in voter choice. *Public Opinion Quarterly, 51*(3), 344–358.

Kinder, D. (1983). Presidential traits. *Report to the NES board of overseers.* Ann Arbor, MI: Center for Political Studies, University of Michigan.

Kinder, D. (1986). Presidential character revisited. In R. Lau & D. Sears (Eds.), *Political cognition* (pp. 233–256). Hillsdale, NJ: Lawrence Erlbaum Associates.

Kinder, D., Peters, M., Abelson, R., & Fiske, S. (1980). Presidential prototypes. *Political Behavior, 2*(2), 315–337.

Kiousis, S., Bantimaroudis, P., & Ban, H. (1999). Candidate image attributes experiments on the substantive dimension of second level agenda setting. *Communication Research, 26*(4), 441–428.

Lang, A. (1995). Defining audio/video redundancy from a limited capacity information processing perspective. *Communication Research, 22,* 86–115.

Lanoue, D. J., & Schrott, P. R. (1991). *The joint press conference: The history, impact, and prospects of American presidential debates.* New York, NY: Greenwood Press.

Lanzetta, J. T., Sullivan, D. G., Masters, R. D., & McHugo, G. J. (1985). Emotional and cognitive responses to televised images of political leaders. In S. Kraus & R. M. Perloff (Eds.), *Mass media and political thought: An information-processing approach* (pp. 85–116). Beverly Hills, CA: Sage.

Lawrence, R. G., McGregor, S. C., Cardona, A., & Mourão, R. R. (2016). Personalization and gender: 2014 gubernatorial candidates on social media. In J. A. Hendricks & D. Schill (Eds.), *Communication and midterm elections: Media, message, and mobilization* (pp. 191–206). New York, NY: Palgrave Macmillan.

Lee, E., & Oh, S. Y. (2012). To personalize or depersonalize? When and how politicians' personalized tweets affect the public's reactions. *Journal of Communication, 62*, 932–949.

McBride, D. M., & Dosher, B. A. (2002). A comparison of conscious and automatic memory processes for picture and word stimuli: A process dissociation analysis. *Consciousness and Cognition, 11*, 423–460.

McKinney, M. S., & Carlin, D. B. (2004). Political campaign debates. In L. L. Kaid (Ed.), *Handbook of political communication research* (pp. 203–234). Mahwah, NJ: Lawrence Erlbaum.

McKinney, M. S., Dudash, E. A., & Hodgkinson, G. (2003). Viewer reactions to the 2000 presidential debates: Learning issue and image information. In L. L. Kaid, J. C. Tedesco, D. G. Bystrom & M. S. McKinney (Eds.), *The millennium election: Communication in the 2000 campaign* (pp. 43–58). Lanham, MD: Rowman & Littlefield.

McKinney, M. S., Houston, B., & Hawthorne, J. (2014). Social watching a 2012 republican presidential primary debate. *American Behavioral Scientist, 58*, 556–573.

McLeod, J. M., Glynn, C. J., & McDonald, D. G. (1983). Issues and images: The influence of media reliance on voting decisions. *Communication Research, 10*, 37–58.

Messaris, P. (1997). *Pictures and reality: Visual persuasion: The role of images in advertising.* London, UK: Sage.

Miller, A., Wattenberg, M., & Malanchuk, O. (1986). Schematic assessments of presidential candidates. *American Political Science Review, 80*(2), 521–540.

Miniard, P. W., Bhatla, S., Lord, K. R., Dickson, P. R., & Unnava, H. R. (1991). Picture-based persuasion processes and the moderating role of involvement. *Journal of Consumer Research, 18*(June), 92–107.

Mitchell, A., Holcomb, J., & Weisel, R. (2016). Election 2016: Campaigns as a direct source of news. *Pew Research Center*. Retrieved from www.journalism.org/2016/07/18/election-2016-campaigns-as-a-direct-source-of-news/

Moriarty, S. E., & Garramone, G. M. (1986). A study of newsmagazine photographs of the 1984 presidential campaign. *Journalism Quarterly, 63*, 728–734.

Moriarty, S. E., & Popovich, M. N. (1991). Newsmagazine visuals and the 1988 presidential election. *Journalism Quarterly, 68*(3), 371–380.

Moy, P., Xenos, M., & Hess, V. (2006). Priming effects of late-night comedy. *International Journal of Public Opinion Research, 18*(2), 198–210.

Nelson, D. L., Reed, U. S., & Walling, J. R. (1976). Pictorial superiority effect. *Journal of Experimental Psychology: Human Learning & Memory, 2*, 523–528.

Niven, D., Lichter, S. R., & Amundson, D. (2003). The political content of late night comedy. *International Journal of Press/Politics, 8*(3), 118–133.

Noller, P. (1985). Video primacy: A further look. *Journal of Nonverbal Behavior, 9*(1), 28–47.

Page, J., & Duffy, M. (2016). What does credibility look like? Tweets and walls in U.S. presidential candidates' visual storytelling. *Journal of Political Marketing*, (April), Retrieved from http://dx.doi.org/10.1080/15377857.2016.1171819

Paivio, A. (1971). *Imagery and verbal processes.* New York, NY: Holt, Rinehart & Winston.

Paivio, A. (1979). *Imagery and verbal processes.* Hillsdale, NJ: Erlbaum.

Patterson, T. (2000). *Doing well and doing good* (Faculty Research Working Paper Series No. #RWP01–001). Cambridge, MA: John F. Kennedy School of Government, Harvard University.

Patterson, T., & McClure, R. (1976). *The unseeing eye: The myth of television power in national elections.* New York, NY: Putnam.

Peters, J., & Parker, A. (2016). Facing a selfie election, presidential hopefuls grin and bear it. *The New York Times.* Retrieved from www.nytimes.com/2015/07/05/us/politics/facing-a-selfie-election-presidential-hopefuls-grin-and-bear-it.html

Pfau, M., Cho, J., & Chong, K. (2001). Communication forms in U.S. presidential campaigns: Influences on candidate perceptions and the democratic process. *International Journal of Press/Politics, 6*(4), 88–105.

Popovich, M. N., Moriarty, S. E., & Pitts, B. (1993). News magazine coverage of the 1988 presidential campaign. *Mass Communication Review, 20,* 99–111.

Powell, L. (2010). Obama and Obama girl: YouTube, viral videos and the 2008 presidential campaign. In J. A. Hendricks & R. E. Denton Jr. (Eds.), *Communicator-in-chief: How Barack Obama used new media technology to win the White House* (pp. 83–104). Lanham, MD: Lexington Books.

Powell, L., Richmond, V. P., & Williams, G. C. (2011). Social networking and political campaigns: Perceptions of candidates as interpersonal constructs. *North American Journal of Psychology, 13*(2), 331–342.

Prior, M. (2007). *Post-broadcast democracy: How media choice increases inequality in political involvement and polarizes elections.* New York, NY: Cambridge University Press.

Ricke, L. (2015). YouTube and the 2012 presidential election: An examination of how Obama and Romney's official YouTube channels were used in campaign communication. In J. A. Hendricks & D. Schill (Eds.), *Presidential campaigning and social media: An analysis of the 2012 campaign* (pp. 246–258). New York, NY: Oxford University Press.

Ridout, T., Fowler, E., & Branstetter, J. (2010). Political advertising in the 21st century: The rise of the YouTube ad. *Paper Presented at the annual meeting of the American Political Science Association*, Washington, DC.

Robertson, S., Vatrapu, R., & Medina, R. (2010). Off the wall political discourse: Facebook use in the 2008 U.S. presidential election. *Information Polity, 15,* 11–31.

Rogers, S. (2014). What fuels a tweet's engagement? *Twitter.* Retrieved from https://blog.twitter.com/2014/what-fuels-a-tweets-engagement

Rosenberg, S. W., Bohan, L., McCafferty, P., & Harris, K. (1986). The image and the vote: The effect of candidate presentation on voter preference. *American Journal of Political Science, 30*(1), 108–127.

Rosenberg, S. W., & McCafferty, P. (1987). The image and the vote: Manipulating voters' preferences. *Public Opinion Quarterly, 51,* 31–47.

Rosenstiel, T., & Mitchell, A. (2012). How the presidential candidates use the web and social media: Obama leads but neither candidate engages in much dialogue with voters. *Pew Research Center.* Retrieved from www.journalism.org/2012/08/15/how-presidential-candidates-use-web-and-social-media/

Ross, P. (2014a). Photos are still king on facebook. *SocialBakers.* Retrieved from www.socialbakers.com/blog/2149-photos-are-still-king-on-facebook

Ross, P. (2014b). Photos get the most engagement on Twitter. *SocialBakers.* Retrieved from www.socialbakers.com/blog/2306-photos-get-the-most-engagement-on-twitter

Ross, P. (2016). Three trends that dominated social video in 2015. *SocialBakers.* Retrieved from www.socialbakers.com/blog/2489-three-trends-that-dominated-social-video-in-2015

Sanders, B. (2016). Instagram image. Retrieved from www.instagram.com/p/9l_N5Agwzc/

Scheufele, D., Kim, E., & Brossard, D. (2007). My friend's enemy: How split-screen debate coverage influences evaluation of presidential candidates. *Communication Research*, *34*(1), 3–24.

Schill, D. (2009). *Stagecraft and statecraft: Advance and media events in political communication.* Lanham, MD: Lexington Books.

Schneider, W., & Maasen, S. (1998). *Mechanisms of visual attention: A cognitive neuroscience perspective.* East Sussex, UK: Psychology Press.

Schweiger, G., & Adami, M. (1999). The nonverbal image of politicians and political parties. In B. I. Newman (Ed.), *Handbook of political marketing* (pp. 347–364). Thousand Oaks, CA: Sage.

Shea, D. M., & Burton, M. J. (2001). *Campaign craft: The strategies, tactics, and art of political campaign management.* Westport, CT: Praeger Publishers.

Shearer, E. (2016). Candidates' social media outpaces their websites and emails as on online campaign news source. *Pew Research Center.* Retrieved from www.pewresearch.org/fact-tank/2016/07/20/candidates-social-media-outpaces-their-websites-and-emails-as-an-online-campaign-news-source/

Shepard, R. N. (1967). Recognition memory for words, sentences, and pictures. *Journal of Learning and Verbal Behavior*, *6*, 156–163.

Stenberg, G. (2006). Conceptual and perceptual factors in the picture superiority effect. *European Journal of Cognitive Psychology*, *18*, 813–847.

Svensson, E., Kiousis, S., & Strömbäck, J. (2015). Creating a win-win situation? Relationship cultivation and the use of social media in the 2012 campaign. In J. A. Hendricks & D. Schill (Eds.), *Presidential campaigning and social media: An analysis of the 2012 campaign* (pp. 28–43). New York, NY: Oxford University Press.

Svensson, J. (2012). Negotiating the political self on social media platforms. *Journal of Democracy*, *4*(2), 183–197.

Theocharis, Y., & Lowe, W. (2016). Does Facebook increase political participation? Evidence from a field experiment. *Information, Communication & Society*, *19*(10), 1465–1486.

Todorov, A., Mandisodza, A. N., Goren, A., & Hall, C. C. (2005). Inferences of competence from faces predict electoral outcomes. *Science*, *308*, 1623–1626.

Towner, T. L. (2013). All political participation is socially networked? New media and the 2012 election. *Social Science Computer Review*, *31*(5), 527–541.

Towner, T. L. (2016). The influence of Twitter posts on candidate perceptions: The 2014 Michigan midterms. In J. A. Hendricks & D. Schill (Eds.), *Media, message, and mobilization: Communication and 2014 mid-term elections* (pp. 145–167). New York, NY: Palgrave.

Towner, T. L., & Dulio, D. A. (2011a). The Web 2.0 election: Does the online medium matter? *Journal of Political Marketing*, *10*(1/2), 165–188.

Towner, T. L., & Dulio, D. A. (2011b). An experiment of campaign effects during the YouTube election. *New Media and Society*, *13*(4), 626–644.

Towner, T. L., & Dulio, D. A. (2011c). The Web 2.0 election: Voter learning in the 2008 presidential campaign. In J. A. Hendricks & L. L. Kaid (Eds.), *Techno politics in presidential campaigning* (pp. 22–43). New York, NY: Routledge.

Towner, T. L., & Dulio, D. A. (2015). Technology takeover: Campaign learning during the 2012 presidential election. In J. A. Hendricks & D. Schill (Eds.), *Presidential campaigning and social media* (pp. 58–73). New York, NY: Oxford University Press.

Towner, T. L., & Munoz, C. L. (2016). Boomers versus Millennials: Online media influence on political perceptions and media performance. *Social Sciences*, *5*(4), 56. doi:10.3390/socsci5040056

Towner, T. L., & Munoz, C. L. (2017). Baby boom or bust? The new media effect on political participation. *The Journal of Political Marketing*. http://dx.doi.org/10.1080/15377857.2016.1153561

Verba, S., Schlozman, K. L., & Brady, H. (1995). *Voice and equality: Civic voluntarism in American politics*. Cambridge, MA: Harvard University Press.

Verser, R., & Wicks, R. H. (2006). Managing voter impressions: The use of images on presidential candidate web sites during the 2000 campaign. *Journal of Communication, 56*, 178–197.

Waldman, P., & Dewitt, J. (1998). Newspaper photographs and the 1996 presidential election: The question of bias. *Journalism & Mass Communication Quarterly, 75*(2), 302–311.

Wallsten, K. (2010). Yes we can: How online viewership, blog discussion, campaign statements, and mainstream media coverage produce a viral video phenomenon. *Journal of Information Technology & Politics*, 7(2/3), 163–181.

Walter, E. (2012). The rise of visual social media. *Fast Company*. Retrieved from www.fastcompany.com/3000794/rise-visual-social-media

Wattenberg, M. (1991). *The rise of candidate-centered politics*. Cambridge, MA: Harvard University Press.

Wattenberg, M. P., & Brians, C. (1999). Negative campaign advertising: Demobilizer and mobilizer? *American Political Science Review, 93*(4), 891–899.

Wells, C., & Thorson, K. (2015). Combining big data and survey techniques to model effects of political content flows in Facebook. *Social Science Computer Review, 35*(1), 33–52.

Whitehouse, A. J., Maybery, M. T., & Durkin, K. (2006). The development of the picture-superiority effect. *British Journal of Developmental Psychology, 24*, 767–773.

Young, D. G. (2004). Late night comedy in election 2000: Its influence on candidate trait ratings and the moderating effects of political knowledge and partisanship. *Journal of Broadcasting & Electronic Media, 48*(1), 1–22.

Zhang, W., Setlzer, T., & Bichard, S. (2013). Two sides of the coin: Assessing the influence of social network site use during the 2012 U.S. presidential campaign. *Social Science Computer Review, 31*(5), 542–551.

Zhu, J., Milavsky, J. R., & Biswas, R. (1994). Do televised debates affect image perception more than issue knowledge? A study of the first 1992 presidential debate. *Human Communication Research, 20*, 302–333.

14

TWEETS AS TOOLS

Exploring the Campaign Functions of Candidates' Tweets in the 2016 Presidential Campaign

Thomas Kim Hixson

In the second debate of the 2016 general-election campaign, Republican presidential nominee Donald Trump described his frequent use of Twitter:

> Now, tweeting happens to be a modern-day form of communication. You can like it or not . . . It's a very effective way of communication. So you can put it down, but it's an effective form of communication. I'm not unproud of it to be honest with you.
>
> (*Newsweek, 2016*)

Trump is correct that Twitter is a modern form of communication, as it was introduced only ten years ago. It has grown in popularity and approximately 49 million adults in the U.S. now use it (Duggan & Smith, 2016). Trump is proud of it, especially his own talent in tweeting. In the early days of campaigning for the presidency he announced, "Somebody said I'm the Ernest Hemingway of 140 characters. Can you believe it?" Yet his opinion that it is an effective form of communication can be debated, particularly its use in political campaign communications. For example, Kreiss (2016) noted that although Twitter has received quite a lot of interest from researchers, little of this work has been directed at campaigns and political actors, and how they might use Twitter in a strategic manner. This chapter seeks to fill some of that void by examining candidates' tweets to answer: How do tweets function in a campaign?, What role do they play in the campaign apparatus?, What content do they communicate?, and How much earned media do they generate?

The 2016 presidential campaign as exemplified by candidates' Twitter use was the apex of mudslinging, name-calling, and nastiness in recent history. In the primary campaign, where as many as 20 candidates formally announced their intention to run, tweets included messages such as "Wow, Lying Ted Cruz really went wacko today" (Trump, 2016, May 3), "Nominating Donald Trump would be a train wreck" (Cruz, 2016, March 29), "After stoking every fire he can think of, Trump encourages his supporters to beat up anybody who disagrees with him" (Clinton, 2016, March 13), and "Be careful, Lyin' Ted, or I will spill the beans on your wife!" (Trump, 2016, March 22). Included in this tweet was an unflattering picture of Ted Cruz's wife. With provocative messages such as these, it was easy for the media to recognize the news value tweets would have in the election.

To be victorious in an election, campaign strategists understand the goal should be to win 50% of the vote plus one vote. To accomplish this success, the belief is that campaigns must communicate with, and persuade, voters. All of the resources of a campaign should be dedicated to that ultimate end. At the most basic level, a campaign has as its resources: time, money, and people, with an emphasis on the most important person, the candidate. There are only 24 hours in a day for a candidate to make appearances, shake hands, give speeches, make fundraising calls, meet with staff, travel, eat, and get a few precious hours of sleep. All of these resources are limited and are used to perform campaign functions such as those described later in this chapter. Twitter has been used to perform these functions and has been complemented with, or has enhanced, other more traditional campaign methods. Whether alone or combined with these older methods, Twitter as a campaign tool has had varying levels of success. Whatever the level of success of a tweet in a campaign, there can be little doubt that the tweet has saved resources to be used elsewhere in the campaign. For example, a tweet such as this one by candidate Ted Cruz: "Join me, @glennbeck, and Chuck Norris on Sunday, March 13, at Charlotte Motor Speedway" (Cruz, 2016, March 7) had the potential of being read by more than 903,000 @tedcruz followers on Twitter (Trackalytics, 2016). It can be argued that many of these followers were not located in the Charlotte area and would have little likelihood of attending the event (or even that these follower numbers are inflated with dormant accounts and Twitter bots). The cost of sending a tweet, however, is much less in time and money as opposed to having volunteers make phone calls or having notices designed, printed, and sent through the mail, especially when these savings are multiplied by the many communications that need to take place in a campaign.

This study explores the use of Twitter by the major candidates Hillary Clinton, Bernie Sanders, Donald Trump, Ted Cruz, Marco Rubio, Ben Carson, and John Kasich. A content analysis was conducted of 4,089 tweets originating from the candidates' Twitter accounts. Retweets were not included unless the tweet included an additional message from the candidate. Only the textual message was analyzed. The analysis did not include tweets made after the candidate dropped out of the race and only included tweets prior to that date. This analysis can be considered as a compendium for the overall campaign. It provides a simple explanation of the campaign tactics involved in the election, but its purpose is more fundamental: to learn the campaign functions that candidates—through their Twitter use—determine are best suited to help him or her win the election. Inherent here are the assumptions that a candidate wants to win, believes victory is possible, and that he or she writes, approves, or has control over the Twitter messages transmitted or the broad communications strategy guiding the messages.

As this chapter shows, the most newspaper coverage of presidential candidate tweets was of those from @realDonaldTrump. The resulting earned media from this coverage is part of the huge advantage that Trump realized in free publicity. This advantage was evident in both the primary and the general election.

Twitter and Social Media in Past Campaigns

Twitter was launched in July 2006, but did not quickly become a force in election campaigns. Little use, without any real strategy, was evident in the 2008 presidential campaign. However, in the midterm congressional elections of 2010, Twitter use increased. By the 2012 presidential election, the 140-character format of campaign messaging had become a much-used medium, particularly by the Obama campaign (Kreiss, 2016). As of August 8, 2016, 20% of American adults use Twitter (Duggan & Smith, 2016). Fifty-nine percent of those Twitter users claim to get news on it with almost half of them actively *seeking* news as opposed to just happening upon news items (Gottfried & Shearer, 2016). Stromer-Galley (2014) agreed that Twitter was only in the beginning stages as a campaign tool in the 2008 election but had become essential for digital campaigning by the 2012 presidential campaign. Indeed, social media has become a fundamental part of the way in which campaigns communicate to the public. Although social media provides for interactivity between the message creator and receiver, the messages sent by campaigns through social media remain highly controlled with less opportunity for the public to take part in the communication (Digital news, 2016). Metzgar and Maruggi (2009) asserted that the use of social media is causing the one-way model of mass media to decline in usefulness as the receivers of the one-way model now need much less resources to reply or to create messages. They noted the benefit of using social media to transmit campaign messages, but indicated that it was also useful to have an "ongoing engagement" with those who receive the message.

The advent of social media has led recent election campaigns to utilize digital communication and to learn how best to use the technology for election success (Stromer-Galley, 2014). This utilization is not surprising, as social media is recognized as being able to more widely distribute messages about campaign issues than traditional media can facilitate (Metzgar & Maruggi, 2009). In campaigns in the past, interpersonal communication has been very important in encouraging political activism. Social media can provide the semblance of interpersonal contact and can be a successful political tool (Kim, Atkin, & Lin, 2016). Twitter, by its nature of seemingly connecting an individual to a candidate, enhances the bridging of the gap between the artificiality of technology and the genuineness of a personal connection. Tweets enable a candidate to have a personal, although mediated, relationship with a follower, thus making the format valuable in campaign outreach. Twitter can be a powerful format for delivering messages, as Metzgar and Maruggi (2009) noted. It enables anyone to post an idea in a short message to a national audience in an unedited and unsuppressed form. A candidate is provided the freedom to directly contact supporters in an immediate manner. There can be little doubt about the potential of a candidate's tweet to be a potent message. Two-thirds of Twitter users report they see a lot or some political related content on the platform (Duggan & Smith, 2016). So, it seems that people using Twitter are open to receiving political information, and are probably much more open to receiving messages when they have to "opt-in" by becoming followers of a candidate.

Twitter followers of politicians can number in the millions. On election day in November, for instance, Trump had 14.3 million followers and Clinton had 10.8 million (Twittercounter.com, 2016). These numbers probably are inflated by "fake" followers that are generated through automated bots or spam accounts, but the real Twitter users are an educated group. Out of the users of five social media networks, Twitter users are the second most college-educated group behind LinkedIn (Gottfried & Shearer, 2016). Therefore, it comes as no surprise that users rank Twitter first among social media platforms for political persuasion. These users trust the platform that can sometimes be as persuasive as family members in its impact on political beliefs (Parmelee, 2014).

Given the nature of Twitter, it seems like it should be a very useful platform for a message to be sent to an opinion leader and then have that person send it to others. However, the level of effectiveness of this two-way flow of communication for political tweets is uncertain. Duggan and Smith (2016) report that 65% of Twitter users claim that what they see on each tweet is political in nature, yet only 20% ever post any political information or opinions. Of course, when candidates include hashtags in their tweets, there is a greater chance of someone other than a follower being exposed to the message. In addition, supporters can be encouraged to tweet about the campaign so that the tweet might trend and perhaps generate earned media (Stromer-Galley, 2014). Supporters can also be encouraged to retweet information to spread a message. "RT" is tweeter-speak for "retweet this message" that will forward the message to all of the supporter's Twitter followers. Clinton used this in several of her tweets, for example: "RT this if you're proud to have Hillary's back tonight" (Clinton, 2016, October 9a). This tweet generated 37,365 retweets. It is easy for a tweet recipient to retweet simply by clicking the retweet link under each tweet. Some messages will get many retweets without the candidate requesting it. For example, Donald Trump's tweet from November 1, "So terrible that Crooked didn't report she got the debate questions from Donna Brazile, if that were me it would have been front page news" (Trump, 2016, November 1) garnered 32,084 retweets. Although these numbers seem to represent a great multiplier effect of the campaign message, both represent less than one-half of 1% of Clinton's and Trump's registered Twitter followers.

Early on in Twitter's use as a campaign communication medium, it had become a platform for one-way communication. Twitter followers use it much more as a way to receive information, as opposed to engaging in dialogue (van Dijck, 2011). Macnamara and Kenning (2014) bemoan the use of social media by political candidates as campaign messages are sent with no emphasis on two-way communication. Indeed, *The Wall Street Journal* labeled Trump's use of Twitter "a powerful broadcast medium" that the candidate used as a method to distribute his message. Furthermore, the newspaper asserted that Trump actually creates his message through tweets (Mims, 2016).

Campaign Functions Twitter Can Perform

Twitter is a campaign communication medium that can be very effective because of the non-existent lead time needed to produce a message and have it immediately distributed at virtually no cost (Kreiss, 2016), saving time and money for a campaign. As mentioned earlier, the resources of time and money are limited in a campaign. The categorization of tweets as campaign communication was completed as part of the research of Macnamara and Kenning (2014) in the Australian elections of 2013. These researchers found 37.8% of tweets consisted of information stating an opinion on national issues; 26.8% were election promises and slogans; 12.9% were attacks on other candidates' policy; 9% were candidate appearance notices; 9% were attacks of other candidates by name; 2.6% was personal information or feeling; and 0.9% were opinions on local issues. Stromer-Galley (2014) also identified the roles Twitter can serve in a campaign: to have insight into what the public is thinking, to let campaigns test how ideas might resonate with supporters, to recruit volunteers, identifying activists for the campaign, and generating contributions.

Tweets can be transmitted at precisely when the best conditions exist; for example, when a candidate performs very well in a debate and a tweet asking for donations is sent out immediately (Kreiss, 2016). For example, "Hillary won tonight. Chip in to help her win on November 8th" (Clinton, 2016, October 9b). This timeliness factor extends to *during* the debates as well. Trump signed off on his Twitter account by announcing he was handing off the tweets from his account to his campaign staff during the debate: "My team of deplorables will be taking over my Twitter account for tonight's #debate" (Trump, 2016, October 9). This enabled the staff to tweet messages reinforcing the words and images of the candidate and/or opponent in real time for those watching and to enlighten those who were not. Although Clinton did not say she was handing off her Twitter account to staff, during the first debate this tweet appeared on @HillaryClinton, "Trump just criticized me for preparing for this debate. You know what else I prepared for? Being president" (Clinton, 2016, September 26).

How This Analysis Was Conducted

A content analysis of 4,089 tweets by presidential candidates was conducted. Tweets from the primaries and the general election were collected. The time frames of this study were January 2 to June 7, 2016 for the primary election and September 1 to November 8, 2016 for the general election. Tweets were drawn from randomly selected weeks in these time periods. Tweets were collected from seven major candidates: Donald Trump, Marco Rubio, Ted Cruz, Ben Carson, John Kasich, Hillary Clinton, and Bernie Sanders. Only tweets originating from the candidates' Twitter accounts were included. Retweets with no comment from the candidates were not included. Although the researcher had no concrete way of determining when a tweet was not written by the candidate himself or herself, the intent of this study is to explore the candidates' tweets as a reflection of how the candidate envisioned his or her campaign.

The campaign functions listed below are the code categories used in this analysis. These categories were derived from the roles Twitter can play in a campaign (Stromer-Galley, 2014), the campaign communication categories found in tweets (Macnamara & Kenning, 2014), and the procedures performed in a campaign (Grey, 2006). Two trained coders, both of whom have campaign management experience, coded the tweets based on the most salient function the tweet served as a campaign tool. Simply put, the coders tried to answer, "What is the tweet about, and what purpose does it serve in trying to make the campaign successful?" The coders based their decisions on the words written and not on any accompanying graphic or video content. Cohen's κ was run to determine the amount of agreement by the two coders on the most salient campaign function present in the wording of the tweet. The agreement between the coders was in the "very good" range, $\kappa = .868$, $p < .001$.

Campaign Functions

Event announcement: a tweet that announces that a campaign event/candidate appearance will occur. Usually contains information about where and when. Often encourages attendance at the event.

GOTV—Get Out the Vote: a tweet that encourages a receiver to go vote, register to vote, or attend a caucus. It also may provide information about how, when, where to do these activities.

Celebration: a tweet that exults glee or joy that is usually connected to an election result, a poll result, or a campaign activity that was a success.

Gratitude: a tweet that is an expression of gratefulness for a kindness done for the campaign or for society. Shows appreciation by the candidate.

Issue or Policy: a tweet expressing a candidate's viewpoint on an issue that has arisen in the campaign or a statement of a policy stance.

Criticism-Opponent(s): a tweet that refers to an active opponent that denigrates, belittles, or disparages that candidate and/or a policy or issue stance. Can also include references to the opponent's campaign or supporters.

Criticism-Media: a tweet that refers to a media organization, media personality, or media report in a manner that questions the truth, judgment, or credibility of the content or the person involved.

Criticism-Other: a tweet that refers to a person other than an active opponent or media personality or to an organization other than an active opponent's campaign or the media that denigrates, belittles, or disparages that person or organization and/or a policy or issue stance.

Fundraiser: a tweet that asks the receiver to make a monetary donation to the campaign.

Volunteer: a tweet that encourages the receiver to take an action other than voting for the candidate or donating money to the campaign. Included would be signing up for some undetermined campaign activity, making telephone calls, distributing campaign literature, retweeting a post, serving as a poll watcher, talking to others.

Endorsements: a tweet that announces an official or implied endorsement from a media entity, a current or former public office holder, a recognized organization, or a well-known celebrity.

Promotion: a tweet containing a statement meant to build up the reputation, credibility, viability, worthiness, likeability of the candidate. Any slogan of the candidate or campaign.

Media appearance: a tweet that announces the candidate or a surrogate can be seen or heard on a designated mass- or social- media presentation.

Other, or Undefined: tweets that do not fit in to the above categories or are too ambiguous to be categorized. These tweets might contain a link to another social media message, or be a tweet that introduces an accompanying image, chart, table, photograph, or video. They also may be expressions of sympathy or some other personal message.

Earned Media Analysis

This study also sought to determine the amount of earned media that was generated by the tweets. Newspapers examined for content about the candidates' tweets were: *New York Times*, *Wall Street Journal*, *USA Today*, *Washington Post*, *Los Angeles Times*, and *Chicago Tribune*. Each day's edition of these newspapers was included during seven randomly selected weeks during the primary (January 2–June 7, 2016) and five randomly selected weeks during the general election (September 1–November 8, 2016). An online search through ProQuest Newsstand was used to find articles in these newspapers that contained the words Twitter, tweet, tweeting, or tweeted and the candidate's names. The articles were then perused to find references to a candidate's tweets or Twitter activity. During the selected weeks in the primaries, 51 articles were identified that met these criteria. In the selected weeks of the general election, 86 articles were found. A further explanation of earned media is included later in this chapter.

The Campaign Functions of the Tweets in the 2016 Elections

Tweets in the Primaries

A chi-square test for association was conducted between candidate and campaign function as found in tweets (see Table 14.1). Statistically significant associations were present in both the primaries and the general election. In the primary election, there was a statistically significant association between candidate and campaign functions as found in tweets, $\chi^2(78) = 850.59$, $p = <.005$. There was

TABLE 14.1 Tweets by Campaign Functions—Counts—Primary Election

Function		*Clinton*	*Trump*	*Sanders*	*Cruz*	*Rubio*	*Carson*	*Kasich*
Event anncmt	Count	0	8	3	2	14	0	5
	Expected Count	5.3	5.4	6.2	3.0	4.7	4.0	3.4
GOTV	Count	6	4	54	18	22	4	4
	Expected Count	18.5	19.0	21.8	10.5	16.3	14.0	12.0
Celebration	Count	8	42	6	4	5	10	23
	Expected Count	16.2	16.6	19.1	9.1	14.2	12.2	10.5
Gratitude	Count	2	26	5	5	6	11	4
	Expected Count	9.8	10.0	11.5	5.5	8.6	7.4	6.3
Issues, Policy	Count	138	13	144	44	40	104	35
	Expected Count	85.7	87.7	101.1	48.4	75.3	64.6	55.3
Crit-Opps	Count	37	77	45	19	31	9	8
	Expected Count	37.4	38.3	44.1	21.1	32.8	28.2	24.1
Crit-Media	Count	0	44	1	1	2	2	0
	Expected Count	8.3	8.5	9.8	4.7	7.3	6.2	5.3
Crit-Other	Count	8	9	11	5	7	22	2
	Expected Count	10.6	10.8	12.5	6.0	9.3	8.0	6.8
Promotion	Count	60	48	49	38	66	45	69
	Expected Count	62.0	63.5	73.2	35.0	54.5	46.7	40.0
Volunteer	Count	11	0	9	7	6	0	3
	Expected Count	6.0	6.1	7.0	3.4	5.2	4.5	3.8
Fundraiser	Count	2	2	3	1	4	0	1
	Expected Count	2.2	2.2	2.5	1.2	1.9	1.6	1.4
Endorsement	Count	5	7	3	5	23	0	15
	Expected Count	9.6	9.8	11.3	5.4	8.4	7.2	6.2
Media appear	Count	5	13	11	12	13	0	15
	Expected Count	11.4	11.7	13.5	6.4	10.0	8.6	7.4
Other	Count	14	10	5	6	21	16	7
	Expected Count	13.1	13.4	15.4	7.4	11.5	9.8	8.4
	Tweet Totals	296	303	349	167	260	223	191

a moderately strong association between candidate and campaign functions as found in tweets, $\varphi_c = .28$, $p = <.005$. Although this campaign will be remembered for the candidates' incivility and no-holds-barred rhetoric, the campaign functions of many tweets during the primary were better identified as traditional and civilized. Of the 1,789 primary campaign tweets analyzed, 518 or 29.0% were devoted to issues and policy statements whereas 375 or 21.0% contained a promotional message of a slogan or reason to support the candidate. To contrast, 340 or 19.0% of the tweets were critical in nature, with the criticism aimed at opponents in 226 (12.6%) of the tweets, aimed at the media in 50 (2.8%) tweets or directed at "others" in 64 (3.6%) tweets (see Table 14.1).

Examining the tweets from the candidates individually, and seeing how they compare with the others, perhaps can provide insights into the strategic thinking of the candidates. Almost half of the tweeted messages from Hillary Clinton (46.6%) and Ben Carson (46.6%) were issue or policy oriented. Bernie Sanders's issue or policy tweets made up 27.8% of all the candidates' issue tweets while accounting for 41.3% of his total tweets. Clinton was close behind Sanders as she tweeted 26.6% of all the issue tweets. By contrast, Donald Trump only devoted 4.3% of his tweets to policy. Overall, the five Republican candidates included in this analysis devoted only 236 (21%) of their tweets to stating policy or addressing issues with Ben Carson, who dropped out of the race first, tweeting almost half of those. In those tweets that were critical in nature, Donald Trump was the leader in this function. Trump's acrimonious, caustic, and belittling tweets totaled 130 or 38.2% of the criticism tweets. Indeed, 42.9% of Trump tweets during the primary were inherently critical. In contrast, all of the other candidates in this analysis had critical-oriented tweets in near equal percentages ranging from Ben Carson (14.8%) to Bernie Sanders (16.4%). Donald Trump was much more likely to criticize opponents, as 34.1% of all these tweets were produced by him. In criticizing the media or its personalities, Trump tweeted 88.0% of all those messages. This extremely high percentage is ironic, given that Trump became best known before the election because of his many media appearances. Also, it is amusing that, as will be shown, Trump was overwhelmingly the recipient of earned media from his tweets. There is a paradox to be found in the analysis. Trump was much more likely than the other candidates to express gratitude for the support he was given. He had 26 tweets that did so, comprising 8.6% of his tweets. Of all the "thank you" tweets in the primaries, Trump transmitted 44.1% of them. Trump was also much more likely to use Twitter to celebrate his success as a candidate. Fully, 42.9% of all the tweets proclaiming some achievement were tweeted by Trump and made up 13.9% of his tweets.

Fundraising appeals via Twitter were surprisingly low given the notoriety that Obama's fundraising through social media, including Twitter, has attained. Only Marco Rubio devoted more than one percent (1.5%) of his tweets to asking for campaign contributions. Likewise, asking followers to volunteer or take action, including requests to simply retweet a message, seemed very low. Trump and

Carson made no such appeal. Ted Cruz devoted only a small portion (4.2%) of his tweets to seeking volunteer effort, but that was the highest percentage of any candidate. When contrasted with the post-primary efforts of the 2012 candidates, this is a huge difference. Romney spent 15% of his social media posts and Obama spent 20% of his posts on messages to encourage fundraising and volunteerism (Messaging, 2012). Endorsements do not have the potential to generate votes as they once did, but still candidates welcome them, if not seek them. In the Twitter world, however, Marco Rubio (39.7%) and John Kasich (25.9%) tweeted approximately two-thirds of those tweets announcing an endorsement by a media entity or a politician.

Announcing a campaign event on Twitter seems very advantageous and practical. As campaign schedules for a candidate are very fluid and often determined with little lead time, the instant messaging that can take place through Twitter seems ready made for this function. Although Marco Rubio (43.9%) and Donald Trump (25.0%) generated the highest percentage of these tweets, they only produced 14 and 8 of these tweets, respectively. In using Twitter to publicize a media appearance and get supporters to tune in, all the candidates except Ben Carson, who did not have such a tweet, and Hillary Clinton who made 5, made a similar number of tweets with this content (see Table 14.2).

TABLE 14.2 Tweets by Campaign Functions—Percentages—Primary Election

Function		*Clinton*	*Trump*	*Sanders*	*Cruz*	*Rubio*	*Carson*	*Kasich*
Event anncmt	% of function twts	0.0	25.0	9.4	6.3	43.8	0.0	15.6
	% of candidate twts	0.0	2.6	0.9	1.2	5.4	0.0	2.6
GOTV	% of function twts	5.4	3.6	48.2	16.1	19.6	3.6	3.6
	% of candidate twts	2.0	1.3	15.5	10.8	8.5	1.8	2.1
Celebration	% of function twts	8.2	42.9	6.1	4.1	5.1	10.2	23.5
	% of candidate twts	2.7	13.9	1.7	2.4	1.9	4.5	12.0
Gratitude	% of function twts	3.4	44.1	8.5	8.5	10.2	18.6	6.8
	% of candidate twts	0.7	8.6	1.4	3.0	2.3	4.9	2.1
Issues, Policy	% of function twts	26.6	2.5	27.8	8.5	7.7	20.1	6.8
	% of candidate twts	46.6	4.3	41.3	26.3	15.4	46.6	18.3
Crit-Opps	% of function twts	16.4	34.1	19.9	8.4	13.7	4.0	3.5
	% of candidate twts	12.5	25.4	12.9	11.4	11.9	4.0	4.2
Crit-Media	% of function twts	0.0	88.0	2.0	2.0	4.0	4.0	0.0
	% of candidate twts	0.0	14.5	0.3	0.6	0.8	0.9	0.0
Crit-Other	% of function twts	12.5	14.1	17.2	7.8	10.9	34.4	3.1
	% of candidate twts	2.7	3.0	3.2	3.0	2.7	9.9	1.0
Promotion	% of function twts	16.0	12.8	13.1	10.1	17.6	12.0	18.4
	% of candidate twts	20.3	15.8	14.0	22.8	25.4	20.2	36.1
Volunteer	% of function twts	30.6	0.0	25.0	19.4	16.7	0.0	8.3
	% of candidate twts	3.7	0.0	2.6	4.2	2.3	0.0	1.6

Function		*Clinton*	*Trump*	*Sanders*	*Cruz*	*Rubio*	*Carson*	*Kasich*
Fundraiser	% of function twts	15.4	15.4	23.1	7.7	30.8	0.0	7.7
	% of candidate twts	0.7	0.7	0.9	0.6	1.5	0.0	0.5
Endorsement	% of function twts	8.6	12.1	5.2	8.6	39.7	0.0	25.9
	% of candidate twts	1.7	2.3	0.9	3.0	8.8	0.0	7.9
Media appear	% of function twts	7.2	18.8	15.9	17.4	18.8	0.0	21.7
	% of candidate twts	1.7	4.3	3.2	7.2	5.0	0.0	7.9
Other	% of function twts	17.7	12.7	6.3	7.6	26.6	20.3	8.9
	% of candidate twts	4.7	3.3	1.4	3.6	8.1	7.2	3.7
	Tweet Totals	296	303	349	167	260	223	191

Tweets in the General Election

In the general election, there was a statistically significant association between candidate and campaign functions as found in tweets, $\chi^2(13) = 484.44$, $p = <.005$. This was a strong association between candidate and campaign functions as found in tweets, $\varphi_c = .46$, $p = <.005$. The general election provides a more discernable picture of the strategy behind campaign Twitter use. With only two candidates splitting the totality of the tweets in this analysis, much more clear distinctions can be made. Clinton and Trump were diametrically opposed most obviously in using tweets to make fundraising appeals, as Trump made none and Clinton made 22. The difference was also great in tweets in criticizing the media; Trump made 36 such tweets whereas Clinton made none in the primary or general election. Again, this use of Twitter by Trump to criticize the media is ironic given that he ended up receiving so much more media attention for his tweets than did Clinton.

Perhaps most surprising is that Clinton devoted a higher percentage of her tweets (34.9%) to criticizing her opponent, than vice versa (30.8%). Of course, this computation does not take into consideration the intensity of the verbal assault in the messages. It may be this intensity, or oddity of the occurrence, that led the media to cover so many more of Trump's tweets than those of his opponent (see Table 14.3). Clinton devoted a higher percentage of her tweets to issues and policy (22.5%) than did Trump (10.7%). Guesses can be made as to why this strategy was followed or developed. Was it that Clinton thought that she could win on the issues? Or was it that her staff wrote more of her tweets than Trump's staff wrote of his? Or did Trump surmise that the voters cared more about the personality of the candidates than the issues? Trump was more gracious, perhaps, in some tweets than he was in campaign appearances. He was much more likely to express gratitude through tweets than was Clinton. Additionally, the successes of Trump's campaign were also much more likely to be announced and shared with followers. During the campaign, Trump was boastful of the large crowds that he claimed attended his campaign appearances.

TABLE 14.3 Tweets by Campaign Function—General Election—Frequency and Percentage

Function		*Clinton*	*Trump*		*Clinton*	*Trump*
Event anncmt	Count	7	70	% of function twts	9.1	90.9
	Expected Count	46.0	31.0	% of candidate twts	0.5	7.6
GOTV	Count	104	27	% of function twts	79.4	20.6
	Expected Count	78.3	52.7	% of candidate twts	7.6	2.9
Celebration	Count	13	71	% of function twts	15.5	84.5
	Expected Count	50.2	33.8	% of candidate twts	0.9	7.7
Gratitude	Count	10	88	% of function twts	10.2	89.8
	Expected Count	58.6	39.4	% of candidate twts	0.7	9.5
Issues, Policy	Count	309	99	% of function twts	75.7	24.3
	Expected Count	243.9	164.1	% of candidate twts	22.5	10.7
Crit-Opps	Count	480	285	% of function twts	62.7	37.3
	Expected Count	457.3	307.7	% of candidate twts	34.9	30.8
Crit-Media	Count	0	36	% of function twts	0.0	100.0
	Expected Count	21.5	14.5	% of candidate twts	0.0	3.9
Crit-Other	Count	6	52	% of function twts	10.3	89.7
	Expected Count	34.7	23.3	% of candidate twts	0.4	5.6
Promotion	Count	231	85	% of function twts	73.1	26.9
	Expected Count	188.9	127.1	% of candidate twts	16.8	9.2
Volunteer	Count	27	4	% of function twts	87.1	12.9
	Expected Count	18.5	12.5	% of candidate twts	2.0	0.4
Fundraiser	Count	22	0	% of function twts	100.0	0.0
	Expected Count	13.2	8.8	% of candidate twts	1.6	0.0
Endorsement	Count	41	16	% of function twts	71.9	28.1
	Expected Count	34.1	22.9	% of candidate twts	3.0	1.7
Media appear	Count	55	50	% of function twts	52.4	47.6
	Expected Count	62.8	42.2	% of candidate twts	4.0	5.4
Other	Count	70	42	% of function twts	62.5	37.5
	Expected Count	67.0	45.0	% of candidate twts	5.1	4.5
	Tweet Totals	1375	925			

If these boasts are not exaggerated, these crowd sizes can hardly be directly attributed to Twitter use, but Trump devoted much more of his Twitter output to announcing events than did Clinton, almost ten times as much. Alternatively, Clinton devoted six times as many tweets than Trump in asking followers to volunteer, but only a very small portion (2%) of her tweets asked for volunteers.

Clinton received endorsements from many newspapers including several that rarely, if ever, had not endorsed the Republican nominee. Perhaps because newspaper endorsements are not as influential as they once were, Clinton devoted little fanfare to this unprecedented situation, at least in the amount (3.0%) of her tweets that mentioned endorsements. Trump did announce the endorsements he received from a few minor newspapers and from some politicians, but still, Clinton accounted for 71.9% of the endorsement tweets. As Clinton became the fourth candidate to win the popular vote but lose in the electoral college, it is perhaps fitting that she had a much higher percentage of her tweets (7.6%) urging her followers to vote than did her opponent (2.9%). Almost 80% of the tweets encouraging voting were tweeted by Clinton.

Earned Media From the Tweets

As discussed above, campaign functions were carried out through the candidates' tweets. The Twitter platform provided campaigns a much less expensive alternative to traditional communication, and it enabled campaigns to produce and distribute messages quickly to a nationwide audience. A candidate's Twitter followers were encouraged to support their candidate by attending campaign events, by making monetary contributions to the campaign, or by volunteering to help. Tweets from a candidate reinforced the candidates' image and promoted the candidacy in an effort to keep followers' support and votes. Candidates used Twitter to criticize opponents and portray them as unworthy to be president. Additionally, tweets were used for the very important GOTV (Get Out the Vote) function by informing voters how to register to vote and reminding them of when to vote. Consequently, what more can a candidate get from a tweet? In some cases, and definitely in the case of Donald Trump in the 2016 election, candidates can get earned media. Earned media is what used to be described as publicity, particularly when that publicity is free; for example, when a brand (or a candidate) is mentioned in a news story and there is no payment to the media for that mention. In the past, Hollywood was the center of generating publicity, as movie studios' publicity departments were famously able to get mentions of their stars in gossip columns and in movie magazines. This earned media fed the movie-going public's desire for information about these actors and the glamourous lives they were said to live. Of course, in doing so, the studios were "advertising" their movies without needing to pay for it. Other industries caught on to this idea and also sought to take advantage of this type of marketing communication that did not cost.

Marketing now refers broadly to three types of media: a) earned media, b) paid media, and c) owned media. Paid media refers to marketing communication that a brand pays for, such as advertising in the traditional media that now includes some social media as well. Owned media is the media that is the property of a brand such as a website, blog, or Twitter account. With owned media the content communicated is under the total control of the brand, at least when first transmitted. In a paid media situation, the original content is under the total control of the brand but it is published or broadcast by the media entity paid to do so. Control of where, and when, and in what environment the message is transmitted is not under the total control of the brand. At times, who might be exposed to the message is also not a certainty. The earned media reported in this chapter is generated from owned media, in this case from candidates' Twitter accounts, but like all earned media, it lacks these controls over message content and placement in the media; there could be a negative mention instead of a positive mention. However, with journalists monitoring and reporting on candidates' tweets (Parmelee, 2014), the earned media created from the candidates' tweets requires an extremely low investment from the campaigns, often requiring no money at all, but rather only time. Earned media has the added benefit of being a more credible message with consumers than owned or paid media because an earned media message comes from a party that apparently would have no bias toward the brand.

Substitute "candidate" for "brand" in the explanation of the types of media above and the benefit of earned media to an election campaign is readily apparent, although prior to the 2016 presidential election negative mentions were normally avoided by the campaigns at all costs. In the earlier media environment, the limited number of media outlets made negative "press" much more difficult for voters to miss or ignore, and that adverse publicity was much more arduous for candidates to overcome. Earned media has come to include mentions not only in traditional media such as newspapers, magazines, radio, and television but also through owned media such as social media. Stephan and Galak (2012) equated earned media with "word-of-mouth" advertising, including mentions of brands in the social media sphere. "Word-of-mouth" communications still have the aura of being believable without any inherent bias in the motivation of the message transmitter. Trying to gain earned media through the use of owned media by election campaigns has become essential in the modern, large-scale campaign.

In a study of earned media for campaigns in local media, Darr (2016) maintains that earned media is a strategic interaction between campaigns and media. Newspapers that lack resources to gather news are much more likely to be influenced by campaigns. Given that today's news-gathering operations are less willing than before to invest resources into reporting, the assumption can be made that traditional media beyond local media could be influenced to cover events or issues by campaigns. The earned media of candidate tweets in the 2016 presidential election bears out this notion. In several instances stories contained a candidate's tweet instead of what in previous elections would have been a quote in response to a reporter's question. Tweets, because they are so readily available and accessible online, have become in this election a digital morgue where journalists can resurrect a candidate's words and give them another life outside the Twitter world.

In a study of the 2012 Republican primaries, Murthy (2015) found that the social media efforts including the use of Twitter by candidates were intended to create "buzz." This type of messaging would, of course, be more likely to produce earned media. Journalists admit they use political leaders' tweets in several ways in their coverage of politics. They use tweets for story ideas, for event notices, to find quotes and polling data, as a source for an alternative viewpoint, a bank to acquire background information, and as a confirmation source for information in existing stories (Parmelee, 2014). Tweets can be valuable in producing earned media also because they might provide insight into the candidates' thinking or feeling. Many campaign managers are not overseeing social media with the scrutiny and vigilance as they did in the past. Voters now receive a more genuine, if still mediated, message in a tweet from the candidates (Fulgoni, Lipsman, & Davidsen, 2016), especially from a candidate such as Trump. As journalists are also monitoring tweets, the possibility of a tweet being the impetus or germ of an earned media materialization is becoming more likely.

In creating "buzz" or earned media, Donald Trump had a lot of practice prior to the 2016 presidential election. In his book, *The Art of the Deal* (1987), Trump had insight into using the media for his own purposes: "The point is that if you are a little different, or a little outrageous, or if you do things that are bold or controversial, the press is going to write about you" (p. 56). Additionally, he apparently believes in the adage that any publicity is good publicity. He wrote, "Good publicity is preferable to bad, but from a bottom-line perspective, bad publicity is sometimes better than no publicity at all. Controversy, in short, sells" (p. 176). Regarding bad publicity, Trump bombastically over-exaggerated his election victory as an "electoral college landslide." He can, however, more accurately describe the amount of earned media he obtained from his tweets as an overwhelming landslide. The reason for Trump's advantage in earned media from coverage of his tweets is not clearly evident, although guesses can be made. For example the analysis here indicates the negative nature of many of Trump's tweets. During the primaries, of the 303 Trump tweets examined, 130 (42.9%) criticized opponents, the media (including personalities), or others. In the general election 40.3% out of his 925 tweets did so as well. And these insult-laden posts were often eye-catching, outrageous, and norm breaking. Given his propensity for name calling—"Crooked Hillary," "Lying Ted Cruz," or "Little Marco"—in his tweets, the *New York Times* famously ran a two-page spread headlined: "All the people, places and things Donald Trump has insulted on Twitter since declaring his candidacy for the presidency" (Lee & Quealy, 2016, p. A10). According to the *Times*, never before had a candidate for president made personal insults such a central part of his or her campaign. Trump's campaign was filled with statements about other candidates, their spouses, media personalities, the media in general, and a former Miss Universe. These statements were made on Twitter and also during campaign appearances and debates. An unprecedented tweet following the first debate even publicly asked voters to watch pornography: "Did Crooked Hillary help disgusting (check out sex tape and past) Alicia M become a U.S. citizen so she could use her in the debate?" (Trump, 2016, September 30).

This analysis of earned media does not include the *New York Times* article, as those mentions of Trump's tweets would have severely skewed the data. Still, it shows the staggering amount of the advantage in earned media that Trump enjoyed. Table 14.4 shows that, in both the primary and general elections,

TABLE 14.4 Earned Media—Newspaper Mentions of Candidate Tweets or Twitter Use

	Articles that Mentioned Candidate's Tweets		*Mentions of Candidate's Tweets*	
Primary Elections Candidate	*Frequency*	*%*	*Frequency*	*%*
Trump	47	92.2	73	89.0
Clinton	3	5.9	3	3.7
Cruz	3	5.9	3	3.7
Sanders	2	3.9	2	2.4
Kasich	1	1.9	1	1.2
Total	51		82	
General Election Candidate	*Frequency*	*%*	*Frequency*	*%*
Trump	76	88.4	103	89.6
Clinton	12	14.0	12	10.4
Total	86		115	

Note: Percentages for articles sum to more than 100% because some articles mentioned more than one candidate's tweets.

Trump's tweets got an enormous amount of earned media through newspaper coverage when compared to the other candidates. Not only was the number of articles that mention a candidate's tweet overwhelmingly in Trump's favor, but the number of mentions of tweets by a candidate was a huge advantage for Trump. As seen in Table 14.4, Trump's tweets were mentioned in 47 of the 51 articles mentioning candidates' tweets. By comparison, only two of his Republican rivals were mentioned. Tweets by Ted Cruz were mentioned in three articles and tweets by John Kasich in one. In the general election, Trump's Twitter activity was mentioned in 88.4% of the articles written about candidates' tweets whereas Clinton's tweets were addressed in only 14.0% of the articles.

Conclusion

Trump had a tremendous advantage in earned media from tweets in both the primaries and the general election. This analysis shows that he set the negative tone of the tweet campaign during the primaries. The insults and name-calling in his tweets broke new ground in presidential candidate messaging by publicly denouncing his opponents in this manner. Trump won the presidency, but Clinton clearly won the popular vote. When examining the messages each tweeted during the general election, Clinton was more traditional in message content. She was more likely than Trump to address issues, urge voters to go to the polls, recruit volunteers, ask for votes, and criticize her opponent. Alternatively, Trump was much more likely to be personable in his tweets by thanking supporters, inviting them to campaign events, and celebrating the successes of the campaign. However, Trump did what was once thought to be suicide for a campaign—criticize the media—and he did it many times. Given the enigmatic and ambiguous result of the election, and the opposing nature of the tweets, it seems precarious to conclude that Trump's tweet content was more, or was less, appealing to the electorate than was Clinton's. Also difficult to determine is the influence that the candidate tweets in this election will have on future campaigns. It seems likely that some candidates will emulate the belligerence of Trump's tweets, but the acceptance of the tweets and the candidate may not match the success Trump experienced. What can be confirmed is that Trump's tweets were much more likely to receive coverage in the press than any of his opponents' Twitter activity. However, identifying a reason for this result is not readily apparent.

Did this earned media advantage result from the media favoring Trump over his opponents? Did it result from the media not favoring Trump and believing that its coverage of his tweeting would result in less support of his candidacy? Did it result from just an anomaly in the unbiased coverage of the candidates? Did it result from the media's obsession with novelty, controversy, and the unusual that Trump's candidacy exemplified? Or perhaps was it a combination of these factors? Whatever the reason is, the result is that Trump's tweets were setting the agenda for much media coverage of the 2016 presidential campaign. Further research may be able to provide greater insight into understanding the earned media advantage of Trump and his tweets. It should intrigue media scholars as they seek to discover the extent of the role the media played as this political neophyte was elected president of the U.S. This election may be the height of interest given to Twitter use by candidates for president. As technology evolves, new platforms will likely become more widely used and probably have greater influence. That may mean that voters in this election will have had the greatest first-hand, yet mediated, insight into a presidential candidate's character and personal idea of strategy.

References

Clinton, H. [hillaryclinton]. (2016, March 13). After stoking every fire he can think of, Trump encourages his supporters to beat up anybody who disagrees with him.—Hillary in OH. Retrieved from https://twitter.com/HillaryClinton/status/709173125246816256

Clinton, H. [hillaryclinton]. (2016, September 26). Trump just criticized me for preparing for this debate: You know what else I prepared for? Being president. Retrieved from https://twitter.com/HillaryClinton/status/780588262402424832

Clinton, H. [hillaryclinton]. (2016, October 9a). RT this if you're proud to have Hillary's back tonight. Retrieved from https://twitter.com/HillaryClinton/status/785143951149899777

Clinton, H. [hillaryclinton]. (2016, October 9b). Hillary won tonight, Chip in to help her win on November 8th. Retrieved from https://twitter.com/HillaryClinton/status/785309814574419968

Cruz, T. [tedcruz]. (2016, March 7). Join me, @glennbeck, and Chuck Norris on Sunday, March 13, at Charlotte Motor Speedway. Retrieved from https://twitter.com/tedcruz/status/707017784685801472

Cruz, T. [tedcruz]. (2016, March 29). Nominating Donald Trump would be a train wreck: It would be handing the White House to Hillary Clinton. Retrieved from https://twitter.com/tedcruz/status/714976221319270400

Darr, J. P. (2016). Presence to press: How campaigns earn local media. *Political Communication, 33*(3), 503–522.

Digital news developments in U.S. presidential campaigns 2000–2016. (2016, July 18). *Pew Research Center.* Retrieved from www.journalism.org/2016/07/18/digital-news-developments-in-u-s-presidential-campaigns-2000-2016/

Duggan, M., & Smith, A. (2016). Political content on social media. *Pew Research Center.* Retrieved from http://pewinternet.org/2016/10/25/political-content-on-socialmedia/

Fulgoni, G. M., Lipsman, A., & Davidsen, C. (2016). The power of political advertising: Lessons for practitioners. *Journal of Advertising Research, 56*(3), 239–244.

Gottfried, J., & Shearer, E. (2016). News use across social media platforms 2016. *Journalism.org.* Retrieved from http://journalism.org/2016/05/26/news-use-across-social-media-platforms-2016?/

Grey, J. L. (2006). *How to win a local election.* Lanham, MD: M. Evans & Co.

Kim, T., Atkin, J. P., & Lin, C. A. (2016). The influence of social networking sites on political behavior: Modeling political involvement via online and offline activity. *Journal of Broadcasting & Electronic Media, 60*(1), 23–39.

Kreiss, D. (2016). Seizing the moment: The presidential campaigns' use of Twitter during the 2012 electoral cycle. *New Media & Society, 18*(8), 1473–1490.

Lee, J. C., & Quealy, K. (2016, October 24). All the people, places and things Donald Trump has insulted on Twitter since declaring his candidacy for the presidency. *New York Times*, p. A10.

Macnamara, J., & Kenning, G. (2014). E-electioneering 2007–2013: Trends in online political campaigns over three elections. *Media International Australia, 152*, 57–74.

Messaging—two different strategies. (2012, August 15). *Pew Research Center.* Retrieved from www.journalism.org/2012/08/15/messaging-two-different-strategies/

Metzgar, E., & Maruggi, A. (2009). Social media and the 2008 U.S. presidential election. *Journal of New Communications Research, 4*(1), 141–165.

Mims, C. (2016, October 17). Keywords: Twitter is more media than tech. *The Wall Street Journal*, p. B1.

Murthy, D. (2015). Twitter and elections: Are tweets predictive, reactive or a form of buzz? *Information, Communication & Society, 18*(7), 816–831. Retrieved from http://dx.doi.org/10.1080/1369118X.2015.1006659

Newsweek. (2016). Trump vs Clinton in second U.S. presidential debate: Full transcript. *Newsweek.* Retrieved from www.newsweek.com/hillary-clinton-donald-trump-2016-presidential-debate-read-full-transcript-508163

Parmelee, J. H. (2014). The agenda-building function of political tweets. *New Media & Society, 16*(3), 434–450.

Stephan, A. T., & Galak, J. (2012). The effects of traditional and social earned media on sales: A study of a microlending marketplace. *Journal of Marketing Research, 49*, 624–639.

Stromer-Galley, J. (2014). *Presidential campaigning in the Internet age.* New York, NY: Oxford University Press.

Trackalytics. (2016). @tedcruz (Ted Cruz). Retrieved from www.trackalytics.com/twitter/profile/tedcruz/

Trump, D. (1987). *The art of the deal.* New York, NY: Random House.

Trump, D. [realDonaldTrump]. (2016, March 22). Lyin' Ted Cruz just used a picture of Melania from a G.Q. shoot in his ad. Be careful, Lyin' Ted, or I will spill the beans on your wife! Retrieved from https://twitter.com/realDonaldTrump/status/712457104515317764

Trump, D. [realDonaldTrump]. (2016, May 3). Wow, Lyin' Ted Cruz really went wacko today. Made all sorts of crazy charges. Can't function under pressure—not very presidential. Sad! Retrieved from https://twitter.com/realDonaldTrump/status/727634574298255361

Trump, D. [realDonaldTrump]. (2016, September 30). Did Crooked Hillary help disgusting (check out sex tape and past) Alicia M become a U.S. citizen so she could use her in the debate? Retrieved from https://twitter.com/realDonaldTrump/status/781788223055994880

Trump, D. [realDonaldTrump]. (2016, October 9). My team of deplorables will be taking over my Twitter account for tonight's #debate. Retrieved from https://twitter.com/realDonaldTrump/status/785274843042230280

Trump, D. [realDonaldTrump]. (2016, November 1). So terrible that Crooked didn't report she got the debate questions from Donna Brazile, if that were me it would have been front page news. Retrieved from https://twitter.com/realDonaldTrump/status/793456094198759424

Twittercounter.com. (2016). Retrieved from http://twittercounter.com/realDonaldTrump and from http://twittercounter.com/HillaryClinton

van Dijck, J. (2011). Tracing Twitter: The rise of a microblogging platform. *International Journal of Media and Cultural Politics*, 7(3), 333–348.

PART 5

Social Media Content

Political Participation and Humor

15

INTERNET MEMES AS POLYVOCAL POLITICAL PARTICIPATION

Andrew S. Ross and Damian J. Rivers

Social media platforms have provided an avenue to more organic and expansive possibilities for individual political participation and engagement during the past decade. Traditionally, individual political participation has been somewhat curtailed to voting (often hailed as the cornerstone of a representative democracy), campaigning, communicating with officials, and other collective activities (Verba & Nie, 1972). Gil de Zúñiga, Molyneaux, and Zheng (2014) have recently argued that these traditional means of political participation have ignored the multitude of channels through which the use of different media typologies and tools can facilitate more inclusive political participation. Widely used social media platforms such as Twitter and Facebook stand as two examples of social media platforms that have been utilized to expand opportunities for individual political participation (see Loader, Vromen, & Xenos, 2014). Although there have been debates concerning the extent to which Internet memes are able to be categorized as a form of social media due to the absence of a personal profile (see Xenos, Vromen, & Loader, 2014), they do represent a tool within the wider social media framework that permits creative content sharing with a political slant.

Internet memes had begun being circulated in previous elections—namely 2008 and 2012—but arguably in 2016 reached a new level of creation and distribution. This is possibly because of their ability to capture "the popular imagination in ways that other visual output has not" (Miranda, 2016, para. 15). Paul (2016) points out that the sheer volume of memes to emerge as part of the election meant that they just could not be ignored, and played a major role in influencing and reflecting both popularity and flailing campaigns. The author also points out that although politicians may not appreciate being the target of a meme, it does at least indicate that they are in some way relevant. It is almost impossible to give an idea of how many memes were circulated during the election such is the volume, but some of the most popular included those related to "Ken Bone," "Birdie Sanders," "Cruz Zodiac Killer," "Deplorables," and "Nasty Woman." Such was the popularity of election memes, the website www.electmeme.lol was established to allow users to vote on their favorites, which gives an indication of the extent to which they featured in online spaces and popular culture throughout the election.

This chapter offers a Critical Discourse Analysis (CDA) of a selection of Internet memes devised and circulated in relation to the 2016 U.S. presidential election. In particular, this study focuses on the discursive (including visual) and social practices associated with the memes in line with Fairclough's (2001) three-dimensional framework to CDA. In order to provide evidence of the multitude of ways that Internet memes developed and demonstrated political engagement parallel to the unfolding electoral process, our study specifically targets the within-group opposition that occurred during the primaries and the active delegitimization of candidates throughout the general-election campaign. It will be shown that the memes exemplify what Milner (2013a) has termed "polyvocality," this being an increasing volume and diversity of "voices involved in public discussion" (p. 2361), voices that often amplify, distort, challenge, and undermine those found within mainstream media. Further, the study will demonstrate how Internet memes can be used in "making a point" (Shifman, 2014, p. 120) in relation to politics and in particular the 2016 election.

Literature Review

Conceptualizing the Internet Meme

Internet memes can be understood on a basic level as a piece of media such as an image or a video that is adapted, typically humorously, and shared among Internet users. On account of the fact that Internet memes are organic in their first iteration and dispersion before being manipulated and further shared, Gal, Shifman, and Kampf (2016, p. 1700) define them explicitly as "groups of items sharing common characteristics of content, form and/or stance, which were created, transformed, and circulated by many participants through digital participatory platforms." Although this definition establishes a conceptual foundation from which to view the Internet meme, it is also necessary to acknowledge the role of human agency and motivation as fundamental in their creation and spread. The route that individual Internet memes and their various iterations take may, at first glance, appear distinctly disorderly—chaotic, even—but Nissenbaum and Shifman (2015, p. 3) highlight how the course plotted "is to a large extent a product of societal and communal coordination." An important aspect of the human agency involved is the way in which generally memes are shared, or adapted to a new iteration, only when agreed with. It is not the usual

FIGURE 15.1 Example of Typical Image Macro Meme

occurrence that a meme is shared if the consumer disagrees with its content or stance.

Although most commonly depicted as a static image macro with bold text overlaying a fixed image, Internet memes are also frequently transmitted as GIF files, Instagram posts, Snapchat snaps, and YouTube videos. The discursive intention of many memes is to express a particular viewpoint or idea, often through different forms of humor including irony, parody, and sarcasm. Figure 15.1 shows an example of a typical image macro meme. During their lifetime, memes such as this will generally retain the static image whereas the text over-laid upon the image will be subject to change.

Within this chapter we intentionally limit the scope of our analysis to image macro memes for two primary reasons. Namely, that a vast quantity of image macro memes relative to other meme forms emerged in relation to the 2016 U.S. presidential election and primaries; moreover, the combination of static image and malleable text offers a simple means of visual-discursive political expression not requiring specialist technical knowledge or ability.

Polyvocal Political Participation: Humor, Delegitimization, and Intertextuality

Considering how Internet memes are able to facilitate political engagement and participation, it is useful to first discuss them in relation to what Milner (2013a) terms "polyvocality." In a study analyzing Internet memes in relation to the 2011 Occupy Wall Street protests (see DeLuca, Lawson, & Sun, 2012 for an analysis of the broader use of social media), Milner demonstrated how participatory forms of media such as memes can bring together and provide a platform for multiple voices to express opinions and take positions in relation to real-time political events. In particular, the author points out that an interesting aspect of this polyvocality is the significance of individuals and collectives formerly positioned on the periphery (or even outside) of real-time political discussion and debate. Dahlgren (2009) previously documented how within any democratic society there exists a need for the citizenry to be able to communicate with each other through the sharing of ideas and opinions. Within the context of the U.S., it is evident that such communication encourages the development of political positions and the performance of roles associated with those positions, typically through identification as either a Democrat or a Republican. In this regard Internet memes can function in service of the nation as an "imagined community" (Anderson, 1991). In other words, through social media, individuals or collectives, no longer dependent on mainstream media attention or coverage, have several outlets "to find information and engage in public conversation on more equal footing" (Milner, 2013a, p. 2361), with Internet memes being one such example.

Humor

One of the most significant characteristics of Internet memes is the use of humor to communicate a social or political critique or commentary. This humor often comes in the form of irony, satire, sarcasm, or parody, subtle or otherwise. In relation to politics, Milner (2013b, p. 65) states that "the ironic lingua franca predominant in memes can afford a political edge," and in a majority of cases this edge is activated. As memes are so rapidly created, manipulated, and shared, they provide an ideal social media tool for responding to current events through humor. Concerning the domain of politics, Internet memes often utilize both overt and subversive humor to provide critique and commentary. This is perhaps owing to the fact that, as Shifman (2007, p. 187) points out, "humor can serve as a unique key for the understanding of social and cultural processes" such as politics. Further, Burgess (2007) contends that an important component of participatory media is a "vernacular of creativity" that emerges from the process of creation and sharing, one which even when bound by "some adherence to technological and cultural limitations . . . is decidedly more open—more the realm of 'the people'" (Milner, 2013a, p. 2360). Essentially, humor is easier to relate to for most people than anything overly political or academic in nature, and also provides an avenue to more easily express views on issues such as politics. When combined with simple technological tools such as memes, accessibility is significantly improved.

A study by Tay (2014) analyzed the use of humor within Internet memes during the 2012 U.S. presidential election, and demonstrated how memetic campaigns can potentially impact upon the voting public. For instance, it was shown that the vast quantity of memes addressing Mitt Romney's "binders full of women" gaffe served to highlight and amplify his unpopularity with women voters. Conversely, the series of memes known as "texts with Hillary," although not overtly political in nature, had a positive impact upon the public image of Hillary Clinton. The memes in both these cases were largely image macro memes and, interestingly, Tay (2014) highlighted the links between this modern digital form of communication and the more traditional political editorial cartoons. Although they both originate in political news and culture, the creators are neither reporters nor editors (Buell & Maus, 1988).

Delegitimization

The most common intention expressed through Internet memes can be understood as an attempt to delegitimize a particular person, idea, or position that is circulating within the wider social sphere or community (often circulated via mainstream media). The particular style of humor used in delegitimization efforts often includes irony, satire, parody, and sarcasm (see Figure 15.2 for examples of each).

Indeed, memes are more likely to mock and to deride a particular person, idea, or position more than to offer messages of support as part of "an agonistic public sphere and media ecology" (Burroughs, 2013, p. 258). In other words, memes are one part of a public sphere and media environment that is polemical and critical. Within most forms of political discourse, legitimacy is sought after and established largely through actions that are in alignment with the dominant social values of the targeted group (Francesconi, 1982). This idea is reinforced when legitimization is viewed as "the creation of a sense of positive, beneficial, ethical, understandable, necessary or otherwise acceptable action" (Vaara, 2014, p. 503). As Internet memes generally seek to demonstrate the *absence* of these characteristics, they can be seen as creations of dissent or forms of resistance. That is, instead of transmitting a positive image of a particular person, idea, or position, memes can be seen as "discursively creating and transmitting a negative image of the Other" (Screti, 2013, p. 212). We should caution here that the binary of positive-negative is highly contentious as the subjectivities are dependent upon group memberships and the dominant ideologies of beliefs within such groups (e.g., an idea seen as positive by one group might be equally seen as negative by another group).

For example, Davis, Glantz, and Novak (2016) demonstrated the delegitimizing capacity of the Internet meme in their analysis of the Greenpeace meme series in their "Let's Go!" Arctic campaign. Figure 15.3 displays an example of a meme from Greenpeace's guerilla campaign that closely mimics the style of the original Shell advertisements, and transplants the same slogan.

This campaign mimicked the advertising of the oil company Shell in a way that challenged Shell's publicly declared positively framed motives and identity. Although this example reflects institutional-level delegitimization, we argue that Internet memes can be used equally in the delegitimization of individuals, groups, and institutions.

FIGURE 15.2A-B Examples of Humor as Delegitimization (From Top, Irony and Satire)

FIGURE 15.2C-D (Continued – From Top, Parody and Sarcasm)

FIGURE 15.3 Example of Greenpeace Meme in Response to Shell's "Let's Go" Advertising Campaign

Intertextuality

The polyvocal nature of Internet memes is underpinned by their intertextuality, this being any text that is "fundamentally related to other texts . . . [with] . . . its meanings being shaped by that relationship" (Androutsopoulos, 2009, p. 43). Further, as Kristeva (1980) argued, the traces of a text existent in subsequent texts carry significant power and can exert influence over the reader/viewer through different perspectives (a kind of snowball effect). Memes are intertextually grounded upon previous texts via the linguistic structure of the text and/or the graphic features involved in the meme. Put more simply, memes tend to adopt images that originated in the news or popular culture. This promotes instant recognition of an idea from future audiences (Varis & Blommaert, 2015), a fact furthered by the relationship between memes and popular culture or real-time events. Knobel and Lankshear (2007, p. 209) acknowledge the "rich kind of intertextuality, such as wry cross-references to different everyday and popular culture events, icons or phenomena" as being crucial to the successful spreading of a particular meme. The "binders full of women" example previously mentioned is testament to this as the audience is required to draw on their cultural knowledge of the presidential debate to make meaning from the meme.

A final important aspect of Internet memes and their polyvocal propagation within the political sphere is the anonymity surrounding their creation and distribution. Davison (2012) contends that memes actually encourage non-attribution and participation beneath a veil of anonymity, which in turn has the effect of nurturing new, more transgressive, and more dynamic forms of communication. In other words, creators of Internet memes can liberally share their political views regardless of how offensive, inaccurate, or unpopular they are as a direct result of not being linked to authorship and thus accountability. We wish to stress that although Internet memes already represent a form of polyvocal political participation, the anonymity involved is crucial in fostering increased participation, especially in comparison to other social media platforms that require individuals to be named participants.

The Study

From the outset of this project, we determined that the study would focus on two phases of the election: the primary and the general-election campaigns. In the context of the primaries, the Hillary Clinton versus Bernie Sanders contest formed the focus of our analysis. Our decision to focus on the Democratic primary was largely due to the fact that the Republican nomination still comprised 12 candidates in February 2016, while at the same time the battle for the Democratic nomination was already a two-horse race and remained so for an extended period, which accounted for the large quantity of memes to emerge from the period. During the actual general-election campaign, our analysis focused on the Republican candidate (Donald Trump) and the Democratic candidate (Hillary Clinton) from the perspective of delegitimization raised by the citizenry through Internet memes. Our data was sourced from two specific sites dedicated to memes (http://politicalmemes.com and http://knowyourmeme.com) as well as from Google image search with terms such as "2016 election memes," "Trump and Clinton memes," and "Clinton and Sanders memes." From the Google search approach, only those memes from the first two pages of results were considered for data selection to ensure the most viewed and shared memes were analyzed. From each phase the 20 memes that the authors both agreed were the best examples of memes utilizing humor and undertaking acts of delegitimization were retained for analysis (40 in total). These were the standards selected due to memes typically incorporating humor and also the manner in which they are typically used to negatively characterize the target. Among these are included those that were especially widely shared or commonly adapted. Given our space constraints only a representative selection of these memes can be shared within this chapter.

Analytical Framework

Our data were analyzed in accordance with the principles of CDA. According to Fairclough (2013) any CDA should relate textual discourses (including memes) to social processes or the social factors that produced the text (including political). In other words, the analysis needs to tend to "the relationship between what is communicated and the social realities tied to that communication" (Milner, 2013a, p. 2362). Considering the varying focus points of the Clinton versus Sanders primary and the Clinton versus Trump general-election contest, a CDA approach enabled us to engage critically with the positions being taken and the arguments being made within the memes. In order to frame the analysis, we adapted Fairclough's (2001) three-dimensional conception of discourse (see Figure 15.4) as a means of conceptualizing the collected memes as examples of participatory political discourse artifacts. We have adapted Fairclough's original conceptualization to reflect the manner in which Internet memes are created, shared, adapted, and shared again in an ongoing, circular manner. In other words, each type of practice in a meme interacts with the next.

Consistent with the three-dimensional conception of discourse presented in Figure 15.4, our analysis began with the identification of the text itself—in this case, each particular meme. As the main area of interest in the present study is understanding how memes have been propagated that "make a point" in relation to the 2016 election, our analysis focused upon the second and third dimensions of the respective discursive and social practices at work. In other words, first the analysis examined the discursive practices involved in producing the meme (e.g., language use, image juxtaposition, or the use of humor or irony). Then, the sociopolitical factors contributing to the production of the meme and the establishment of the point or message were explored, including

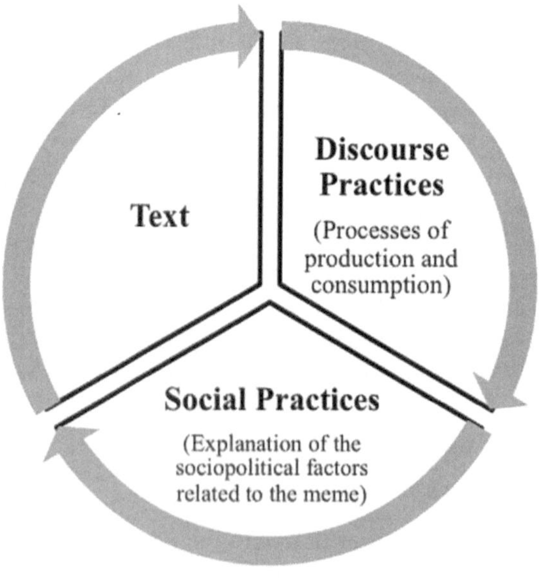

FIGURE 15.4 Adapted from Fairclough's (2001) Three-Dimensional Conception of Discourse

relevant intertextual relationships. An important part of the third dimension of social processes was considering the other semantic properties of the meme that draw on the audience's background knowledge in relation to other aspects of the campaign or candidate histories. As all individuals bring different knowledge backgrounds, influences, and ideologies to a text, the interpretations and explanations can only ever be viewed as subjective. This observation is amplified in the case of memes, where any hope of identifying a more objective message is hidden by the anonymity that memes offer to the creator. We propose two research questions in order to structure the following analysis and discussion:

RQ1: What discursive practices were used in the 2016 U.S. presidential election meme's production and how do they represent Milner's (2013a) concept of polyvocality?

RQ2: How do social practices reveal the point or political stance of the meme and how is this established through humor, delegitimization, and/or intertextuality in relation to the sociopolitical environment of the 2016 U.S. presidential election?

Analysis and Discussion

As foregrounded above, the memes selected for analysis were drawn from two phases of the election, different both in temporality and in focus: the Hillary Clinton versus Bernie Sanders primary contest and the Donald Trump versus Hillary Clinton general-election contest.

Hillary Clinton vs. Bernie Sanders: Democratic Party Presidential Primary

Although it varied, the majority of memes in the Democratic Party primary appeared to support Bernie Sanders. One frequently shared and iterated meme highlighted the polyvocal nature of memes. The image mimicked the type of poster commonly seen before any election, with headshots of Hillary Clinton and Bernie Sanders in front of the U.S. national flag (see Figure 15.5 for two derivations of this meme). The candidates were positioned next to each other under a banner asking the audience to compare the candidates on issues that matter. Three blank boxes can be seen, one for the purpose of defining the issue and one under each of the candidates. This image macro meme template therefore invites participants to express a political opinion that will favor one candidate over the other. The responses triggered typically utilized various forms of humor to express a political preference for Bernie Sanders.

In terms of the discursive practices involved, in these examples the visual component plays a minor role, identifying the targets of the meme by juxtaposing their headshots. Beyond this, the discursive practices centered on the use of

FIGURE 15.5A-B Examples of Hillary Clinton vs. Bernie Sanders Memes

humor as a means of delegitimizing. Regarding humor, the two memes adopt sarcasm, as the issues of *Star Wars* or Radiohead could hardly be considered "issues that matter". Concerning the textual component, there are similarities in the way in which Hillary Clinton and Bernie Sanders are presented, which in turn represents "the text producer's experience of the natural or social world" (Fairclough, 2001, p. 93). Each meme portrays the candidates differently through the text used, and this reflects a relational value in that the creator is establishing a social distance between the audience and the subjects, and also between the candidates themselves.

With the humorous framing of the memes established in the irrelevant and non-consequential issues defined, the memes take a more critical stance via the use of sarcasm to delegitimize Hillary Clinton. The first example presents the supposed views on Star Wars of each candidate. Whereas Bernie Sanders is depicted as providing an in-depth comment on the movie franchise as a whole, Hillary Clinton is depicted as producing a gesture associated not with *Star Wars*, but *Star Trek*, thereby portraying her as lame and disconnected from common popular culture. The second example frames the English rock band Radiohead as the issue that matters. Bernie Sanders is again depicted as demonstrating a depth of knowledge through critically analyzing part of the band's catalogue and its importance, therefore positioning him as a man of the people through a shared awareness and understanding of popular music. In contrast, Hillary Clinton is depicted as having nothing more to say other than her appreciation of the band's most successful mainstream track (i.e., "Creep"). The selection of Radiohead as an issue that matters may well have been used as the set-up to deliver a punchline that associates Hillary Clinton with the word "Creep."

In relation to making a point (Shifman, 2014), the two delegitimizing memes outlined make use of a strategy known as "moral evaluation" (Van Leeuwen, 2007), whereby through comparison one idea, person, or position is characterized positively or negatively. From a positive, legitimizing perspective, one person will be shown as similar to another in light of some specified or implied value and/or belief. Conversely, from a negative, delegitimizing perspective, such as that occurring in the Hillary Clinton/Bernie Sanders memes, the memes show difference between the two actors, with one of the individuals negatively cast in relation to the other individual. The *point* of these memes and the numerous other iterations is that Bernie Sanders is understood as well informed and in touch, whereas Hillary Clinton is shown as superficial, ill informed, and out of touch. When reduced to their most basic meaning, the discursive practices adopted in creating the memes have established the message of Bernie Sanders = good and Hillary Clinton = bad. The discourse practice then in turn highlights the "social processes they are a part of" (Fairclough, 1992, p. 80) in that a distinct political stance or ideological preference is revealed by the creators.

The memes in Figure 15.5 display a relationship with other texts and a full interpretation and explanation can only be achieved through the audience drawing on their knowledge of other texts, of which traces or social cues are evident within the meme. For example, the memes shown in Figure 15.5 draw heavily on popular culture. If, for instance, the audience was not familiar with the work of Radiohead, the intended message and point of the meme would not be effectively interpreted. In other words, the intention of the creator would be lost. Similarly, if the audience was unfamiliar with the cinematic texts of *Star Wars* and *Star Trek*, the intended act of delegitimization would also be rendered unsuccessful. Therefore, the expression of political opinions or political participation through memes comes with a certain amount of risk and demands that the creator produce humorous content that is highly relatable to a large audience. Although popular culture can be seen as a somewhat safe option, there is still no guarantee that the intention of the creator will be understood by a general audience, as other variables such as audience demographics including age and gender will also likely have an impact.

In comparison to the general-election campaigns, a point of interest within the primaries is that the memes (or any other form of media) favoring either Hillary Clinton or Bernie Sanders were created by supporters of the Democratic Party, or at the very least, non-supporters of the Republican Party. This creates a situation of two possible effects that highlight the social practices in the memes. The first is that the creator will vote for the Democratic Party even in the event of their preferred candidate being unsuccessful in the primary. On the other hand, this situation could fall under the "divisive primary hypothesis," which Kenney and Rice (1987, p. 33) argue can have a negative impact on a party's likelihood of victory in a main election as intense and competitive primary campaigns "forge strong in-group loyalties and out-group hostilities, leaving many of the supporters of losing candidates unwilling to vote for their party's candidate." The result being that an individual either votes for the opposition or abstains from voting (Wichowsky & Niebler, 2010), which ultimately can be perceived as a form of self-sabotage from a political party perspective. Put more simply, as an example, imagine the many Sanders supports who created and/or shared memes that criticized and delegitimized Clinton in an attempt to help Sanders win the nomination. When this failed, if the Sanders supporters and others who may have been influenced by political memes decide not to vote, they are essentially aiding the opposing party in their election campaign. Thus, memes encountered as part of the Hillary Clinton/Bernie Sanders contest should be considered in relation to both of these possibilities, although the ultimate effect can never truly be measured.

All said, the memes presented in Figure 15.5 in relation to the Democratic primary take a stance in favor of Sanders through the use of humor, delegitimizing discourse, and intertextuality. Variations on only one meme template have been presented, but there were hundreds of other Clinton/Sanders memes circulating throughout the primaries, many of which appeared to support Clinton and oppose Sanders. This further highlights Milner's (2013a) idea of polyvocality in public discourse, which is further compounded when we consider that the memes presented represent a minute portion of those that emerged during the primaries for both parties.

The Delegitimization of Donald Trump in the General Election

A plethora of Donald Trump memes emerged throughout the presidential campaign. Many of these portrayed him in a negative light, and this was generally done on the basis of his assumed persona, his alleged personal affairs, and his questionable policies. The memes presented in Figures 15.6, 15.7, and 15.8 either relate to statements he allegedly made during and prior to the election campaign and the policies that the media highlighted as being central to his campaign.

FIGURE 15.6 Trump Delegitimization Meme 1

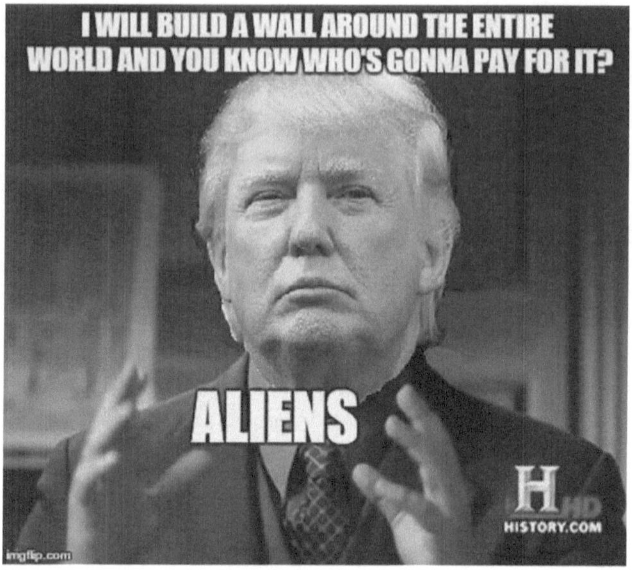

FIGURE 15.7 Trump Delegitimization Meme 2

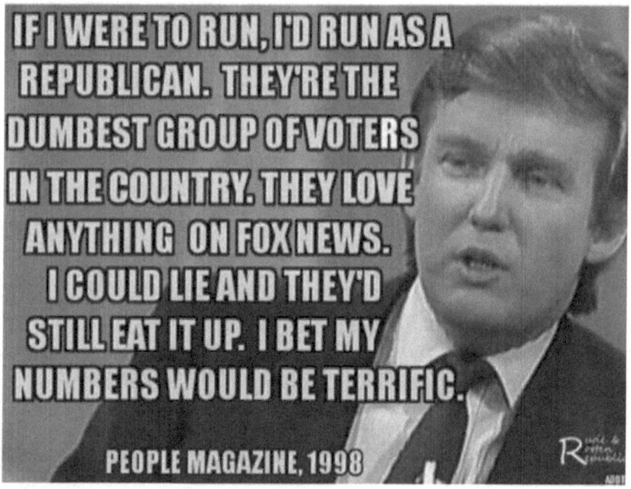

FIGURE 15.8 Trump Delegitimization Meme 3

Each meme adopts different discursive practices. Visually, the meme in Figure 15.6 adopts a split-screen format, placing an identical image of Trump in the first, second, and third positions in which he appears to be expressing anger or rage (many populist politicians attract voters on the basis of their perceived strength in the face of an impending threat). The fourth image in the bottom right shows Donald Trump somewhat flippant and dismissive. Alone, these images are meaningless beyond the presentation of emotional states, but with the addition of text they discursively create politically laden humorous meanings. The meme in Figure 15.6 can be said to delegitimize Donald Trump through a comparison of his comments about his position on different groups. Towards Mexicans, Muslims, and the Pope—groups and individuals with no inherently major negative connotation on their own—he is portrayed as insulting and discriminatory. In contrast, the final image presents Trump in a less aggressive mood with reference to the Ku Klux Klan (KKK), known for pushing a White nationalist agenda, where he takes the position that the KKK may not be as unfavorable as is often automatically assumed. The meme is to be interpreted, first, through the readers' awareness of these aspects of his campaign, and secondly by observing the order of the text. In the first three images the textual subjects are Mexicans, Muslims, and the Pope—groups who have no inherently negative connotations attached—and this is followed by Trump's views on them. Conversely, in the final image, the subject is the KKK, a group generally known negatively for promoting racist views and bigotry. In this image, this group, however, is followed by Trump's opinion, which is markedly neutral in comparison to the other groups. This approach to the use of images and the arrangement of the textual components adds emphasis to the message the meme conveys.

Intertextuality also plays a role in the interpretation of the meme in Figure 15.6, as without prior knowledge of Donald Trump's comments towards the groups featured, it would be more difficult to establish meaning or, more importantly, to believe the point being made in the meme. The discursive practices employed merge with the sociopolitical practices in the sense that the creator's political standpoint is shown to be that Donald Trump's position towards minority groups or religious leaders, as in the case of the Pope, is offensive, discriminatory, and therefore not presidential. At the same time, this is juxtaposed against his tolerance or indifference towards groups such as the KKK, a move intended to delegitimize his candidacy further.

Depicting Donald Trump with a contemplative facial expression, the meme shown in Figure 15.7 rephrases Donald Trump's border wall policy proposal with exaggerated sarcasm, highlighting the creator's "evaluation (in the widest sense) of the bit of reality it relates to" (Fairclough, 2001, p. 93). Through the discursive practices used, the creator appears to be drawing attention to the irrationality and unlikelihood of the policy and the effect is to highlight that "humor, ridicule, and mockery are part of an overall architecture of delegitimization" (Hodson & MacInnis, 2016, p. 69). As in the previous example, to interpret the humor adopted in the meme, the audience must first draw on their intertextual understanding and awareness of Donald Trump's stated policy with regard to the proposed U.S.-Mexico border wall. There is an additional intertextual reference here to the History Channel series *Ancient Aliens* featuring Giorgio A. Tsoukalos, from which the still image forming the basis of this meme was taken. Thus, there can be seen a reference to a prior text from a TV program, but then also a new derivation of a previous meme (this "aliens" meme featuring the original image of Tsoukalos has been widely adapted and shared, attributing the cause of a wide variety of often unrelated events to aliens). Then, there is also an inherent requirement that the reader sees Donald Trump's proposed policy as totally irrational—particularly with regard to his suggestion that Mexico would be required to pay for the construct of the wall. With these conditions in place, the meme utilizes sarcasm as a means of establishing a lack of social reality in the relationship between the proposed policy and its likelihood of implementation and success. In other words, such is the absurdity of the proposed policy as a foundation for a presidential candidate: the meme expresses that it is just as likely that aliens would be willing to pay for a wall around the entire world.

Through the discursive practices involved, the meme shown in Figure 15.8 makes a concerted attempt to delegitimize Donald Trump by trying to establish an antagonistic divide between Donald Trump and his own political party. This meme demonstrates the great change that has occurred in polyvocal political participation through greater access provided by social media and in particular Internet memes. To preface this explanation, in relation to the 1988 presidential election, Blumler (1990) described how ordinary citizens had been almost totally excluded from participating in the election from their place in the public sphere as a result of political professionals and advocates assuming dominate positions (in the distribution and control of information). This exclusion created a "cycle of cynicism and fakery, contributing to a climate of mutual antagonism" (Bucy & Gregson, 2001, p. 363) among politicians and media. However, in the current environment that supports participatory digital cultures and the emergence of many voices, this type of antagonism can be instigated *by* ordinary citizens, and not through *excluding* them. Taken at face value, the meme in Figure 15.8 shows Donald Trump as being disrespectful towards Republican voters, which could *potentially* have the effect of influencing their vote if they accept the information shown at face value. At this point, a new perspective on intertextuality emerges, as the textual component of the meme is founded on a prior text (attributed to an interview in *People* magazine) that does not actually exist—it is a fake and can therefore be seen as an effort to sabotage the relationship between the Republican party supporters and the candidate chosen to represent them.

Therefore, there is an *implied* intertextuality, which is a new phenomenon in media contexts. Building a negative characterization upon a total falsehood could not be done so easily in the past, perhaps due to greater integrity within the journalistic profession and the reliance that many people had upon traditional forms of news media. The anonymity of the creator therefore assumes a status as crucial in this instance, as whomever created and proliferated this meme is protected by anonymity and need not be concerned with the potential consequences of producing false and misleading information, or fake news, such as this. Importantly, the sociopolitical practices at play here are founded on dishonesty and fraudulent claims, but the stance of the creator can be seen through the creation of a social disconnect between Donald Trump and the Republican Party, which in effect shows Donald Trump as being disrespectful and arrogant, thereby attempting to delegitimize him as a candidate. However, and as the election result suggests, a miscalculation was made here as these typical characteristics and qualities that may be used to delegitimize a presidential candidate (even Hillary Clinton) were seen by a significant number of Republican Party voters as being desirable. Therefore, the meme shown in Figure 15.8, although attributing a false quotation to Donald Trump, may, in this instance, have worked in his favor.

Overall, the memes discussed featuring Donald Trump mocked and derided him and as such were an attempt at delegitimization through transmitting a negative image of him. By placing emphasis on the policies he has proposed and on some of his views towards groups of people, the memes depict him as having values not aligned with those who support legitimacy, including compassion, respect, and honesty. The effects of these memes are to add to the polyvocal nature of political participation as citizens engage with events as they happen in real time in the lead-up to the election and to highlight further the avenue that Internet memes provide to citizens of the electorate.

The Delegitimization of Hillary Clinton in the General Election

As with Donald Trump, a large number of memes targeting Hillary Clinton emerged during the election contest and generally portrayed her negatively. A particular focus for this negative depiction was her ongoing email controversy, as shown in Figures 15.9 and 15.10. The meme in Figure 15.9 depicts an image of former President Richard Nixon, and his image attributes the textual component, in this case a narrative admission and observation, to him in a statement comparing his own behavior with the alleged behavior of Hillary Clinton. The textual element represents Richard Nixon's own voice in comparing the severity of Hillary Clinton's email deletions to his own actions and suggests that Hillary Clinton's actions are more severe or morally questionable. The comparison established between the actions Richard Nixon and Hillary Clinton allegedly took and the subsequent effect on both individuals creates the delegitimizing tone, not only of both, but also with specific degrees of wrongdoing. This meme incorporates an ironic tone in that, for Richard Nixon, the result of his Watergate involvement was ultimately his resignation, whereas Hillary Clinton remained a presidential candidate. Another significant connection to be made here is again with intertextuality as "each word tastes of a context and contexts in which it has lived its socially charged life" (Bahktin, 1981, p. 293). Internet memes, as has been shown, are often a form of text influenced by the content of previous texts, in this case Richard Nixon's press conference denying involvement in the

FIGURE 15.9 Hillary Clinton Delegitimization Meme 1

FIGURE 15.10 Hillary Clinton Delegitimization Meme 2

Watergate scandal and the well-known quote "I am not a crook." In short, and showing how memes are able to transcend across time and space in relation to the public record, this meme recalls an historic comment made by a former president and formulates a closely related question directed at a presidential candidate.

Similarly, the meme shown in Figure 15.10 creates a comparison that sets up a delegitimizing comparative that transcends time and space. However, in this case it is whistle-blower Edward Snowden, the former CIA employee who leaked classified information pertaining to U.S. government surveillance programs that Hillary Clinton is aligned with. As was shown in relation to Richard Nixon, the comparison is used to delegitimize Hillary Clinton by juxtaposing her image (notably, the same image from the "texts with Hillary" memes—another example of memes referencing prior memes) with Edward Snowden's and executing a relatively small alteration to the text that suggests that Clinton is alleged to have carried out the same action as Snowden, but with significantly different results for each party—Snowden is exiled and Clinton almost became president. These results are highlighted through the discursive use of irony or shock in the manner in which the question "wanted for president?" is posed, and this discursive practice then merges with the social practices as the creator uncovers the hypocrisy of the scenario. It is in this merging of the discursive and social practices that the point of the meme becomes clear. In terms of how these memes delegitimize Clinton, we argue that the memes in both Figure 15.9 and Figure 15.10 put greater distance between acceptable and unacceptable behavior for a presidential candidate.

Conclusion

The 2016 U.S. presidential election was a demonstration in the continuously increasing use of media as a form of political engagement and active citizenship. As platforms such as Facebook and Twitter remain the most frequented platforms for accessing information and sharing viewpoints online, the propagation of Internet memes has continued to rise. Due to the relative simplicity of creating and sharing memes in parallel with actual election events, creators and consumers utilized humor and delegitimization strategies as a means of making a point and sharing an opinion, perspective, or preference. With the circular flow of creation, diffusion, and re-iteration involving various discursive and social practices and processes, the Internet memes shown in the present chapter have provided an insight into how they were employed during the Democratic presidential primary and the general-election campaign to, on the surface, make a joke or a comment, but on a more critical level to engage with the political process and reveal a political position.

Although only a representative sample of the memes collected for the study are presented and discussed in this chapter, there were important insights gleaned from the entirety of the collected memes in relation to how they are utilized as a form of political participation. For example, the sheer mass of variety was evident, ranging from memes that were very widely shared in the form of minor adaptations of images emerging from the elections such as "Birdie Sanders," to memes referencing prior memes and other media texts such as the "ancient aliens" meme in relation to Trump's proposed wall. Added to this are memes that could be considered one-off image macros that are created and made public but do not achieve any virality, yet represent an example of a citizen (creator) making a statement in relation to their political position that may or may not be seen, believed, and adopted by others. It is the variety of meme types and sharing potential that expand the possibilities of their use as a tool of political participation.

In relation to the research questions posed in the present chapter, the range of discourse practices Internet memes employ has been demonstrated in relation to both production and consumption. The consumption of the memes then linked with the social practices involved, which arose from the point the creator was trying to make and the sociopolitical environment from which the meme emerged. All memes presented represent the concept of "polyvocality" in that they were a small selection of a plethora of memes emergent from the 2016 election, and as such once each meme was created, a new voice and a new perspective was added to the online public discourse surrounding the election. Although it remains a challenge to measure the direct influence of Internet memes, the anonymity that protects creators and allows the sharing of controversial ideas and even false news is critical, and is something that must be carefully considered in future political processes.

References

Anderson, B. (1991). *Imagined communities*. London, UK: Verso.

Androutsopoulos, J. (2009). Language and the three spheres of hip hop. In H. S. Alim, A. Ibrahim & A. Pennycook (Eds.), *Global linguistic flows: Hip hop cultures, youth identities, and the politics of language* (pp. 43–62). New York, NY: Routledge.

Bahktin, M. (1981). *The dialogic imagination: Four essays*. (C. Emerson & M. Holquist, Trans.). Austin, TX: University of Austin Press.

Blumler, J. G. (1990). Elections, the media, and the modern publicity process. In M. Ferguson (Ed.), *Public communication: The new imperatives* (pp. 101–113). London: Sage.

Bucy, E. P., & Gregson, K. S. (2001). Media participation: A legitimizing mechanism of mass democracy. *New Media & Society*, *3*(3), 357–380. doi:10.1177/1461444801003003006

Buell, E. H., & Maus, M. (1988). Is the pen mightier than the sword? Editorial cartoons and 1988 presidential nominating politics. *Political Science and Politics*, *21*(4), 847–585. doi:10.2307/420024

Burgess, J. (2007). *Vernacular creativity and new media* (Unpublished PhD thesis). Queensland University of Technology, Brisbane, Australia.

Burroughs, B. (2013). Obama trolling: Memes, salutes and an agonistic politics in the 2012 presidential election. *The Fibreculture Journal*, *22*, 257–276.

Dahlgren, P. (2009). *Media and political engagement: Citizens, communication and democracy*. Cambridge, UK: Cambridge University Press.

Davis, C. B., Glantz, M., & Novak, D. R. (2016). 'You can't run your SUV on cute. Let's go!': Internet memes as delegitimizing discourse. *Environmental Communication*, *10*(1), 62–83. doi:10.1080/17524032.2014.991411

Davison, P. (2012). The language of Internet memes. In M. Mandiberg (Ed.), *The social media reader* (pp. 120–136). New York, NY: New York University Press.
DeLuca, K. M., Lawson, S., & Sun, Y. (2012). Occupy Wall Street on the public screens of social media: The many framings of the birth of a protest movement. *Communication, Culture & Critique, 5*(2), 483–509. doi:10.1111/j.1753–9137.2012.01141.x
Fairclough, N. (1992). *Discourse and social change.* Cambridge, UK: Polity Press.
Fairclough, N. (2001). *Language and power.* London, UK: Longman.
Fairclough, N. (2013). *Critical discourse analysis.* New York, NY: Routledge.
Francesconi, R. A. (1982). James Hunt, the Wilmington 10, and institutional legitimacy. *Quarterly Journal of Speech, 68*(1), 47–59. doi:10.1080/00335638209383591
Gal, N., Shifman, L., & Kampf, Z. (2016). 'It gets better': Internet memes and the construction of collective identity. *New Media & Society, 18*(8), 1698–1714. doi:10.1177/1461444814568784
Gil de Zúñiga, H., Molyneaux, L., & Zheng, P. (2014). Social media, political expression, and political participation: Panel analysis of lagged and concurrent relationships. *Journal of Communication, 64*(4), 612–634. doi:10.1111/jcom.12103
Hodson, G., & MacInnis, C. C. (2016). Derogating humor as a delegitimization strategy in intergroup contexts. *Translational Issues in Psychological Science, 2*(1), 63–74. doi:10.1037/tps0000052
Kenney, P. J., & Rice, T. W. (1987). The relationship between divisive primaries and general election outcomes. *American Journal of Political Science, 31*(1), 31–44. doi:10.2307/2111323
Knobel, M., & Lankshear, C. (2007). Online memes, affinities, and cultural production. In M. Knobel & C. Lankshear (Eds.), *A new literacies sampler: Everyday practices and classroom learning* (pp. 199–228). New York, NY: Peter Lang.
Kristeva, J. (1980). The bounded text. In L. S. Roudiez (Ed.), *Desire in language: A semiotic approach to literature and art* (pp. 36–63). New York, NY: Columbia University Press.
Loader, B. D., Vromen, A., & Xenos, M. A. (2014). The networked young citizen: Social media, political participation and civic engagement. *Information, Communication & Society, 17*(2), 143–150. doi:10.1080/1369118X.2013.871571
Milner, R. M. (2013a). Pop polyvocality: Internet memes, public participation, and the Occupy Wall Street movement. *International Journal of Communication, 7*, 2357–2390.
Milner, R. M. (2013b). Internet memes, identity antagonism, and the logic of lulz. *The Fibreculture Journal, 22*, 62–92.
Miranda, C. A. (2016, October 20). From Clinton's shimmy to Pepe the frog: Memes and the LOLcat effect on the 2016 election. *The Los Angeles Times.* Retrieved from www.latimes.com
Nissenbaum, A., & Shifman, L. (2015). Internet memes as contested cultural capital: The case of 4chan's/b/board. *New Media & Society, 19*(4), 484–501. doi:10.1177/1461444815609313
Paul, K. (2016). *How Memes Shaped the 2016 Presidential Election.* Retrieved from http://au.complex.com/life/2016/05/election-memes
Screti, F. (2013). Defending joy against the popular revolution: Legitimation and delegitimation through songs. *Critical Discourse Studies, 10*(2), 205–222. doi:10.1080/17405904.2013.764614
Shifman, L. (2007). Humor in the age of digital production: Continuity and change in Internet-based comic texts. *International Journal of Communication, 1*, 187–209.
Shifman, L. (2014). *Memes in digital culture.* Cambridge, MA: MIT Press.

Tay, G. (2014). Binders full of LOLitics: Political humour, Internet memes, and play in the 2012 US presidential election (and beyond). *The European Journal of Humour Research, 2*(4), 46–73. doi:10.7592/EJHR2014.2.4.tay

Vaara, E. (2014). Struggles over legitimacy in the Eurozone crisis: Discursive legitimation strategies and their ideological underpinnings. *Discourse and Society, 25*(4), 500–518. doi:10.1177/0957926514536962

Van Leeuwen, T. (2007). Legitimation in discourse and communication. *Discourse & Communication, 1*(1), 91–112. doi:10.1177/1750481307071986

Varis, P., & Blommaert, J. (2015). Conviviality and collectives on social media: Virality memes, and new social structures. *Multilingual Margins, 2*(1), 31–45.

Verba, S., & Nie, N. H. (1972). *Participation in America: Political democracy and social equality*. New York, NY: Harper & Row.

Wichowsky, A., & Niebler, S. E. (2010). Narrow victories and hard games: Revisiting the primary divisiveness hypothesis. *American Politics Research, 38*(6), 1052–1071. doi:10.1177/1532673X10369660

Xenos, M., Vromen, A., & Loader, B. (2014). The great equalizer? Patterns of social media use and youth political engagement in three advanced democracies. *Information, Communication & Society, 17*(2), 151–167. doi:10.1080/1369118X.2013.871318

16

ENGAGED BRIGADE

Digital Platforms and Millennial Engagement in the 2016 Election

Alison N. Novak

Less than one week after *Vanity Fair* published a ringing endorsement of Hillary Clinton for president of the U.S., the magazine tweeted a follow-up article where they questioned her ability to win the election because of lackluster support from a critical group of voters: the Millennial generation (Nguyen, 2016). Since 2008, Millennials (those born between 1981 and 2001) have dramatically shaped the political landscape and been credited with two major presidential victories (CIRCLE, 2012). However, like other news publications at the time, *Vanity Fair* wondered if Clinton, or any 2016 candidate for that matter, could capitalize on the generation's interests, power, and political engagement (Nguyen, 2016). Amongst their reasoning for this critique was the sudden disappearance of Millennials within political groups in traditional social media platforms such as Facebook and Twitter (Rucker, 2016). *Vanity Fair* and numerous other publications cited an August 2016 Pew study that revealed Millennials were exiting the platforms and participating in less political communication than in previous election cycles (Fry, 2016). *The Guardian, Washington Post*, and *The Atlantic* all suggested this was a sign of the political disengagement of the generation—a common narrative of youth political participation through history (Brownstein, 2016; Nguyen, 2016; Rucker, 2016).

However, this was not Pew's interpretation of their findings. If Millennials were not talking politics on Facebook and Twitter like they were in 2008 and 2012, then they had to be somewhere else (Fry, 2016). Perhaps they were on the latest social media platform designed for Millennials and their political interests: Brigade. Publicly launched in April 2016, Brigade reported that three million Millennials created accounts within the first six months of operation (Nevius, 2016). The platform, designed to facilitate Millennial involvement in the upcoming election, host debates over campaign issues, and produce a user-generated guide for new voters, was instantly recognized by other media outlets for its popularity and potential to impact the 2016 electoral outcome through the Millennial generation's engagement (Castillo, 2015; Mangalindan, 2015).

Although previous research has examined extensively how social media platforms impact political engagement (especially by Millennials), few studies have had the opportunity to look at how this process begins, in the earliest phases of a new platform. Previous studies on political debates, discourses, and discussions on Facebook and Twitter occur years after the platform gained popularity. Due to Brigade's newness, this project can lend insight into how political engagement manifests within a digital space as it popularizes and matures against the backdrop of a national election. This chapter addresses the following questions: How did Millennials users engage the 2016 election in a new social media platform? How did Millennial users view their own political agency, particularly as it is mediated by Brigade users, mass media, and older generations? Finally, how did the structure, affordances, and design of Brigade encourage or facilitate political engagement in the 2016 election?

Millennials and the 2016 Election

Despite record-breaking youth voter turnout during the 2008 and 2012 presidential elections, media coverage questioned if Millennials would participate in the 2016 election. As the Millennial generation matured into voting eligibility, their maturation was heavily narrated by discourses of political disengagement and apathy (Novak, 2016). Largely, mass media criticized the group for their perceived lack of interest in politics and failure to follow traditional paths to political engagement (e.g., Seipel, 2014).

However, scholars question if these mass media narratives are based on empirical observations of Millennials or rather a continuation of cultural discourses that position youth and new adaptations of civic engagement as inferior to older, established models (Stewart & Bernhardt, 2010). Researchers in the spirit of Stuart Hall argue that media narratives of youth engagement are almost always emblematic of tensions stemming from a new, younger generation replacing an older, traditional group or audience (Hall & Jefferson, 2006; Jordan, 2015; Montgomery, 2009; Novak, 2016). As a result, the journalistic treatment of Millennial participation is shrouded in falsehoods and intrinsic biases against youth groups (Turner, 2009).

Negative press coverage of political agency is coupled with the generations adoption of new, digital technologies that challenge and possibly harm the political economics of traditional media journalism (Spurgeon, Ferrier, Gunders, & Graham, 2012). Researchers propose that Millennial adoptions of digital news platforms and technologies have produced negative coverage of the group in traditional news publications (such as newspapers and television broadcasts) (Novak, 2016). Millennials are frequently blamed for recent hardships (i.e., declining advertising revenue) faced by traditional media because of their adoption and popularization of digital media platforms that have profited from the attention of the world's largest generation (Kelly, 2006). Coupling the normative tension of one generation replacing the other (described above) with this anxiety over the proliferation and possible replacement of digital news media over traditional sources results in critical and negative media narratives of Millennials in many facets of American culture, including politics and civics (Kelly, 2006). Other research has demonstrated how these negative Millennial discourses are then adopted by the mass public or audience and further integrated into the structure of daily life (Spurgeon at al., 2012).

Partially, the diversity of America's largest generation complicates media narratives of the Millennial engagement with politics. Although research from CIRCLE (2012) argues the Millennial generation is largely liberal leaning, there are few issues, politicians, and organizations that centrally unify the group (Milkman, 2017). The economic, racial, educational, and geographical diversity of the group challenges researchers and media to completely understand and predict the behaviors of the group, particularly in an electoral context. Despite the uncertain and somewhat negative discourses that surround the Millennial generation, a growing body of scholarship identifies the age group as being incredibly relevant and effective in American elections (Huntley, 2006). In both 2008 and 2012, Millennials broke American records by having the highest generational percentage of turnout of any group (over 50% in both elections) (CIRCLE, 2012).

Although Millennials understand their own political impact, they are also sensitive to the negative media discourses that surround their political engagement (Kelly, 2006). Previous scholarship finds this has caused Millennials (and other coalition members) to report feeling left out or unwanted in traditional channels, thus they seek alternative forms of civic engagement (Novak, Johnson, & Pontes, 2016). For example, Hispanics and African Americans turned to coordinating civic movements such as "Black Lives Matter" through social media rather than working with established political action or social justice groups because they felt unwelcome in those channels (Novak et al., 2016). Similarly, scholars propose this movement online (and the popularization of digital platforms) is partially explained by the desire of coalition members to engage civically, politically, and socially against a political environment that made it difficult for them to find routes to participation.

Millennials, in particular, identify the ways that traditional routes to political engagement are blocked. First, Millennials reported they were turned away from volunteering for candidates (or were only assigned remedial tasks when volunteering) (Rabina, 2009). Second, the group faces a complicated voter-registration procedure (including controversial voter ID laws that inhibit young, minority voters) (Bennett, 2015). Finally, they felt that candidate platforms excluded or countered their interests and well-being (Ross & Rouse, 2015). Again, Millennials reported they went online to participate in order to overcome and bypass these obstructions to their engagement.

These new paths to civic engagement are criticized by the media as less authentic, effective, or useful than traditional participation (Metzger, Erete, Barton, Desler, & Lewis, 2015). Journalists have taken to calling this digitally oriented engagement "slacktivism," (implying the generation's engagement takes less effort and is less important) and have frequently debated its merits and worthiness (Zuckerman, 2014). Social movements that proliferate from digital spaces and new forms of engagement (such as Black Lives Matter, Occupy Wall Street, and Adios Arpaio) are often criticized and labeled as inferior or problematic because of their digital origins (Zuckerman, 2014). And, although the users who originate and support these movements argue against this narrative, their status as members of the coalition and minorities limits their ability to challenge these mass media discourses (Metzger et al., 2015).

It is against this political backdrop that Brigade was beta-tested in 2015. Platform developers recognized the digitization of political engagement and the efforts of coalition members (and Millennials in particular) to participate in the political process despite being turned away from traditional paths (Mangalindan, 2015). The growing political power of Millennials (as members of the group continued to reach voting age) justified the development of a new digital application in which Millennials could enact their political participation and agency away from the reaches of negative traditional media coverage (Rabina, 2009). Although political pundits continually debated if the group would impact the 2016 outcome, in the months leading up to the election, Millennials were vocal and active in digital platforms on political and electoral topics.

Scholars and Brigade creators were not the only ones to recognize the new, digital forms of engagement enacted by the Millennial generation. Presidential candidates (and their campaign teams) attempted to woo the group (and others) through digital media. For example, Hillary Clinton attempted to start a Twitter conversation on student loan debt with emojis; John Kasich made a bacon snapchat filter; and Rand Paul released a photo app that strongly resembled Instagram. In short, candidates attempted (some better than others) to appeal to young voters through the development of digital content (Stanek, 2015). It is worth noting that many young Millennials were critical of these "inauthentic" attempts to attract the group through surface-level digital content, calling them "humiliatingly lame" and summarizing these efforts with, "Often, they end up looking like my 64-year-old dad—who is still convinced Facebook steals your identity and has asked "What's a Twitter?"—if he suddenly tried to act like he was super savvy at sending snaps" (Stanek, 2015, para. 2).

In effect, Millennials voiced that they felt attacked by the amount of attention they were now receiving in digital spaces by political campaigns and candidates. Platforms of engagement such as Facebook, Twitter, and Instagram, where they turned to avoid negative narratives of apathy in 2008 and 2012, were quickly co-opted and overrun by the same political machines that once alienated and barred them from entry (Stanek, 2015). Brigade creators stepped in, proposing their digital platform as a new space for Millennials to form collective action and engage politically (Mangalindan, 2015). Brigade was positioned as a new space for Millennials to engage the political process, participate in civic issues centered on social justice, and enact their political agency within the upcoming election. However, what that engagement might look like, and its value within the 2016 election, was still up for debate.

Digital Platforms of Voter Engagement

As noted, traditional media narratives of digital political engagement have been largely critical and negative, particularly as they are related to the Millennial generation (Novak, 2016). Although scholars debate the origins of digital campaigning, the 2004 presidential election was one of the first to use social media (beyond websites) for campaign purposes. Governor Howard Dean's use in 2004 of MeetUp.org to locate supporters online and form groups that could later meet in physical spaces to campaign for the presidential candidate was considered one of the first multi-modal, multi-directional social media campaigns to capitalize on youth digital preferences (Trippi, 2005). As noted by campaign manager Trippi (2005), this digital grassroots movement for Governor Dean was ignored and discredited by the mass media who discursively described digital engagement as less valuable than the traditional get-out-the-vote efforts of then-Senator John Kerry (McGrath, 2011). Four years later, Barack Obama turned to Facebook and other social media platforms to recruit youth, register voters, and fundraise micro-donations (Hais & Winograd, 2008). Although President Obama was applauded by traditional media for his innovative approach, these accolades were minor compared to the critical discourses that lamented Millennials' reluctance to volunteer traditionally (in this case physically) for the campaign (Hais & Winograd, 2008).

Social movements associated with Millennials are criticized for their origins within digital media. As noted, Black Lives Matter, Occupy Wall Street, and Adios Arpaio (all social protest movements that began online with heavy Millennial participation) were criticized by journalists who questioned if any social movement could truly have strong membership ties or a centralized sense of identity if it began online (Novak et al., 2016; Zuckerman, 2014). Often, journalists compared these movements to past organizations that were deemed successful because of their non-digital, physical origins (Calhoun, 2013). According to Gitlin (1980), this is one way that journalists can discredit or position a protest movement (and its membership) as problematic or ineffective.

Scholars too have failed to reach a consensus regarding the effectiveness and value of digital engagement in politics. Digital engagement is both hailed as a great advancement to democracy and the political process, and simultaneously lamented as the end of civilized political debate and yet another barrier to political entry (Twenge, 2006). In an effort to evaluate the impact and effect political platforms may have on elections, few studies have looked to provide descriptive analyses of how voters use these platforms to engage the process (and how this engagement may be similar or different to previous work).

This uncertainty in the effectiveness and value of digital engagement in presidential elections has coupled with scholars' uncertainty over the identity and value of Millennials in politics. For example, the works of Mindich (2005); Twenge (2006); and Bauerlein (2009) propose Millennials as disengaged in the political process and threatening the foundations of informed citizenry and public opinion that make up the U.S. Each scholar questions if Millennials will outgrow digital preferences that hinder more authentic and effective political engagement practices (such as voting) (Bauerlein, 2009). Previous scholarship has identified that two bodies of research on Millennials exist: one set that perceives their form of digital engagement as an innovative and new approach to politics that should be valued for its difference from traditional norms (Huntley, 2006). Alternatively, a second body of scholarship argues that Millennial reliance on digital platforms for participation is inferior to traditional approaches and, therefore, reflects badly on the ethos and identity of the group (Deal, Altman, & Rogelberg, 2010; Hoffman, 2017; Twenge, 2006).

Noted by previous scholars, political and civic conversations by Millennials on social media platforms are critical to understanding the socio-cultural position of the generation (Mascaro, Novak, & Goggins, 2012). By studying these conversations as a type of engagement, researchers can learn about the motivations and rationale for political engagement. This study follows in the tradition of scholarship that look at new platforms and how they may impact or shape political engagement. In short, a study of Brigade allows researchers to look at how Millennials digitally engage an election, and perhaps generates insight into the value and impact of this engagement.

Brigade

In fall 2015, Napster creator Sean Parker debuted Brigade, a digital application designed to motivate and facilitate political and civic discussion between young voters. Piloted in Manchester, New Hampshire and San Francisco, California, the app provided users with issue preference quizzes, candidate information, and issue-centered debates that were designed to help voters decide who and what to vote for or against. Designed specifically for new voters, a 20-question quiz attempted to triangulate user interests, values, and beliefs, then match those qualities with local and state candidates and policies. Users were also asked to provide a birth year, with a reminder the site was built for "Millennials," but other users could join if they wanted. Users were also encouraged to "pledge" their votes to specific candidates and recruit friends to join the network by sharing their pledges on other social media platforms (specifically Facebook).

In an effort to promote the platform and its civic intentions, Brigade partnered with the *San Francisco Chronicle* and *Philz Coffee* (a San Francisco coffee chain popular with Millennials) to disseminate information about the upcoming 2015 California state elections (Cutler, 2015a, para. 2). Brigade sponsored a series of political discussions, led by editors of the *San Francisco Chronicle* throughout October.

Brigade's targeting of a popular hangout in San Francisco was not accidental. In launching the platform, CEO Matt Mahan described the app intentions to "quickly get regular people engaged in articulating and debating political positions" (Cutler, 2015a, para. 2). He went on to explain that by regular people he meant young Millennial voters whom he viewed as being particularly disadvantaged and ignored by the complex political environment of attack ads and changes in candidate positions. Parker further described Brigade's mission as "disrupting" traditional political agendas and mass media narratives through Millennial civic discussion and action. Both Parker and Mahan positioned the app as a means for Millennials to enact their power and agency within an electoral space that was primarily oriented towards the needs of big businesses, established ideologies, and traditional voters. In effect, Brigade was designed to return power to young voters by providing a collective space for Millennials to organize and enact their political agendas, particularly in the aftermath of Facebook, Twitter, and Instagram being adopted and co-opted by political candidates.

The application launched nationally in April 2016 in time for users to begin downloading and creating profiles during the Democratic and Republican Party primaries. By September 2016, the application boasted three million user accounts. CNN hailed the new application as "the tinder for politics," referencing its Millennial popularity and ability to connect users from around the country to each other (Castillo, 2015). New Hampshire Public Radio applauded Brigade's ability to inform voters of local election issues, locate polling places, and support local-candidate get-out-the-vote efforts in New Hampshire (McDermott, 2015). *The San Francisco Business Times* called Brigade a force that could save the public from "apathy, ignorance and cynicism" in the days before Super Tuesday primaries (Gaus, 2016). In general, media reception of Brigade was supportive, hopeful, and even overly dramatic at times.

As the platform evolved throughout the 2016 election cycle, Brigade's creative team added more elements designed to encourage user participation and discussion. This included: (1) information on ballot measures in all 50 states; (2) up-voting user comments (similar to Reddit); (3) push-notification alerts tailored to issues, candidates, and parties selected by each user; and (4) debates moderated and contributed by users. Brigade also eliminated the need for users to "friend" or connect in order to share content or interact. All users could now engage with each other (unless they were identified and blocked by an individual). Brigade presented these modifications as the creation of digital affordances that facilitate engagement between users, political issues, and civic collectivity. In 2016, Brigade's stated goal was to eliminate any barriers between a user and political engagement, presenting voters with streamlined information and pathways to political participation (Cutler, 2015a, para. 5).

Rather than present an interpretation of candidate policies or statements, Brigade triangulates voter information based on user quizzes. For example, after taking a nine-question quiz on gun control, users can then look to see what percentage of Clinton or Trump supporters (aka pledges) they match. So, for Brigade, the question is not how well user interests or opinions match the candidate, it is how well they match that candidate's supporters/pledges (or committed voters). This is evidence that there is an underlying engagement framework at work within the platform. It relies upon crowd-generated information (assessed from user quizzes) to make recommendations for new users and voters. Users must engage, share their opinions, up-vote comments, and pledge support to candidates for the algorithms to work. The site requires users to be social and engage each other and the platform, not merely lurk on the site, in order for the platform to be effective.

Fortunately, three million users adopted the app, generating a plethora of information to connect new users to candidates, policy platforms, and issues. In addition, the debate and discussion portions of the platform, where users post opinions and comments, respond to others' comments, and up-vote user content they support, were popular. These posts give insight into the decision-making process of Millennials as they navigate the 2016 election and engage the political process.

Method

In an effort to study the ways a digital platform designed for political engagement facilitated Millennial user participation in the 2016 election, this study used a discursive approach to analyze Brigade and the messages exchanged within the system. Discourse analysis methods are used to interpretively study how individuals position their political opinions and ideologies, and communicate them through debate, discussion, and action. Previous scholarship has used discourse analysis of messages to understand how a population engages each other in digital spaces or on digital platforms (e.g., Novak, 2016).

Discourse analysis relies upon user messages to look at the inward meaning-making process that occurs when individuals attempt to enact political action or turn opinion into behavior. Scholars note that looking at the discourses that emerge within a digital space can give insights into the political ideology, process, and ontology of a larger group (in this case Millennials) (Delahunty, 2012; Gee, 2014).

In order to study the discourses present within Brigade, a random sample of 2,000 debate posts were selected for this study. These posts (including the response comments) were collected from April 1, 2016 until November 9, 2016. This time period represents the first six months of Brigade's availability to the mass public and the period of time when public attention to electoral politics was at its peak (Fry, 2016). As a result, this six-month period before the national election is when the public solidifies voting preferences, researches and forms opinions about candidates, and communicates with others about campaigns. Thus, studying posts made during this time can illuminate citizen mindsets and group decision-making processes as arbitrated by a digital platform.

It is important to note that Brigade has not sold or shared its user database with any entities. As a private company, its end-user license agreement does allow the selling of user information (like the Facebook end-user license agreement). However, Brigade creators made it clear they would not do this before the 2016 election. As a result, it is unclear how well Brigade users represented the larger Millennial population (Republican, Democratic, or independent identifying). It should further be noted that conversations and debates on Brigade are not generalizable to the entire Millennial population; however they can suggest the possibility of a development of a new politically oriented platform for the generation. Future research can and should look at how Brigade user data compares to other social media sites and the general population.

To study the discourses, the 2,000 posts were read by the researcher holistically. Using Gee's (2014) seven meaning-building tasks, the posts were examined for patterns of significance, practices, identities, relationships, politics, connections, and sign systems/knowledge. Findings were then combined to a set of three discourses that summarize how Millennials politically engaged the 2016 presidential election through Brigade. For qualitative reliability of discourses, examples of each discourse and quotes are provided. All comments are taken verbatim from the platform and are not corrected for spelling or grammar.

Findings

Brigade and Civic Engagement

The structure and design of Brigade provides insight into how these previously described discourses of identity and politics take place. Here, some of Brigade's features are interrogated for their impact on the development of civic and political dialogue within the platform. First, the framing of posts on the site complements the designer's intention to facilitate engagement and network conversation. Rather than post comments (as on Facebook or Twitter), users post "debate" positions, which other users can reply to. Rhetorically, this situates statements on the site as inviting (and nearly requiring) replies to another user.

Further, in order to start a "debate" on Brigade, users must post a statement that readers can "agree" or "disagree" with. In order to post a textual response to the user's statement, readers must select "agree" or "disagree," thus contributing to a numerical total of users who agree or disagree with the statement. For users who simply want to view the debate, they also must select agree or disagree before responses are displayed. Thus, the platform encourages engagement (not lurking) because users are required to answer questions and take positions in order to read more about a topic.

Users are also rewarded for participation within debates through earning up-votes. Users can earn spots on the leadership board for "most posts," "started most debates," or "top recruiters" (requesting friends to join the network). Like a game, Brigade encourages a layer of competition between users to obtain status on the leaderboard. In addition, the more quiz questions a user answers, or debates a user agrees or disagrees with, the more complete your profile recommendations will be. As the site learns more about each account, it recommends other politicians who share interests or views, other issue that may be relevant to the voter, and other areas of the country that share the user's views. With more participation in the network, the site becomes more personalized for the user.

Finally, Brigade provides users with direct information (through emails, push notifications, and in-site alerts) regarding important events or issues. For example, Brigade emailed users when voter-registration periods were ending and absentee ballots were due based on user addresses. In addition, Brigade emailed users when Trump and Clinton were visiting their area. Finally, the platform provided push notifications (for users who accepted them) when a debate topic was added that was similar to earlier debates they participated in. Again, although it is unclear how much this impacted the political engagement of Millennials, it is likely that the information provided on the platform did facilitate some traditional voting.

It is important to note topical conversations on Brigade were largely centered on the national election. Primarily, users debated the merits of each of the major presidential candidates, current events, and civic and political issues. For the most part, users shared their opinions, but provided evidence in the form of news articles, quotes, images, and examples to support their arguments. There were limited instances of trolling or personal attacks on a person's character, but rather instead focused on the merits of each other's arguments. Topically, there were no specific issues or foci that received more attention than others, but instead each discussion board seemed to garner a similar number of responses and depth of those responses. The next two sections focus on these debates and responses posted throughout the platform.

Election Discourses

Among the 2,000 posts collected in this analysis, 1,143 posts (57%) included five or more responses from other users. On average, each post had nine responses, and the post with the most responses had 130 comments from other users. Although not generalizable, the frequency of responses within this dataset suggests that most posts shared with the Brigade community generated a conversation among Millennials on that topic. As noted by Mascaro et al. (2012), social networks with political discussion posts that generate responses more than 50% of the time improve user affinity, civic engagement, and likelihood to vote. Although studying if Brigade conforms to the social networks studied in this earlier project is outside the scope of this chapter, the depth and descriptive nature of the debates and discussion on Brigade can generate insight into how these relationships are formed and how they may impact civic and political engagement.

Topically, the majority of debates on the platform originated from current events or updates about the election. For example, in the hours and days after each of the presidential debates, users started their own debates on topics such as who won, interpretations of quotes, and fact-checking candidate's answers. In the aftermath of the third and final presidential debate, one user posted, "I actually feel bad for Hillary in the 3rd debate. She looks like her feelings are really hurt throughout. I don't enjoy seeing anyone suffer, even Hillary Clinton." This particular Brigade debate over the first Trump-Clinton debate resulted in 31% of users agreeing to the above statement, and 69% disagreeing. After selecting "agree" or "disagree," users were able to post responses to this topic. Using Gee's (2014) meaning-making categories, many users participated in debates like this one through "sense-making" or attempting to interpret and understand a current event.

Sense-making involves the audience engaging with media events by questioning its relevance to their own lives, its impact on other issues, or its value to social or cultural groups. After the earlier comment about feeling bad for Hillary during the last debate, users constructed responses that invoked sense-making discourses (or collections of responses). For example, users replied and exchanged messages with each other:

User A: She kicked his whiny ass.

User B: I didn't think it was possible for me too feel bad for her, but I agree . . . Trump has no mercy.

User A: No mercy is the approach that should be taken when battling ISIS.

User C: But, that is what she does. A great Trump debate. He won hands down. Hillary continued to lie and as usual refused to answer a direct question.

User B: [User A] please she didn't win. A fraud and a fake to the bitter end. A nasty woman for sure.

User C: Aww, widdle Hillary needs to find her safe space, lol.

Again, these replies invoke a sense-making discourse as the users attempt to determine who won the third presidential debate, thus making sense of the debate's impact on the electoral outcome and on who would therefore receive a boost in the polls. Again, this sense-making has a future predictive component in which the users attempt to interpret recent events so they can reduce anxiety about an uncertain future. The users above varied in their interpretation of the victory, but later on questioned how this might impact either candidate's likelihood to win the election. Moments after posting about "widdle Hillary," User 1 started his own debate with "'Keep You in Suspense': Masterful move (agreed) Cooked his Goose (disagree)." User C's new post again invoked sense-making, as the Brigade community attempted to understand how Trump's quote regarding accepting the election results would impact political strategy and the 2016 outcome. Unlike the previous debate in which users attempted to engage each other (even by calling them out by name), users responded to this post by reflecting on their own feelings and experiences (rather than the responses from fellow users).

User D: Donald knows how to manipulate the media better than anyone I know. I believe this is just one more masterful move that will keep the media on their toes and at Donald's beck and call for the next 7 days.

User E: Mr. Trump is an entertainer and he's a brand manager—regardless of anyone (or my own) feelings for any candidate in this race (I would absolutely have welcomed Gov. Johnson in these debates), what worries me is his cavalier attitude with basic civics. Yes, he will likely get media folks to talk about it, but that's not a good reason to get them to listen to him. Everyone must accept the certification of our elections, it would have been easy for him to note "I will absolutely support the results; we also must be vigilant against any threat to our votes, and I will make sure that we keep a strong watch on everything for the sake of the American people."

User D: Sticking his fingers in his ears and singing lalalalala would have been an equally eloquent response.

User E: That comment was his own hammer driving in the last nail of his own coffin.

Responses such as these provide researchers with evidence of media engagement and emotional reflections on the electoral process. In addition to providing their own points of view, they respond (albeit with humor) emotionally to the recent presidential debate, especially as they attempt to understand what future events may take place. Gee's (2014) sense-making discourse identifies passages like this as intending to help the audience reduce anxiety over an uncertain future. By participating in this type of sense-making discourse, users attempt to gain understanding and perspective that would aid in predicting the future.

Although it is impossible to identify if all users are Millennials, the appearance of a sense-making discourse suggests consistency with other studies of the generation. As noted by Vidali (2010), Millennials are often characterized as being apathetic to politics, when in fact they demonstrate high levels of self-reflection, subjectivity-insight, and reflexivity that is related to increases in civic engagement. Vidali (2010) terms the types of comments above indicative of "active disengagement," in which Millennials engage with the process internally and then share these interpretations with digital communities of other Millennials. She notes that Millennials are reflexive and insightful when it comes to sense-making of civic and political events, but they struggle to communicate this insight with the larger public. Vidali (2010) also notes that because Millennials have extensive histories producing and interpreting media artifacts (such as social media posts or images), they are able to communicate these insights through diaries and journals. Brigade's textual platform, in which users are encouraged to debate individuals' interpretations of political events seamlessly, advantages Millennials' sense-making abilities by providing a textual place to demonstrate their engagement. Again, these skills were previously honed on traditional social media platforms such as Facebook and Twitter, but were now applied exclusively to a political context on Brigade. For users, Brigade isn't so much a departure from the norms and existing structures of Facebook or Twitter, but rather a focusing of these behaviors onto one topic. Social media platforms support Millennials' textual active disengagement by encouraging users to share their sense-making process. Sharing their own interpretations is rewarded by the platform through tailoring messages, notifications, and content to a user's interests. In short, the site uses Millennials' textual active disengagement predisposition to facilitate political engagement.

The majority of posts examined in this study reflected on Clinton and Trump and the value they brought to the 2016 election. Gee's (2014) politics category of discourse analysis asks researchers to evaluate how users may interpret the political relevancy of an issue, individual, or concept. Largely, posts invoked the politics framework by questioning Clinton and Trump's potential, eligibility, and likelihood to become president. For example, users engaging each other in the comments section of the post: "Trump will be the most innovative president ever":

User F: There is little hope at this point that anyone who supports in ANY manner Trump . . . I can not even begin to explain as I have posted so many anti-Trump debate topics that I am the recognized anti-Trump mouth piece . . . among the many here on Brigade . . . If you post debate topics and request my response I'd love to engage but link evidence for you [*sic*] reasoning.

User G: [User F] as I have stated I in no way want Trump, however the lesser of two evils. I will submit the links to the proof that I talked about tomorrow, it is late and I am getting bleary eyed. Time for meds and sleep. I understand your position, but I think once I can get you the links to what I have been talking about you will understand where I am coming from. I will do exactly that tomorrow. Thanks

User F: You can't change people's minds at this point; we are less than a month away from the election.

Here, users invoked the politics framework by debating Trump's position within the political race. Importantly, the users questioned the larger election background by considering "the lesser of two evils." This type of debate, juxtaposing Trump with other candidates, was common throughout, reflecting a type of significance discourse. Users questioned the significance of Trump as a candidate and potential world leader. As with many posts throughout Brigade, users posted content (usually links to external websites and news articles) to support their conclusions and attempt to persuade others. Here, User G adds that he or she has directly messaged User F with two links to support his pro-Trump stance. Posts such as these also reflect Vidali's (2010) meaning-making suggestion that Millennials are thoughtful and can provide evidence in their sense-making reflection on politics.

Although it is difficult to determine if people who committed their votes on the platform actually voted in the election, 80% of users said that they did intend to vote and were strongly committed to one candidate. The high percentage is likely a result of the community's interest in politics (they did join a political social network after all) rather than the effect of Brigade on voter turnout. However, it is also possible that, as previous research suggests, Millennial political engagement online does positively influence voter turnout (Mascaro et al., 2012). Most Millennial users engaged in the political debates, took the voter interest quizzes, and shared their political alignment with other users. In many ways, Brigade reified the functions of other popular social networks that facilitated political engagement on its own platform. This adaptation of the affordances and design of other social media platforms into Brigade will be discussed fully in the coming section, but what is immediately important is the acknowledgement of this practice by Millennial users within their own comments. Many Millennials discussed the effect Brigade was having on the election, their own interests, and larger narratives of civic and political engagement. The next section reflects on these discourses in order to understand Millennial reflections on civic engagement in the digital space.

Millennials on Civic and Political Engagement

As noted by Novak (2016), Millennials are largely aware of mass media stereotypes and narratives of their disengagement, apathy, and digital reliance. Novak (2016) and Vidali (2010) used digital diaries to study how Millennials encounter, accept, or challenge these often negative stereotypes. Similarly, the textual affordances of social networks provide insight into this interpretation process of Millennials and their political engagement. Debate posts on Brigade often asked the community about the *identity* of their generation, the *practices* of the group, and their *relationship* to other American institutions (e.g., older generations, media industry, and political structures).

For example, consider this debate post "Reverse ageism disproportionately affects the Millennial generation." Here, a Millennial user questions the negative narratives told about the Millennial generation (even outside the scope of politics). Through the discursive framework of "relationships," posts such as this one ask users to compare and contrast the experience of generational groups to each other. This debate post generated a lot of user responses, which provide evidence and their own interpretation of "reverse ageism" and its impact on Millennials.

User H: Wtf is with these old geezers hating on millennials when it's their generation's policies that have harmed us so much and hampered our growth and success.

User I: very similar experiences where I live [User H] I'm tired of the lamentations for "the good old days"

Users such as these provided reflections on the media and general public's treatment of Millennials. Most concluded that the generation was being unfairly and unnecessarily criticized for attributes and problems that were not their own. Frequently, users called the public's positioning of the generation a type of ageism (or reverse ageism—there was some debate if reverse ageism is even possible). Characterizing this positioning as ageism allowed a discourse of identity to persist on the platform that defined the group specifically through the characteristics they were not—mostly the negatives stereotypes communicated through traditional news media. Frequent stereotypes that users identified as incorrect include: "apathetic," "dumb," "entitled," "whiny," "incapable of making informed decisions," "easily manipulated," and "politically vacant." Here Gee's (2014) discourse of identity is constructed based inversely in the negative of popular depictions of the group. Rather than present their own narrative or description of the generation's identity, users instead focused on why the above list of terms of reference were incorrect. Importantly, this challenges the popular depiction, but fails to provide a corrected (or approved) version, which Hall and Jefferson (2006) conclude makes it difficult to change the media or control cultures' narrative. The implications of this will be provided in detail in the discussion.

Debates over Brigade's place in Millennial digital life often appeared within discussions over Millennial-centered issues such as student loan reform and changes to health insurance coverage for those under 26 years of age. Again, Millennial identity was constructed in these debates through what the generation believed was not working, or would not appeal to their group. For example, one person replied to a post about Clinton's email scandal with "People in my generation don't really care about such incidental things." Like in earlier conversations over Millennial attributes, most issue-focused comments were similarly disagreed with. Again, Millennials did not provide an issue that they thought was more important or relevant, but were clear about the incidents and topics that they felt did not matter or were not important for their age group, such as Hillary's emails, Medicare, and foreign policy initiatives with Russia.

Millennial users also affirmed that their own use of the site was largely inspired by the adoption of other social media platforms by candidates and traditional political structures. Often integrated into debates over "Millennial issues" (such as what would and would not make the generation vote for a candidate), Millennials reflected that they adopted Brigade because their previous social networks were "taken over by the people we are trying to avoid." For Millennials, Brigade was a protected space, where candidates, political party organizers, and even pollsters could not interfere. One user wrote "four years ago, I went on FB [Facebook] to learn about the election. I can't do that anymore because all the candidates have taken over the real information." Statements like these provide affirmation of the Brigade creators' intentions, that other social media was now co-opted by the candidates themselves, and Millennials desired a social space away from the purview of these parties to discuss politics. Although open to any user who signed up, Millennials in the online space commented on feeling like it was a "private" space to "share my point of view without worrying that I was then going to get bombarded by Trump's paid ads or Hillary's voter registration team." Some users added that they hoped Brigade wouldn't fall into the same trap as "Twitter and Facebook—they use [*sic*] to be for us, now they are for the [political] elites." Statements like these invoke Gee's (2014) sign systems/knowledge framework of discourses, in which Brigade is first likened and connected to other social media platforms, then constructed as different due to its seemingly private nature. Interviews with the Brigade creators suggest that this discourse is precisely what the platform hopes to achieve: the connection to the features and purpose of social media, but a type of Millennial exclusivity that has seemingly been lost by earlier social media giants (Cutler, 2015b).

The creators of Brigade were certainly outspoken about their desires to grow their social media platform by identifying and optimizing the generation that felt like earlier platforms were now co-opted by media and political elites. Brigade users (while not directly acknowledging these comments), largely identified as feeling left out of the political process, thus their turn online to the digital space. One user shared his experience about feeling left out:

> What they [older generations] don't get is that we want to participate in politics, but we aren't wanted. I want to volunteer, but last time I tried they acted like I wasn't smart enough to phone bank and made me clean the office. I'm not too proud to do that, but its [*sic*] not exactly inspiring me to take up a life of politics. In 2008, when I went online I was able to help Obama get elected by talking to people and helping. In person I was basically laughed at, but online I made a difference. That's why I was so sad when I felt like I lost when Facebook became more loyal to the politicians and not to the people.

Like the user above, many Millennials discussed feeling they were not welcome in traditional physical campaigns and felt shunned in traditional social media spaces such as Facebook, but on Brigade they were empowered to become active parts of the process. Brigade can then help the generation achieve engagement, especially in the aftermath of a turn in Facebook's design or operation. Several users referenced the way they perceived Facebook (and Twitter) used to be, reflecting that they used to feel more in control of the platform. Instead, today they viewed these platforms as more "profit-driven" and "less interested in my [user] needs and wants." Although there were no posts that specifically described how these changes took place, what caused them, or what the changes in the platform designs were, it is clear that the changes were partially responsible for users turning to Brigade for political engagement purposes.

Discussion

In the six months since Brigade's launch, users have flocked to the site as a space of political debate, information sharing, and engagement. In doing so, a set of discourses regarding the proliferation of a new social media platform during the 2016 election was constructed by Millennial users, especially as they engaged in sense-making of current events. In their pre-launch interviews, Brigade creators readily reinforced the site's focus as a space for the Millennial generation to enact political and civic engagement practices (Mangalindan, 2015). Throughout the site are specific references, by users as to this focus, such as in the conversations on ageism and reverse ageism, reflections on being left out of traditional political spaces, and even in the debates over what issues matter most to the group. This type of reflection reinforces that users are primarily Millennials, although user data from Brigade is needed before this can be confirmed.

Posts on Brigade confirmed Vidali's (2010) assertions that Millennials are capable of critical insight into political climates in textual form. Millennials were quick to point out electoral issues and media depictions of their own group that they found problematic. However, without replacing them with clearer statements of their own identity, the value of these conversations on Brigade is a bit mottled. Although some scholars would say that this misses the critical part of challenging the cycle of identity (Hall & Jefferson, 2006), it may also reflect the newness of the platform and the distraction of the election. In time, Millennials may use Brigade to start their own social movement that may proliferate beyond the screen (such as other groups that have used Twitter's platform to start movements such as Black Lives Matter or Occupy Wall Street). Although this did not occur in the first six months of Brigade's release, it does not mean the generation cannot do so in the future. Again, this is indicative of the new platform Brigade, not necessarily all social media platforms. Although sources such as Pew question the frequency of Millennial political engagement on more traditional platforms such as Twitter and Facebook, it appears that they may have returned to those platforms after the election (Baker-Bell, Stanbrough, & Everett, 2017).

Brigade's 2016 release was specifically designed to coincide with the presidential election. However, Millennial long-term commitment and interest in the site remains to be seen. As a platform that has designed itself around the election, its layout, purpose, and structure will likely be changed when there are no candidates running for public office. Brigade creators have clearly stated their intentions to continue to grow the site to foster political engagement, but how they will do this outside of the election is unclear. In addition, user reactions to these changes should be monitored to understand how the generation engages a changing and evolving platform, particularly in the aftermath of the user complaints about Facebook and Twitter changes.

Conclusion

Brigade's rise in popularity within its first six months of operation suggests that Millennials have been looking for a new social media platform that is perceived to be outside the purview of traditional political elites. Although it is unclear how long this exclusivity may last, Millennials clearly embraced the platform throughout the 2016 cycle as a space to debate and engage the political process. Although more empirical research is necessary before an effects-based conclusion can be drawn regarding its ability to generate votes or physical participation in the 2016 election, this interpretive analysis demonstrates how users embrace and use a new politically oriented platform to engage a national election.

References

Baker-Bell, A., Stanbrough, R. J., & Everett, S. (2017). The stories they tell: Mainstream media, pedagogies of healing, and critical media literacy. *English Education, 49*(2), 130–142.

Bauerlein, M. (2009). *The dumbest generation ever: How the digital age stupefies young Americans and jeopardizes our future.* New York, NY: Penguin Group Inc.

Bennett, C. J. (2015). Trends in voter surveillance in western societies: Privacy intrusions and democratic implications. *Surveillance & Society, 13*(3/4), 370–377.

Brownstein, D. (2016, September 19). Millennial voters may cost Hillary Clinton the election. *The Atlantic.* Retrieved from www.theatlantic.com/politics/archive/2016/09/hillary-clinton-millennials-philadelphia/500540/

Calhoun, C. (2013). Occupy Wall Street in perspective. *The British Journal of Sociology, 64*(1), 26–38. doi:10.1111/1468-4446.12002

Castillo, W. (2015, June 23). Introducing Brigade, 'the tinder of politics'. *CNN.* Retrieved from http://edition.cnn.com/2015/06/21/politics/brigade-app-politics-iphone-android/

CIRCLE. (2012). Updated estimate: Youth turnout was 50% in 2012; youth turnout in battleground states 58%. *CIRCLE: The Center for Information and Research on Civic Learning and Engagement.* Retrieved from www.civicyouth.org/updated-estimate-50-of-youth-turnout-in-2012-youth-turnout-in-battleground-states-58/

Cutler, K. M. (2015a, June 17). Sean Parker's Brigade app enters private beta as a dead-simple way of taking political positions. *Tech Crunch.* Retrieved from https://techcrunch.com/2015/06/17/sean-parker-brigade/

Cutler, K. M. (2015b, October 12). Brigade, the political engagement platform backed by Sean Parker, launches a new voter guide before November elections. *Tech Crunch.* Retrieved from https://techcrunch.com/2015/10/12/brigade/

Deal, J. J., Altman, D. G., & Rogelberg, S. G. (2010). Millennials at work: What we know and what we need to do (if anything). *Journal of Business and Psychology, 25*(2), 191–199.

Delahunty, J. (2012). 'Who am I?': Exploring identity in online discussion forums. *International Journal of Educational Research, 53*, 407–420.

Fry, R. (2016, August 29). This may be the last election dominated by Boomers and prior generations. *Pew Research Center.* Retrieved from www.pewresearch.org/fact-tank/2016/08/29/this-may-be-the-last-presidential-election-dominated-by-boomers-and-prior-generations/

Gaus, A. (2016, March 2). As Super Tuesday sparks debate, can Brigade's app drive voters to the polls? *San Francisco Business Times.* Retrieved from www.bizjournals.com/san-francisco/blog/techflash/2016/03/as-super-tuesday-sparks-debate-can-brigade-voters.html

Gee, J. P. (2014). *How to do discourse analysis: A toolkit.* New York, NY: Routledge.

Gitlin, T. (1980). *The whole world is watching.* New York, NY: Routledge.

Hais, M., & Winograd, M. (2008, December 18). It's official: Millennials realigned American politics in 2008. *Huffington Post.* Retrieved from www.huffingtonpost.com/michael-hais-and-morley-winograd/its-official-millennials_b_144357.html

Hall, S., & Jefferson, T. (Eds.). (2006). *Resistance through rituals: Youth subcultures in post-war Britain* (2nd ed.). New York, NY: Routledge.

Hoffman, A. J. (2017). Millennials, technology and perceived relevance of community service organizations: Is social media replacing community service activities? *The Urban Review, 49*(1), 140–152.

Huntley, R. (2006). *The world according to Y: Inside the new adult generation.* Crows Nest, Australia: Allen & Unwin Press.

Jordan, A. B. (2015, May). Do communication technologies define a generation? *Paper Presented at the annual meeting for the International Communication Association*, Puerto Rico.

Kelly, D. M. (2006). Frame work: Helping youth consider their misrepresentations in media. *Canadian Journal of Education, 29*, 27–50.

Mangalindan, J. P. (2015, June 17). Introducing Brigade beta, Sean Parker's civic-focused social network. *Mashable.* Retrieved from http://mashable.com/2015/06/17/sean-parker-brigade-beta-civics-social

Mascaro, C. M., Novak, A., & Goggins, S. (2012). The daily brew: The structural evolution of the coffee party on Facebook during the 2010 United States midterm election season. *The Journal of Information, Technology and Politics, 9*(3), 234–253.

McDermott, C. (2015, October 26). With eye on local elections, 'Brigade' app rolls out new feature in N.H. *New Hampshire Public Radio.* Retrieved from http://nhpr.org/post/eye-local-elections-brigade-app-rolls-out-new-feature-nh

McGrath, M. (2011). Technology, media, and political participation. *National Civic Review, 100*(3), 41–44. doi:10.1002/ncr.20075

Metzger, M. W., Erete, S. L., Barton, D. L., Desler, M. K., & Lewis, D. A. (2015). The new political voice of young Americans: Online engagement and civic development among first-year college students. *Education, Citizenship and Social Justice, 10*(1), 55–66. doi:10.1177/1746197914558398

Milkman, R. (2017). A new political generation: Millennials and the post-2008 wave of protest. *American Sociological Review, 82*(1), 1–31. doi:10.1177/0003122416681031

Mindich, D.T.Z. (2005). *Tuned out: Why Americans under 40 don't follow the news.* New York NY: Oxford University Press.

Montgomery, K. C. (2009). *Generation digital: Politics, commerce, and childhood in the age of the Internet.* Cambridge, MA: The MIT Press.

Nevius, C. S. (2016, September 17). Tech companies must wake up and smell the politics. *San Francisco Chronicle.* Retrieved from www.sfchronicle.com/bayarea/nevius/article/Tech-has-to-wake-up-and-smell-the-politics-9208701.php

Nguyen, T. (2016, September 19). Hillary Clinton could lose the election because Millennials don't like her. *Vanity Fair.* Retrieved from www.vanityfair.com/news/2016/09/hillary-clinton-millennial-voters

Novak, A. (2016). *Media, millennials, and politics: The coming of age of the next political generation.* New York, NY: Lexington Books.

Novak, A. N., Johnson, K., & Pontes, M. (2016). LatinoTwitter: Discourses of Latino civic engagement in social media. *First Monday, 21*(8). Retrieved from http://firstmonday.org/ojs/index.php/fm/article/view/6752/5604

Rabina, D. L. (2009). [Review of *Millennial Makeover: MySpace, YouTube and the Future of American Politics,* by M. Winograd & M. D. Hais]. *Government Information Quarterly, 26*(4), 613–614. doi:10.1016/j.giq.2009.05.001

Ross, A. D., & Rouse, S. M. (2015). Economic uncertainty, job threat, and the resiliency of the millennial generation's attitudes toward immigration. *Social Science Quarterly, 96*(5), 1363–1379. doi:10.1111/ssqu.12168

Rucker, P. (2016, August 13). For Millennial voters, Clinton v. Trump feels like a joke. *Washington Post.* Retrieved from www.washingtonpost.com/politics/for-millennial-voters-the-clinton-vs-trump-choice-feels-like-a-joke/2016/08/13/306d85a2-609c-11e6-8e45-477372e89d78_story.html

Seipel, A. (2014, October 4). Millennial voters are paying attention, so why don't more actually vote? *National Public Radio.* Retrieved from www.npr.org/sections/itsallpolitics/2014/10/08/354187589/millennial-voters-are-paying-attention-so-why-dont-more-actually-vote

Spurgeon, C., Ferrier, L., Gunders, L., & Graham, P. (2012). Youth citizens, values, and new/s media. *Continuum: Journal of Media & Cultural Studies, 26,* 911–922.

Stanek, B. (2015, November 26). 11 humiliatingly lame ways 2016 candidates are trying to appeal to young voters. *The Week*. Retrieved from http://theweek.com/articles/589208/11-humiliatingly-lame-ways-2016-candidates-are-trying-appeal-young-voters

Stewart, K. D., & Bernhardt, P. C. (2010). Comparing Millennials to pre-1987 students and with one another. *North American Journal of Psychology, 12*, 579–602.

Trippi, J. (2005). *The revolution will not be televised: Democracy, the Internet, and the over throw of everything*. New York, NY: HarperCollins.

Turner, G. (2009). Millennial journalism. *Journalism, 10*(2), 390–392.

Twenge, J. (2006). *Generation me*. New York, NY: Atria Books.

Vidali, D. S. (2010). Millennial encounters with mainstream television news: Excess, void, and points of engagement. *Linguistic Anthropology, 20*, 372–388.

Zuckerman, E. (2014). New media, new civics? *Policy & Internet, 6*(2), 151–168. doi:10.1002/1944–2866.POI360

17

DONALD TRUMP AND THE LATE-NIGHT POLITICAL HUMOR OF CAMPAIGN 2016

All the Donald, All the Time

Stephen J. Farnsworth, S. Robert Lichter, and Deanne Canieso

Political humor has become a staple of late-night television talk-shows. Large parts of the media audience turn to the post-prime-time comics for entertainment and even for an alternative source of news (Baym, 2005). Starting with Richard Nixon's appearance on *Laugh-In* during the 1968 presidential election, presidents and presidential candidates have sought to humanize their image and bolster their standing by appearing on evening comedy programs (Gould, 1968; Lichter, Baumgartner, & Morris, 2015). In 1992, those entertainment venues came into their own as sources of political news. That year Ross Perot launched his candidacy via appearances on *Larry King Live*, and Bill Clinton sought to win over younger voters by playing his saxophone on *Arsenio* (Davis & Owen, 1998; Kolbert, 1992).

The late-night talk-shows have remained prominent political venues in subsequent election cycles. By 2008, a candidate who canceled a late-night TV appearance (as Republican presidential nominee John McCain did to David Letterman) faced a barrage of criticism from the talk-show host (Farnsworth & Lichter, 2011). After three weeks of comedic criticism, the chastened Republican nominee went on *Late Night* to apologize profusely, thanking Letterman several times after the host said he would put the incident behind them (Lichter et al., 2015). Letterman observed that the tables had turned in recent years: "The road to the White House runs through me," he joked (Lichter et al., 2015). As the saying goes, many a truth was said in jest.

Indeed, the same might be said of late-night humor in general. Partly owing to Donald Trump's outsized personality and outrageous pronouncements, the hosts had an unprecedented amount of material to work with, and the line between campaign news and campaign humor became increasingly blurred. In addition to the nightly talk-shows, *Saturday Night Live* skits provided a weekly counterpoint to campaign events, which were chronicled by journalists and produced sharp ratings increases among audiences.

All the attention boosted the profiles of new hosts on several shows, following the greatest shake-up of late-night talk since Jay Leno succeeded Johnny Carson on *The Tonight Show* in 1992 and David Letterman launched *The Late Night* on CBS the following year. During the 20 months prior to the onset of our study period, Jimmy Fallon succeeded Leno, Letterman gave way to Stephen Colbert, who migrated from his Comedy Central parody show *The Colbert Report*, and his erstwhile colleague Jon Stewart left *The Daily Show*, to be replaced by Trevor Noah. Another *Daily Show* alumnus, John Oliver, began a weekly political talk-show on HBO. Unlike Leno and Letterman a quarter century earlier, this new crop of hosts benefitted from their ability to reach secondary audiences via YouTube and other social media, not to mention the websites that reprinted much of the material from their skits and monologues.

In this paper, we report on results of a new content analysis project that examined the jokes aired by late-night comics, using two different studies of late-night humor conducted by the Center for Media and Public Affairs (CMPA) of George Mason University. For the primary campaign, we examine the 2,854 jokes that targeted political figures, whether or not they were running for president, from September 1, 2015 through April 30, 2016, by which time it had become clear which candidates were going to be the Republican and Democratic presidential nominees. The jokes relating to the two nominees received extra scrutiny: we also examined the subjects of the 3,008 jokes that focused on the two presidential nominees between September 1, 2015 and November 11, 2016, a few days after the presidential election. (Jokes relating to the eventual nominees are in both studies, of course). To illustrate the significance of the data, we first examine the ways in which late-night comics have increasingly shaped political discourse over the past several decades.

Late-Night Comics: Content and Effects

Some scholars believe that late-night television talk-shows, particularly *The Daily Show*, deserve to be considered as an alternative news source (Baym, 2005). During his heyday as host of the Comedy Central program, survey respondents identified Jon Stewart as one of the most trusted journalists in America, comparable to Tom Brokaw or Anderson Cooper (Baumgartner & Morris, 2011). As a result, presidential candidates have increasingly treated these talk-shows as a means of reaching potential voters who have little interest in traditional political news but are exposed to campaign information on infotainment programming. During the 2008 campaign, for example, presidential candidates and their family members made 80 appearances on these shows (Lichter et al., 2015). Although most of the attention was focused on the favorites for winning the nomination, these shows also offered opportunities for those further back in the pack, who otherwise received little to no media coverage.

Research into the content of talk-shows has found that they do a better job of focusing on substantive issues during presidential campaigns than do journalists, who place greater emphasis on the campaign horse race and the candidates' strategies and tactics. A Center for Media and Public Affairs study of national TV talk-shows during the 1992 campaign found that 74% of the political segments focused on substantive matters (primarily policy issues and candidate qualifications). By contrast, campaign coverage on the ABC, CBS, and NBC evening news programs that year ranged from 26% to 34% substantive content (Farnsworth & Lichter, 2011).

Scholars have also identified partisan differences in the targets of late-night jokes. Republican presidential nominees were joked about more often than their Democratic counterparts during each of the six presidential election campaigns from 1992 through 2012 (Lichter et al., 2015). For example, during the 2012 election, 16.2% of all political jokes were directed at Mitt Romney, compared to only 6.2% that targeted Barack Obama (Lichter et al., 2015). Late-night political humor has gained in attention and influence as people reduce their consumption of traditional media, like the daily newspaper and the broadcast television networks' evening news shows. This trend has been particularly pronounced among younger adults, many of whom turn to soft news as a major source of political information (Baumgartner & Morris, 2011; Mitchell, Gottfried, Kiley, & Matsa, 2014). On balance, research has found that viewing late-night political humor is associated with higher levels of political knowledge (Brewer & Cao, 2006). These late-night political conversations appear to increase political knowledge by providing information in a digestible and interesting manner (Xenos & Becker, 2009; Young, 2006). Among their viewers, late-night humor also increases political participation in a variety of formats (Moy, Xenos, & Hess, 2005). This wide range of political activities may be a result of increased internal political efficacy, which is associated with viewing late-night political humor (Baumgartner & Morris, 2006).

The overwhelmingly negative nature of political humor can lead to more negative evaluations of the political figures being skewered (Baumgartner & Morris, 2006). Politicians often try to minimize the negative impact, or even try to "work the refs" of political comedy, by appearing on these political humor shows as guests (Lichter et al., 2015). Selective news exposure by consumers may limit the impact of these comic takedowns on the general public, however. The first and/or most significant exposure some viewers and readers receive relating to politicians and to policy topics frequently come from partisan media sources (Iyengar & Hahn, 2009; Stroud, 2008; Taber & Lodge, 2006). A 2014 Pew Research Center survey, for example, found that liberals were more likely to trust and conservatives more likely to distrust *The Colbert Report* and *The Daily Show*, two of the late-night comedy programs included in its survey (Mitchell et al., 2014).

Data

This primary campaign portion of the study examines 2,854 jokes about political figures that were made by the late-night comics during the last four months of 2015, before the start of the primaries, and the first four months of 2016. By April 30, 2016, there was little doubt that the party nominees would be Donald Trump and Hillary Clinton, despite increasingly desperate efforts by their remaining opponents to stem the tide. During this eight-month nomination campaign period, we tracked political jokes by Jimmy Fallon (*The Tonight Show* on NBC), Stephen Colbert (*The Late Show* on CBS), Jimmy Kimmel (*Jimmy Kimmel Live!* on ABC), and *The Daily Show*, the Comedy Central program with new host Trevor Noah. In the case of the latter, we began our study on September 28, 2015, when Noah formally took over from Jon Stewart. The three broadcast network shows had the largest audiences of any late-night talk-shows, whereas *The Daily Show* has been especially popular with young adults. We tracked both the traditional joke formats, the "one-liners," and the more extensive lead-in humor more commonly employed on Comedy Central's *Daily Show*.

The second analysis looks at the topics of late-night humor directed at the two major party nominees during more than a year of campaign discourse, starting on September 1, 2015 and ending on November 11, 2016, a few days after the presidential election. A total of 3,008 jokes about Clinton and Trump were analyzed as to whether they had significant policy, political, and/or personal content. (Many jokes covered more than one issue area.) Coding was done by college students who were trained by senior staff. Training continued until the coders attained at least 80% reliability ratings. Videos of all relevant materials were examined rather than transcripts.

These two studies represent an updating of the CMPA database, which includes more than 100,000 jokes by hosts on popular late-night TV shows from 1992 through 2012. This material includes not only jokes about political figures but also those directed at government institutions and social institutions, such as churches and the military, as well as jokes that addressed a general social or economic problem, such as inflation, gay rights issues, or climate change. Due to limited resources, however, the current study was limited to jokes directed at individual political figures.

Results and Discussion

During the eight-month presidential nomination period examined, presidential candidates dominated the late-night humor discourse. As shown in Table 17.1, during the run-up to the state primary and caucus period from September through December 2015, the four late-night comics routinely devoted a majority of their political jokes to presidential candidates. Jimmy Fallon told the most candidate jokes (487 or 77% of his jokes), but Jimmy Kimmel told the greatest

TABLE 17.1 Candidate Late-Night Joke Analysis, Late 2015

	Sept.	*%*	*Oct.*	*%*	*Nov.*	*%*	*Dec.*	*%*	*Total*	*%*
Total Candidate Jokes										
Fallon	166	69	99	72	142	88	81	84	487	77
Colbert	176	65	73	53	73	82	25	86	347	66
Kimmel	129	78	74	89	75	92	57	93	335	86
Noah	5	*	108	69	90	76	65	88	268	68
Total	**476**	**66**	**353**	**69**	**380**	**85**	**228**	**88**	**1437**	**74**
Republican Candidate Focus										
Fallon	133	56	53	39	108	67	62	65	356	56
Colbert	108	40	56	41	61	69	21	72	246	47
Kimmel	123	75	52	63	60	74	55	90	290	74
Noah	4	*	61	39	74	63	64	86	203	51
Total	**368**	**77**	**222**	**63**	**303**	**68**	**202**	**78**	**1095**	**56**
Democratic Candidate Focus										
Fallon	33	14	46	34	32	20	19	21	130	21
Colbert	56	21	20	15	09	10	4	*	89	17
Kimmel	4	*	22	27	15	19	1	*	42	11
Noah	1	*	48	31	14	12	1	*	64	16
Total	**94**	**20**	**136**	**39**	**70**	**42**	**25**	**10**	**325**	**17**

Source: Center for Media and Public Affairs, George Mason University

*Fewer than ten jokes in the category for a comic for that month, too few for analysis.

Notes: Some political jokes relate to more than one candidate and cannot be classified as clearly directed towards one party or another.

percentage of jokes devoted to political candidates (335 or 86%). Similarly, Trevor Noah consistently devoted more than two-thirds of his jokes at political figures during the three months that he was part of the analysis.

Of the 1,437 political jokes told during those four months, 1,095 were focused on Republican candidates, which represented a larger field than the Democratic contenders (see individual candidate data in Tables 17.3 and 17.4). Jimmy Kimmel had the highest percentage of jokes aimed at the Republican candidates (74%) and Trevor Noah the least (51%). The highest percentage of jokes directed at Democrats came from Fallon (21%) and the lowest from Kimmel (11%). Among the four months, the high-water mark for Democratic jokes was in October, when Fallon directed 34% of his jokes at the Democratic field. No other month or individual comic in late 2015 devoted even one-quarter of the jokes to that party. (Because some political jokes were directed at more than one candidate, not all jokes were categorized as specifically Republican or specifically Democratic in orientation.)

In Table 17.2, we examine the late-night jokes during the first four months of 2016, when the nomination campaigns took place in earnest. Once again

TABLE 17.2 Candidate Late-Night Joke Analysis, Early 2016

	Jan.	%	*Feb.*	%	*March*	%	*Apr.*	%	*Total*	%
Total Candidate Jokes										
Fallon	118	77	116	88	106	72	97	78	437	78
Colbert	104	84	89	86	63	63	48	66	304	76
Kimmel	58	87	89	78	104	73	58	84	309	79
Noah	91	81	92	89	95	66	89	82	367	79
Total	**371**	**82**	**386**	**85**	**368**	**69**	**292**	**78**	**1417**	**78**
Republican Candidate Focus										
Fallon	83	54	84	64	75	51	51	41	293	53
Colbert	72	58	57	55	48	48	38	52	215	54
Kimmel	38	57	69	61	79	55	44	64	230	58
Noah	75	67	77	75	79	55	67	62	298	64
Total	**268**	**59**	**287**	**64**	**281**	**53**	**200**	**53**	**1036**	**57**
Democratic Candidate Focus										
Fallon	35	23	32	24	28	19	44	35	139	25
Colbert	31	25	19	18	13	13	8	*	71	18
Kimmel	17	25	16	14	20	14	8	*	61	16
Noah	16	14	12	12	15	10	19	18	62	13
Total	**99**	**22**	**79**	**17**	**76**	**14**	**79**	**21**	**333**	**18**

Source: Center for Media and Public Affairs, George Mason University

*Fewer than ten jokes in the category for a comic for that month, too few for analysis.

Note: Some political jokes relate to more than one candidate and cannot be classified as clearly directed towards one party or another.

candidate jokes dominated late-night humor, with 78% of the jokes focusing on the presidential field. The results were very similar for the four comics during these four months, with candidates being the subject of the jokes between 76% and 79% of the time. Of the 1,417 political jokes offered during those four months, 1,036 were directed at the Republican field. During this four-month period, Noah's show devoted 64% of all jokes to Republicans, the highest level, and Fallon's show had the lowest percentage, with 53% of the jokes targeting Republicans. No more than one-quarter of the jokes were directed at the entire Democratic presidential field, with a high of 25% by Fallon and a low of 13% on *The Daily Show*.

In the three remaining nomination phase tables, we look at the individual candidates whose actions and attributes generated the comedy. As shown in Table 17.3, Donald Trump ranked first in all four months of late 2015 and, in three of the four months examined, he was the subject of twice as many jokes as the runner-up in the joke race. (The one exception was November, when Ben Carson was a relatively close runner-up.) Carson finished out of the top

TABLE 17.3 Top Late-Night Joke Targets, Late 2015

September		*October*		*November*		*December*	
Trump	204	Trump	104	Trump	101	Trump	109
H. Clinton	61	H. Clinton	46	Carson	79	Cruz	23
Jeb Bush	50	Carson	40	Jeb Bush	49	Jeb Bush	21
Obama	46	Sanders	33	Sanders	32	Christie	13
Sanders	25	Chafee	31	H. Clinton	22	H. Clinton	13
Boehner	24	Jeb Bush	26	Jindal	18	Carson	12
Walker	20	Biden	25	Obama	17	Obama	10
Christie	18	McCarthy	20	Cruz	13	Sanders	7
Paul	14	Christie	13	Huckabee	12	Kasich	6
Putin	12	Webb	12	O'Malley	10	Cheney	4
Carson	11	B. Clinton	8	Rubio	7	O'Malley	4
Fiorina	11	Gowdy	7	Christie	5	B. Clinton	3
Rick Perry	11	Rand Paul	6	Fiorina	4	Fiorina	3
Brady	8	Fiorina	5	Eisenhower	4	Graham	3
Gilmore	8	O'Malley	5	Kasich	3	Rubio	2
Graham	8	Putin	5	Lessig	3	M. Obama	2
Rubio	6	Obama	4	Putin	3	McConnell	2
Jindal	5	Amin	4	B. Clinton	2		
Jinping	5	McCain	4	Both Clintons	2		
Cheney	4	Rubio	4	Vitter	2		

Source: Center for Media and Public Affairs, George Mason University

Note: Targets have to be the subject of at least two jokes to be listed. In addition, only the Top 20 targets per month are listed.

ten in September, but was third in October, second in November, and sixth in December, when his poll numbers had started to fade.

Carson's experience demonstrates that saying little on the campaign trail does not spare a candidate from ridicule. Consider a *Tonight Show* jab at Ben Carson, who was the subject of 142 jokes during that three-month period. "Ben Carson's the first human to get 25 hours of sleep per day. I feel bad making fun of Carson, but it's not like he's gonna see it," Fallon said following one of Carson's understated debate performances (Lichter, Farnsworth, & Canieso, 2016).

Among the Republican candidates, former Florida Governor Jeb Bush was consistently popular with humorists. He finished third in joke rankings for September, sixth in October, and third in both November and December. Senator Ted Cruz (R-Texas), who ended up being the chief rival to Trump, did not even make the top 20 jokes targets during September and October of 2015. But when Cruz surged in the polls, he surged in the comic rankings: he ranked eighth in November and moved into second place in December 2015.

As was the case in national news coverage before the start of the primaries and caucuses, Republicans received most of the attention. Although the Democrats did not face as much ridicule on late-night TV during these four months, Hillary Clinton finished second in the humor sweepstakes in September and October and fifth in November and December. Vermont senator Bernie Sanders, who emerged as her chief rival for the Democratic nomination, was consistently further back, ranking fifth in joke totals for September, fourth in October and November, and eighth in December.

Not all leading political joke targets were running for president in 2016. President Obama ranked fourth in the humor contest during September and former House Speaker John Boehner (R-Ohio) ranked sixth that month. Russian President Vladimir Putin was the highest-ranking international political figure in September, ranking 12th, and he remained in the top 20 for the final three months of 2015. Putin was in the top 20 all four months analyzed, as was Obama.

A few unusual names made the top 20 lists during the fall of 2015. New England Patriots quarterback Tom Brady, famous more for winning Super Bowls and for allegations of deflated footballs than for politics, endorsed Donald Trump and ended up being the source of eight jokes during September 2015. And Uganda dictator Idi Amin, who died in 2003, was the source of four jokes during October.

Table 17.4 shows that Donald Trump also finished first in the joke rankings during all four months of the nomination season examined: January through April 2016. Once again Trump consistently finished well ahead of the second-place finisher every month. These months were particularly "good" for Bernie Sanders, who finished second in the joke tally during January, February, and March, as he scored a number of early primary wins and gave the Clinton campaign more competition than had been expected. Sanders also finished third in April, behind only Trump and Cruz, who at that point was one of the few remaining Republican candidates for president who was still standing. Cruz also moved up the rankings during the latter period, with fifth-place finishes in January and February and a third-place finish in March. Jeb Bush finished third in January and February, but dropped out of the Top Ten once his campaign fizzled.

Perhaps surprisingly, Hillary Clinton did not dominate the joke conversation on her way to becoming the Democratic nominee. She was sixth in January and fourth in February, March, and April. President Obama, though term-limited, was the subject of more jokes than any Democrat running for president other than Sanders or Clinton. He ranked fourth in January, ninth in February, fifth in March, and sixth in April. Moreover, all the major Democratic contenders other than Clinton and Sanders had dropped out of the race by February. These also-rans included former Virginia Senator Jim Webb, former Rhode Island Governor Lincoln Chafee, and former Maryland Governor Martin O'Malley.

Mitt Romney, the Republican Party's 2012 presidential nominee who became active in the "Never Trump" movement, ranked eighth as a humor subject

TABLE 17.4 Top Late-Night Joke Targets, Early 2016

January		*February*		*March*		*April*	
Trump	137	Trump	150	Trump	187	Trump	113
Sanders	67	Sanders	51	Sanders	44	Cruz	60
Jeb Bush	47	Jeb Bush	49	Cruz	38	Sanders	43
B. Obama	46	H. Clinton	36	H. Clinton	33	H. Clinton	29
Cruz	33	Cruz	30	B. Obama	26	Kasich	18
H. Clinton	17	Rubio	27	Rubio	26	B. Obama	13
O'Malley	17	Carson	25	Carson	21	Fiorina	7
Christie	16	Christie	11	Romney	20	Priebus	6
Carson	15	B. Obama	9	Kasich	17	Hastert	4
Palin	15	Kasich	7	Christie	7	Ryan	4
Rubio	8	O'Malley	6	Jeb Bush	6	Jeb Bush	2
Fiorina	6	Paul	5	Garland	5	O'Malley	2
Paul	6	Gilmore	4	McConnell	5	Huckabee	2
Jindal	5	Fiorina	3	Trudeau	4		
Ryan	3	G.W. Bush	3	Graham	3		
B. Clinton	2	Romney	3	Ryan	3		
Graham	2	Santorum	3	Palin	3		
Haley	2	Biden	2	Lincoln	2		
Putin	2	Pope Francis	2	Schwarzenegger	2		
				F. Castro	2		
				Biden	2		
				Kerry	2		
				Queen Elizabeth	2		
				R. Castro	2		

Source: Center for Media and Public Affairs, George Mason University

Note: Targets must have at least two jokes to be listed.

in March, up from 16th in February. Several foreign figures were the subject of humorous discussion on late-night shows. Newly elected Canadian Prime Minister Justin Trudeau was the subject of four jokes in March, when Queen Elizabeth II of the U.K. was joked about twice. Putin was the target of two jokes in January and Pope Francis was the subject of two jokes during February.

In Table 17.5 we combine the monthly results to provide Top Ten lists for late 2015 and early 2016. In both periods, Donald Trump was the target of the late-night comedians' zingers more than one time out of four. Hillary Clinton was second during late 2015 and fourth in early 2016. Bernie Sanders was second during early 2016, after ranking fifth during the final months of 2015. Ted Cruz was third during early 2016, a significant increase from his eighth-place finish during late 2015. Nine of the top ten political figures targeted

TABLE 17.5 2016 Top Late-Night Joke Targets, Top Ten Totals

Late 2015	*Jokes*	*Percentage*
1. Donald Trump	518	26.7%
2. Hillary Clinton	199	10.2%
3. Ben Carson	142	7.3%
4. Jeb Bush	146	7.5%
5. Bernie Sanders	97	5.0%
6. Barack Obama	77	4.0%
7. Chris Christie	49	2.5%
8. Ted Cruz	35	1.8%
9. Marco Rubio	29	1.5%
10. Carly Fiorina	23	1.2%
10. (tie) Bobby Jindal	23	1.2%
Early 2016	*Jokes*	*Percentage*
1. Donald Trump	587	32.3%
2. Bernie Sanders	205	11.3%
3. Ted Cruz	161	8.9%
4. Hillary Clinton	115	6.3%
5. Jeb Bush	104	5.7%
6. Barack Obama	94	5.2%
7. Ben Carson	62	3.4%
8. Marco Rubio	61	3.4%
9. John Kasich	43	2.4%
10. Chris Christie	34	1.9%

Source: Center for Media and Public Affairs, George Mason University

in late 2015 were candidates for president. The one exception was President Obama, who ranked sixth. Obama also ranked sixth in the early 2016 rankings, and once again was the only name on the list who was not a candidate for president during 2016.

In Table 17.6 we turn to our detailed focus of the humor directed at the major party nominees. Stephen Colbert told the most political jokes during the general-election study period (from the start of the first major party convention on July 18 through November 11, a few days after the election). The pattern for three of the four late-night comics examined was consistent: 81% of Colbert's jokes focused on Trump, as compared to 80% of Noah's and 78% of Kimmel's. Fallon's famous head-rubbing and otherwise congenial September interview with Trump faced criticism for not being more critical (Merry, 2016), and the data show that Trump fared better on *The Tonight Show* than on the offerings of the other networks. But even on Fallon's show, Trump was still the subject of notably more ridicule than Clinton (64% versus 36%).

TABLE 17.6 2016 General Election Joke Totals

	Trump	*%*	*Clinton*	*%*	*Total*
Fallon	180	64	101	36	281
Colbert	284	81	65	19	349
Kimmel	176	78	50	22	226
Noah	199	80	51	20	250
Total	**836**	**76**	**267**	**24**	**1103**

Source: Center for Media and Public Affairs, George Mason University

Note: Jokes were aired from the start of the first major party convention through election week, from July 18 to November 11, 2016.

TABLE 17.7 Topic Areas of Presidential Candidate Jokes

	All Jokes	*Policy*	*%*	*Politics*	*%*	*Personal*	*%*
Before the Iowa Caucus (9/1/15 through 1/31/16)							
Trump	672	58	9	161	24	605	90
Clinton	161	9	6	66	41	150	93
Total	**833**	**67**	**8**	**227**	**27**	**755**	**91**
From the Iowa Caucus to the Start of the Party Conventions (2/1/16 through 7/17/16)							
Trump	844	114	14	359	43	802	95
Clinton	222	31	14	140	63	193	87
Total	**1066**	**145**	**14**	**499**	**47**	**995**	**93**
Party Conventions through General Election (7/18/16 through 11/11/16)							
Trump	836	156	19	547	65	662	79
Clinton	267	19	7	190	71	222	83
Total	**1103**	**175**	**16**	**737**	**67**	**884**	**80**
Full Campaign Period (9/1/15 through 11/11/16)							
Trump	2351	325	14	1059	45	2058	88
Clinton	657	59	9	396	60	565	86
Total	**3008**	**384**	**13**	**1455**	**48**	**2623**	**87**

Source: Center for Media and Public Affairs, George Mason University

Note: Percentages do not sum to 100 because jokes can refer to more than one topic area.

In addition to whom the comedians were joking about, we examined what they were joking about. In Table 17.7 we examine the jokes for three subject areas: policy content, non-substantive political content (such as political strategy and the horse race), and personal matters (such as the candidates' character and personality traits). We examined the jokes during three separate segments of the campaign: before the Iowa Caucus (September 1, 2015 through January 31, 2016), from the start of the nomination contests up to the start of the first nominating convention (February 1 through July 17, 2016) and from the start of the nomination conventions through the election and a few days beyond (July 18 through November 11, 2016). For both candidates during all three periods, personal matters dominated the humor: more than four out of every five jokes included some material regarding character, personality, or other personal traits, including 88% of the jokes focusing on Trump and 86% of those focusing on Clinton. Many of those jokes also focused on political calculations and the horse race, particularly in the late summer and fall, where 65% of jokes relating to Trump and 71% of the jokes relating to Clinton included references to political calculations. Political matters were notably less prominent in the pre-season campaign jokes, referenced in only 24% of Trump's jokes and 41% of Clinton's.

Few jokes offered policy content: not once during those three periods did the percentage of jokes that focused on policy exceed 20%. This is not particularly surprising (Niven, Lichter, & Amundson, 2003). One might expect the late-night comics to focus on personalities—human foibles are often rich veins for humor—and perhaps never more so with the larger-than-life personalities offered on the ballot in 2016. Likewise, the heavy news media emphasis on political calculations offers joke writers a ready source of information from the daily news (Farnsworth & Lichter, 2011; Patterson, 2016). Even so, greater policy content in the jokes would provide more information for those voters who are using the late-night comedy shows as a source of campaign information (Baumgartner & Morris, 2011).

Discussion and Conclusion

This study of the attention late-night comics paid to politicians during late 2015 and 2016 confirms the impression that Donald Trump was in a class by himself. He ranked first in terms of the number of jokes he received during all eight months of the primary study period, which started well before he was seen as a favorite for the nomination. The blustery billionaire may be a rich source of material for comedy, and it seems the attention he received from the late-night comics varied little depending on his poll standings or his record in primary contests. When the two major party nominees squared off in the general election, the comics remained consistent: all four focused primarily on Trump, with relatively little to say about Clinton.

Although Hillary Clinton was the second-most-frequent source of humor during late 2015, the relative attention paid to her declined during the winter and spring of 2016. Although Sanders proved an unexpectedly strong threat, Clinton remained consistently ahead in pledged Democratic convention delegates during the process and was always a favorite to win the nomination. As her path to the nomination became clearer in early 2016, she was the subject of less attention from the comics, a sharp contrast from the more consistent way

Trump was treated across the eight months of primary jokes examined here. Perhaps the length of time she has been in the public eye—she was First Lady for eight years, a U.S. senator from New York for another eight years, a failed presidential candidate in 2008, and secretary of state for Barack Obama's first term—meant that by early 2016 the comedians were running out of new and different funny things to say about her. This could also be true during the general election, where voters started the campaign season more familiar with Clinton, and when Trump showed an ability to dominate both public attention and news discourse (Patterson, 2016).

One of the larger surprises of the 2016 nomination season was the relative success of Bernie Sanders, who had little support in the polls before the nomination contest began. But as he won more and more contests, the comedians took an increasingly strong interest in him, moving from fifth in the humor rankings in late 2015 to second in early 2016. As with Trump, Sanders's personality may have lent itself to humorous commentary. For example, his rumpled demeanor may have stimulated more jokes than that of a conventional, disciplined, button-down candidate. But the Sanders experience does seem to show that relative political success begets more attention from the comics.

The increased attention to Cruz during early 2016 also suggests that comics respond to political success, at least for politicians who were not yet household names. Cruz ranked eighth during late 2015, when he was just another name in the crowded Republican field, but moved to third during early 2016 as he emerged as the main rival to Trump. The same pattern can be seen for Ohio Gov. John Kasich, who also lasted longer in the Republican contest than most other would-be nominees. Kasich did not make the Top Ten until early in 2016, as his ability to survive as a candidate throughout the nomination process became increasingly apparent. Dr. Ben Carson represents a confirmation of this pattern in the opposite direction: his political fortunes sank once the nomination contests were underway and the comedians lost interest.

Of course, just because you are losing does not always mean comedians let up on you, particularly if your last name is Bush. Jeb Bush ranked fourth in the number of jokes during late 2015, when he seemed as likely as other Republicans running for president to receive the nomination, and he continued to rank fourth in the number of jokes in early 2016, when his extremely well-funded campaign failed to secure even modest success in early primary and caucus states. (Bush finished sixth in Iowa and fourth in New Hampshire before suspending his campaign on February 20, 2016.)

Barack Obama's consistent sixth-place finish during the two periods we examined during the nomination cycle represents something of an anomaly for a sitting president nearing the end of his second term. In 2000, Bill Clinton placed second in the number of late-night jokes he received, behind George

W. Bush. In 2008 George W. Bush placed second in the number of jokes he received, behind John McCain, that year's Republican nominee (Lichter et al., 2015). Since his 2008 candidacy for the presidency Obama has always been a difficult subject for the late-night comics, perhaps because his cool demeanor did not lend the first African American nominee and president to the sort of broad-brush character-related humor that would flow naturally from the humor-rich public perceptions of Bill Clinton as an aging lothario and George W. Bush as a dim bulb (Lichter et al., 2015).

One must also note that the late-night comics tend to focus on the themes in the news. Personality and political machinations routinely dominate campaign news stories, even though such topics may be less important to voters than the policy initiatives that the candidates would offer. But in the same way that some reporters may hesitate to offer much policy coverage, the comics likewise may consider policy themes too complicated or simply too unfunny to deserve much attention. This is a disadvantage for those citizens who might otherwise become informed about substantive issues as they listen to the four horsemen of late-night comedy, but it reflects the news coverage that is often the source of their inspiration.

For all the drama, suspense, and unexpected turns of the 2016 elections, late-night comedy differed surprisingly little in many regards from that of other recent presidential campaigns, at least insofar as we were able to measure them. There were new faces among the hosts (as there were among the leading candidates), and old routines such as Letterman's Top Ten lists gave way to new ones like Jimmy Fallon's "slow jamming the news." But these were more a matter of form than substance. The heavier focus on Republican than Democratic candidates continued for the seventh straight election and (as noted above) the emphasis on personality over policy remained unchanged as well. Candidates continued to frequent the shows and were treated relatively well by their hosts, but the brief moments of civility disappeared once the guests had departed.

On the other hand, the sheer volume of jokes about Trump was certainly unprecedented; even Bill Clinton was never so frequent a target during his election campaigns (Lichter et al., 2015). And at least qualitatively, there seemed more of an edge to much of the humor, as the comedians' distress and disdain toward the Donald sometimes seemed palpable. For example, Colbert tried to "connect the dots" among Trump's ideas and behavior and ended up drawing a swastika. But even this was in line with highly negative news coverage of Trump that included discussions of whether it was appropriate to call him a Fascist or compare him to Hitler. Thus, Trump posed a challenge to comedians, as he did to journalists. Even when making light of Trump, there was a dark edge to the outpouring of late-night comedy. It remains to be seen whether the distinctiveness of late-night comedians' takes of candidate Trump will continue to color their treatment of President Trump.

Acknowledgements

The authors would like to thank Aisha Shafi of George Mason University and Joshua Wartel of Brown University for research assistance, and to thank the University of Mary Washington and the Center for Media and Public Affairs at George Mason University for financial assistance.

References

Baumgartner, J., & Morris, J. S. (2006). *The Daily Show* effect: Candidate evaluations, efficacy and American youth. *American Politics Research, 36*, 341–367.

Baumgartner, J., & Morris, J. S. (2011). Stoned slackers or super citizens? 'Daily Show' viewing and political engagement of young adults. In A. Amarasingam & R. W. McChesney (Eds.), *The Stewart/Colbert effect: Essays on the real impacts of fake news* (pp. 63–78). Jefferson, NC: McFarland & Co.

Baym, G. (2005). *The Daily Show*: Discursive integration and the reinvention of political journalism. *Political Communication, 22*, 259–276.

Brewer, P., & Cao, X. (2006). Candidate appearances on soft news shows and public knowledge about primary candidates. *Journal of Broadcasting and Electronic Media, 50*, 18–30.

Davis, R., & Owen, D. M. (1998). *New media in American politics.* New York, NY: Oxford University Press.

Farnsworth, S. J., & Lichter, S. R. (2011). *The nightly news nightmare: Media coverage of US presidential elections, 1988–2008* (3rd ed.). Lanham, MD: Rowman & Littlefield.

Gould, J. (1968, September 17). Laugh-in team back with a Nixon line. *New York Times*, p. 95.

Iyengar, S., & Hahn, K. S. (2009). Red media, blue media: Evidence of ideological selectivity in media use. *Journal of Communication, 59*, 19–39.

Kolbert, E. (1992, June 5). The 1992 campaign: Media; whistle stops a la 1992: Arsenio, Larry and Phil. *New York Times*. Retrieved from https://nyti.ms/1G7hUqp

Lichter, S. R., Baumgartner, J. C., & Morris, J. S. (2015). *Politics is a joke! How TV comedians are remaking political life.* Boulder, CO: Westview.

Lichter, S. R., Farnsworth, S. J., & Canieso, D. (2016). Late night tells 3 times as many jokes about 2016 Republicans as Democrats. *Washington Post* (The Fix blog). Retrieved from www.washingtonpost.com/news/the-fix/wp/2016/03/08/late-night-tells-3-times-as-many-jokes-about-2016-republicans-as-democrats/

Merry, S. (2016). No one should have expected Jimmy Fallon to go tough on Trump: That was Letterman's job. *Washington Post.* Retrieved from www.washingtonpost.com/news/arts-and-entertainment/wp/2016/09/16/no-one-should-have-expected-jimmy-fallon-to-go-tough-on-trump-that-was-lettermans-job

Mitchell, A., Gottfried, J., Kiley, J., & Matsa, K. E. (2014). Political polarization and media habits. *Pew Research Center.* Retrieved from www.journalism.org/2014/10/21/political-polarization-media-habits/

Moy, P., Xenos, M., & Hess, V. (2005). Communication and citizenship: Mapping the political effects of infotainment. *Mass Communication & Society, 8*, 111–131.

Niven, D., Lichter, S. R., & Amundson, D. (2003). The political content of late-night comedy. *Harvard International Journal of Press/Politics, 8*, 118–133.

Patterson, T. (2016). News coverage of the 2016 general election: How the press failed the voters. *Shorenstein Center on Media, Politics and Public Policy, Kennedy School, Harvard University*. Retrieved from https://shorensteincenter.org/news-coverage-2016-general-election/

Stroud, N. J. (2008). Media use and political predispositions: Revisiting the concept of selective exposure. *Political Behavior, 30*(3), 341–366.

Taber, C. S., & Lodge, M. (2006). Motivated skepticism in the evaluation of political beliefs. *American Journal of Political Science, 50*(3), 755–769.

Xenos, M., & Becker, A. (2009). Moments of zen: Effects of the *Daily Show* on information seeking and political learning. *Political Communication, 26*, 317–332.

Young, D. (2006). Late-night comedy and the salience of the candidates caricatured traits in the 2000 election. *Mass Communication and Society, 9*(3), 339–366.

INDEX

Page numbers in italic indicate a figure.